Apotheosis, LLC.
P.O. Box 441721
Aurora, Colorado 80044

Printed in the United States of America First Edition 2019, Revised Edition: 2024

Unless otherwise indicated, Bible quotations are from the New American Standard Bible, THE LOCKMAN FOUNDATION.

Book Cover Image (Revised Edition): Apotheosis

Library of Congress Cataloging-in-Publication Data Allen, Ellis D.
Volume One: Hidden Challenges of People of Faith and How to Navigate Them | Phantoms of Faith Series | Volumes 1-7 Ellis D. Allen

Revised Title: OVERCOMING HIDDEN CHALLENGES- APOLLOS I
ISBN: 978-0-578-22021-5

In the first installment of the Phantoms of Faith Series, Dr. E. D. Allen offers spiritual, professional, and practical encouragement regarding major obstacles that challenge individual faith and our connections to God and others today. This is a must-read for anyone who desires to examine and affirm their faith and relationship with God and life. More importantly, this book is for those having difficulty identifying or navigating personal struggles in life.

D. Lovato
Aurora, Colorado

Overcoming Hidden Challenges provides a comprehensive exposition of what it means to be human while navigating a relationship with a Divine Creator who loves unconditionally. This relationship, declares the author, comprises a variety of modalities ranging from sexual ambiguities to social and ethical considerations regarding race and racism. The book embraces the spiritual, the mental, the emotional, and the psychological; it is, in a word, a 'brilliant' approach to some of life's challenges. It is a must-read for anyone seeking to make sense of the complexities of human existence and a myriad of moral and spiritual discourses.

-Dr. Darrell Wesley | Senior Minister |Ethics Professor
U.S. Navy Chaplain Ret.

I am honored to contribute to an exciting and unique composition of truth designed to aid the sojourning Believer from Earth to Heaven and ultimately glorify God. Some of the revisions in this composite are simplifying otherwise complicated sections, doctrinal clarity, and an index to locate exciting words and phrases quickly. Notwithstanding, the body of this work remains a compelling asset for those serving in the kingdom and for the lay member who may be simply trying to navigate life.

-Apollos I
Exegetical Theologian

THE PHANTOMS OF FAITH

VOLUME I

OVERCOMING HIDDEN CHALLENGES

E. D. ALLEN

Revised by: Apollos I

THE

CONTENTS

Preface to Series

The Phantom of Faith Series holds a crucial proposition that those immersed in sacred texts, religion, social sciences, and medicine should document their experiences in these fields, particularly where these principles intersect with the public square to the glory of God. Additionally, one of the significant challenges the 21st-century Church faces is her preoccupation with remaining relevant in a progressive world while preserving the integrity of the Word and fulfilling its divine mandate.

Fearing antiquity, she chases reformation. I do not mean reformation in the traditional theological sense but the perpetual restructuring of the church in its futile attempt to appear relevant, appease its membership, and remain competitive with the secular world. In her efforts to garner legitimacy as an institution that speaks for God and seeks the good of humanity, segments of the faith community have developed spiritual and cognitive distortions, inadvertently presenting the church as a group of people who are immature, weak-minded, and delusional. However, recognizing these distortions opens the door to growth and learning.

Cognitive distortion is a clinical term that describes a faulty thought process where one holds specific ideas or beliefs contrary to normalcy and does not reflect truth. Among those who misapprehend the true essence of the Church's faith and mission are those who wrongly equate maturity with the capacity to accommodate a secularized reading of Scripture and its application in the world. The church shows maturity when it becomes proficient in responding to every segment of society without prejudice or preferential treatment while remaining scriptural. Distortions of faith and mission often lead to a frenzied response to declining membership and communal demands with solutions counterintuitive to divine mandates. In its fear of becoming obsolete, keeping members, recruiting new members, and withstanding the pressure of secularization, some religious entities have relaxed their values and reconfigured God's Word to allow what God denies and jettison what He codifies as essential for a relationship with Him.

Some segments of the faith community understandably go to great lengths to preserve God's mandates by viewing modernity as sacrilegious and, in effect, cling to a 1950s model of ministry in a 21st-century environment. These see contemporary approaches to ministry (even those not violating Scripture) as a departure from the Faith. Attempting to combat modernity, they fixate on the "One Church" doctrine and the interrogatory, 'What must I do to be saved?' even for members who have long since embraced this biblical concept. They outsource other aspects of the church's mission to nonprofits in the community. This model of ministry does not address the phantoms of faith or real challenges facing people in the pew and public square.

Meanwhile, the onlooker (those unchurched and de-churched) sees the faith community as an out-of-touch entity irrelevant to the fundamental dynamics behind the scenes in their lives. In their minds, they have not abandoned God but have abandoned traditional forms of church and worship. Hence, the familiar statement, "I believe in God and Christ, but not an organized religion or denomination." They continue to search for God and spirituality in unorthodox ways and contexts.

They seek actual answers to real questions or resolutions pertinent to their circumstances. These do not see the church as relevant or practical. The Pew Research Center's study America's Changing Religious Landscape (2015) captures this unfortunate reality.

The report highlights that over 100 million people have abandoned traditional forms of the church. The center notes that the Christian share of the population has declined by 8% over seven years. In addition, in 2011, David Kinnaman pointed out that the mosaic group of the population (between ages 18 and 29) believes the church makes little sense, and they cannot raise their most pressing life questions to the church. Matters that concern them most, the church frequently avoids or sweeps under the rug. Subsequently, their quest continues but in the other direction and context. In areas in which the church is vocal, mosaics describe the teaching as "shallow."

These findings arouse my attention. I tested the findings by examining a small sample of churches in the Denver Metro area, including Churches of Christ, denominational, and independent churches. Examining Church websites provides a snapshot of congregational life and their perception of the community they serve.

What was most interesting was how sermons, bible studies, and church programs contrast with issues facing church members and the community. Most often, there were no signs of a correlation between lesson topics and mundane problems facing members and the community. For instance, generic issues such as What must I do to be saved, the church, righteousness, and the love of God were frequent. Whether these lessons adequately respond to hidden issues of members and the community is debatable. But to an unchurched person looking for solutions to their challenges, answers are not apparent through these.

I contrast this information with narratives and issues of my former clinical clientele (most of whom identify as Christian) and those encountered during my pastoral experience. In addition, casual conversations with Christians attending church in this area and conversations with over 5,000 followers on social media over four years suggest that while most believe the church addresses their primary issues, the more complex and unorthodox challenges remain unattended. Some people feel they cannot raise their problems or concerns about life to the church they are attending. From this, I surmise there is a disconnect between religious entities and the more complex and unorthodox challenges parishioners and surrounding communities face. In my mind, (at least) this gives credence to Kinnaman's argument about the mosaic group of our population and the findings by the Pew Research Center. Orchestrating and delivering programs and services that meet the community's needs requires a thorough understanding of the issues and questions facing the church and the community.

If the chief purpose for humanity is to glorify God, the church must become the primary entity through which God is known and realized as the singular antidote to the ills and issues facing the community. This reality leads me to write volume one, OVERCOMING HIDDEN CHALLENGES.

During this effort, and through intellectual conversations and debate, I surmise the issues facing both those in the church and the community are complex, multifaceted, and protracted sometimes. Subsequently, it became necessary for me to not only create one volume or book but also develop a series. Hence, the series titled Phantoms of Faith. The series exposes the hidden challenges of people of faith, most often orchestrated by Phantom forces seeking their demise. As examples, the writing highlights narratives of Christians and people of other religions who have experienced challenges in unorthodox contexts and the impact of these on their lives and resolutions.

It includes practical perceptions and wisdom regarding unique challenges befalling people of faith and the phantom forces from which they originate. As a Christian and African American writing through the lens of the Western-European culture, the framework presented in this series regarding challenging issues may differ from those living and practicing faith outside my culture.

However, I hope this framework provides insight, direction, and resolution for those seeking answers or looking to thwart the forces that undermine God's intended purpose for their lives. This can be a resource for those looking to improve the quality of their lives and relationships. Phantoms of Faith is a series. It is my effort to write each book in this series to honor God and enrich people's lives across various sectors of life. I hope this volume and the series will serve as a resource for the church and the unchurched, the minister and the academician, clinicians and counselors, and religious experts and novices. This is my legacy and contribution to the greater good, to the glory of God. In this, I pay homage to ministers, practitioners, and scholars for their writing and contribution to the existing literature. This work reminds family, friends, and detractors that this scholarship is possible because I acknowledge the irrevocable gifts God has given me and God's presence in me. I give all the glory and praise to Him.

-E. D. Allen, D Min. PhD.

ACKNOWLEDGEMENTS

It is derelict if I do not acknowledge and express gratitude for other professional consultations while developing this volume. Their expertise in Psychology, Women and Gender Issues, World Religion, Critical Thinking, and Chaplaincy were valuable assets to me. Although this volume's data are anecdotes from my former clinical and pastoral experience, specialized training, and unique contexts, its composition would have been more complex and protracted, independent of their consultation and insight. I appreciate the appraisal and wisdom to simplify, synthesize, and deconstruct data to prevent the average reader from alienation and drowning at such depths.

Thank you for vesting time in educational discussions and invigorating debates that spawned intellectual debt, for which I am grateful. Special thanks to my family, who saw the value of this work or the effort (at least) and, as such, helped preserve the space necessary for this undertaking by assisting me with my daughter's specialized care and well-being. Your help in this regard is immeasurable.

In addition, I am grateful for Dr. Thomas Holland, former Senior Minister of the Crieve Hall Church of Christ in Nashville, former Chair of the Bible Department at David Lipscomb University, and Director of the Nashville School of Preaching and Biblical Studies, who operated and situated at David Lipscomb during my tenure. Although our curriculum then included the study of every book of the bible, denominational dogma, Christian ethics, marriage and family counseling, and requisites necessary at that level of study, it was your class and instructions in hermeneutics and exegesis that remain paramount and have stood the test of time.

The strategic utility of grammatical and lexicographical tools aimed at mining the mind of God revealed in His word and unearthing directives toaid people in the human experience are invaluable. It was not only the acquisition of these tools but your caution that we use these in tandem with theHoly Spirit and preserve the integrity of the holy text. Even though many years have passed, this teaching continues guiding my homiletics and applying God's sacred mandates. You are a champion of truth, a treasure, and a blessing to the brotherhood. Thank you for your service and counsel.

IN LOVING MEMORY

OF

MY FATHER

SANDY J. ALLEN

EXPIRED: APRIL 18, 2018

DEDICATION

I want to dedicate this volume to the following people:

My Family

Had you not been, I would not be. Thank you for your support, patience, and faith in the gifts of God in me. I am grateful for all of you. Besides these, Keyla, Shay, and Ellisia are children with special needs and the purest human I have ever experienced.

Minister Dennis Bruce Gamble, I

I have been blessed to have you as my father-in-the-gospel, life coach, and mentor during my early ministry and young adulthood years. You are the epitome of a Christian, a Man of God... joyous, caring, loving, patient, forgiving, and an ambassador of truth. I appreciate your counsel, direction, and prayers over the years. Ithank God for your life and being. Thank you.

Ivan Delgado

Your friendship and brotherhood are timely and invaluable. I appreciate your support, encouragement, confidence, and trust in me during this writing. Thank you for being my confidant. May God bless your life and soul.

INTRODUCTION

Overcoming Hidden Challenges is the first volume of the Phantoms of Faith series. The Phantoms of Faith series is a biblical, theological, and psychological analysis and response to the challenges of people of faith in unorthodox contexts. While not an exhaustive work on these issues, it unveils and discusses a few of the hidden unorthodox challenges of Christians and other religious bodies. Written through an interdisciplinary lens, the problems in this volume unfold in scriptural contexts and processes through theological, psychological, and neuropsychological conversations, as these are critical tenets of humanness.

Theology usually refers to one's interpretation and application of Scripture. An individual's training, home, and church environment, life experiences, and the measure of the Holy Spirit given predicate their theology. I am cautious about the amount of theology I impose on these issues. I do not allow my theology to extend beyond what we can confirm in God's Word's original Hebrew and Greek texts.

Theology has within it a human element that cannot rise beyond one's fragmentation, except unless there are practical undergirdingsources upon which such theology can rest. The original language in which God allows His men of old to write His Word and guidance by the Holy Spirit are the pillars upon which my theology rests. This means that before concluding spiritual matters, I separate the brotherhood doctrine or the tenets of Christianity from those not supported or confirmed in the original language of the Word of God. This then presents conclusions that are sound and in the purest form possible. Second, processing these issues in psychological conversations refers to how an individual's challenges impact behavior and the cognitive functions that form an individual's mental framework before and after the onset of their issue. It provides insight into why people do what they do and how this impacts them and others.

When I refer to placing some of the issues raised in this book in neuropsychological conversations, I am referring to observing a tetralogy consisting of behavior, mind, brain, and the nervous system and how these operate in tandem, forming issues or responding to them. In some instances, discussing behavioral issues in this context broadens our spiritual understanding of the individual before, during, and in the aftermath of their disaster, i.e., life stressors, death of loved ones, and sexual thoughts and behaviors are candidates for discussion in this context. Suppose the faith community wants to bridge the gap between it and the 100 million souls seeking God and spirituality outside traditional norms. In that case, we must learn to deconstruct and appreciate the challenges facing communities in the 21st century. Suppose individuals (churched or unchurched) want to understand the meaning of life and experience a state of bliss. In that case, they, too, must deconstruct and appreciate the challenges facing them and how this influences their relationship with the Creator.

I will try to contribute to this ideology and discussion by offering this series. Overcoming Hidden Challenges removes the veil behind which lies the genesis of perpetual, enigmatical issues taking the lives of people hostage. Although this volume presents likely familiar challenges, its approach and in-depth deconstruction differentiate it from ordinary conversation and analysis of these issues. Because this volume reaches a broad readership, the writing style is fluid. Sections appear homiletical (preachy), and others are more technical, scientific, and serious and evoke a range of emotions throughout. Some sections are very elementary(at least for the seasoned analytical practitioner of faith and psychology), and others are profound and extraordinarily complex, even for those seasoned.Its composition considers the novice and ensures it does not alienate such a person from the conversation.

In addition, it provides encouragement and direction for existing Saints, as well as tools and concepts for scholars to extend research. Although the Word of God guides topics presented in this book, it does not follow traditional Christian writing. It is a scholarly approach to the issues and includes language that both church and unchurch individuals can understand. Sometimes, terminology conventionally used in psychology and medicine is interjected in the narrative, which may be challenging in a Christian context for some. I use references from sources in and out of the church and across various professional disciplines, as is common in scholarship. I do not use these as substitutes for Scripture, but on the contrary, they confirm God's truth. For instance, Flavius Josephus was a Jewish historian writing during the time of Christ. April 3, A.D. 33, in theAntiquities of the Jews, he notes they condemned Jesus Christ to a cross.

We believe and teach the crucifixion and death of Christ not because of Josephus and others but because of Scripture. Josephus and other historians confirm the integrity of such teaching. In this vein, references in this book support Scripture and are not a substitute for the Holy Mandate. In addition, referencing the works or thoughts of others is not an endorsement of beliefs or practices contradicting Scripture, nor a blanket endorsement of this writing by those I reference in this work.

Except for a few chapters, each begins with a narrative and ends with The Guidepost, a section with ideas, suggestions, and directives regarding the subject matter. The narratives in this book are authentic. However,names and places are altered to preserve anonymity or confidentiality where necessary.

1

The Adam Complex

Misunderstanding God and Miscalculating Satan

"Every man carries within himself a world made up of all that he has seen and loved, and it is to this world that he returns incessantly, though he may pass through and seem to inhabit a world foreign to it."

- Chateaubriand

A Critical Beginning

If you were asked what the four most distinctive and definitive sounds in the history of the world are, how would you respond? Would your mind think back to the 1945 Trinity Blast in Alamogordo, New Mexico, or the nuclear explosion at Chernobyl in 1986? What about the infamous volcanic eruptions of Vesuvius in 79 A.D. and Krakatoa in 1883, hallmarked as the loudest sounds ever heard by humans in known history?[1] Perhaps your calculus is more galactic and offers the explosion from a supernova or neutron star, which are unbelievably massive! Sounds represent meaning because they are the effect or result of a cause.

They are precursors of critical events or transitions. Four definitive sounds within time and space inevitably emerge as essential precursors to man's meaning, identity, and destiny. The first is scientifically regarded as a singularity, an entity unimaginably larger than any other power within the human realm. This singularity ingeniously introduced an epic liberation of indestructible energy. This energy was paradoxically incomprehensible and more complex than anything that followed in its aftermath. This first sound is none other than the recognized origin of the universe, which many scientists dub the "Big Bang."

Contrary to the scientific interpretation of the 'Big Bang' as a cosmic event, Theologians perceive it as the manifestation of the First Cause, the Sovereign God and Creator of the Universe. His intelligence and power transcend human comprehension, defining His nature and being.

Having predetermined in His unfathomable mind the purpose, parameters, and extent of man's existence, He created the universe by codifying an incredibly dense point to inflate and expand faster than the speed of light to speeds too inconceivable to note. [2] The rapidity of such transformation caused an unparalleled bang, correctly pointed out as the "mother of all blasts!"[3] Cosmic material screeched into a vast void, creating an auditory symphony of sub-blasts, collisions, and fluctuations assembling in temperatures likely in the trillions[4]. Lucifer and other angels may have witnessed an incredible fireworks show. This was the original shock and awe! God gives the universe's elements, atoms, and particles their marching orders at that moment. Under His guiding eye, they collect, separate, and organize substances suitable for His agenda -the creation of the universe.[5] After the violence of this epic artistry settles, the earth cools, and then it happens! He prepares the Earth for habitation, after which He takes dust from the ground and astonishingly sculpts the king of His creation- a tripartite being called man. God gave man life, identity, and purpose; the so-called "Big Bang" is the first precursor to man's identity.

Next is the sound of God walking and presumably calling the man in the Garden of Eden after Adam and Eve's fall. [6] Although comparatively softer, its distinctiveness and the context in which it manifests make the second sound as powerful as the first. They heard the sound of pending judgment, the pronouncement of a looming identity crisis, displacement, spiritual misalignment, and an altered destiny in its wake. Third are the sounds heard at Calvary, hallmarked by:

(1) the deafening silence during the epic darkness at Calvary. Few give adequate attention to the theology behind the darkness that unfolded during Jesus' crucifixion. While some point to this event as proof of God's alienation of the "human" part of Christ, it is, more critically, indicative of the Father's presence and judgment. It was not until after three hours that Jesus cried out, feeling abandoned following a possible Trinitarian dialogue. This dark period is the exact moment the pinnacle of the punishment for sin is exacted. It is subsequently the moment that the believing man is set free from the penalty of his sins;

(2) The powerful earthquake that occurred at Christ's death simultaneously tore the thick veil of the Temple, highlighting man's restitution and reconciliation.

(3) The earthquake that marked the Angel removing the stone from the Lord's tomb on Resurrection Sunday was the bookend to the justification process.[7] Together, they cradle the antidote for the misguided notions and sin that unfolded in Eden. Independent of any other source or human

contribution, these divine acts restore man's identity, purpose, and destiny.[8]

(4) Although unrealized, that unique "shout and trumpet" earmarking the end of the church age and the beginning of the final consummation of human affairs is equally noteworthy. The reality of God "calls things into being that which does not exist" and, in effect, impacts as though they already are. These eschatological sounds solidify man's destiny.[9]

The Search for Self

From the beginning of human existence, people have struggled to understand themselves in contrast to the Creator. This struggle intensified after the fall of man in the Garden of Eden, which resulted in displacement, spiritual alienation, confusion, and a loss of purpose. As humans search for meaning and identity, we must strive to maintain a balance between our lives and the God who created us. Even if some people don't acknowledge His existence, a natural hunger, and yearning are embedded into the human experience that arises from this strategic disruption of the fundamental balance between humans and their Creator. At first glance, finding answers to questions like "Who am I?"

and "Why am I here?" can seem complicated and unclear. This is evident by the various lifestyle choices people embrace to help find their version of fulfillment while reducing anxiety caused by the constant struggle for self-discovery and belonging. However, negative influences can distract and disrupt this vital journey. These forces can make staying true to oneself and finding inner peace challenging.[10]

Consider two individuals whose everyday lives reveal common human challenges. On a Saturday morning, Phalonia awakes to the sweet chirping of robins and blue jays outside her window. The chirping of birds breaks up intermittent silence. She blinks a few times to break free from deep sleep. Her spouse remains fast asleep while the children are still knocked out from their Xbox overdose the night before. Despite the need to move before everyone else, she is captivated by the reality that her 9 to 5 hustle is in recess. There are no traffic jams now, and the sounds of city traffic are subdued. The office phones are routed to voice mail; there are no harassment issues or conflicts to resolve between employees.

Suddenly, the still of the morning is disturbed by the percolating sound of the automatic coffee pot. The gurgling sound and the arousing aroma of coffee are so stimulating that they force her out of bed. Entering the bathroom, she looks in the mirror... then leans in for a closer look and notices the changes in her face, likely due to stress and fatigue. She says, "I don't even recognize who I am anymore... my goodness, where did I lose myself?"[11]

Simultaneously, on the other side of town, in an upscale neighborhood, K.T. broaches the day differently. Tossing and turning all night, he finally fell into deep, rejuvenating sleep at 6 am. Unfortunately, this experience is short-lived. The warmth and brightness of the sun beaming through his window slides across his face and awakes him. His world and experience are different from Phalonia's. The left side of his bed is empty. No tiny feet race down the corridor, or children argue over video games. He does not welcome the silence of the morning; for him, it is deafening. It is so still and quiet that he can hear his footsteps cross the carpet to the bathroom. Although he owns a Porsche, Mercedes, and Hummer and a vibrant medical practice downtown, he still feels empty. Looking at himself in the mirror, he murmurs, "I don't even know what I am doing anymore." This confuses K.T. because his life reflects everything his parents, community, and culture suggest he should become and do. Yet, he feels like a man without a purpose.

Both narratives reveal the ongoing need for fulfillment and identity, which mundane pursuits cannot consistently satisfy. Phalonia is one of many individuals who are not pursuing their preferred or desired paths. Their lives are stuck in a cyclical experience that lacks fulfillment and consequently steals their joy. Self-misalignment occurs when one's divine gifts, relationships, and direction are not in harmony with one's overarching life purpose, which is unrealized by most and is defined by the creation of life itself. In an interview about brokenness and wholeness, Dr. David G. Benner (2016) notes that this misalignment lends itself to the imaginary alienation commonly at the heart of brokenness. [12] Because many people do not know or understand God, the internal feeling of alienation is not viewed as something connected to God or the breached relationship between the creature and the Creator. Like Phalonia, K.T.'s life is misaligned too. The alienation he experiences manifests as a loss of purpose, and Phalonia's as a search for identity.

After considering their narratives, how do you define yourself? When you see yourself in the mirror or when someone asks you, "Who am I?" what comes to mind? Do you define yourself based on your parents and their characteristics? Or do you identify yourself as a Believer, Christian, Spiritualist, Atheist, or Humanist? If you choose any of these, what does it mean to you? Are you being honest with yourself or hiding any part of yourself in your answer? Do you think your credit score, address, or mode of transportation defines you? Or do you believe that your education, job title, or lack thereof is what defines you? Have you lost your individuality amid work and family responsibilities? Are you so busy with work and family that you feel like you're at the center of never-ending drama? In some instances and communities, a person's skin pigmentation is a defining criterion. Are your investment portfolio, bank account good looks, anatomical gifts, and sexual orientation a part of the nexus that defines you? While it is true that no person is one-dimensional,[13] the sum of our being is not without identity and purpose, the reality of which must also be evaluated in the context of a Divine Creator. Irrespective of an individual's consciousness of or belief in this fundamental reality, it is the innate premise for questions about identity, purpose, and the human pursuit of the same.

Every human's response to these questions and motivations is subjected to what this author dubs the Adam complex. The word complex in this writing is more psychological and spiritual than corporeal or tangible. Therefore, it connotes a composite of behavior, repressed thoughts, emotions, and dynamic experiences.[14]

The Adam complex is the ability to stabilize the interpersonal trifecta between God, the inner self, and external forces that try to undermine the union between the creature and the Creator. Humanity must see themselves in the shadow of a Divine Creator, who gives life, identity, and purpose, and to whom our entire being (body, soul, and spirit) is tethered and held in tandem.

Our ability to understand this is strongly associated with two significant factors.

> **First**, understanding God as He truly is, as opposed to how many see Him. One of the most critical errors people make in their appraisal and attempt to know and develop a relationship with God is reducing Him to human terms and perceptions. He is often perceived as a distant and unrelatable being by both Christians and non-Christians. Although the totality of God is incomprehensible, humans' difficulty with Him is primarily influenced by our natural condition and the subsequent demand to adjust spiritually, cognitively, and behaviorally to have a meaningful relationship with Him.[15] Many see these changes as something they are unwilling to make consistently. Subsequently, people attempt to simplify their relationship with Him by diminishing Him.

To many, He is "the man upstairs," "mother nature," and other idioms that make Him no more significant than the best of us.

Periodically, a late-night TV host includes segments during the show in which he imagines interviewing God regarding mundane issues, such as the death penalty, one celebrity's decision about campaigning for the presidency, and additional appearances about other contemporary problems. In these segments, God is presented as a white-headed and bearded Caucasian with a wife, a credit card, and a tattoo. This fictional deity discusses current events with human understanding, logic, and language. It is assumed that no disrespect is intended because this is a fictional or Hollywood interpretation of a divine being. Several comedians often use irreverent and derogatory remarks about God while performing. This conventional approach to God normalizes man's ongoing attempts to make Him like the "average Joe," which instantly reduces guilt and the fear of judgment commonly associated with it and deceives humans into thinking they are more significant than they are really. Granting Him Divine status while not adhering to His expectations gives a false sense of security and justification for improper behavior. This liquefaction of Deity erroneously empowers people to interrogate Him and challenge what He determines essential for life and godliness.

Sometimes, the church, other denominations, seminaries, religious committees, pastors, teachers, theologians, psychologists, and activists have imprudently interpreted God's word. They alter His image and Word to suit modern humans, absolving them of godlessness.

The **second** factor that influences who we are and why we exist comes from our ability to decipher and resist Satan's attempt to destroy our relationship with the Creator.

There is a narrative about the antelope in the jungle who wakes up every morning running because he knows a lion is on the hunt. The antelope does not graze, toy, or assume a lackadaisical approach to the lion. He is fully aware that the lion will kill him. Consider this for clarity: what if, upon exiting your garage or front door, a lion is in the yard... would you proceed to exit your home? Would you not take precautions or not leave at all? Seeing a lion on your front lawn or driveway will startle you! You will seek help immediately and will likely find another way around it. It is essential to recognize that failing to acknowledge Lucifer (Satan) as a destructive force can lead to negative consequences such as confusion, surprise spiritual attacks, disintegration, and a constant need to fill voids in one's life. It is beneficial for all individuals to comprehend and assimilate these two factors. Correctly understanding God and recognizing the Devil as a formidable threat are critical constituents that frame our identity, purpose, and the proverbial pursuit of them.

The absence of such wisdom affects micro and macro orientations, contributing to some of society's mundane ills and challenges. [16,17] People with faith in God often feel a strong urge to maintain a connection with their Creator, which is not typically felt by those who do not follow any religion or have a temporary disinterest in their faith. Those who believe in the Law of God and follow the teachings of Jesus Christ understand the significance of building a relationship with Him while striving to lead a righteous life. This ongoing effort is precisely what the Adam complex defines. The phantom forces exacerbating this process are not always apparent to the affected people.

This is likely due to the subtle and sometimes cloaked vein through which these forces emerge. Here are a few examples:

- religious institutions prioritize training clergy in general leadership rather than developing hermeneutical and exegetical skill sets.
- The second is born out of the first, evident by the steep rise of ministers and teachers purporting a diluted and non-offensive version of the gospel, which doesn't challenge anyone nor clearly define attributes of God as vital tenants for a relationship with Him. This diluted presentation does not entirely expose Satan's schemes to the Saints. The importance of the biblical church is often emphasized at the expense of other scriptural teachings, which can hinder individual and collective growth and maturity.
- The persistent casual attempt to balance or replace scripture with humanism and the weak portrayal (or, in many cases, total absence) of God in the home are other phantom forces disrupting the covenantal relationship with God.

Humanity needs to understand the Adam complex to progress and achieve spiritual balance. Two opposing forces constantly act upon man's existence: God, the Creator, who can make demands on the entire being, and Satan, the Deceiver, who can only influence the physical body, which includes the mind. Notwithstanding, as depicted in the simple illustration in Figure 1, both forces are influential, but God is the most powerful.

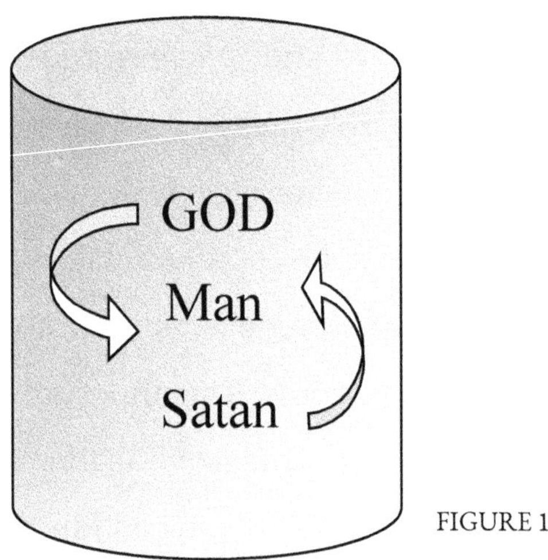

FIGURE 1

The Divine Agenda

The first question about the human experience and its purpose must include the fact that we are created in the image and likeness of a divine Creator, which is evident in the following passages of Scripture:

> ...let Us[18] make man in Our[19] image, according to Our likeness...[20] (Gen. 1:26, 27)

> For by Him, all things were created, visible and invisible, in the heavens and earth.[21] He is before all things, and in Him all things hold together.[22] (Col. 1:16-17)

We harness energy in a body with extraordinary capabilities, resilience, and an intelligent mind, reflecting a Creator. What does it mean to be created in His image and after His likeness? Ultimately, these are those communicable attributes of God placed in man at his creation.[23] The Hebrew word for image contains a root that means to shade and indicates resemblance, a representative figure, or a phantom.[24] Ralph Elliot's (1961) research suggests that linguistically, the word "image" implies a hewn or carved statue or a "copy," and the word likeness similarly means a facsimile.[25] In addition, Spiros Zodhiates (1984) identifies the word "likeness" as a "pattern or shape."[26] However, we must exercise caution and not assume that God has a body like humans. God is a spirit and therefore does not have or need any body parts or their functions for Him to exist, which is amplified by analysis of Philippians 2:5-8.[27]

Here, Jesus became the "likeness of men," confirming that He became something He was not before that moment.

> Have this attitude in yourselves which was also in Christ Jesus, who, although He existed in the form of God, did not regard equality with God a thing to be grasped, but emptied Himself, taking the form of a bond-servant, and being made in the likeness of men. Being found in appearance as a man, He humbled Himself by becoming obedient to the point of death, even death on a cross.

The conduit or medium through which the likeness and image of God manifest in man is three-dimensional: **First**, one segment of the immaterial nature of man is the soul. What part of man is like or reflects God's nature? It cannot be the flesh or the body itself because the body is made from the dust of the ground, which contains elements of the universe. God is the First cause, does not have origin, and therefore cannot be made of the same substance (flesh) or any other tangible substance. The man was formed from the ground, but his soul was not created from tangible material. It appears that the spirit of life, which came directly from God's breath, resides in the soul of man, making it a reservoir for a part of God Himself. [28] The soul, like God, is immaterial, on a spirit order, like how John 4:24 describes God. A spirit does not have DNA, flesh, and bones. It is invisible to the naked eye and can exist outside the body. Therefore, it is immortal, and most importantly, it is the true essence of our being. [29] Carl Jung (1875-1961), a noted psychiatrist and psychoanalyst, understood the self (the inner person) as the image of God within man and capable of existing outside of space and time. [30,31] Alter a man's inner core or soul; you will, in effect, change who he is.

The body was designed as a conduit for the soul and a medium for interpersonal relationships and socialization between humans. Given the vast chasm between the creature and the Creator, God needed to create a medium and process through which the creature could experience Him, commune, and communicate, as well as an avenue through which man could express himself in response to a Holy God. Additionally, God allowed man to duplicate this process through procreation, thereby presenting an incomprehensible number of souls serving and praising the Creator, ideally. [32] Service to and relationship with God extends beyond the body to the soul. The scripture is clear: the flesh cannot please God,

> "[7]because the mind set on the flesh is hostile toward God; for it does not subject itself to the law of God, for it is not even able to do so, [8]and those who are in the flesh cannot please God." (Rom. 8:7-8) NASB

It is important to note that the word "flesh" refers to man's corrupt and weak nature, which is susceptible to sinful desires and appetites.[33] The point of emphasis is that the human body is the conduit through which man's corruption is experienced. Subsequently, the body has long been a synonym for this mindset and behavior. Part of the human dilemma is to bring the body into subjection and alignment with a soul guided by the Spirit of God. This is what the Apostle Paul means by

> I discipline my body and make it my slave... (I Corinthians 9:27) NASB or the King James version, which reads, I keep under my body, and bring it into subjection...

The Immutable Value of Humanity

The evolutionary fallout from the events that took place in the Garden of Eden presents a body designed and wired in a way that makes it vulnerable to temptation and lust. It is logical to think that before man's fall, his mind and body were in a different state, a pristine form, and in perfect harmony with the Creator.[34] Because of God's transcendent nature, no human can commune with Him without divine properties made available for that fellowship. At the apex of his creation, man was equipped with everything necessary to interact with God meaningfully, which included the degree of righteousness essential for a human-divine relationship. This produces an unavoidable reality, which many, from antiquity to modern day, have difficulty digesting, which is man has always been and will always be incapable of acquiring and maintaining righteousness independently. The Apostle Paul correctly captures this truth in Romans 3:9-10, 23, in which he notes all are under sin; there is none righteous; all have sinned and fallen short...

Christopher (1876), while discussing man's constitution, brilliantly notes:

> "In order that there may be rational communion between the infinite Jehovah and his finite creatures,... it is necessary that there shall be in the being of each party to the communion a medium of connection or communion through which thought and sentiment may flow from the one to the other; by which interflow joy, happiness, and pleasure may come to each."[35]

We must admit that the human body is a remarkable entity strategically designed for relationship, socialization, and service to God through the community and society. The Psalmist exclaims that we are "fearfully and wonderfully made!"[36] Isaac Asimov, a biochemist, stated, "The human brain is the most complex and orderly arrangement of matter in the universe."[37]

Even in its most pristine state, a divine element was necessary for the body to complete man's existence in God's image, and this element (dimensions of the Spirit) solidifies the human's inherent value. Man's inherent worth rests in the fact that we are created in His image. As previously mentioned, Theologians interpret this concept in several ways. But what is undeniably chief among them is the idea that the image of God in this context speaks to God's communicable attributes He shares with man and by which humans are capable of exemplifying holiness.

The image of God in man is so highly revered that God instituted capital punishment for anyone taking the life of another, i.e.:

> Whoever sheds man's blood, by man, his blood shall be shed, for in the image of God He made man.
>
> Genesis 9:6 (NSAB)

This measure is lost in the erroneous notion that humans result from a cosmic accident, not a living Creator. The reflection of God's image and presence in man enriches every soul. As such, one's race, ethnicity, or nationality is of no effect in this estimation. White is without privilege, and black does not oscillate justice because the soul and spirit have no color. By this measure, the immigrant has dignity, and the poor are just as significant as the wealthy.

The criminal (although worthy of reprimand) is just as valuable as law-abiding citizens because each person is created in God's image. More critically, this image remained intact even after man's fall in the Garden of Eden. At the precise moment God ordains capital punishment, humanity has already fallen and shown itself wicked. The fact that humans are created in the image of God is immutable. A person's sin does not mar, alter, or adjust this image but instead accentuates their failure to be image-bearers reflecting the divinity of the Creator. Looking at Romans 3:23 again, this is, in some measure, what the latter part of Romans 3:23 teaches:

> For all have sinned and fallen short of the glory of God. (NASB)

Glory in this verse refers to the image of God and signifies that in his sins, man is not what God wants him to be or displays God's image and character. This ideology highlights man's conundrum as a created being attempting to reflect an uncreated image. It is undeniable that man was created in God's image, and this image defines and secures a person's dignity. It must be understood clearly that there are no circumstances under which this can be altered. The anatomical differences, inequality, imperfection, and failure commonly highlighted by culture gatekeepers do not automate licensure for inhumane or undignified treatment, judgment, and isolation of people. A person's value is not measured exclusively by what societies determine but by what God places in them.

Irrespective of the grandeur of the human body, it is lifeless without the presence of the immaterial parts of God's creation, the soul, and the dimensions of the Spirit.

The word soul originates from the Hebrew word Nephesh, which means respiration, breath, a breathing creature.[38] The corresponding Greek word for soul is pusuche. Notably, it is a term from which the English word psychology derives. Psychology studies human thought, emotion, and behavior, an exciting definition derived from a word that reflects a person's inner being. It has since been determined that the soul of man is the seat of thought and emotion and, subsequently, the principle of all behavior. The first example is in Deuteronomy 12:20, where desire is associated with the soul. Additionally, the soul can love, [39] rejoice, express sadness and desire, long for a relationship with God, exhibit knowledge and understanding, and have memory.[40]

In chapter 11 (The Final Verdict), the soul's capacity is much more distinguishable in the afterlife. At death, the soul departs, leaving the body utterly lifeless, yet it (the soul) continues to exhibit some of the five senses associated with the body and additionally, continues to express emotion, knowledge, memory, reason, and the capacity to communicate, but only within the new world it finds itself. This fact solidifies the argument that the soul is the natural person, not the body. In this approximation, the body is merely a conduit and means to an end physically and spiritually. Determining the true essence of a person requires looking beyond the body to their inner being.

This detail is too often lost or ignored when appraising candidates for relationships. This kind of shallowness diminishes the richness of relationships and socialization and potentially foils communal harmony. It certainly misplaces the more essential elements of relationship, a thought explored in more detail in chapter three, Irreconcilable Differences.

What is critically noteworthy here is that humans are intentionally created as relational beings, and every person is to reflect the image of the Creator in this context.

Relationships become another medium through which we seek identity and purpose. The soul operates and influences the body in this same way. The body carries out the desires of the heart or soul. Like the brain, the soul is impressionable and seeks out knowledge and experience; it is responsive and adaptive to data and experiences it encounters in its environment. In other words, it is shaped or fashioned by what it knows and experiences.

The brain is the point of contact between the two. Information between the body and the soul is multi-directional, meaning that the soul sends information to the body. Conversely, the body receives information externally and transmits the data to the brain for processing, the outcome of which grows into the tapestry of the soul. [41] However, categorization and interpretation of this information depend upon the condition of the soul, especially its spiritual condition. The psychological equivalent to this is referred to as schematic processing. Schema is a framework that organizes and interprets data received through the body's senses and the environment around it.[42]

Our schema is a processing center that determines our mental and attitudinal approach to life. As we go through different stages in life and gain new experiences, our brains and souls constantly work to understand and make sense of the latest information. This process involves clarifying the new information and comprehending initially unknown things. How a person processes new information or new experiences is based on an existing framework composed of prior experiences (traumatic or pleasurable), training, education, and godly characteristics or the lack thereof. Psychology dubs this process as assimilation.

Additionally, our schemas are adaptive, meaning people can adjust their perceptions or frameworks to integrate new data. This is known as accommodation.[43]

As such, it directs and influences how a person responds to other people and situations. Naturally, this capacity is designed to ensure a qualitative, optimal earthly experience within the confines of the human-divine relationship.

Concepts regarding the separation of the body and soul usually develop within dualism, an ideology proposed by Rene Descartes, a 17th-century philosopher. Descartes held that the body and mind (soul) are separate. In this context, Descartes believed that the body (most notably the brain) functions like a machine and that mathematical laws of physics elucidate these.[44] However, Descartes is incorrect in that the body and the mind do not influence each other because they are separate entities. As suggested earlier, it is accurate to surmise that the soul can function as a separate entity, a fact that is more explicit in the afterlife.[45] Descartes' view is philosophical. However, psychology sees dualism as an independent, formidable force with properties of equal significance that affect the inner person. Numerous instances and data suggest that what happens internally manifests externally through a person's health and behavior. While residing in the individual, the soul works with the brain. Beauregard and O'Leary (2007), in their book, The Spiritual Brain: A Neuroscientist's Case for the Existence of the Soul, note that religious experience expands beyond physical explanation and, in effect, sure up the existence of the immaterial nature of man, the soul.[46] A person's inner reality is displayed through the body. One of the first examples of the body and soul working synchronously is found in the Genesis account after Cain's crime against his brother and sin against God. Note what God says to Cain upon approach:

> "[6] Then the Lord said to Cain, why are you angry? And why has your countenance fallen? If you do well, will not your countenance be lifted up..."[7] (Genesis 4:6-7)

Another way of explaining this point is to consider the effects of stress on the body. Meyers (2008) notes that stress "is the process by which we appraise and cope with environmental threats and challenges."[47] Additionally, R.S. Lazarus (as cited in Meyers, 2008) states that our stress "arises less from the events themselves than from how we appraise them."[48] Many years ago, researchers determined that significant impacts and life-altering events such as trauma, disaster, the revelation of infidelity, divorce, death, and the day-to-day effort to succeed in life create substantial levels of stress that ultimately manifest physically. Any of these protracted over an extended period will change a person's attitude and appearance, induce illness, and even cause death.[49]

When stress occurs, three significant systems are stimulated into the response: the voluntary nervous system, which communicates with your muscles in preparation for the fight-or-flight mode; the autonomic nervous system, which helps increase blood flow to muscle while reducing blood to kidneys, digestive tract, and the skin; and the

neuroendocrine system, which regulates the body's internal operation. Meyers points out that sugar and fat stored in the body are released into the bloodstream under stress.[50]

> "Mind and body interact; everything psychological is simultaneously physiological. Psychological states are physiological events that influence other parts of our physiological system."[51]

Meyers goes on to note research suggesting a correlation between stress and cancer. This does not confirm that stress produces cancer cells, but relatively, its weakening effects on the immune system potentially lay the groundwork for the advent or advancement of the disease.[52]

Although God could know what was going on with Cain without any external cues, He noted the physical changes in Cain's face and that these were unintended disclosures of what was happening with him internally. Like a psychological paradigm, where the mind and body interact, the soul and body interact in a spiritual paradigm. All things spiritual become simultaneously physiological to the extent possible bodily, as already demonstrated through Cain. The word countenance originates from a Hebrew word that reflects facial expression of emotion.[53]

The body is influenced by the condition of the soul, as thoughts and behavior are guided by the soul's feelings and desires. The soul gives the body life, identity, and purpose, making people individuals. The soul is uniquely created. It is the essence of our being, the source in which the spirit of life dwells. The seat of every emotion, desire, or thought that makes us who we are. However, the soul is susceptible to life experiences, whether joyous or traumatic. Additionally, the soul can be changed and weakened if not nurtured properly. It is a relational being explicitly designed for that purpose.

Distilling the motivation behind so much detail about God's creation of humanity is critically noteworthy. Humans experience the world and its failures and corruption through their bodies. Still, they experience restoration and reconciliation with their Creator through their inner spirit. The daily dynamics imposed upon humans externally and internally are worthy of ongoing evaluation and appreciation in this reality. The soul is influenced by the world through the body and influenced internally by a divine Spirit.

The **second** dimension of the image and likeness in which we are created and that define us is the divine spirit, which is also referred to in this writing as the God module.

As such, it is immaterial, invisible, immortal, and dwells in the body temporarily while influencing the soul under specific prerequisites. H. Christopher (1876) states:

> "Man is, therefore, at least a dual being; more frequently is he spoken of as a trinity, having body, soul, and spirit."[54]

The immaterial nature of man is divided into two parts. Although many churches teach the indwelling of the Holy Spirit, many Christians see the Spirit as an outside influence instead of a being and force synchronized with man's inner being. This concept is not a new discussion. Witness Lee (1968), in his book The Economy of God, expands on research conducted in 1927.[55]

Furthermore, several scriptures confirm the separation between the soul and spirit. However, two are presented here for reference:

> Now, may the God of peace Himself sanctify you entirely, and may your spirit, soul, and body be preserved completely, without blame at the coming of our Lord Jesus Christ. I Thess. 5:23 NASB
>
> For the word of God is living and active and sharper than any two-edged sword and piercing as far as the division of soul and spirit, of both joints and marrow, and able to judge the thoughts and intentions of the heart. Hebrews 4:12 NASB

The Dimensions of the Inner Man

While these two passages and approach trichotomize the creation of man, which is the view adopted here, there is another vital text we should reflect upon:

> ...then the dust will return to the earth as it was, and the spirit will return to God who gave it.
>
> Eccl. 12:7 (NASB)

In some sense, the traditional view is acknowledged here, which states that humans consist of two substances: flesh and soul, a dual being. However, there is biblical precedence for suggesting the immaterial part of man is two-dimensional, as implicated in Eccl. 12:7. If dust is identified in this verse as one element and the spirit returning to God as another, where is the soul in this equation? Some argue that the spirit returning to God in this passage is nothing more than the element of life and corresponds to that moment in which God breathes into Adam's nostrils, "the breath of life." It's important to note that the estimation being discussed here doesn't account for the soul. Additionally, the referenced verse doesn't necessarily suggest that the soul and spirit are interchangeable. We understand that the soul is the individual's conscience and doesn't return to God.

At issue is the multiphasic nature and usage of the Hebrew word for spirit, rûwach (pronounced "roo′-akh), which is air, wind, or breath and certainly includes the concept of the element of life. Notwithstanding, even as the element of life, rûwach is depicted as the force through which life has character, reason, and other elements of being. For instance, Proverbs 16:2,

> All the ways of a man are clean in his own sight, but the Lord weighs the motives. (NASB)

The word "motives" in this verse means spirit (rûwach), and as such, it reaches beyond the elements of life to suggest characteristics consistent with being. Because of Scriptural instances like this, some see the soul and spirit as synonymous parallelism and point to Isaiah 26:9 as one example:

> At night my soul longs for You, Indeed, my spirit within me seeks You diligently.

Yet, from one view, Psalm 32:2 depicts the word spirit as a person's disposition or mental framework. Conversely, the slight dimension or division exacted between the soul and the spirit in Hebrews 4:12 is undeniable. There is precedence for the argument that three substances contribute to who we are—the body, soul, and spirit. Further, the view of man as a trichotomy makes him akin to his Creator, in that God is a

Triune being, three persons (Father, Son, and Holy Spirit) yet one essence. Even with a body, soul, and spirit, the man is considered one being. The body is a medium through which we can experience the external world, the soul gives us self-consciousness and understanding of personality, and the spirit gives us God-consciousness.[56] But what is this spirit, and why do we have it? What is its role generally and within the context of the Adam complex?

There are distinctions between how God rules the material world (i.e., the universe) and the immaterial world. The material world is managed through His infinite power. He can begin or end anything anywhere at any time. No power is more significant than Him, and no cosmic event is beyond His knowledge and influence. Conversely, the immaterial world (i.e., the souls of men and angels on high) is managed by divine objectives, reasoning, directing His subjects through relationship, moral influence, and a type of love that motivates, navigates, and synchronizes our will to His. Because we were created to glorify Him within the context of a relationship, there needed to be a conduit or medium through which His created beings can communicate, fellowship, and interact spiritually through prayer, praise, and worship; that there is a channel by which happiness and other emotions could flow, as well as divine directives assisting men during life's challenges; and a medium suitable for relationship during the human plight from earth to heaven.

In anticipation of the relationship, the Creator instills in humans a divine spirit, a medium connecting humans to their Creator, allowing them to embody the image and likeness in which they were created.

In this context, the Spirit of God synchronizes with man's spirit.

The aim is for man's inner being to function in tandem with the spirit. The Spirit's first objective is to establish awareness of God.[57] The chasm that exists between man and God is incomprehensively vast. The unregenerated human is not even aware of Him appreciably without divine intervention, and upon awareness of Him, the human is clueless and incapable of approaching Him. Although God probably adjusted Himself before allowing Adam to stand before Him, Adam needed some aspect of the Divine One before he was aware of himself and his environment and became conscious of and knowledgeable about the Creator. Hence, God breathed into His nostrils' life and some degree of knowledge and appreciation for Him as Creator. Adam was formed from dust, but God didn't bring him to life until He placed something divine in him. The sequence of events is intentional. As Creator, God is mindful of man's limitations and saw the end from the beginning, including man's fall. The foreknowledge is accompanied by wisdom that necessitated man's creation in a manner that accommodates essentials for redemption and includes a reservoir for the Holy Spirit.[58] This way, after making man aware of God, the Spirit living inside man's human spirit lays the groundwork for the resurrection from the fallen state in which he finds himself. This begins with what theologians call regeneration and what the Bible declares. In contrast, it is a divine act that starts the salvific process by awakening a man to the reality of God and his corrupt condition.[59] The Holy Spirit is the agent of physical life, spiritual life, and transformation through sanctification. It is not the preachers, pastors, elders, or even church members who bring about a change in people's lives. Instead, the Holy Spirit works within us according to the Father's divine plan that was determined before the world began. These great servants can only announce and explain the Good News. Redemption and salvation are the work of God. The Spirit lives at depths so profound that such space can only be reserved for the Creator. As such, no human should ever allow any foreign presence (person, substance, or situation) in a space invaluable and reserved for something as holy and mighty as the Spirit of God. Never allow anyone or anything so deeply into your core space that the experience changes who you are.

And yet, many have allowed just that... alcohol, drugs, sex, money, power, and relationships profoundly alter people for the worse every day.

The Spirit's function then is strategic and multiphasic, aimed at equipping the soul with tools necessary for spiritual success.[60] "...His divine power has granted to us everything about life and godliness..." (II Peter 1:3). We have what we need to succeed, which is established through the Spirit's role and function. Making us conscious of God, we are subsequently convicted by the Spirit. One cannot be mindful of God without recognizing his imperfection, fallenness, and the inherent need for salvation.[61]

PART TWO

THE PSYCHOANALYTIC VIEW

The Psychology of it All

Through revelation of moral agency, consciousness, and the word of God, the Spirit convicts the person He inhabits. As such, He becomes the influence behind the voice in your head, speaking to the soul to govern thought and behavior. Robert Feldman (2013) describes this: "The superego includes the conscience, which prevents us from misbehaving by making us feel guilty if we do wrong."[62] A person misbehaving, seemingly without thought or consideration of others, is noted as a person without a conscience.

These internal dialogues and voices (metaphorically) are often called the conscious. Have you ever thought about where does consciousness originate? Where does this voice come from? Can it be the Spirit's gentle nudge to do what is right whenever the opportunity presents itself? Perhaps another way of understanding this is to parallel Sigmund Freud's structural theory of the mind[63] with the model under discussion here. Although Freud (a stark atheist) held that belief in God was a form of neurosis and a longing for a father, his work and research on critical composites of personality leaves an indelible impression in psychology specifically and society generally. Additionally (likely to his and other atheist's annoyance), Freud's model affirms how the Spirit's presence in man leads him to consciousness that informs thought and behavior. Freud believed that our hidden personality influences our behavior and decision-making. Our personality is divided into three overlapping and interactive regions: ID, ego, and superego. Many psychology textbooks use the iceberg model to illustrate the structural theory of the mind.[64] The idea behind this illustration is that the part of the iceberg protruding out of the water is a small portion compared to the volume of ice beneath the water. Conversely, the significant components and dynamics contributing to people's identity are largely hidden. The **ID** is identified as the part of the mind that stores all fears, hyper-sexual desires, deviance, trauma, or emotional injury. It is where irrational impulses and aggression originate. It is both insensitive and thoughtless, pleasure-seeking, [65] and therefore purely driven by instant gratification. Durand and Barlow (2006) give us a clearer perspective by stating that the ID "is basically, the animal within us; if unchecked, it would make us all rapists or killers."[66] This concept may be difficult for some to digest. Societies all over the world have people within them who are demented or psychologically and physiologically fragmented. As such, there is no check and balance system within them, which allows the ego to process whatever is in the ID in real-time. It becomes their reality.

This kind of person operates without consciousness or a moral compass. Whether we buy into this notion or not, we must admit that deviant and erroneous unorthodox behavior is driven by and derived from dynamical forces externally and within the individual.

How do people become this way? What are the factors contributing to deviant and ungodly behavior? How are these motivations and experiences logged and registered in the ID? Do we enter life with a clean slate emotionally, mentally, and spiritually? Are some born with these ill tendencies?

The answers to these questions may be twofold. First, the advent of these characteristics commonly associated with the ID is not innate to humans generally. Under normal circumstances, a person's entry into the world and initial trek to adulthood is not marred by the tenets we have come to associate with this part of the mind. Second, what settles in the ID is often the fallout from physical and emotional trauma and exposure to various experiences in revolving contexts. The ID is built out of the stuff we call life experiences. However, there is a biological and evolutionary approach to personality development.

Carl Jung (pronounced "young") (1875-1961) was a noted Swiss psychiatrist and psychoanalyst who rejected Freud's structural theory of the mind, namely the notion that the unconscious primary significance revolved around sexual urges. [67] Jung points more toward what he dubbed the "collective unconscious," a typical "set of ideas, feelings, images, and symbols that we inherit from our ancestors, the whole human race, and even animal ancestors from the distant past." [68] The biological and evolutionary approach (primarily built on research by behavioral geneticists and their argument that personality is predicated on our genes) is also a competing factor. Elements of all three of these theories are likely involved in personality development. As an example, as indicated earlier in this chapter, we are the biological and evolutionary by-products of Adam and Eve's spiritual, psychological, and neurological state after their fall in the Garden of Eden.

Additionally, there are noted instances in which a person is born with chemical imbalances and impaired cognitive and neurological conditions that affect behavior. Where these are present, it is almost certain that they are produced by biological error or a traumatic event. We can rest assured that where a person is imprisoned by psychological and neurological defects beyond their control, the fate of their soul lies in the hands of a just God. However, in relatively healthy individuals and everyday circumstances, the **superego** (the second region of the mind) regulates behavior, especially those irrational and animalistic behaviors lodged in the ID. The superego is where internalized ideas reside. Spiritual connections, parents, caregivers, and society instill positive values, moral conscience, religious instructions, righteousness, judgment, and aspirations.[69]

Ideally, the superego acts as a filter and barrier to avert irrational behaviors from surfacing from the ID and filter incoming data and experiences that perpetuate similar ideologies and behaviors. You are standing behind someone who unknowingly drops a one-hundred-dollar bill. The ID may suggest that you say nothing and keep the money to buy the new tennis shoes you are eager to purchase. However, moral standards lodged in the superego, your mother's voice about always doing the right thing, or the Sunday school lesson from the prior week kicks in... noting that it is wrong to keep the money and, therefore, should be returned to its rightful owner. The desires or drives housed in the ID are latent, meaning they can become conscious at any moment.

As most people know, conceiving and enacting a lousy idea only takes a moment. Subsequently, irrespective of how horrific or ungodly some of these desires may be, they can live in the superego temporarily. At this stage, the possibility of them is that much riskier. Without a healthy superego, a person will indeed enact whatever lies deep in his unconscious region and will likely see no wrong. The superego most often functions in opposition to the ID. However, when the desires of the ID work in tandem with the goals of the superego, the two regions may appear to be one. The dynamics of internal conflict are more apparent in this context. The ID and the superego make opposing demands that have real consequences. A mental and emotional brawl develops as one tries to overthrow the other. However, an internal referee, a mediator, and a chief executive of the mind seek to temper the demands of the superego and ID. This is called the **ego**. The ego operates on what is known as the reality principle[70], which seeks to satisfy the superego's desires and ID in reasonable and harmless ways to self and society. Another way of understanding this model is to label the components as unconscious, preconscious, and conscious segments. The ID is the unconscious, the superego is the preconscious, and the ego is identified as the conscious mind. Irrespective of the approach, careful analysis of this model reflects the trichotomy of humans and, more specifically, our internal modus operandi, which includes the work of the Spirit. As contrasted in the image below,

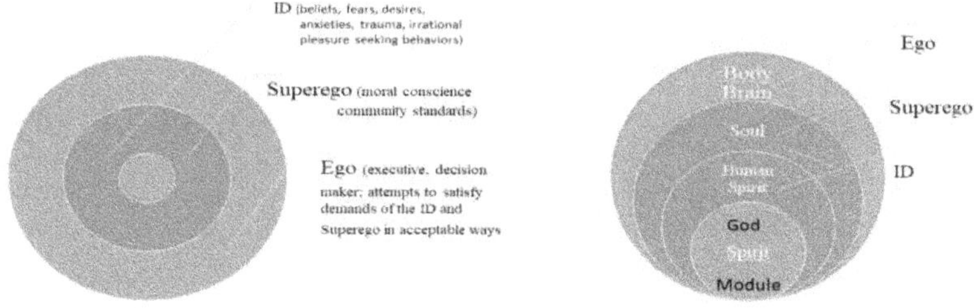

What Freud and others identify as the ID, ego, superego or unconscious, preconscious, and conscious parallels man's immaterial nature, the work of the Spirit, opposing phantom forces, and how these are processed.

The most critical among these is the superego. Adapting either system, we surmise that the soul resides in or is equivalent to the superego (preconscious), the part of the person with moral consciousness that regulates irrational behavior. However, it is essential to remember that the desires or drives in the ID or unconscious are latent and transitory. They can surface in the superego, even if it is temporary.

In other words, it is possible for some of the irrational behaviors that live deep inside a person to become a part of their soul, a part of who they are, long enough to enact them, at least. Whether this happens or not depends upon the health of the superego and if the ID (unconscious) is more dominant. One will do well remembering that although this part of a person is largely hidden, it is powerfully influential and can alter your soul subsequently. The Spirit seeks to take residence deep within a person and, through His presence and sanctifying work, destroy and bury the debilitating and ungodly part of the individual. The human spirit is the conduit through which God accesses the soul to guide and influence it through relationship, love, and divine leadership. This human/divine communion produces the conviction that ultimately leads to change.

The Spirit not only convicts and gives consciousness but also sanctifies those He inhabits. [71] In layperson's terms, He cleans and purifies to present and dedicate the soul to a relationship with God.

PART THREE

THE RELATIONSHIP

Far too many do not consider that a person cannot approach or interact with God in any condition. A man must prepare and qualify to enter God's presence and commune with Him. This does not suggest that one needs to be flawless before entering a relationship with God, but that each person must allow and engage the Spirit that lives within, who, in effect, qualifies us for a relationship with the Divine. The perfection necessary for man to have is impossible without God's aid. The first step is always through Jesus Christ, the propitiation[72] for our sins and the conduit through which a relationship with God is possible. Note:

> "I am the way and the truth, and the life; no one comes to the Father but through me." (John 14:6) NASB.

The Spirit (through Christ) prepares us for divine relationships and enables us to live out God's plan for us, even during challenging moments. Note:

> "In the same way, the Spirit helps our weakness; for we do not know how to pray as we should, but the Spirit Himself intercedes for us with groanings too deep for words;" (Romans 8:26).

Those problem areas, such as temptation, moments when our moral compass and priorities are misplaced, and when we experience states of confusion or habitual behaviors antithetical to righteous standards, are the areas the Spirit seeks to help resolve. He fights the enemy with us and through us. Subsequently, submitting to His leadership and counsel is of utmost importance. However, all too often, people, either because of total ignorance of this power and the processes associated with it or because of mere neglect of the Spirit's presence, interfere with His operation by routinely interjecting self, denying the Spirit venue and opportunity to work. Note:

> "Do not quench the Spirit;" (I Thessalonians 5:19) NSAB.

> "Do not grieve the Holy Spirit of God, by whom you were sealed for the day of redemption." (Eph. 4: 30) NASB

The idea behind the words "quench" and "grieve," as rendered here, is sadness, pain, and agony elicited from behavior and lifestyle antithetical to the work and purpose of the Spirit. When a person re-engages behaviors and ideologies the Spirit has worked diligently to pull one out of; it causes significant pain, sorrow, and frustration of the Spirit. Intriguingly, Zodhiates notes that the Greek synonym for these words is “stenochereo,” meaning “to crowd into a narrow space.” [73] In this context, it suggests denying the Spirit appropriate room to work in the individual. The Spirit is our source of power for challenges in life and godly living.[74] However, it is not like a magic wand that a person can wave at will. This power is cultivated through relationships and familiarity. Every person is a human spirit, but the Holy Spirit is reserved for the people of God.[75] It is stimulated by prayer and ongoing meditation on the word of God and things of Him. Intentionally embracing behaviors contrary to the work of the Spirit forfeits the power within. Attempting to fight phantom forces without adequate tools and preparation is spiritual suicide. When God strengthens and prepares us, He does so from the inside out, not the outside. Note:

> “that He would grant you, according to the riches of His glory, to be strengthened with power through His Spirit in the inner man.” (Eph. 3:16) NASB

> “I can do all things through Him who strengthens me.” (Phil. 4:13) NASB

There are a few critical aspects regarding how the Spirit enables and empowers that are worthy of note. Rarely discussed, the Spirit equips us with intellectual gifts, unique talents, and abilities contributing to success and fulfillment. For instance:

> [30] Then Moses said to the sons of Israel, "See,
> the LORD has called by name Bezalel the son of Uri, the
> son of Hur, of the tribe of Judah. [31] And He has filled
> him with the Spirit of God, in wisdom, in
> Understanding, and knowledge and all
> craftsmanship; to make designs for working in gold
> and in silver and bronze, [33] and the cutting of stones
> for settings and in the carving of wood, to perform in
> every inventive work. [34] He also has put in his heart to
> teach both he and Oholiab, the son of Ahisamach, of
> the tribe of Dan. [35] He has filled them with the skill to
> perform every work of an engraver and of a designer
> and of an embroiderer, in blue and in purple *and*
> scarlet *material*, and fine linen, and of a weaver, as
> performers of every work and makers of designs.
> Exodus 35:30-35

Most people don't contribute their success (academically or otherwise) to inherent abilities given to us by the Holy Spirit. Additionally, the Holy Mandate notes that Christ gave gifts to men, which can edify the church (Eph. 4:1-7, 11-16) and the community. Our ability to learn and develop skillsets is consequential to the blessing of God through the work of the Spirit. The professor, psychologist, CEO, physician, and self-made IT guru are by-products of the gifts of the Spirit. Many will do well, remembering there is force antithetical to success and happiness. It is a force working strategically against wellness, productivity, and spiritual development. It manifests through various people (family, friends, co-workers) and multiple contexts (in marriage, business, and communally, such as churches), creating a domino effect in the lives of many.

The second way the Spirit empowers is through hope, providing hope.

> "Now may the God of hope fill you with all joy and peace in believing, so that you will abound in hope by the power of the Holy Spirit." (Romans 15:13)

This may seem elementary to the seasoned Christian and corny to the unchurched reader. However, hope, as used in this verse, reflects one's desire for something good and confident expectation of receiving it.[76]

Think of it this way: it's Thursday, and you know Friday is payday. There is ongoing hope and anticipation for the day because of what it yields: a paycheck. Generally, most workers are happiest when remuneration for services is rendered- payday! Over time, the employer/employee relationship proves the employee can trust payment on the designated day. There is so much hope and trust in it that the employee is motivated to follow company rules even on the day farthest from payday, i.e., Monday. They are encouraged to show up, even with the Monday blues. Moreover, while putting on a stellar performance (because it increases value, personally and numerically), an employee will tolerate challenging people around them to get what is promised on Friday.

Similarly, the person who hopes and trusts in God and the blessing wrought through a relationship with Jesus Christ is empowered with the hope that satisfies, motivates, and creates a positive outlook that consistently promotes happiness. This process enables a person to stand up, do right, and live happily and in harmony with God. This type of hope translates into a unique inner peace.

Irrespective of what is happening around or to a person, they will stay the course because of their hope, trust, and belief in the power of God.

Next, the Spirit strengthens us to overcome problem areas and complex circumstances. Anything disturbs equilibrium and continuity between an individual and the Creator is problematic. Some dilemmas are internal and self-imposed, while others are external and produced by forces seeking to obscure, bind, and destroy individuals and families. [77]

There are many other things, duties, and privileges ascribed to the work of the Spirit, i.e., He teaches, comforts, and counsels, to name a few. These are enumerated here to clarify that man's immaterial being is divided into the Holy Spirit's presence, leadership, and power.

When God created man in His image, He made him with the inclination for good, just, and holy things. [78] It is like a child born to their parents. The child has similar DNA. Subsequently, the child either favors the father or mother, or in some cases, both. Additionally, the child is prone to mannerisms and behaviors consistent with the parents. For instance, one former global superstar resembled his late father in more ways than one. Not only were there similar features, but he also had a tireless work ethic, which contributed to his success, multiple NBA records, and a billion-dollar empire. Right before he dismantled his opponent above the rim, that patented wag of the tongue derived from watching and spending time with his father, whose tongue routinely protruded while performing activities around the house.

Because God instilled a part of Himself in man, he, similarly, bears the natural characteristics of his Creator. Other similar traits are developed through a relationship with Him over time. God is the standard for life and holiness; the origin of all that is good, just, caring, and loving.

How do we determine that something is wrong, except there is a consciousness of right? What motivates the unchurched, nonbelieving humanitarian and philanthropist to have compassion for someone they do not know halfway around the world? What causes a president not to abuse his power but to exercise integrity while satisfying their responsibilities? Where does the need to protest the abuse of children or the compelling need to give food and shelter to a homeless person originate?

If we surmise that caregivers and parents embedded these, where did they get it from? We can go on and on attempting to ascribe the origin of morality to other causes and agencies, but in the end, we are faced with the reality that the spirit of these originates with God, and because of His Spirit in us, morality or the need for it is innate to humans. However, morality can be destroyed by the absence of a godly spirit and the advent of an evil one. If the presence of God's Spirit promotes godly consciousness and moral agency, the lack of such fosters behavior contrary to these.

Given that a significant portion of this chapter highlights details of man's creation (essential to understanding the Adam complex), let's focus now on the other two dynamics within this trifecta. As a reminder, *the Adam complex is the ability to stabilize the interpersonal trifecta between God, the inner self, and external forces that try to undermine the union between the creature and the Creator*.

Man's analysis and view of self contribute to his ability to acknowledge and respond to his Creator appreciably. People routinely make decisions based on their understanding of themselves or the lack thereof. Friends, soul mates, careers, and recreational habits are all predicated on who a person believes they are and what they prefer in life. The revelation that we are part spirit suggests expectations beyond our fleshly existence. Given that the Creator made man in His image and after His likeness, He seeks communion or fellowship with His subjects.

Knowing that we are souls with thoughts and emotions that affect behavior is crucial to interacting with the Holy God.

Misunderstanding God

We are created to be in harmony with Him in ways that promote inner peace, self-actualization, and life-long happiness. However, if we do not know or understand who we are, our appraisal of Him is dramatically misapprehended, and our relationship with Him is altered or nonexistent. Misunderstanding God contributes to unbecoming behavior and instability that evokes unnecessary challenges, pain, and loss, if not in this life but certainly in the future. Misunderstanding means that the interpretation and value of something are misapplied or underappreciated; it means to confuse one thing as something else, to mix something up, or to make an error in response to it. As noted earlier in this chapter, man's attempt to relate to God is softened and simplified by reducing Him to a level no more significant than the best of us. Among the new shows dawning the airways this fall is a show in which God is on Facebook befriending people. One's initial appraisal of this may see no harm in the modern playful portrayal of Deity. God is wholly invested in our joy and happiness, but certainly not at His expense.

He has given us various gifts, venues, and ways to live happily. Note:

> "Every good thing given, and every perfect gift is from above..." (James 1:17) NASB.

> "I know that there is nothing better for them than to rejoice and to do good in one's lifetime; moreover, that every man who eats and drinks sees good in all his labor is the gift of God." (Eccl. 3:12-13) NASB

As you learn and understand yourself, who is God to you? There is no way to document all that God is in His totality, nor can our finite minds comprehend all He is. This does not mean that He is condensed to the sum of our thoughts. However, does it mean that He is unknowable? Does it mean that He is too complex to relate interpersonally? Any answer in the affirmative is erroneous. If God is unknowable yet condemns man for not knowing or entering a relationship with Him through Christ, He is unjust in His administration. This notion is impossible for two reasons. First, God is just in all His theocratic government. He can't go against or contradict Himself.[79] Secondly, the essentials necessary for a relationship with Him are declared through His word and the person of Jesus Christ.[80] Everything else about him that is either mysterious or too complex to comprehend is not essential for a relationship with Him, i.e., a person can enter a covenant relationship with God through Christ without complete knowledge of how God constructed heaven, angels, and hell. These are only a few of several profound mysteries of God, which, in effect, is part of what makes Him God. Why do so many believe we must know and understand everything about Him and His work to be God? God cannot be discovered, He cannot be figured out, He is only revealed, and even that is at His discretion.

Among all the things God has disclosed to us about Himself, the most substantial aspect of His character that is significant to the Adam complex is His holiness. Too many Christians treat God's holiness trivially. Unfortunately, His holiness is not always reflected in our approach to Him, whether in worship, prayer, or praise. Too many churches and families prepare extraordinarily little for human-divine encounters. For instance, it's Sunday morning, and the Saints have assembled. Many come into the sanctuary with their extreme hats, tight dresses, and suits; there is a joyful atmosphere with laughter and smiles, as it should be to some extent. There is discussion about the pot roast in the oven, the events that took place over the weekend, and the outlook for the week ahead. In other areas, an opposite environment exists with flip-flops, short pants, and wrinkled shirts.

Although there is no dress code per se or a ruler to measure the length of a skirt, attire, and behavior reflect one's attitude toward the environment, the occasion, and the people involved. In some places, there is a haphazard and apathetic approach to the house of God, which is naturally holy. Additionally, in some assemblies' members are disgruntled over 'Sunday morning displacement' (when a person's regular seat is occupied), and the energy from interpersonal train wrecks (members who can't get along) saturate the environment.

In these environments, there are often no defining transitional moments from the social gathering to a consciousness of the holy assembly. A person's heart or soul must prepare for the human-divine encounter. However, the fact that one's décor and behavior reflect one's inner-person and attitudinal approach is indisputable.

A person is less likely to appear for a job interview in flip-flops and shorts unless the position requires such attire. If invited to a White House State Dinner, you better believe that a person will ensure that the décor and attitude are appropriate for the occasion. Generally, people (seemingly) do not mind respecting or honoring those things and other people we have dubbed significant. For example, it is a standing rule that when entering the presence of the King of

Saudi Arabia or the Queen of England, a person bows, doesn't speak unless spoken to, or don't extend your hand to greet unless they have extended theirs; when the President of the United States enters or leaves a room or a judge entering and exiting a legal forum, we are taught to stand in honor and respect of the office, if not the person. It is a concept we understand and practice without hesitation. However, these and their office are minuscule to the Creator, God of the universe, the Holiest of Holies. Yet, His Supremacy is not always front and center, but all too often at recess, even in the minds of some people of faith.

This is likely because of insufficient attention to God's holiness in contemporary preaching and teaching. For instance, one aspect of God's holiness unknown to the average church member is His transcendent nature. When today's Christians usually think about God's holiness, they only reflect on His moral purity. However, when the Bible refers to God's holiness, it speaks of His transcendence, making His moral character secondary but equally critical. The "come as you are mantra" may help the stranger feel comfortable, but it does little to prepare the soul for the presence of a Holy God. Remember, when we assemble (especially for worship), we are, in effect, entering His presence [81] , which should always prompt adequate preparation. If congregants are not taught to recall and recognize God's holy presence, they will not keep this in their minds as they approach God through prayer, praise, worship, and other aspects of their lives. The people must be taught and routinely reminded of the holiness of God.

Note:

> "Guard your steps as you go to the house of God and draw near to listen rather than to offer the sacrifice of fools; for they do not know they are doing evil." (Eccl. 5:1) NASB

> "By those who come near Me, I will be treated as holy, and before all the people I will be honored." (Leviticus 10:1-3) NASB

> "...be holy, for I am holy..." (Leviticus 11:44-45; 19:2; 20:7)

The holiness of God sets the tenor for one's approach and relationship with Him. We must get out of our minds that God can be approached in any manner. He is not cousin Vinny or "June-bug" or like your "bestie." He doesn't have a Twitter handle, Snap Chat account, or surf Facebook in ways like humans. One of the most iconic stories depicting the significance of our approach to and presenting ourselves before God is found in Exodus 3:1-9. While pasturing in the fields near Mt. Horeb (the mountain of God), Moses is alerted to God's presence. Subliminally, Moses is summonsed into the presence of God. He ascends the mountain for this purpose. Notice what takes place upon his arrival. Moses turned his attention toward God, mainly to see Him, but God called out to him first! This initial encounter and discourse with Moses are directive, protective, and informative. God determines how He should be approached, not man.

He instructs Moses to remove his shoes or sandals because the ground is Holy. Typically, most readers and narrators are consumed by the inextinguishable burning bush, so little significance is given to Moses' shoes. However, the request to remove his shoes has a profound message. First, the request is protective because entering God's presence and looking upon Him without prior sanctification and preparation is certainly death! It is a fact that is so mind-blowing that our little finite minds cannot grasp the notion appreciatively. God is so pure and righteous that His holiness will instantly destroy anything or anyone defiled before Him, for no one is as holy as he is. It is a knee-jerk reaction of sorts to that which is unholy.[82] This explains the ongoing need for covering and cleansing in the presence of God. Many people fear and dislike the wrath of God. They do not like thinking or talking much about this part of Him. However, the fact is that His holiness generates His wrath. The wrath of His holiness destroys, but the loving nature of Him saves. His holiness is nothing to take for granted or play around with. He must be respected and treated as holy consistently. As previously noted, this fact is echoed in Exodus 19:21; 33:20

> "Then the Lord spoke to Moses, "Go down, warn the people, so that they do not break through to the Lord to gaze, and many of them perish."

> "[20] But He said, you cannot see My face, for no man can see Me and live!"

In this light, Moses is instructed to remove his shoes. In one aspect, shoes indicate something lowly, filthy, and defiled. In other aspect, shoes are symbolic of power, victory, and dominance (Ps. 8:6). Soldiers of old would place their feet on the head or neck of the enemy they defeated, symbolizing victory (Joshua 10:24). Even in the 21st-century shoes carry significant cultural connotations, i.e., during an Iraqi press conference in 2008, an Iraqi journalist stood up and hurled his shoes at then-president George W. Bush. As he shouted in Arabic, he indicated that one shoe was a farewell gift from the Iraqis and the other for the widows and orphans killed by the U.S.-led invasion and occupation.[83] Moses' removal of his shoes is significant.

The prerequisite for anyone coming before the Creator is to have a covering and purgation of anything that defiles and, in effect, appeases the wrath of a Holy God. There must be an attitudinal adjustment, which must include humility and capitulation of all power and dominion. In this regard, kings, queens, lords, and presidents must surrender their crowns and power to Him upon approach. He is the King of kings and Lord of lords[84] and before whom, or in contrast, no equitable power or measure of holiness exists.[85] It is no wonder that it was appropriate for Moses to rid himself of any symbolic gestures of defilement.

Upon approach, God immediately makes Moses conscious of the significance of the environment and place he has now entered. The ground was holy because God was present. When God descended on Mt. Sinai, the mountain and its environment were dramatically altered in response to His presence. An impressive amount of fire and smoke inundated the environment; the brash trumpets, thunder, lightning, and violent mountain shaking marked God's presence.[86] Any man or beast making the slightest contact with the mountain would be executed.[87] The scene and sounds at Mt. Sinai were so immense it terrified the people.[88] One of several lessons we learn from this is that wherever God is present, the spatial orientation and experience are like no other. It's not a softball game or a trip to the amusement park. It is not a music concert or anything like Hamilton and the Nutcracker. It is and should be distinctively different. This notion should foil contemporary attempts to make the church and worship experience like anything to which it is antithetical. Although the Sinai summit is significant, what is even more noteworthy are the prerequisites God ordered before his arrival. Note: Exodus 19:10-13 NASB

> 10 The LORD also said to Moses, "Go to the people and consecrate them today and tomorrow and let them wash their garments; 11 and let them be ready for the third day, for on the third day the LORD will come down on Mount Sinai in the sight of all the people. 12 You shall set bounds for the people all around, saying, 'Beware that you do not go up on the mountain or touch the border of it; whoever touches the mountain shall surely be put to death. 13 No hand

> shall touch him, but he shall surely be stoned or shot through; whether beast or man, he shall not live.' When the ram's horn sounds a long blast, they shall come up to the mountain."

The key word here is consecrate or sanctify, which means "to be holy," solidifying the notion and fact that any contact or communion with the Holy One requires that the comer's approach and relationship with Him is undefiled. The Old Testament Tabernacle system of worship[89] was predicated on this fact. During this period, the people of God worshipped and communed with Him from a distance. The structure of the Tabernacle ensured man's safety while paying homage to God. Some people view these narratives as Old Testament jargon, implying that the principles highlighted therein are for those alive at that time. However, God is immutable and remains as holy now as He was then. Subsequently, His expectations have not changed. Today, man is blessed by the vicarious atonement of Jesus Christ, mitigating the process and sanctions against those unjustified to enter God's presence and relationship subsequently.

Notably, Hebrews chapter ten encapsulates the sufficiency of the death of Christ in this regard. Additionally, chapter twelve contrasts Sinai and Zion (the city of God) and correctly notes Jesus as a mediator of a new covenant. Instead of this, the people of God (now covered by the blood of Christ) can "draw nigh" and come closer and enter the holy place without experiencing instant death or the dreadful scenes that played out on Mt. Sinai. However, it is critically noteworthy that Christ's work did not diminish God's holiness. It is not that God is less holy because Christ paid the penalty in our stead; it is not that because we can enter His presence by the blood of Christ, holiness is no longer demanded or expected of those who seek Him. God is holy by nature. As noted earlier, He cannot change or go against Himself. Principally speaking, what was unholy to Him then is unholy still. That which was an abomination then is an abomination now. The demand for holiness, then, is demanded today. Note:

> "[13] Therefore, prepare your minds for action, keep sober *in spirit*, fix your hope completely on the grace to be brought to you at the revelation of Jesus Christ. [14] As obedient children do not be conformed to the former lusts *which were yours* in your ignorance, [15] but like the Holy One who called you, be holy yourselves also in all *your*

> behavior; [16] because it is written, "YOU SHALL BE HOLY, FOR I AM HOLY." I Peter 1:13-16 NASB

> "Therefore, I urge you, brethren, by the mercies of God, to present your bodies a living and holy sacrifice, acceptable to God, *which is* your spiritual service of worship." Romans 12:1 NASB

> "Pursue peace with all men and the sanctification without which no one will see the Lord." Hebrews 12:14 NASB

The ongoing work of the Holy Spirit and the vicarious death of Christ lay the groundwork and chart the path that leads to a relationship with God. Jesus poignantly and emphatically states

> "...no one comes to the Father but through Me." (John 14:6) NASB.

Since man's fall in the garden, God has been on a mission to restore a relationship with the creature He made in His image and likeness and deliver what He intended for man to have all the while—eternal life with Him. The initial pristine state of man (which was contaminated by the onslaught of evil) is restored through the work of the Holy Spirit and the death of Christ. As mentioned, the Holy Spirit sanctifies us, making us holy and acceptable to God.[90]

The first dynamic within the Adam complex is born out of the intricate nature of His holiness and man's failed condition. As such, it creates a dichotomy and paradox that generate ongoing tension between the creature and the Creator. The word 'tension' etymology originated in the 16th century, meaning "a stretched condition" in French; in Medieval Latin, it meant "stretching." Today, the word includes these connotations and mental or emotional strain.[91]

The tension is multifaceted, generally ascribed to people of faith and humans. We must remember that when the Holy Mandate states that.

> "For God so loved the world, He gave His only begotten Son, that whoever believes in Him shall not perish, but have eternal life."

It is a gift not only for Christians today and those of old but for the entire world. There are those (even people of faith) who erroneously assert that the death of Christ was for limited individuals. Christ died for all.[92] Although many will be lost, God is interested in a relationship with every soul He has created. Subsequently, salvation and the gift of eternal life are extended to everyone, not by force, but by invitation through faith in the Gospel.[93] Humans were created to live in harmony with God and not die. Sin introduced death into the world system. God does not take pleasure in death, although it is required.

> "For I have no pleasure in the death of anyone who dies, declares the Lord God. "Therefore, repent and live." (Ezekiel 18:32) NASB

Consequently, God desires that everyone be saved by entering a covenant relationship with Him to restore this relationship and make good on the gift of eternal life. Note:

> [8]But do not let this one *fact* escape your notice, beloved, that with the Lord one day is like a thousand years, and a thousand years like one day. [9] The Lord is not slow about His promise, as some count slowness, but is patient toward you, not wishing for any to perish but for all to come to repentance. (II Peter 3:8-9) NASB

> [3]This is good and acceptable in the sight of God our Savior, [4]who desires all men to be saved and to come to the knowledge of the truth. (I Timothy 2:3-4)

This divine determination is pressed against man's expedition for significance for himself and the people around him, man's need for definition and clarification, evolution, and communion with people and things his society dubs critical to the human experience.

Prime education from the nation's ivory towers and the subsequent pursuit of high-end occupations, property in elite zip codes, and head-turning transportation are chief among his concerns. Additionally, God's quest for a relationship with man is confronted with his capitalist drive, investment portfolio, sexual gratification, elite and sometimes unorthodox relationships, as well as the need to identify with groups championing his agenda or interests, even to the discrimination of others. It is not that all of these are criminal or corrupt; instead, they become the essence of man's life. These things become meaning and identity for those who pursue them at the expense of everything else. In a worst-case scenario, these lifestyles become a god for many. Life is solely about the chase and any pleasure or gratification. As God investigates the lives of men, he seeks opportunity and room to enter and authentically complete man's need for meaning and identity.

However, in some cases, the trek man takes, and the lifestyle he chooses exacerbates the natural tension between him and God. Anything that opposes God or is unholy and contrasts with His will is hostile to Him and interferes with cultivating a relationship with the creature He loves. Understanding His holiness is critical in this regard.

The only means to enter a relationship with the Father is through the essential atoning work of Christ. God is busy drawing us closer to Him by navigating these relationships within the context of our lives, i.e., before his rendezvous with God at Sinai, Moses walked the royal halls of Egypt. As the Prince of Egypt, he was held in high regard. Educated in the best schools of his day, experiencing luxury at its finest, he embodied a quality of life likely coveted by many during that time. However, his experience in Egypt would later be nothing more than a training camp for the new relationship and the ineffaceable and historic task awaiting him.

The transition from royalty to a fugitive of justice allowed room for God (who had His eyes on Moses from the trip in a basket to the dusty topography of the desert) to develop a relationship with him and give new meaning and identity to his life. God's desire to establish a relationship and man's search for meaning and identity must align. The two must find each other and connect. Man's goals and desires should synchronize with God's will for his life. Any misalignment will perpetuate tension and evoke forces and challenging circumstances aimed at nudging and adjusting one's life back into alignment. This process stabilizes the equilibrium between the creature and the Creator.

Notably, this process is not always pleasant. It may manifest as illness, financial trouble, relationship issues, and career challenges for yourself and others directly connected to you. Additionally, some of our hardship is the fallout of that phantom force seeking to undermine the union between the creature and the Creator. The inevitable outcome from pseudo promises made by that force includes chaos and confusion, generally. However, symmetry is sustained through pain and challenge and moments of blessing and comfort. God routinely blesses the lives of men (often undeservingly) and establishes He is a good, gracious, loving Father. Note:

> "Come to Me, all who are weary and heavy laden, and I will give you rest. Take My yoke upon you and learn from Me, for I am gentle and humble, and you will find

> rest for your souls. For My yoke is easy, and My burden is light." (Matthew 11:28-30) NASB

> "...so that you may be sons of your Father who is in heaven; for He causes His sun to rise on the evil and the good and sends rain on the righteous and the unrighteous." (Matthew 5:45) NASB

Humans are at liberty to enjoy life to the fullest, but ideally, they must do so within the confines of a relationship with a holy God. This is the human dilemma, seeking to live symmetrically with the Creator while being human. Every move and moment is weighted against whether the person we are allowed to develop is the one God wants and intends us to become. Does a person surmise they are more informed about what's best for their life? If so, what is the premise for such a conclusion? How does your reality fair against the One who created you? Does your version of a relationship with God consider His holiness? If so, or not, how is it informed? Do you understand what God is looking for in your relationship and why? If not, how then can you sustain a relationship with him?

Remember, Moses does not show up instructing God about the parameters of their relationship; God informs him.

Unfortunately, once people finally decide "to give God a try," they make too many attempts to enter a relationship with Him on their terms or in ways that seemingly benefit them rather than serve Him. All too often, what is missing is a natural spiritual response to an aggressively loving Father. Holiness or sanctification is the standard and means by which we temper the tension generated by the contrast between God and His creation. It is how one stabilizes equilibrium with Him. Holiness is not perfection in the sense that one is consistently flawless in their pursuits in life and relationship with the Holy One. Although there is a constant drum beat and calls to perfection, i.e.

> "Therefore, you are to be perfect, as your heavenly Father is perfect." Matthew 5:48 NASB

The meaning does not reflect flawlessness but a completion of standards or goals prescribed.[94] It cannot refer to sin-less-ness in that God and only Him measure up.

> "For all have sinned and come short of the glory of God." Romans. 3:23 NASB

Another way of looking at this is to consider the wrench mechanics use. The wrench accurately fits around the nut or bolt and thereby loosens or tightens; the wrench is the "perfect tool" in that it functions how it is designed. Similarly, when we function or live in ways God has codified, we complete the task and standard, reach the goal, and are perfect in this context.

This is what Paul means in II Corinthians 7:1,

> "Therefore, having these promises, beloved, let us cleanse ourselves from all defilement of flesh and spirit, perfecting holiness in the fear of God." NASB

Holiness is complete when people liberate themselves from things that defile them, perfecting holiness. The Spirit helps navigate life to this end. He attempts to influence our choices and decisions about where to hang out, with whom, and the context. He leads us away from people and things contaminating the effort to be pure and holy. Choosing to avoid scenarios that lead to illicit sexual behavior, pornography, and thoughts that are discriminatory, envious, and corrupt are among a plethora of situations that defile a person. These are amazingly easy to fall in and out of, especially without spiritual guidance. Today's social media platforms make these efforts and behaviors easy to develop but difficult to end. Ideally, the closer we move to holiness or sanctification, the less tension in the relationship between the creature and the Creator. There are periods in which some people toggle in and out of these things. However, if individuals keep the Spirit ahead of them, they will remain conscious of the need to stabilize the equilibrium between them and God. In this context, we do well, remembering that we do not have to do this alone. It is impossible to arrive at perfection or the divine goal for our lives without the strategic work of the Holy Spirit.[95]

Although this is certain, the process is protracted, and the outcome is difficult to sustain consistently. This is especially true for those who have already exposed themselves to people, things, and situations to which the body and mind have become sensitive. For example, addictive behaviors such as indulgence in alcohol, drugs, sex, and, yes, shopping or defiled thoughts, jealousy, and hatred lend themselves to reciprocal influences. These are the by-products of existing environments or contribute to their structure.

Albert Bandura's (1986)[96] research identifies how "behavior, internal personal factors, and environmental stimuli work tandemly." [97] He dubs this process as reciprocal determinism[98]. Personality shapes the environment, and the environment shapes personality. There is an integral dance between the environment and one's personality. People choose their environments based on who they believe they are. The type of church you attend (or the lack thereof), the radio station you tune into, the movies you see, and the people or groups you associate with are predicated on your temperaments. A person's past exposures, current activities, and interests propel them into or create a longing for environments that reinforce similar behaviors and thoughts. In effect, the environment ultimately shapes the individual. For example, suppose a person (white, black, or other) is raised in a home in which racism and prejudice are acceptable. In that case, this person is inclined to seek out people and environments that perpetuate similar concepts and, in effect, further shape and harden the individual's personality as racist. We now know reinforced behaviors will likely escalate or increase. In psychology, this is referred to as operant conditioning. [99] Personality develops from activities and environments in which it is exposed and filters how a person engages or responds to specific events in the future. Additionally, a person's personality is instrumental in duplicating or creating situations that mirror them and producing predicaments to which they like reacting. For example, a person with anger will see and respond similarly to others. Generally, people react to others in the same way they treat them.

A person with a sexually immoral personality sees and interacts with others in ways that perpetuate who they are. They will attempt to set up situations in which they can respond sexually.

For example, sexualizing general conversations, using eye contact, touch, and voice as a stimulus to create sexual desire and response in the other person, which in effect sets up situations in which sexual desire can unfold.

Situations like these complicate a person's effort to stabilize the equilibrium between them and God. If holiness is the key element or ingredient for a sustained relationship with God, these behaviors and circumstances are a constant threat to that union. In response, there are frequent reminders and nudges by the God module or Spirit within, creating a perpetual tug and push in the individual.

The daily hustle, push and pull, and manipulation of the tension between the creature and the Creator establishes an annex of thoughts, emotions (repressed or otherwise), and behaviors that shape the inner-self, either in ways that stabilize the equilibrium between man and God or that precipitously misaligns the union between them. Failure to see who God is and His love manifest in the request to be holy perpetuates inner conflict. Misunderstanding God's person obscures the richness of His love and blessings for those with whom He is connected. Equally, the inability to synchronize the Spirit's assistance with the Soul's effort creates uncomfortable realignment.

Through the mundane issues of life (health and sickness, poverty and success, the effort to mean something and become someone), God constantly arouses man's attention, alerts him to His presence, and beckons him into a relationship like no other.

Phantom Forces (Miscalculating Satan)

However, just as there is a constant tug to enter a covenant relationship with God and, in effect, adopt an authentic blissful life, there is a consistent pull in the opposite direction to embrace a pseudo-life of success and fulfillment. It is precipitated by a dynamic often inadequately approximated by many, including people of faith. The lure is so enticing and seems so immensely gratifying and gratuitous few can discern its true nature. The medium and conduit these pseudo promises derive is a formidable force with extraordinary capacity and beauty. This is part of the deception. The art of which is noted in the fact that the one deceived is unaware of the deception. Knowledge and wisdom poisons deception, rendering it ineffective. Therefore, it is essential that people of faith appropriately distinguish and comprehend the dynamic routinely and aggressively disturbing the symmetry between a loving Father and the jewel of His creation.

Remember, t*he Adam complex is the ability to stabilize the interpersonal trifecta between God, the inner self, and external forces that try to undermine the union between the creature and the Creator.*

Satan is humanity's chief opponent. What comes to your mind when that name is evoked? Does it contra up images of some red creature-like person? Does he have enormous wings dripping in red and yellow flames, a long, perfectly straight nose, and horns protruding from his head? Does he have a pitchfork, a long tail with black tips, and a deceptive smile like Batman's Joker?

Are you thinking of the American police drama series-Lucifer, in which the Devil is unhappy in hell and decides to move to Los Angeles chasing women, wine, and entertainment?[100] Is he (in your mind) the ex-spouse or the boss with whom you have ongoing difficulties?

No. Although some of these may appear devilish, none of them are accurate. They pale in comparison to the real deal. Herein lies the underlying cause of miscalculating the force working against humanity: inadequate appraisal of the enemy. Knowing your enemy is the first key to winning any battle in any forum. Any military general will tell you one must see the enemy before launching an attack. Militaries, such as U.S. forces, are equipped with incredible tools to assess the strengths and weaknesses of the enemy. In business, we are taught to know our competition, the industry, and the viability of our business efforts. The Strengths, Weaknesses, Opportunities, and Threats (SWOT) analysis is typically used to measure an entity's viability and impact. First, it is vital to acknowledge the existence of your competitor or opponent and understand their inner workings. Lucifer (Satan) is an enemy, competitor, and opponent, not a friend.

Contemporary art does not capture the true essence or inner workings of him with whom humanity is in constant battle. The names ascribed to him give us a glimpse of the inner workings of his spirit and method of operation, which have remained the same for thousands of years. First, the name Lucifer debunks common depictions of him as a red, demon-like image or some dark creature. The red dragon in the Book of Revelation is symbolic and not to be taken literally.[101] Given who he is, what he does, and the fact that he is associated with a smoke-filled fiery abyss, it is no wonder many describe him as a creature of sorts. However, the truth is that the name Lucifer translates as the shining one or light bearer. It is a Latin translation of the morning star, as used in Isaiah 14:12, which many scholars believe refers to his original fall from heaven.

Notably, when Jesus references the moment in which Lucifer is kicked out of heaven, he says:

> “I was watching Satan fall from heaven like lightning.” (Luke 10:18) NASB

In fairness, some scholars oppose the idea that Isaiah 14:12 and Ezekiel chapter 28 (which will be addressed momentarily) refer to Lucifer. They believe that these passages refer to rulers during the writer's time. However, the passages note things that cannot be ascribed to humans, i.e., Ezk. 28:13-14, 16 and Is. 14:12 references the cherub (an angel), the mountain of God (God’s dwelling place in this case), and the garden of Eden, to name a few. Subsequently, these references point to Lucifer directly.

Lucifer was conscious of his beauty, magnificence, and power for an extended period (who knows how long before the world was created). He felt that such beauty and power deserve recognition and praise. Due to his glorious nature, he thought he should be elevated, lofty, and practically worshipped.

He and the other angels under his influence likely lacked knowledge and wisdom regarding where such thoughts and emotions would take them.[102]

This is logical, given that God did not need to provide specific instructions about good and evil or right and wrong to a pristine world never exposed to evil or beings without knowledge of such reality.[103] God issued commands, and His angels would obey without question.[104]

However, Lucifer is so intoxicated over his beauty and power that he develops amnesia, forgetting that he is a created being and that the creature (in this context) is never greater than his Creator. Lucifer and his followers may not have known that such thoughts would evoke God's wrath. The tenor and content of their thoughts and desires broached the Throne room reserved for the Holy One, the Almighty. Lucifer's desire to rise and make himself equal to the Holy One, in effect, foolishly challenges the God of the universe! Such provocation causes the Almighty to act instantaneously! With one swipe of His mighty hand, he clears out a third of heaven, permanently sending Lucifer and all the angels championing his ideals to a new dark address.[105] Lucifer's new revelation and knowledge deceptively empower him. Later (how much later is unknown), he takes his experience (knowledge of good and evil) and the deceptive degree of fulfillment and uses it to take down the first two creatures placed on earth- Adam and Eve.[106] Given that Satan is often associated with all things dark and evil, the typical appraisal of him does not include or consider the fact that Lucifer and his demons are fallen angels. There is limited information about angels, but what we do know is revealed to us in the Holy Mandate. Although the information seems minuscule, it is rich and highly informative when analyzed carefully. For example, Ezekiel 28:13-19 describes Lucifer's exceptional beauty, responsibilities, power, and the steep rise of pride and arrogance contributed to his fall.

This passage and others aid our understanding that angels are extraordinarily stunning and brilliantly magnificent creatures. In addition, they harness supernatural abilities and powers.[107] Any tangible substances, like dust or dirt, did not shape them. Conversely, like Adam, they were created (likely God-breathed) or commanded into existence individually and in full maturity. However, like humans, they are dual beings with a body and a spirit. Their bodies are not human but are designed specifically for their world and the responsibilities imposed on them by the Creator. As such, they are not part of a secondary reproductive system in which more angels exist through birth.

They are gender-neutral. Subsequently, they do not have ancestral relationships like humans. There are no grandpas, parents, siblings, or spouses among them. This is (in part) what Jesus is referring to in Matthew 22:30

> "For in the resurrection they neither marry nor are given in marriage <u>but are like angels</u> in heaven." NASB

Like the soul of man, their nature is like God's spirit. This, in effect, makes them invisible [108] and immortal. [109] They possess emotions[110], interests, and curiosity.[111] Additionally, angels can take on human form at times. This is a fact all will remember well. Consider Genesis chapter 18, as well as Hebrews 13:2, which states:

> "Do not neglect to show hospitality to strangers, for by this, some have entertained angels without knowing it." NASB

Look at the text closely. Reread it. What do you see? Does it challenge your thinking or perceptions about humans and angels? How can one entertain an angel if they are invisible? Angels are immaterial (spirit-natured). As such, they cannot change; they are like God, who does not change.

Subsequently, it is not that an angel can modify to become human, but that an angel can indwell a human body temporarily, at least.[112] Unlike Hollywood's portrayal, their wings will not inadvertently pop out from beneath the flesh they are indwelling. They can assume a human body without physical detection. Given this, how do you know you have not already encountered and entertained an angel? If so, how do you know that the angel you encountered is of God or Satan?

This interrogatory set up the second error contributing to miscalculating Satan, which is the assumption that he no longer has abilities he harnessed as Lucifer, the angel in heaven. Anyone drawing this conclusion immediately underestimates his power and ability. Subsequently, a person is already vulnerable and disadvantaged before the battle rages. By nature, toe-to-toe, he is much more powerful. This foe is formidable, unlike the unruly neighbor, irritating co-worker, or ex-spouse. As such, the world (people of faith especially) must take his presence and threat seriously. Too many are showing up to battle with baseball bats when the enemy has a tank!

Such a force requires instinctual and spiritual cathexes[113] to produce effective strategies for success. We are encouraged to suit up for battle.[114]

Since his fall, he is correctly dubbed Satan, which means adversary. In addition, he is known as the Devil, which refers to a person who constantly falsely accuses and divides people without legitimate reasons. It is a technique of one who divides and conquers. He is given this name because he falsely charged God with antagonism to the idea of man developing knowledge, wisdom, and happiness. Such a charge slandered God's name and holy agenda and altered the relationship between the creature and the Creator, ultimately.[115] Additionally, he constantly accuses men before God, i.e., in Job 1:6, Satan comes before God with accusations against Job's devotion to God.[116]

Satan is equipped with many tools and schemes aimed at our demise and in antagonism to God's holy agenda. He has many demons (fallen angels) and souls of men and women he has recruited over the life of humanity. He is dubbed the god of this world, [117] who blinds, possesses, [118] deceives, [119] ensnares, [120] tempts, [121] and troubles many. [122] However, according to passages like Job 1:6-7 and Luke 22:31, Satan cannot do any more than God allows because he, too, is subject to the Sovereignty of God, ultimately.

Regardless of the context in which he operates (God's permissive will) and attacks, everyone needs to understand how he wrecks the lives of so many.

Subsequently, on the other side of the spectrum within the Adam complex are devices[123], wiles, or schemes that affect, disrupt, and can even destroy equilibrium between the creature and his Creator. The words used to describe this outcome are significant and noteworthy. Satan's devices, as used in II Corinthians 2:11, have sinister implications and are symptomatic of his character, which is evil. Subsequently, the Greek word for devices here is noemata, which refers to the mind as a device with strategic purpose and, in this text, means "evil scheming originating from thought."[124] It is indicative of a mindset or thought process formulated tactically, surgically, and imaginatively to destroy the people of God mainly. Additionally, the words wiles and schemes used in Ephesians 6:11 are Methodia in Greek, the word from which the English word method derives. Its Greek connotation reflects "cunning arts, deceit, and trickery." Wuest also notes that the Greek verbal form of the word means "to investigate by method."[125] It is a systematic plan of attack.

This originates from phantom forces seeking to under mind union between the creature and the Creator. How these are engaged is worthy of discussion, briefly. There are several methods, tools, and venues by which Satan employs his agenda. However, there is one exceptionally critical to the

Adam complex. But before detailing this one, note Eph. 6:12, in which the word struggle or wrestle is used. It states:

> "For our struggle is not against flesh and blood, but against the rulers, against powers, against the world forces of this darkness, against the spiritual forces of wickedness in the heavenly places." (NASB)

Thayer explains that the word refers to a competition between two individuals, where each person tries to throw the other to the ground. The contest is concluded when the winner can pin down and, with both hands, press upon their opponent's neck until they are flattened. Additionally, Wuest points out that this description is noted within the context of Greek culture, in which the loser of a struggle or wrestling contest had his eyes gouged out and blinded for the rest of his days.[126]

If you have not gotten the message by now, take note. Satan is a skilled and formidable enemy who wants to choke the life and soul out of you! He is not someone whom you take lightly. "The battle is real, difficult, and dangerous."[127] Satan is so smooth and strategically deceptive that he will corrupt a person's soul with a promise and a gift. He will twist your soul and mind until they are inverted, calling wrong right and right optional. He will turn a virgin bride for her husband into a promiscuous reality in marriage; he will cause a person to breach sanity by erroneously thinking they are better than others simply because of the color of their skin.

In the drive for wealth and power, he orchestrates some capitalists and corporations to rape the environment and oppress the poor. He is persuasive, making many believe he is just a myth. In Scientific American's article, the Psychological Power of Satan, the late Justice Antonin Scalia and Keyser Soze correctly note, "the greatest trick the Devil could ever pull is convincing the world he didn't exist."[128]

Given that humanity is up against such a formidable foe, is there any area he would not breach? Is there anything he would not attempt to forward his agenda? Would he not assume the honorable seat of a judge in a courtroom in a way that paralyzes the wheels of justice? Do you think he would not attempt to influence a Prosecutor to fudge evidence to convict someone they do not like? Would he not influence university professors to teach and encourage students to out-think God and question what He has codified as essential? What would stop him from producing havoc in families through financial upheaval and physical and sexual abuse? Why would he not influence a supervisor to deny promotion solely based on gender if he believes it will rob a person of happiness? Would he not influence churches, denominations, and subsequent committees to alter the Holy Script in ways that permit things God has denied? Would he allow the world to believe in God and the universe we all live in? Would he not want the world to think that religion and faith is confusing and therefore optional or, worse that God does not exist?

Why would he not evoke these or other deceptive acts and roguish deeds? What would be his rationale for not entering and attempting to sabotage every aspect of life? Why would he not interfere with a person's relationship with God?

Satan's repertoire and arsenal are extensive. An explanation of Ephesians 6:10-18 tells us that through his demons, his tentacles are far-reaching and devastatingly impactful. Like a masterful magician and a slick con artist, Satan hoodwinks and deceives many into thinking that the war is between us. Subsequently, many turn on others through discrimination, nationalism, caste systems, economic privilege and disparity, gender bias and confusion, political posturing, and religious preferences. However, the fight isn't human per se but spiritual. Note these words:

> "For our struggle is not against flesh and blood, but against the rulers, against the powers, against world

> forces of this darkness, against spiritual forces of wickedness in the heavenly places." Ephesians 6:12 (NASB)

In other words, satanic forces are notably present in principalities or rulers. These are evil spirits in leaders and governments of countries or nations, oppressing the lives of their citizens in numerous ways. In some cases, they lead people away from God and His truth. Some of these places employ corrupt politics that bind and harm their people. Additionally, as the inner self attempts to balance its relationship with the creator, he is pressed by the evil agenda of world forces.

These are Satan's demons at work in other ways in the world and who work in tandem with spiritual forces in heavenly places. This is the phantom force operating in the heavens of the world, not the holy place of God and angels.[129] Their sole purpose is to turn your life upside down and, in effect, destroy you.

All of these and the motivations behind them are at work within the Adam complex. As noted, Satan has a plethora of methods to employ to this end. Among them, the sifter is the most dangerous part. Naturally, Satan lures a person into the sifter by first disguising[130] himself and his agenda; second, by tempting a person with something that is already apparent within them; third, by deceiving[131] the person about the outcome should they surrender to the attraction; and fourth ensnaring[132] a person, which holds and set them up for sifting.

In a dialogue with Peter, Jesus warns of Satan's desire or request to sift him and the rest of the disciples like wheat. It is a text that too many of God's people either do not fully understand or completely ignore, or worse, those who are not "into church and God" at all are dangerously oblivious to such tactics. Wuest's translation from the Greek text captures the appropriate tenor, practicality, power, and daunting dynamics of this text. First, Luke 22:31 as it appears in the New American Standard Bible (NASB) and its translation from Greek subsequently. However, note that the emphasis is on this author. The text and translation are as follows:

> "Simon, Simon, behold, Satan has demanded permission to sift you like wheat." -NASB.
>
> Translation
>
> "Simon, Simon, behold, Satan, by asking **obtained** you and your fellow disciples **for himself and from my power to his,** so that **he may shake you in a sieve**

> **as grain is sifted**, by an **inward agitation, trying your faith to the verge of overthrow**."[133]

First, note that Satan (just as he did with Job) must request permission to attack our lives. [134] Satan and his demons cannot attack anyone without God's knowledge and will. Why, then, do you think God allows such attacks and hardship? What Satan aims to destroy us with, God uses to perfect His will, a concept explored in more detail in succeeding chapters. Second, the message is not solely for Peter but for all the disciples of Christ, including those today. Additionally, Satan's request includes the capitulation of power over the individual for the sole purpose of ruling over them himself. This must consist of control of their mind or heart and soul. Satan always works from the inside out. Think about the various things and people in your life that agitate you, ruffle your feathers, or get under your skin, disturbing your inner peace and tranquility; those desires keep you restless until they are fulfilled. These phantom forces aim to assume dominance by taking what lives in a person and shaking them so violently that they disintegrate; they come apart at the seams, developing a person into someone they were not prior. However, this is only effective if there is something in a person to which they are sensitive, naïve, and vulnerable. This concept is more transparent through the etymology of the word agitate, which is as follows:

> In 1540, for example, the word originated from the Latin word agitates and agitate, meaning to disturb; to put in constant or violent motion, drive onward, impel; to set in motion, to drive forward, "figuratively" incite to action; keep in movement, stir up. Additionally, by the 1590s, the word meant to shake or move to and fro. By the 1640s, it was indicative of keeping questions of significance in constant public view,[135] i.e., why are they doing this? What happens if I do this? Did she mean what I think she meant? Why do people behave this way? Why can I not have this?

As we march toward a life of fulfillment and optimality, we must deny Satan the opportunity to destroy by discharging things within us that belong to the world of which he is the ruler. The more we limit our exposure to the junk that interests us, the less likely or minimal the attacks on us or the need for them. This is what Jesus alludes to in John 14:30

> "...for the ruler of the world is coming, and he has nothing in Me;"

Sin always originates from within.[136] The desires of a person's heart or mind will either draw Satan and his forces to them or drive them away, making room for God and a more fulfilling and balanced life. What our hearts are made of and how our schemas are developed are predicated on exposure and experiences (disreputable or otherwise) that constitute knowledge, wisdom, and the tapestry of the soul. Satan can only tempt us with what is already dormant in us or is already interesting to us. Oddly, man is his distraction and destruction. Phantom forces merely exploit what is already present.

Evil's intrinsic and intrusive force arrests and disturbs humanity's spiritual equilibrium. Man constantly conflicts with his complex (a composite of behavior, repressed thoughts, emotions, and dynamic experiences), which obfuscates his associations, identity, and sense of fulfillment.

While passionately lulled into the heart of the loving Creator, he is jerked and pulled by an entity aimed at his demise. The daily hustle and mayhem produced by the need for self-actualization is intensified by balancing relationships with the Creator. Families are attempting to “get enough church and bible into their lives” while trying to satisfy the demands of the other aspects of the inner self and expectations of the community in which they live. The academic needs of three children, the two extracurricular activities each is involved in (because society teaches things must be done to enrich life), and the demands at the office call for extended hours. In addition, marital needs and interests, the self-imposed need to shop for shoes one does not need, and manufactured pressure to improve one's golf game are a few examples of the mundane stressors of life.

As families like this one live out their lives, Satan anxiously observes, waiting for the opportunity to wreak havoc in the family that appears kosher.

One wrong move, one window left open, or a door cracked, he enters... his presence manifests in several ways. Suddenly, little Michael is hesitant to go to school because he is bullied; mom has been swept off her feet by a co-worker into a forbidden relationship; Marina "cutting" [137] in her bedroom at night to make herself feel better about herself, which on its face upend common explanations given for this psychological phenomenon. Meanwhile, Dad is drinking from his evolving depression over erectile dysfunction. Although it is not atypical for these issues to manifest in one family simultaneously, it is not surprising in the 21st century. Conversely, the other side of the coin paints a different picture. There are no big houses, career jobs, or financed extracurricular activities, but there are stressors. Life is about the constant effort to survive adequately, which is compounded by the fallout from a life disintegrated and fragmented by abuse via illicit substances, violence, child abuse, and incest. The lives of some of these endure the routine bombardment of the issues from these injuries. God is absent in some of their lives, which in effect renders them not only clueless of Satan's tactics but also defenseless against such forces. It seems that they cannot catch a break. There is no respite.

There is constant concern about drug addiction and the promiscuous behavior of youth in the family; bill collectors, intermittent employment, and unresolved issues between siblings inundate their lives. They are oblivious to the power of the Spirit of God upon accepting and capitulating to His loving call and grasp. These are those Satan seeks to trap in their circumstance and close their eyes to the light and route out of their calamity. The unchurched and de-churched[138] are not exempt from the dynamics involved in the Adam complex. This does not mean they do not experience seasonal success, comfort, and blessings. The goodness and graciousness of God extend to everyone temporarily, including those who deny Him or are not interested temporarily.

While incredibly busy with life, these are subject to the call of God and the distraction and demise of phantom forces.

Although Satan is an external object, the impact and pressure are within; the tug of war happens deep within the individual, especially the Christian. Subsequently, an internal war and conflict rages perpetually.[139] One of the verses that capture this reality so starkly is Galatians 5:17

> "For the flesh sets its desire against the Spirt, and the Spirit against the flesh; for these are in opposition to one another, so that you may not do the things that you please." NASB

When a man sets his mind on that which is good, he begins to have problems with the evil nature of his flesh, his being.[140] However, God, who has history before Him, has not left His people unequipped and ill-prepared for forces that seek to eradicate them. He has not just equaled the battlefield; He tipped it in our favor! He created man so His Spirit lives in him, giving him all he needs to secure victory over these phantom forces. It is Satan's neck that will be choked and held to the ground, ultimately (I John 4:4).

A person can overcome depression or heal from the scars and anguish of abuse, survive the collapsing walls of marriage and finance, and the stinging reality of loneliness. A person can find direction and identity and evolve through what God has provided. However, this resolution is only realized through the life and presence of the Spirit. Through the Spirit, man must stabilize the trifecta that is his by nature. The Spirit in him must be fed and nurtured consistently. The force a person feeds most will dominate and shape the inner self. Subsequently, all will do well, remembering that without the Spirit thriving in us, these phantom forces will shatter our lives into a million pieces.

CHAPTER ONE NOTES & REFERENCES

---

[1] However, these sounds must be placed outside the sounds of God's voice depicted during the Sinai event in Exodus 20:18, 19, over which the people feared death.

[2] 670,616,629 mph

[3] Ibid

[4] How the Universe Works. The History Channel

[5] The sheer precision necessary for the universe to work, the structure of the solar system, the earth's position, the magnetic field, and other elements and processes that sustain and conserve life are not accidental but intentional and directive- because God is on a mission.

[6] Gen. 3:8-10. This reference to sound coming from God after man's fall should not be underestimated. Its mere mention in the Holy Scriptures highlights its significance. This likely points to what Theologians dub a "theophanie," a time in which God appears in human form but is fully and truly God. This adjusted manifestation likely still produced heavenly radiance, enough to display God's transcendent nature (because glory and holiness are never without radiance) but cloaked sufficient to prevent the instant deaths of Adam and Eve. Apollos I treats the "sound" in this passage in greater detail in God A Consuming Fire.

[7] Romans 4:25

[8] SEE: Matthew 27:33-28:6

[9] I Thessalonians 4:16-5:11; II Peter 3:10-13; Rev. 19:17

[10] True to "oneself" denotes the divine purpose for which the human was created, which brings glory to God as an image-bearer.

[11] Author's file

[12] Benner, G. David (2016) Interview on Brokenness and Wholeness. Retrieved from: www.drdavidgbenner.ca/brokenness-and-wholeness/

[13] There are multiple aspects to an individual, i.e., spiritual, biological, economic, and psychological, to name a few, and each of these influences is.

[14] The way that two or more people behave with each other because of a particular situation.; something that causes change or growth in something else. Dynamics. Merriam-Webster, Retrieved from: https://www.merriam-webster.com/dictionary/dynamic

[15] Every human entering the world is naturally corrupt, darkened, displaced, and bent toward sin and evil. As such, the human is naturally an enemy of God. See Jer. 17:9; Rom. 3:10-18; 5:1-21; Eph 2:1-3;4:17-24

[16] In this writing, micro is agency and interpersonal interactions between individuals, family, and other small groups.

[17] The collected effect of micro levels influencing organizations and institutions (i.e., churches, human services, and nonprofit sectors) that impact individuals and small groups.

[18] God the Father, Son, and Holy Spirit

---

[19] Ibid
[20] Genesis 1:26
[21] Colossians 1:16 NASB
[22] Ibid, vs. 17 NASB
[23] Communicable attributes of God contrast with the Incommunicable characteristics of His nature and, therefore, correspond to characteristics or capacities found in humans. These traits include grace, mercy, longsuffering, goodness, holiness, righteousness, and spirituality. The Incommunicable attributes of God are the opposite, in that god and Him alone possess these traits, i.e., His omnipresence.
[24] Spiros Zodhiates (1984) Hebrew/Greek Study Bible: Lexical Aid to the Old Testament, pg. 1653: 6754
[25] Ralph H. Elliot, 1961. The Message of Genesis, (Broadman Press, Nashville, TN.)
[26] Ibid, pg. 1607: 1823
[27] Ibid
[28] Genesis 2:7; 35:18; I Kings 17:19-23
[29] The immortal nature of the soul must not be conflated with the inherent eternality of God. The promise of eternal life indicates its absence among the created order. God gives it eternal life, not that it naturally possesses it.
[30] The collective psyche of an individual in which cognition and emotion derive
[31] Encyclopedia of Psychology and Religion (2014) Retrieved from www.link.springer.com/referenceworkentry/
[32] Gen. 1:28; 9:1; Revelation 7:9-10
[33] Ibid, Zodhiates pg. 1755:4561 (Sarx)
[34] Evolutionary in the sense that the effects of Adam and Eve's sins in soul and body are passed on through their children and the human race, ultimately.
[35] The Remedial System (1876) Christopher, H. pg. 19. Transylvania Press Lexington, Kentucky
[36] Psalm 139:14
[37] As noted in Fearfully and Wonderfully Made (2018) Retrieved from https://www.AllAboutGOD.com/fearfully-and- wonderfully- made.htm. Whether Asimov understood it or not, this statement is antithetical to the evolutionist theory, ultimately.
[38] Ibid, Zodhiates pg. 1637: 5315
[39] Song of Solomon 1:7
[40] Lamentations 3:20
[41] I am aware that there are circumstances in which behavior is mediated by psychosis or some other form of neurological impairment and that a person may not be aware (at the soul level) of such behavior their impact and consequences. For example, a businessman slips falls, and suffers a severe head injury that contributes to sexual predatory behaviors that do not exist before his fall. Additionally, addiction of any kind is a disease that leads to behaviors that influence and shape the soul.
Even within this estimation, those (usually ultra-conservatives) are concerned about accountability. In such cases or situations in which a person is dominated by neurological impairment or addiction, we do well remembering that God is just in His administration.

[42] Ibid, Meyers pg. 104

[43] Ibid

[44] Richard Restak (1991) The Brain Has a Mind of Its Own: Insights from a Practicing Neurologist. Crown Publishers

[45] Luke 16:19-31

[46] Marios Beauregard and Denyse OLeary (2007) The Spiritual Brain: A Neuroscientist's Case for the Existence of the Soul. Harper One Publishing

[47] Ibid, Meyers pg. 396

[48] Ibid, pg. 396

[49] Ibid, pg. 398-407

[50] Ibid, pg. 397

[51] Ibid, Meyers pg. 405

[52] Ibid, pg. 404

[53] Ibid, Zodhiates, pg. 1650:6440

[54] Ibid, pg. 25

[55] Witness Lee (1968) The Economy of God. Living Stream Ministry

[56] Kenneth S. Weust (1973) Weust's Word Studies Vol. III, pg. 48

[57] Mention of the Spirit's work here is not intended to capsulate His work in the salvific process, in which He regenerates, directs, illuminates, sanctifies, and intercedes for the Saints. See: Jo. 3:7-8; Titus 3:5; Acts 16:6-7; Rom. 8:26, to name a few.

[58] The key word to understanding this statement is "foreknowledge" prógnosis in Greek, which speaks to God's predetermination to have a relationship with His creation and include necessary resolutions for such a relationship to exist. This concept is convoluted and obscured by the suggestion that God's foreknowledge is merely cognitive perception garnered solely by looking through time to the moment described. In contrast, the word speaks to a relationship formed before the world began. Hence, the human body is designed with this determination in mind. For more information about foreknowledge, see Zodhiate Lexical Aids to The New Testament, code: 4267, 68; Strong's Greek Dictionary to The New Testament, pgs. 210-211; New International Dictionary of New Testament Theology and Exegesis, pg. 139; The New Linguistic and Exegetical Key to the Greek New Testament, pg. 566

[59] See again, John 3:1-8; Titus 3:5

[60] The Holy Spirit is given to those who believe and accept Jesus Christ as Lord. He is a down payment for the promise of ultimate salvation. The Holy Spirit awakens us to the reality of God and our sinfulness, a process called regeneration. A person can not respond to God's call independently of this process. As He lives in the Christian, He becomes a conduit for spiritual communion with the Father. He convicts us of sin, illuminates the Word of God, guides, counsels, intercedes on our behalf, and helps during moments of weakness and failure. He resurrects us to a new life. The Spirit is ultimately responsible for applying the work and outcome of redemption to

the believer through "sanctification." (See: Jo. 3:5-8; 14:16, 26; Rom. 8:11, 26-27; Titus 3:5;

[61] Isaiah 6:1-7

[62] Robert S. Feldman (2013) Understanding Psychology 11th Edition. McGraw-Hill Publications

[63] Sigmund Freud (1927) The Future of an Illusion Hogarth Press, London

[64] Durand, Mark V., and Barlow, David H. (2006) Essentials of Abnormal Psychology 4th Edition Thomson Wadsworth Publishing

[65] Ibid, Feldman Pg. 453

[66] Ibid, Durand, and Barlow pg. 19

[67] Ibid, Feldman pg. 457

[68] Ibid

[69] Ibid, Meyers Pg. 423

[70] A Freudian concept in which instinctual dynamics are governed in a way consistent with societal norms.

[71] II Thessalonians 2:13, 14

[72] The sole sacrifice that appeases the wrath of God and enables reconciliation between God and man, which cannot exist otherwise. The theocratic system of justice demands a special death penalty for the sins of humanity. This is satisfied through Christ's death on the cross. See also Romans 5:1, 8-10

[73] Spiros Zodhiates (1992) The Complete Word Study Dictionary: New Testament. Pg., 929:3076

[74] Rom. 15:13, Eph. 1:19; 3:16, 20

[75] Acts 5:32

[76] Ibid, Zodhiates pg. 1713: 1680

[77] James 1:14,15; I John 2:15,16

[78] Kenneth S. Weust (1973) Weust's Word Studies Vol. One pg. 111 Eerdmans Publishing Company

[79] Hebrews 6:18

[80] John 1:18; Col. 1:15

[81] Matthew 18:20

[82] Ibid, vs.24

[83]Steven J. Meyers and Alissa Rubin (Dec. 14, 2008) Iraqi Journalist Hurls Shoes at Bush and Denounces Him on TV as a'Dog' Retrieved from https://www.nytimes.com/2008/12/15/world/middleeast/15prexy.html

[84] I Tim. 6:15

[85] Rom. 3:10; Job 37:5, 23

[86]Exodus 19:16-19

[87] Ibid, vs.12

[88] Ibid, vs.16

[89] Exodus chapters 25-40

[90] II Thessalonians 2:13

[91] www.dictionary.com

---

[92] I John 2:2. Every man is allowed to respond to God's call. When a man is lost, he is lost by his own account; when a man is saved he is so because call chose him. Eph. 1:4-5

[93] Acts 2:14-47; I Corinthians 15:1-4

[94] Ibid, Zodhiates pg. 1880: 5048

[95] II Thessalonians 2:13-14

[96] Bandura, Albert (1986). Social foundations of thought and action: A social-cognitive theory. As stated in Meyers (2008).

[97] Ibid, Meyers pg. 443

[98] As stated in Meyers (2008) pg. 443 "the interacting influences between personality and environmental factors.

[99] "A type of learning in which behavior is strengthened if followed by a reinforcer or diminished if followed by a punisher."
Ibid, pg. 232

[100] www.wikipedia.org

[101] Revelation 12: 3-4

[102] I am cognizant that thoughts and discussion regarding the events that took place in heaven before the world began contras up questions, such as how an angel conceived such ideas and eventually sinned against God? How can something like this happen in heaven? Although these questions are worthy of contemplation and extended discussion, I will not address them in the body of this writing and chapter, specifically. (See Appendix for an extended note on the subject)

[103] (although evil automatically exists in contrast to a Holy God- See Appendix)

[104] Psalm 103:20

[105] Revelation 12:4, 7-9

[106] Genesis 3:1-7

[107] Ps. 103:20

[108] Numbers 22:22-31 (Although this narrative has a serious message, it is very amusing!)

[109] Luke 20:36

[110] Luke 15:10

[111] I Peter 1:12

[112] Matthew 8:28-29 (this verse refers to demons, which are fallen angels)

[113] Investment of mental or emotional energy in a person, object, or idea. Retrieved from www.merriam- webster.com/dictionary/cathexis

[114] Ephesians 6:10-18

[115] Genesis 3:5, John 8:44

[116] There is significant ongoing debate regarding these verses. In question is whether Satan appears before the Throne of God after his fall. The phrase "sons of God" is indicative of angles according to some scholars. Conversely, others hold that these were not angels. However, according to verse 7, the meeting is not on earth. If not on Earth, then where was this meeting?

[117] II Corinthians 4:3-4

[118] Luke 22:3

[119] Revelation 20:7,8

---

[120] I Timothy 3:7

[121] I Chronicles 21:1;

[122] I Samuel 16:14

[123] II Corinthians 2:11

[124] The Complete Biblical Library Romans-Corinthians Vol. pg. 521

[125] Ibid

[126] Ibid, Weust Pg. 141

[127] The Complete Biblical Library (1986) Vol. 8 Study Bible Galatians-Philemon pg., 169

[128] The Psychological Power of Satan. Piercarlo Valdesolo on October 29, 2013 Retrieved from: https://www.scientificamerican.com/article/psychological-power-satan/

[129] Ibid, Wuest pg.141

[130] II Corinthians 11:14

[131] Revelation 20:7-8

[132] I Timothy 3:7

[133] Ibid

[134] Job 1: 6-12

[135] Ibid

[136] James 1:13-15

[137] A psychological phenomenon in which one engages non-suicidal, self-imposed injury as a coping mechanism for emotional pain, frustration and anger.

[138] As defined by Mary Tuomi Hammond(2001) "those who have lost a faith that they once valued or have left a body of believers with whom they were once deeply engaged. The Church and the Dechurched: Mending Damaged Faith. Chalice Press

[139] Romans 7:23

[140] Romans 7:21

2

In a Million Pieces

Stitches of an invisible hand

Early Saturday morning, Fresca is up and rushing through her house. They inundated her with projects at work the day before, and she left the office much later than planned. Exhausted after getting home, she flops into her gravity chair to relax but drifts into a deep sleep. As she awakened from her coma-like rest the following morning, she realized that she had slept in the chair through the night. Jumping up and undressing, she races to the shower. Oh gosh! I must get ready! She says. Fresca is hosting her book club members at her place in less than two hours. Given that she had no opportunity to prep the day before, she is beside herself as she attempts to prepare for guests. She emerges from the bathroom in her robe and a towel wrapped around her head. She rushes into the kitchen to start brunch. The sound of pots, pans, skillets, and other dishes echoes throughout the house as she prepares the meal.

While the coffee pot percolates, she chops fruit to go with breakfast. Her stomach growls, reminding her she slept through dinner last evening. While preparing for guests, she cooks bacon and sausage for herself. She also remembers that the living room needs dusting. As she races into the living room, she slips! Instinctively, she grabs the mantle over the fireplace to break her fall. Her hand knocks off a valuable antique vase handed down from her great-grandmother. She screams as the vase spins through the air. Unable to catch it, the vase slams on the hardwood floor, shattering into pieces. Fresca gasps and then covers her mouth with her hands. The rocking sound of a larger piece of the vase settling from the violent impact intermittently interrupts the silence. Looking at the disaster, she realizes there are too many broken pieces to repair. As she drifts into sadness, the crackling sound and piercing aroma of burning bacon arrests her attention...

Have you ever broken anything valuable? Have you ever experienced a broken heart, soul, or spirit? Do you know what it is like to have your mind broken? There are not a lot of everyday things that can shatter into a million pieces. A volcanic eruption could blast a mountain into a million pieces, the debris from one of the space shuttle disasters, or the fallout from two rogue planets colliding in the universe. Reducing something into a million pieces requires a significant impact. Pieces indicate something fragmented or severed so that the object is no longer whole or complete and, in effect, incapable of functioning the same way or for the same purpose. In chapter nine, this is referred to as disintegration, the complete shattering of the inner self. It is a complete disfiguring of one's core being and sifting of the self or the soul in ways that alter a person's identity.

Old Testament Hebrew depicts brokenness as "shaver," meaning the literal and metaphoric mangling, shattering, or smashing of bones[1], which represents destruction at great depths within a person. Brokenness alters and sometimes obscures one's vision, impeding the ability to navigate the next steps. It is a shoplifter of dreams in that a person's brokenness can become so troubling that they marinate in their swamp pool of anguish and hopelessness. Their dreams are assassinated and substituted with the nightmare of their reality.

Brokenness is not foreign to humans living in the 21st Century. We can trace the tentacles of brokenness throughout the annals of history. Realizing the pervasiveness of brokenness might cause professionals to declare a global epidemic. There are many types, facets, and degrees of brokenness. Benner (2016) sees brokenness as something within a person, an estrangement of God and the authentic self. [2] Others might surmise that brokenness is relative, meaning that the individual predicates their understanding and impact and the context of their circumstance. What brokenness is to one person or group is not for others.

Brokenness to some people is the realization of their fears and vulnerability, the fragility of one's capabilities and hollowness of their power to effect change, or the revelation and awareness of their sinfulness, which is "a broken spirit." Others see brokenness as displacement (in the sense that one is divided and dispersed from self and God), which comes from an overwhelming circumstance, a force, or a gut-wrenching experience beyond one's control. All too often, brokenness is a discourse of injury by someone else's selfishness or neglect, their sins, or misguided notions. In this writing, brokenness is the decentering, dismemberment, and devastation of the inner self in ways that hinder an individual in critical areas.

In whatever way brokenness is defined, its presence in people's lives worldwide is undeniable. Brokenness is not always atypical. The components of brokenness can be hidden in plain view. Although the intricate details or pieces of a person's circumstance are unseen, their brokenness is visible. Sometimes, we see it in the co-worker's attitude at the office. Dressed to impress, she steps in her 6-inch hills, loud perfume, and made-up flawlessly. However, as she navigates the office, she doesn't greet and, when greeted, emanates a cold-like stare as if she is thinking, 'Why are you even speaking?' You can see it in the gentleman who sits in the third row every Sunday. His face is so conditioned to anger that he looks like he is frowning when he's smiling. It's visible in families where members are in constant conflict over grudges held so long that they have forgotten the premise of the issue. It's noted in some clergy members' arrogance over the 'office of the ministry' and the perpetual need for self-actualization and significance. We see it in leaders obsessed with power and luxury, and in a demented way, some people rape, kidnap, and enslave women and children around the world.

People associate brokenness as evidence of one's mental health. This writing does not make light of the fact that mental illness is a severe issue. People should treat those experiencing this human dilemma with dignity and respect. Although mental illness is not the sole element of brokenness, it is one we should not ignore. The World Health Organization reports that over half a billion people in the world suffer or have suffered from mental illness or some form of neuropsychiatric disorder.[3] In 2013, the National Alliance on Mental Health Illness reported that 61.5 million Americans experience mental illness in a year.[4] 13.6 million people live with severe mental illnesses such as schizophrenia, major depression, or bipolar disorder.[5]

In addition, 26 percent of homeless adults staying in shelters live with serious mental illness, and about 46 percent live with severe mental illness or substance abuse disorders.[6] Forty-two million people live with anxiety disorders, such as panic disorder, obsessive-compulsive disorder (OCD), posttraumatic stress disorder (PTSD), generalized anxiety disorder, and phobias.[7] Seventy percent of youth in juvenile justice systems have at least one mental health condition, and at least 20 percent live with a severe diagnosis.[8] It is conceivable that sometimes, mental illness contributes to illicit behavior in some, i.e., a person who has a sexual addiction, which will embrace habitual sexual behaviors precipitated by psychological impairment.[9] This does not discharge a person's accountability to God and those injured by such unbecoming behaviors. The act or behavior itself is sinful.[10] However, faith communities dealing with such people must consider the person's addiction in their spiritual assessment and theological directives.

Brokenness is not limited to mental disorders or disadvantaged or disenfranchised groups. Several great men and women in the Bible experienced periods of brokenness. For example, King David experienced the steep rise of jealousy and hate from his enemy, Saul, and the daunting weakness of his flesh, which is evident through adultery with Bathsheba flanking his trek to greatness.[11] Disintegrated and displaced by his experience, he refers to himself as broken two times during his prayer, as noted in Psalm chapter 51.[12] In Luke 4:14-19, the Holy Mandate suggests that the human condition is in a perpetual state of brokenness. Jesus identifies brokenness as a central part of his public ministry. His ministry aims at the reality of brokenness. Among the people in the world experiencing brokenness are those either unaware or denying the existence of their brokenness, which is of utmost concern to society and the church. Unconsciousness and denial of brokenness will only lead to deepening their condition and breaking or abusing others along the way. Broken people break people.

The Distinction Between Brokenness and Suffering

Where does this brokenness in the world originate? Its origin is multifaceted or multidimensional. The differentiation between brokenness and suffering is noteworthy in our effort to identify and distinguish these. As a working definition, this chapter defines brokenness as the decentering, dismemberment, and devastation of the inner self in ways that incapacitate an individual in critical areas. Suffering is something different. Biblical definitions suggest the word means a weakened state, anxiety, physical and emotional pain, and a period of tribulation. In one way, suffering is the fallout of brokenness, a cause-and-effect relationship. Brokenness is the cause, and suffering is the impact of brokenness in some cases.

However, these can invert. Suffering protracted over an extended period can lead to brokenness. Suffering can surface independently of brokenness, i.e., as best as determined, Job's suffering wasn't the fallout of brokenness. God declared that Job was unlike any other human. In other words, his righteousness and relationship with God set him apart from any other human living that day. Yet, he experienced profoundly impactful multidimensional suffering that few would survive in our time.[13] Jesus Christ suffered immensely, yet there was nothing broken in Him except the brokenness of humanity He assumes.[14] He was known as the "man of sorrows."[15]

Throughout history, especially in ancient Israel, people associated brokenness and suffering with sin. If a person was suffering, they assumed they must have sinned to bring such hardship into their lives. Job's friends charged him with this as he attempted to navigate his situation. They believe such hardship would not occur to a person if they had done nothing wrong. Job defends his character and commitment to God throughout the book.

Ultra-conservative Christians and other religious bodies living today still hold to these ideals and believe a person experiencing trouble and suffering indicates sin in their life. Although the consequences of rebellion and sin may include hardship and trouble,[16] the latter does not always indicate the former. In other instances, brokenness results from the sins and rebellion of others because sin impacts the individual and the people around them.

The assumption that brokenness and suffering are the fallout of sin is not unreasonable. Sin is often the reason or origin of brokenness and suffering.[17] In Jeremiah 19:1-11, God summons the prophet to break a vase before the people of Judah as a sign of their sinful condition and His response.

Note:

> [10]"Then you are to break the jar in the sight of the men who accompany you [11]and say to them, 'Thus says the Lord of hosts, "Just so will I break this people and this city, even as one breaks a potter's vessel, which

> cannot again be repaired; and they will bury in Topheth because there is no other place for burial."

I Corinthians 5:5 (though controversial) gives an example of brokenness or destruction because of sin. [18] Surrendering a person over to Satan for destruction annihilates those desires and behaviors indifferent to God's prescribed mandate for holiness. As noted, Satan designs the sifter to destroy a person. The destruction here is not the literal death of a person but the subjugation of illicit desires and behaviors set in motion by excommunication. We know from the context of this verse that Paul was chastising the Corinthian church for their relaxed attitude or approach to the sexual sin of a person who had intercourse with his stepmother—a gross violation in any civilized society. Paul's point was that there should have been an aversion and irritation that warranted swift action against such behavior. However, this does not sanction the church to punish people physically. It reads, "Deliver such a one to Satan for the destruction of the flesh." Allow the sin itself and the one authoring it (Satan) to destroy the wickedness living in that individual. Send him back to the world from which such behavioral concepts derive, and it (the sin and the world from which it comes) will destroy, break down, and humble him to his senses.

William Barclay (1975) states the following regarding this text:

> "An easy-going attitude to sin is always dangerous. Carlyle said that men must see the infinite beauty of holiness and the infinite damnability of sin."[19]

We know that this does not refer to the death of a person (although some sinful behavior can cause death) because Paul points to the man's potential salvation and encourages the church to reaffirm their love for him. [20] Additionally, Barclay states:

> "It was to humiliate the man, to bring about the taming and the eradication of his lusts so that in the end his spirit should be saved."[21]

Brokenness (and suffering) rises from the need to reduce arrogance, self-righteousness, and independence. It is the independent attitude of self (I need nothing or anyone) that God wants to break. Some are too big for their britches (as they used to say) and too "headstrong," haughty, and high-minded for God to use and be in relation without change. Arrogance reminds God of Satan and, in effect, subjugates

Him by the delicate declaration that everything a person needs is within themselves. God is irrelevant. Although this is likely unconscious and unarticulated, it manifests in thought and behavior. This kind of mindset contributes to self-righteousness, which develops "kingdom priests, god-divas and prayer warriors, bishops of blessings and anointed soul sisters of glory, which in reality for some is a pseudo testament and deception that one has arrived at the place he is yet to experience. Self-righteousness suggests that a person has reached a point in their journey where they sever dependence on God. The standard and measure by which they navigate life are derived from their law developed from life experiences and their personal, private interpretation of God's laws during those experiences. The unchurched individual develops their standards through personal experiences and communal values around them. They arrive at a point and standard that renders God and the church obsolete. These are socialized and not always clear in either of the two, yet they manifest appreciably. A person's dependence rests within them and not in God, which replaces God as God, violating the first commandment given to humanity, "You shall have no other gods before Me."[22]

Such a declaration reaches far beyond the concept of carved wood, stones, and other images evoked as gods and goes into man's heart, the tapestry of his soul to that which he serves depends on and worships himself. It is this person who must experience brokenness. Any other source of dependence one might have apart from God protracts the experience of brokenness. [23]

Brokenness emerges as the agent of change and the conduit through which God becomes relational. Dr. Charles Stanley, writing about Brokenness as a life principle, stated:

> "Most Christians do not understand brokenness and try to avoid it. We like healing and blessings. But God gives His best only to those He breaks. The underlying principle behind brokenness is death to self." [24]

Psalm 51:17 is a text that captures this concept. Note:

> "The sacrifices of God are a broken spirit; a broken and a contrite heart, O God, you will not despise."

The word contrite in this verse indicates something crushed to powder. [25] The undesired condition of the heart is nonexistent. This allows room and opportunity for God to reconstitute an individual for a relationship with Him. This is likely what Paul instructed the Corinthian church to do: to start responding to the one who sinned among them. One of the significant components targeted for brokenness is those things a person depends upon in place of God. The Holy

Father wants to remove anything a person places more stock, trust, and interest in over Him or that sees these as a more viable source. This kind of relationship and mindset toward any person, thing, substance, or desire for them inadvertently elevates over God. He targets these areas for brokenness.

The process of brokenness could be more pleasant for everyone. Its duration depends on the nature and necessity of brokenness and whether the individual understands its divine message. How and where brokenness manifests in an individual's life determines the break. The suffering emanating from the break highlights the severity of the situation. In this light, brokenness and suffering are distinguishable.

It is noteworthy to delineate three types of suffering:

- Consequential- suffering because of decision, behavior (i.e., crime or sins), and action not otherwise specified.
- Congenital- suffering inadvertently and inherited from the world's fallen nature or the direct impact of sins/and/or crimes of a person(s) within your family or environment.
- Commissioned- suffering from an external stimulus imposed on one who assumes hardship and plight

out of a sense of love and duty. Christ is the ultimate example in He is humanity's substitute for the physical pain, emotional anxiety, and penalty for sin. Another practical example of this is grandparents assuming the heartaches and hardships of raising an impacted teenager of a rogue parent. A scenario played out too many times across this country.

It is plausible for any of these to arise out of brokenness. Suffering and brokenness are unique experiences. The categorization of suffering, as noted above, lends itself to concepts around the origin of brokenness, which either originates from God or Satan. Still, even brokenness imposed by him is subject to the sovereignty of God. Satan's sifter, as presented in chapter one, can certainly produce the destruction brokenness delivers. The problems sifting causes will mentally dismember a person, but as we will see what Satan uses to destroy, God orchestrates and bends to His will. Whether a person's suffering is consequential, congenital, or commissioned, it originates from brokenness precipitated by God or Satan working in the lives of people. Brokenness intertwines with the continuum dubbed the Adam complex in chapter one. Irrespective of its origin, brokenness is a force to reconstitute the individual.

As mentioned, brokenness may not be the by-product of God or Satan. Sometimes, brokenness is the fallout of incidences and unintended consequences, i.e., the engines of a passenger jet malfunction, causing the plane to plunge into the ocean, not only taking the souls on board but shattering the lives of loved ones left behind. In other instances, brokenness is the by-product of the inner self, whom God has given will, desire, and the capacity for a schema or mental framework from which judgment and decision-making arise. We often make these resolutions through perceptions developed by past experiences, not only of the individual but also the people and groups by whom they associate. These perceptions feed people's thoughts about who they are or should become. Brokenness stokes the realization of one's failure to evolve into the person created by one's perceptions.

It generates a crippling, manufactured fear of being suspended and separated from that reality. Benner (2016) refers to this as "illusory alienation from one's authentic truth" and estrangement from God.[26] He states: "This illusory sense of estrangement and separateness forms brokenness."[27]

Although God does not author every experience of brokenness, He knows of the intricate details leading into, and that matures during periods of brokenness. As noted, there are no surprises for the sovereign and omniscient One.

God uses humanity's fragmented experiences as a channel and sequence to transform an individual into a meaningful relationship with Him and a more qualitative human/divine experience. Satan is always looking for opportunities to devour a person. He exploits brokenness, which he has not authored, as a device to dismantle a person at their core. [28]

Again, brokenness is the decentering, dismemberment, and devastation of the inner self in ways that incapacitate an individual in critical areas. The definition explains how and why Satan exploits these opportunities. People do not function best during these moments. Decision-making and judgment are impacted when a person is living in emotional duress. Have you ever been in so much pain you can't think straight? Have you ever been so overwhelmed and overtaken you live on autopilot? These disjointed states produce confusion and irrationality. For example, a person entertains transactional sex to meet demands from financial pressure. In other instances, a male overtaken by the demands of manhood and his inability to satisfy them succumbs to alcohol and crack to escape his nightmare.

As noted in chapter one, we must not miscalculate Satan's resolve by underestimating his ability to search and discover vulnerabilities as a conduit to upend a person.

STICHES OF AN INVISBLE HAND

One way to foil Satan's demonic attempts is learning to see brokenness not just as a process of bitterness, difficulty, and deterioration but as an unseen reality aimed at developing a relationship with God and improving society. It is the reconstitution of the soul in ways that qualify and enable intimacy with God, making the comer's earthly experience as heavenly as possible. Unsuspected by most (including people of faith) are stitches threaded between tears, breaches, cracks, and crevices of life and the soul. Weaved by an "invisible hand," the soul broken into pieces and reduced to powder, God gathers, threads, and twists into something unrealized and inexperienced.

A new person is born, developed, and cultivated to a new end. The invisible hand intersects between the point of brokenness and suffering.

The renowned economist and moral philosopher Adam Smith, whom history dubs the father of capitalism, coined the phrase "invisible hand."[29] 1759, he published The Theory of Moral Sentiments.[30] However, his revolutionary work, An Inquiry into the Nature and Causes of the Wealth of Nations (aka The Wealth of Nations), was published on March 9, 1776. The writing influenced other economists, philosophers, and governments around the world.[31]

It became the blueprint for building wealthy nations through what some saw as unbridled greed. [32] Although Smith advocated the economic advancement of society and individuals, he noted and warned against the commercialization of culture, inequality, and neglecting people with low incomes. There is an ongoing debate regarding Smith's work between economists on the left and those on the right. However, although his work is informative and fascinating, Smith's concept of the invisible hand is of utmost concern in this chapter and, therefore, extrapolated from this debate.

The Economic Times of India defines the invisible hand:

> "The invisible hand is the unobservable market force that helps the demand and supply of goods in a free market to reach equilibrium automatically."[33]

Investing Answer's website defines the invisible hand as

> "... An unseen mechanism that maintains equilibrium between the supply and demand of resources. Smith states that the invisible hand functions under the innate inclination among free market participants to maximize their well-being. As market participants

> compete, driven by their needs and wants, they involuntarily benefit society."[34]

In each definition, the invisible hand is an unseen force or mechanism that establishes and maintains equilibrium between two objects. The invisible hand is such because it orchestrates man's pursuit (often driven by self-interest) to benefit him and society clandestinely. Similarly, God (the invisible hand within the context of this chapter) rewrites the mission and game plan for brokenness, often driven by phantom forces perpetuating the break.

As a result, these forces enact what they oppose and do what they declare never to do. These forces and the souls it seeks to break are bent to the will of the sovereign Creator –equilibrium between Him and His creation. This does not suggest that man is without will and choice or that God programs him with no alternative but to follow God. He is a free moral agent and can accept God or not. Like Adam and Eve, we are prone to take our liberty too far, asserting our self-sufficiency and freedom without considering the consequences.

The magnitude of unbridled and boundless independence is injury, brokenness, and pain. As mentioned, relationship predicates the human and divine encounter, which God navigates by love and holiness. God determines the details and composites that make up our relationship with Him. He decides what this relationship should look like. Our task is to preserve equilibrium with Him and sustain alignment as we trek through the human experience.

Everyone's journey is unique because we do not experience suffering and life similarly. God tailors the relationship with Him to the individual, but within the confines of His will as God of the universe. Although we are led to believe all roads lead to God, sometimes this is untrue. Such reasoning allows a person to author their salvation and to do so within the confines of their comfort zones, even when God is calling them out. It is the comer who must adjust because God never changes.[35] The erroneous notion that we can come to God just as we are and believe in Him without change is ridiculous. Echoing the song Just As I Am does not mean staying as you are; change must happen; a person must be born again.[36] This is a point in which understanding God as He is, rather than how we see Him, is most critical. Chapter One notes that His holy nature and man's sinful reality perpetuate a hostile[37] environment and relationship that must change. Donald Guthrie (1981), a noted theologian, captures this truth in this manner:

> "Holiness is essentially an attribute of God. It marks him out as being utterly pure in thought and attitude...

> This quality of holiness creates a barrier in man's approach to God since man becomes conscious of his lack of holiness in the presence of God."[38]

For healing and renewal to truly impact an individual, we must undergo a paradigm shift in how we perceive brokenness. Coined by American physicist Thomas Kuhn, the term "paradigm shift" refers to a profound change in our fundamental models or perceptions of events.[39] It shapes our outlook, mindset, and mental approach towards circumstances and people as a snapshot of our mental framework. Our experiences, thoughts, and emotions shape this framework, ultimately creating a foundation for processing new experiences. Like the concept of "attitude adjustment," which involves modifying our mental approach or response to a situation or person, we must change how we view brokenness to understand its value and potential outcomes. Brokenness and the contributing processes provide awareness that a person is decentered and needs perfecting in particular areas. God has and will strategically use this process to effect change, provide direction, and summon a person to a task unique to them and the relationship between the two. The invisible hand utilizes brokenness as a purification, amputation, and supplemental process. There are instances in which God breaks an individual or allows one to be broken to take something out of them or to place something in them. This process alters a person to their profit and God's glory.

In almost all instances, man comes to God with experiences and perceptions antithetical to God's nature and mission, making a meaningful relationship with Him implausible. God must change a person to qualify them for the relationship and the spiritual blessings or benefits produced.

What is noteworthy is that the brokenness God is authoring or allows breaks in profound ways, shattering a person into a million pieces. One must be reconstituted. People interrupt this process by reinserting themselves because Satan has convinced a person they know better than God or because the process of brokenness and stitching is too uncomfortable. However, we must deny ourselves[40] and allow the process to mature and perfect the individual.[41] Too many are squirming, dipping, and dodging the process because of inconvenience. The path that leads to the end of a trial or tribulation is the one taking you straight through it.

If we do not allow brokenness and its associated processes to mature or complete, we reserve for future heartache and hardship because change must happen. The most painful times of life occur during moments of brokenness. This experience is often viewed as something we should avoid.

Brokenness draws us into communion with God and His people. We reach out to God and others for direction and healing during tumultuous times.[42]

If not understood over time, the message and lesson of brokenness can lead a person into a life of wilderness. The wilderness is a unique and powerful place or experience because it strips away layers of thoughts and desires that cover the heart, revealing the true essence of our being. It removes excess; everything is dry, and there is only enough to keep you alive, but not much more. Have you ever felt lonely among people? You have family, friends, co-workers, and fellow believers, yet you are lonely. You are among them, but you are not fully present. They reach out, but you feel nothing, numbed by brokenness...you are in the wilderness.

THE WILDERNESS OF BROKENNESS

Have you ever considered the characteristics that define such a place? The characteristics of a wilderness have an interesting connection to this discussion. First, it consists of forces beyond humans, i.e., forces of nature or, better, the hand of God. It is a space where man's impact is nonexistent; it is a venue for solitude, "primitive and unconfined recreation," with adequate space to use its preservation in unimpaired conditions.[43] Theologically, the wilderness, like a desert, is a motif that runs through scripture and Christian history. It is often dry and considered a hard place, not conducive for long-term residence. It is the place where God sends the broken soul for surgery and recovery. God orchestrates forces shaping the wilderness. The wilderness brings a person into solitude, which in this context should be a time of inward reflection and survey of one's walk and relationship with God, a review or analysis of all the wrong turns you have made and their consequences. It is solitude that incites or encourages review of a person's spiritual progress; it forges introspection or self-examination; prayer, including the solemn and determined rededication of self and its future relationship with God. It referees the struggle between the inner self's desires and God's call. It produces sacrifice, as a person realizes that desires of the inner self are incongruent with the call of God.

However, one must enter solitude because it is in these moments that Satan does the most incredible damage. What you dub as your sanctuary, Satan sees as a place for opportunity to dismantle and destroy who you are at your core. He wages a threefold assault:

- He uses your desire to break you mentally and spiritually (Lk. 4:2)
- Challenges your identity in God (Lk. 4:9)

- But the ultimate spiritual assault is Satan's attempt to get us to worship something or someone other than God. (Lk. 4:5-8) As a person tries to find an antidote to their situation, Satan offers other solutions, leading one to depend upon and worship something other than God as a resolution.

The wilderness forces us to give up or see the vanity of the resources we trust. The lives of individuals resisting and refusing to learn this lesson are caught up in a cyclical experience of brokenness. Often clueless (including the unchurched) about why things are in constant mayhem, they gripe, moan, complain, and self-medicate by inventing ineffective resolutions to their issues. These are temporary fixes and likely variances to the proper antidote to their situation. The same person is oblivious that the stitching or repairs to their life cannot happen while the pieces are still in motion from the break. If a person has not learned or sometimes refuses to learn the lesson from their disaster, they break repeatedly and, in effect, live in brokenness consistently. When the pieces are no longer toggling, rocking, or moving from the violent break, rearrangement, substitution, and stitching can begin.

Stitching, although uncomfortable, is a part of the healing process. Stitches of the invisible hand include those moments of healing and holiness, clarity and direction, strength and resolve leading to a new person, a new mantra and mission that brings the creature into a qualitative life and ever closer to a loving Creator. What God uses to thread and stitch a person's life and soul back together may not be atypical. Life may not be or look as before brokenness, the whole intent of change. As the new person evolves, he restores God to His rightful place. Misalignment is often the source of the problem and the origin of brokenness. Man has stepped out of his place, or worse, attempted to move God out of His, disrupting the equilibrium between the two. Averting brokenness requires things in their rightful places. God must be King in the individual's life. Restoring God to His natural place in our lives re-establishes symmetry codified at the start of human existence. Pushing or pulling a soul out of alignment with God can perpetuate brokenness that shatters into a million pieces.

But the Father is a master strategist who can weave life's messes into a beautiful tapestry that is more potent than before. His Holy Spirit is an antidote that heals, comforts, and guides the Believer to wholeness and reconciliation.

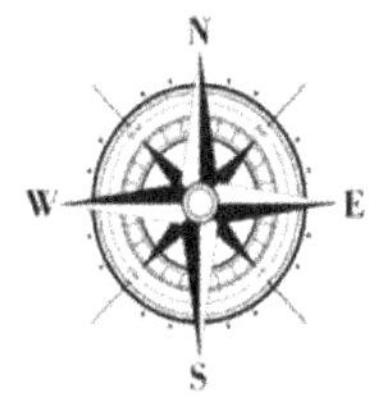

THE GUIDE POST

Seven Steps Through Brokenness

1. Restore God and your relationship with Him to natural order.
2. Create a paradigm shift that allows you to see brokenness differently.
3. Identify the area of your life that is broken. This will identify the severity of the situation.
4. Ask for guidance and understanding throughout the process.
5. Do not interrupt the process; allow it to perfect what is necessary for you.
6. Strengthen the areas identified as problematic through prayer, study, and counseling.
7. Seek spiritual guidance and therapeutic orientation where necessary by a licensed professional.

CHAPTER NOTES AND REFERENCES

[1] Complete Biblical Library (2000) Vol. 7 Hebrew-English Dictionary World Library Press, Inc.

[2] Benner, G. David (2016) Brokenness and Wholeness. Retrieved from: https://www.drdavidgbenner.ca/brokenness-and-wholeness/

[3] World Health Organization (2003) Investing in Mental Health. Retrieved from: http://www.who.int/mental_health/media/investing_mnh.pdf

[4] National Alliance on Mental Illness | Westchester (2013) Retrieved from: https://namiwestchester.org/about-mental-illness/facts-figures/

[5] Ibid

[6] Ibid

[7] Ibid

[8] Ibid

[9] Abnormality in thought or mood contributing to diminished ability; elevated, risky behaviors and difficulty fulfilling responsibilities in critical areas.

[10] In DSM-IV and DSM-IV-TR, the diagnosis of 'sexual disorders not otherwise specified [NOS]' (302.9) was included; this allowed for a diagnosis that included hypersexual behavior. Kaplan M.S., Krueger R.B. Diagnosis, assessment, and treatment of hypersexuality. J Sex Res 2010; 47: 181-98. These findings are under debate currently.

[11] I Samuel 23:15-ff; II Samuel 11:1-27

[12] Psalm 51:8, 17

[13] The Old Testament book of Job

[14] Mark 9:12; Luke 24:26, 46

[15] Isaiah 53:3

[16] I Peter 2:20-21; Galatians 6:7

[17] I Peter 4:15-19

[18] I am cognizant of the variances surrounding this verse, which some ultra-conservative groups hold. Namely, that the text supports physical punishment and death for those practicing sin. This author dubs such notions and practices as erroneous and misapprehensive of the text. II Corinthians 2:7-8 points to discipline as temporary and has nothing to do with physical harm or death. However, this does not trump other places in Scripture, such as Leviticus 10:1-3 and Acts chapter 5, where death was the immediate consequence for violating God. Conversely, in these examples, death was authorized by God, who holds life in His hands.

[19] Barclay, William (1975) The Letters to the Corinthians Revised Edition Westminster Press. Pg. 44

[20] II Corinthians 2:7-8

[21] Ibid, Barclay pg. 44

[22] Exodus 20:3

[23] Philippians 3:9

[24] Stanley, Charles. In Touch Ministries. Retrieved from www.intouch.org

[25] The Complete Biblical Library Psalm.

[26] Ibid

[27] Ibid, Benner

[28] Job 1:7; I Peter 5:8

[29] Investopedia Retrieved from: https://www.investopedia.com/updatcs/adam-smith-economics/

[30] Ibid

[31] Adam Smith Institute Retrieved from: https://www.adamsmith.org/the-wealth-of-nations/

[32] Rasmussen, C. Dennis (June 9, 2016) The Problem with inequality, according to Adam Smith. Retrieved from: https://www.theatlantic.com/business/archive/2016/06/the-problem-with-inequality-according-to-adam-smith/486071/

[33] The Economic Times (2018) Retrieved from: https://economictimes.indiatimes.com/definition/invisible-hand

[34] Investing Answers.com Invisible Hand. Retrieved from: https://investinganswers.com/financial-dictionary/economics/invisible-hand-771

[35] Ps. 102:27Hebrews 1:12; 13:8

[36] John 3:3, 7

[37] Romans 5:1, 9-10

[38] Guthrie, Donald (1981) New Testament Theology Iner-Varsity Press. Pg. 99

[39] Retrieved from: https://en.wikipedia.org/wiki/Thomas_Kuhn. It is meant to describe the nature of scientific revolutions or fundamental changes in the basic concepts and experimental practices of a scientific discipline

[40] Mark 8:34

[41] James 1:2-4

[42] Rom. 15:2; Gal. 6:2

[43] Characteristics of wilderness Retrieved from: http://blmsolar.anl.gov/glossary/dsp_wordpopup.cfm?word_id=147

3

Irreconcilable Differences?

Navigating Challenging Unorthodox Relationships

The dinner table is an inimitable iconic symbol of blessing, thanksgiving, and spatial orientation for connection, celebration, recess, and renewal. It is where people discover friendships, marriages develop, and dissolves. Distinguished expressions of individuality and thought are evident here, i.e., a teenage daughter descends from her bedroom with a new piercing and tattoo unbeknown to her parents; a son discloses his sexual orientation in the form of a familiar interrogatory; guess who's coming to dinner? The dinner table's mere existence is diacritical to culture. It symbolizes families' intermittent escape from life's monotonous shuffle and humdrum in America. It plugs into a collective solitary refined for relatives and others with whom they are close. Irrespective of its iconic symbolism, the dinner table hosts contradictory experiences.

In a transformative moment, Jesus uses the dinner table to redefine His ministry. Through the Parable of the Guests and the Parable of the Dinner, He teaches the principles of humility and servitude, embodying the dinner table's symbolic power. However, the dinner table is not always a place of enlightenment. It can also become a venue for conflict, as Jesus experiences when dining with a Pharisee who seeks to trap Him. Jesus elects to introduce "The Lord's Supper". This incident captures the dichotomy of the dinner experience, where the same table can be a source of profound spiritual lessons and a setting for malicious intent.

As contemporary lifestyles impose increasing demands on families, the dinner table adapts from its traditional symbolism and transforms into a hub for brief conversations and disseminating critical information. The dinner table takes on a new significance during one of the Gensic family's annual gatherings when they come together to share their lives and reconnect. As the designated time and day approach, those living abroad prepare to return to the family home. They make travel arrangements; others service their cars for the trip. As the family readies for the annual gathering, one daughter prepares for a gathering far different from her six siblings. Diana, a 33-year-old mother and wife, marks the family's annual gathering for the moment she reveals a long-held secret. As Diana prepares to leave, she enters moments of reflection, contemplating what has been weighing on her heart for years. Understanding her need for solitude, her husband respects her silent moments. Diana rehearses the conversation she envisions, a dialogue she has written, erased, and rewritten countless times.

The day arrives. The family and their spouses return home the evening before the big dinner. They greet each other, teasing one another about who has gained and lost weight during the interim. Diana, with a knot in her stomach, engages in conversations. As night falls and everyone retires for the evening, she becomes restless and unable to sleep. However, at some point, she drifts off into sleep and wakes up the following morning. As the day matures, Diana's nervousness becomes clear. Her sister pulls her aside and asks, "Diana, what's wrong?" She stares. In a fleeting moment, she thinks of telling her sister what she is about to do but changes her mind and replies, "Nothing... I am ok.... Tired, I guess."

Sounds of conversation, loud laughter, and music inundate the house. The children are noisy as they play games and hold their level of conversation. The aroma from the kitchen reminds everyone of the purpose for which they come–family, fellowship, and good-ole-eating. Each of them makes their way to the dining room. Seated and with the food on the table, chatter fades into silence as Diana's father prepares to offer grace and thanks for food and family. As one might imagine, the food is excellent, the fellowship and camaraderie between them appear seamless, and everything else is as expected. As Diana loses herself in her thoughts, the sounds of rattling forks, dispensing beverages, chatter, and laughter fade into the background of her mind. Suddenly, she says, "I have something to say!" Holding their youngest child in his lap, her husband takes a sip of water and a deep breath because he knows what is coming. Holding a big grin, one of her sisters says, well... what is it? Diana freezes for a moment. Her father notices her eyes are tearing and her lips are trembling. Concerned now... he says, honey, what is it? The room enters a deafening silence. Then, she yells it out!

Casesarion (her older brother) sexually abused me for years during our childhood. Sounds of forks dropping onto plates, gasps, and sighs inundate the room. One of her siblings sprues out the beverage he was drinking at the time; her mother cries uncontrollably. Her sister spits the food in her mouth, saying, "I've lost my appetite." Believing Diana's story, her other brother jumps up, curses Casesarion, and storms out of the dining room with his wife trailing him to calm him down. Diana says, "For years, I have been too afraid to say anything about it..." Feeling guilty about the impact of her statement, she says, "...and maybe I would say nothing still if it were not for the scars." –Author's file

Casesarion blushed with clenched fists and remained silent. His wife turns to him with teary eyes and a trembling voice, saying, Casesarion, please tell me this is not true! Unbeknown to Diana, Casesarion's marriage is already in trouble for other reasons. He does not answer his wife. Dropping her napkin on her plate, she says, "That's it. I am getting a divorce. She turns to Diana and says, "I am sorry... I don't know what else to say." She leaves the room. Casesarion is fuming by now. He breaks his silence, screaming at Diana, "See what you've done!" He leaves the table abruptly.

Concurrent with the family's response to Diana's shocking revelation, her father is grappling with restoring order after a joyful dinner descends into chaos. Stunned, he is trying to figure out what to say or do. He remains silent for a few minutes longer. Then, he calls for calm and attempts to lead everyone into prayer when one of his daughters slams her hand on the table, shouting, "Dad! Is that the first thing you can think of to do? You are doing what you have always done: shoving religion down our throats! Well, look how that turned out!" His daughter's scolding is more about Diana's need for comfort than anything else. Feeling helpless, the father pushes back from the table, gets up, and turns to the window with tears. He feels like a failure. He walks over to the end of the table where Diana is sitting, embraces her, and cries over her pain and his son's error. At some point, the father emerges from the dining room to look for his son, Casesarion. The two of them enter his home office to converse, the details of which are unknown to this writing.

Some likely question the wisdom of Diana's approach, timing, and motives. What was on her mind? Was it the injury and pain protracted over several years? Was it revenge? What did it accomplish? Whether or not botched, the move was a first step toward healing for her if no one else. As time moves forward, the dust from this calamity lifts. However, as expected, their lives are not the same. Casesarion and his wife divorced because of the allegations and the totality of things that had gone wrong in their marriage. Diana's youngest sibling is not communicating with her because she believes that Diana botched up the annual family event by choosing that time and place to unveil her injury and anger. As she sees it, "This messes up the family now..." A few years have passed, and the Gensics have not convened for a family meal since that day. Diana's parents are struggling with the fallout of the event and how to deal with the issues from now on. Her father is illusive and almost pacifies the situation because it is a testament to his failure, in his eyes at least. Diana's attempt to recover, live out her faith, and maintain a relationship with her family in this context is ongoing. There are moments in which she feels that the differences developed behind this ordeal leave some of the relationships between them irreconcilable.

Diana's horrific narrative and experience are not new to the ears and minds of families living in the 21st century. It is likely correct to assume and add that stories like hers exist as far back as man's revelation of his sexual desires. However, irrespective of how commonplace these things appear, society and the church must repudiate behaviors that contradict societal norms and violate divine expectations within the human experience. This issue is problematic for any family in or out of the faith and across geographical boundaries. The challenge for many people is learning to live harmoniously with people whose thought processes and behaviors create irreconcilable differences.

What are irreconcilable differences?

What do parents of faith do when their child discloses that they are now an atheist? How does a mother deal with the new reality that her daughter wants to become a man yet still see and relate to her as the daughter to whom she gave birth? What does Diana do with the brother who abused her, and is the sister now at odds with her over the event that took place at dinner? First, the two-dimensional definitions of irreconcilable differences. Most people are familiar with this term in the context of Family Law. It refers to couples seeking a divorce without identifying the fault. In this context, it means substantial incompatibility between marriage partners or inability to agree on most things, significant things.[1] However, the irreconcilable difference in this writing is the perceived inability to navigate disruption that seems insurmountable but is contextual, situational,[2] and finite.[3]

This definition does not limit the indifference and disruption under discussion in this chapter to those borne out of contexts with which we are familiar or that seem commonplace, but rather, other unorthodox challenges and differences that are irreconcilable and strain relationships. Indifference and disruption sometimes manifest in simple ways but have complex outcomes. Sometimes, indifference and disruption matriculate into the lives of Christian families through unorthodox contexts, such as custody battles between parents and guardians, or derive from a unique nexus between personality flaws and moral challenges. For instance, in one family, the mother's last will identifies a daughter struggling with self-actualization and self-interest as the executor of her estate. She executes her mother's wishes, which include paying for all expenses related to her death out of the money left behind for the family. However, the daughter sees total power over her mother's possessions as a unique opportunity to advance her interests and desires. She deviates from her mother's wishes, deciding (even before leaving the hospital) not to pay for funeral expenses associated with her mother's death. The rationale for this 'cognitive-commercial-break' is that she will have more money if she does not pay these expenses. Such a move caused instant disruption and conflict between family members. The intensity of the situation quickly built into a physical confrontation. The conflict delays funeral arrangements and burial, which adds more cost for such services.

As the siblings and other family members fought, the mother's cold body lay in wait while costs were mounting. After understanding that the lengthier the wait, the more expensive the mother's death is becoming, the daughter capitulates and duly enacts her mother's last will. However, the irrational event left rifts in this family's relationship afterward.

Sometimes, disruption develops through indifference borne out of cultural assumptions and expectations. These can become a barrier to forming relationships. When people do not behave in ways conducive to cultural expectations, faithful constituents of the culture view and treat them differently; sometimes, these are unintentionally bleak, harsh, derogative, and discriminatory. For example, when cultural constituents see a woman entering their environment (work, school, etc.) with attire covering her entire body or exposing too much, they view her (whether conscious of it or not) as one disloyal to cultural tenets or religious beliefs. Conversations about the woman's attire are communicated between peers or in solitary with one's thoughts. Regardless, their perception develops out of the woman's contrast to their cultural expectations and one's orientation and measure of the exact expectations. Although the woman in this example may not have uttered a word or exhibited inappropriate behavior, her attire speaks volumes. They then interpret the language of her attire through the lens of that culture, including its religious beliefs. Unlicensed cultural commentators and religious gatekeepers see her attire as her inability to perceive and navigate certain environments or her refusal to accept tenets codifying specific cultures or faiths. These perceptions almost always cause indifference, which creates spatial orientations that prohibit effective communication and act as a roadblock to developing meaningful relationships.[4] In this case, the woman becomes disaffected without having entered a relationship with cultural commentators or spiritual gatekeepers. It is disruption before the requisites for harmony can initiate and mature.

Sometimes, conflict and disruption occur among those less likely to experience it and in unorthodox contexts. Several years ago, an elderly Christian couple was in an unorthodox predicament. It is unorthodox because usually, at their ages, life is much seasoned and settled, and when people are generally at the apotheosis of marriage and relationship. But this marriage is different. The husband is addicted to pornography. His wife discovers that in her absence, he was often viewing pornographic material. This caused a rift between them. The wife believes the issue is insurmountable if he continues viewing the images. Although the husband knows his behavior is inappropriate, he continues. Subsequently, the wife leaves the home to protest his unbecoming behavior. But, because of the husband's periodic illness, she remains engaged and assists him where and when necessary but refuses to move back into the home under those conditions. In her mind, they are too old to be contemplating divorce. Given that resolution is improbable, resignation becomes the alternative in this case. People's lifestyles that contradict principles of faith can create spatial orientations contributing to irreconcilable differences.

When hard-pressed against a person whose being or decision-making contradicts your faith and values, the first thing to remember is that every person's life and walk with God is personal, tailored to that individual and the call of God upon them. As mentioned in previous chapters, this does not mean there are 9 billion ways to God. No. God sets the parameters and goalposts through His word for human and divine relationships and life. In this context, what God requires of one, He requires of all. There is no respecter of persons with Him. [5] The phrase "personal relationship" shows a coveted, intimate bond between the creature and the Only Creator–God. It is the manifestation and realization that God is interested and invested in the souls of every created being and those formed through post-secondary reproduction.

How He interacts with each person is consistent with His nature (i.e., holy and loving) and synchronizes with His call and expectation. Each person's walk (meaning their life experience with or without Him) harbors elements distinctive from all others while navigating the terrains that lead to God. People of faith who believe they have it all together must respect that not every person's life, spirituality, and relationship with God develop simultaneously or at the same pace as theirs. Not every person's life is at the same point on the spiritual continuum as others. The lives of people can be messy. Those living a successful godly life should know (from personal experience, if by no other means) that cultivating faith, developing spirituality, and deepening personal relationships with God is incremental, protracted, and requires patience and ongoing support from other members of faith and family. These should know that the word of God and the regenerating work of the Holy Spirit are vital to growing in faith and godliness. People with issues that are or appear to contradict divine principles and family values need time and opportunity for their problems to intersect with the Word and the Spirit for healing, modification, and revolution. This process begins with acknowledging these facts by those closest and most influential to them.

The realization and acceptance that people's position on the spiritual spectrum varies create no duplicity within a person of faith. All too often, Christians and ultra-conservative groups see such realization and acceptance as compromising principles of faith, Scripture, or their value system. Post-traditional application of the biblical tenets is possible without compromising faith and doctrine. Recognition of salvation autonomy, individual responsibility, and accountability to God does not translate into a full-throated endorsement of sin. It is not a blatant disregard for inappropriate thoughts and behavior.

Conversely, it accentuates the fact that each person must "workout"[6] (not work for) their salvation; and this does not mean (as noted previously) that each person creates their version of divine deliverance. It means one must complete what God determines and expects of those in a relationship with Him. It means that a person must see this through. What is it that one must see through? These are the things God requires of every individual seeking Him and in a relationship with Him. The Greek word used for "workout" in Philippians 2:12 means to bring something to fulfillment. This does not mean salvation by works but instead highlights the Christian's responsibility for pursuing obedience necessary for sanctification. A man is saved by God's work of grace, not by his works (Eph. 2:8-10). It is about remaining committed to God through obedience. Several Scriptures support the concept of individual commitment and responsibility to God.[7]

Notice that the chapter title is in the form of an interrogatory, a question. Irreconcilable difference (as defined in this chapter) includes the word "perceived," which refers to looking at someone particularly to envision and interpret something through that point of view; it is strategic judgment grasped in one's mind.[8] In this light, and the operational definition for irreconcilable difference, insurmountability and inability are matters of mind, not fact. The premise for adverse spatial orientations[9] created within the context of the relationship is often unsubstantiated, creating a fabricated space. This means that one's rationale for the space between them and the one with whom they oppose is situated against something that is not absolute or the basis of which is an undetermined impossibility. This does not nullify the authenticity of any sin, crime, or injury that a person commits or experiences. For example, spatial orientation from the act of adultery is absolute because the act of infidelity severs the bond codifying marriage.

The reality of sin, interpersonal errors, and the associated pain is not fictional. However, an individual's background and the situation's dynamics often shape the perceptions by which someone judges the person. This doesn't diminish the fact that for some people in unique contexts, the fallout from the disruption is so severe that it hinders the paradigm shift necessary for overcoming indifference. This hindrance often stems from significant emotional injury. Insurmountability is relative, subjective, and, in effect, contextual, situational, and finite. The complexities around the concept of insurmountability are evident. What is insurmountable to one person or group may not be for others. A person's belief system and cultural nuances influence their perception of these situations. Most human experience is perception; perception is reality, out of which judgment and decision-making develop.

If a person is still living, there is always an opportunity to address indifference and discord. There are only two mediums creating inability and insurmountability. The first is death. There is no venue for rectification of any kind in death. However, if a person lives, there is always an opportunity to reach a resolution and equilibrium between opposing forces. As alluded to earlier, the second (although situational) happens when severing the bond of the marriage relationship. To emphasize insurmountability through brokenness, consider its impact on the bond of marriage in specific contexts. When disruption (which in this example is infidelity) severs the bond of marriage, that union and relationship no longer exist in its initial form. The relationship dynamic changes. The bond unifying the couple is broken. We know that sexual adultery severs the bond by the exempt clause imposed by Jesus in Matthew 19:9. The Master's select terminology helps us understand that sexual immorality alters the marriage union in such a way that one has the right to discontinue marriage with that individual and without communal stigmatization. Indifference and disruption become insurmountable when infidelity destroys the bond of marriage.

If reconciliation occurs after the marriage bond breaks, it does not restore the condition of the initial union, which is severed by disruption from infidelity. For the sake of argument, divorcees remarrying each other after a case of infidelity creates a new bond. They do not and cannot continue the bond severed by infidelity. A new agreement and bond must emerge.[10] In this sense, and the former example, disruption becomes insurmountable. However, indifference and disruption are surmountable in all other relational dynamics. To simplify the concept, let us divide the five categories of relationships noted in this book into five baskets. Most people's lives intersect with one or more of these categories.

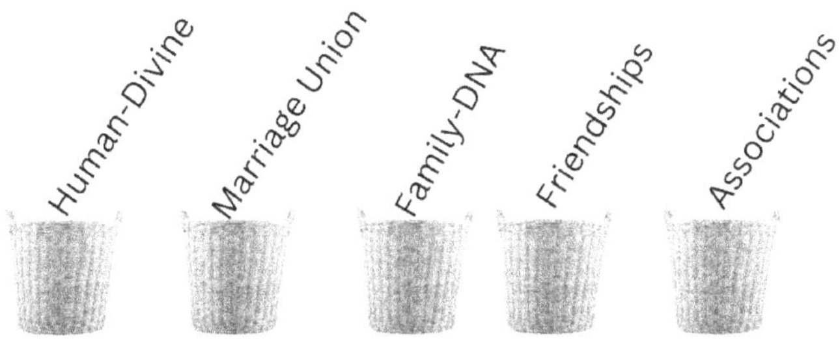

Figure 1

First, it is noteworthy to differentiate kinship and relationship. In this context, kinship is a consistent state of being that does not require ongoing interaction between people, constituting the connection for it to exist. The relationship is a connection that characterizes how two people engage and regard one another in particular contexts. Although marriage and friendship are relationships, they are distinguishable by the parties that identify and engage with each other.

Expectations between the two are different. However, both require ongoing interaction, communication, intimacy (on various levels), association, and mutual agreement to exist. Effective relationships always define the expectations within that relationship. The relationship will likely thrive when each party meets those defining characteristics.

The five categories noted above are the primary contexts in which humans have kinship or experience relationships. Two of the five are static,[11] and the other three are dynamic[12]. Basket 1 contains the human/divine connection, a static kinship; it never changes. It identifies as kinship here because humans (soul and body) are created, establishing a relationship with the Creator.[13] Humans are God's offspring.[14] As long as the creature and Creator exist, this kinship is permanent. Irrespective of a people's choice to follow God or not, He still considers them created beings, and God is still the Creator. Therefore, the kinship between the two is concrete, and the connection ordains expectations.

The second static connection is basket three, family by DNA. This refers to a blood connection and is a kinship. Like the former, it could be more flexible regardless of the relationship quality between family members. Whether a person loves or hates their relatives or does not enact essential elements necessary for a relationship, they are still family, still related. However, marriage unions and friendship associations are distinctive from kinship. Relationships can exist within the kinship. However, the relationships between a spouse, friends, and associations are dynamic, meaning they can change at their core and become nonexistent.

The term associations refers to those relationships that are contextual or situational, i.e., we associate two people working for the same company or within the same department of a company as co-workers. Their relationship is time-limited, exists within defined parameters, and often does not exist outside of work. The length of employment and work within the department predicates the duration of the relationship. There is no contact outside the workplace. However, it is common for two people working together to move from mere associates to friends and sometimes develop kosher or illicit relationships.

Another example is relationships that develop within the context of church or faith communities. Sometimes, these functions more like family in that there is a relationship beyond the place of worship, and they often include dynamics consistent with the traditional family. Relationships require that the essential components and dynamics that cultivate and perpetuate them are consistent and inclusive of all parties. Although disruption can affect any of the five categories, it can only annihilate three: marriage, friendships, and associations.

Constructing Insurmountability

How do people in kinships and relationships get to the point of insurmountability? As you review your current interpersonal conflicts (if any), how do you think you and the party(s) involved got to your impasse? Can you identify essential pieces or factors making the situation insurmountable? Did you, by your own volition, devise and orchestrate a resolution that benefits you and not the other party(s)? Would leaving the issue unaddressed cause it to evaporate?

There are likely many avenues contributing or leading to the perceived point of insurmountability. However, what appears commonplace when there is interpersonal conflict or confrontation with a person whose being contradicts another person's belief system is the immediate devaluation of the opposing party. In most cases, this happens unintentionally. In other cases, people seek the demise of those whose lives are antithetical to their own. The prefix in the word devaluation means to reduce something, to separate and remove, like in the word "dehumidify." Devaluation means to underestimate the value or significance of something through reduction and separation.[15] Devaluation manifests in the language used to respond to the person with whom indifference or conflict exists. Language is the product of one's perceptions, emotions, and knowledge. Language often contributes (if not determines) to the outcome of conflict between individuals. For example, a conservative Christian family enters counseling to discuss a plethora of issues disrupting their family. Chief among them is their only son's decision to embrace homosexuality. This caused a significant rift in their family. The mother is conscious of her son's need for emotional support. But she is struggling with how to do that while maintaining her faith. The father does not have any of it. He is angry and unknowingly verbally abusive. In his mind, Scripture has given him the right to respond the way he is responding to his son. He asserts that Leviticus 18:22, 20:13, and Deut. 23:17 dubs the behavior an abomination, and Romans 1:26-27 classifies such behavior as vile and unnatural.

The demeaning way he applies the text manifests in the language he uses to communicate with his son. His son hears something his father may not have meant or intended. Here is what his son hears or how he interprets what his dad is saying. "You are an abomination," as opposed to the behavior he embraces; "vile," as opposed to the act itself; "an unnatural person," as opposed to the practice itself.

The father's point that such behavior is incompatible with the Holy Mandate is correct. Notably, destruction must always aim at the sin, not the person. As noted in the earlier chapter, Paul's message to the Corinthians is about the man who had sexual intercourse with his stepmother. He notes, "...deliver such a one to Satan, to destroy his flesh" (his sinful nature), not the person. He later encourages the church to reaffirm their love for the one committing this horrific act. Paul notes that too much grief or sorrow "katapothe"[16] the man, meaning swallow him up with total extinction.[17]

The son's effort to defend his choice and express hurt over his father's response includes language that demeans and devalues the father. What the father hears attacks him, his faith, and God, not what his son intended. Both sides harden their position. Both view the other as having crossed the line, moving beyond the point of no return. In each of their minds, the issue is impossible.

In another example, a mother learns that her teenage daughter is pregnant by a person of color. It outrages the mother on two fronts. One, the mother is from a family that sees people of color as inferior, problematic, and contaminative when integrating or associating with their race. The daughter's relationship with the young man has been clandestine up to this point. However, upon disclosure, the mother surmises that her daughter has disregarded significant family values. Two, as a person of faith, the mother understands sex outside of marriage as inappropriate. The mother's language compares her daughter to Jezebel, and she uses the word contamination to describe her daughter's body and relationship. [18] She devalues her as a person and disowns her as a relative. Given the daughter's issues, the mother believes the proper thing to do here is for her daughter to leave their home to live with her father or other relatives. The daughter feels like an outcast and struggles with how her biological mother could treat her in this manner.

Conflation

There are many more examples available, some more horrific and unorthodox. However, these show how important language and communication are during the initial stages of conflict and injury. [19] Insurmountability begins when devaluation becomes both the subject and tenor of one's initial response to a breach, conflict, and clash arising from interpersonal dilemmas.

As used in this chapter, two distinctive invaluable components lie at the core of devaluation: conflation, the blending, fusing, and confusing of two sets of information and concepts. Conflation is often integrated into the initial response to conflict in religious contexts. The first answers the questions of what and why. The second identifies the dynamics constituting the process and event.

During my former experience as a forensic psychology consultant, I answered the question of why and helped direct the orientation and evaluation of clients referred by law offices, the trier of fact, or other branches of the judicial system.[20] In this setting, the client population comprises people whose thought processes and behavior infringe on the law, endangers others, and often contradicts societal norms. Most times, clients show up sheepish about their behaviors practiced in secrecy, such as sexual perpetration. These clients enter sessions expecting what they did to be the center of the discussion, as it should be.

There is a fear of judgment, which, in effect, makes the client less candid about the issues of record. When people (in or out of the faith) fear judgment, feel threatened by ostracism, or are treated indifferently because of their errors, transparency and cooperation are less likely. They often hide from or circumvent the truth, become dishonest, and cannot internalize treatment or corrective measures, making rehabilitation and resolution improbable. These become emotional and stressed-out over the ever-pressing need to capitulate to familial and communal demands (including the church) to rectify the issues. [21]

Sometimes, expectations reach far beyond what is necessary or what Scripture codifies.

When a person or group approaches indifference, conflict, or disruption fixated on what happened (the event), judgment settles in creating spatial orientations that obscure answers to the question, why? Upon realizing what happened, the parties must transition and seek answers to the question, "Why?" This has proven to be much more productive in clinical and spiritual environments. This approach to indifference, conflict, and disruption is more beneficial in congregational life and pastoral service because it does not come across as judgmental.

Answering why circumvents insurmountability by creating an approach and language that speak to the reasons for indifference, disruption, and failure within interpersonal dynamics and spiritual contexts. It causes understanding that lends itself to critical discovery, which flushes out the mental framework, thoughts, and motivation contributing to adverse behavior. It analyzes the nexus affecting a person's spiritual journey. Conservative segments of the faith community are excellent in investigating truth and identifying and magnifying errors. However, it struggles with understanding the dynamics leading to spiritual collapse and the process leading to recovery and restoration. Fixation of a person's sin event will obscure evidence of repentance and protract any insurmountable issues between the faith community and the individual. [22] In this context, reconciliation becomes impracticable. In such instances, the person will likely leave that faith community or, worse, the whole community altogether, further complicating the resolution and searing perceptions about the event and the people involved.

Conflating Process and Event

The second set of components often conflated by people in conflict (especially people of faith) is process and event. Process in this context is a series of action steps leading to a desired outcome. It is a navigation tool for resolution, the compass directing the parties to define the constituents of the disruption and carry out corrective measures. An event is more than just what happened (act/cause); it includes the emotional and spiritual impact (injury/effect) on the parties involved. Because American culture recognizes the correlation between childhood experiences and adult development and perception, many regularly attribute contemporary challenges to past abuses and failures so extensively that some disregard such findings as practical causes of today's issues. In other words, there are instances when people read a person's injury as something related to their past instead of recognizing it as a legitimate impact of the current situation. They believe insurmountable issues in the lives of some people are a by-product of personality issues such as narcissism, the need for entitlement, and self-actualization, to name a few.

Sometimes, a person's mental construct, personality, and the need for self-actualization drive their definition and understanding of traumatic events when there is a reward or benefit. The impact of traumatic events can be life-altering for individuals. Trauma at the point of disruption calls attention to the event (act/cause) and impact (injury/effect). For instance, if someone drops a bowling ball on your head, it will upset and hurt you. Dropping the bowling ball on your head tells what happened but says nothing about why. Whether it threatens you or causes pain predicates what happens next. If dropping the ball on your head did not produce pain or injury or produced no threat, you will see the act as uneventful. Nothing happened as a result.

But the act (what was done) becomes an event the moment you are threatened or experience pain and injury associated with the act. If fear and pain drive an immature person's emotional response, the propensity to devaluate the one with whom they are in conflict is more likely. Devaluation, in effect, sets in motion the conflation of process and event. Because the event synchronizes with fear, pain, or injury, one assesses the issue from this vantage point and attempts to deal with the situation through this lens. The other critical and distinguishing component of an event is the trauma often associated with it. This is the second factor differentiating an event from the act (what was done) and the emotional and psychological fallout. When injury develops from an act or behavior, people tend to fixate on the act or behavior, causing pain or separation. The one impacted by the act identifies, understands, and responds to the opposing person through this lens, even if the act was a point-action.[23]

Conflating events and processes obscure necessary steps to resolution. This creates an instant barrier to resolution and reconciliation, causing cognitive and spiritual dissonance. Indifference and disruption protract, appearing insurmountable after an extended period. An unimpeded process allows room for analysis of constituents or elements, causing an impasse between persons or groups.

The right approach creates mediums for conversation and clarification of the motives behind the disruption's most porous and impactful elements.

Cyclical Forces Working Against Resolution

However, people can avoid deception by realizing that forces are situated against genuine concepts and attempting to resolve issues between individuals and groups. These are strategic, influential, and aimed at upending healthy relationships. Satan is the culprit behind the force seeking to destroy individuals through relationships. It is in his interest that there is mayhem and confusion in your life. He writes the script and narrative that provides commentary on a person's circumstance, causing them and the people around them to believe bad choices and decision-making are at the heart of their failure. Although individuals must claim ownership of some things, people cannot be ignorant of Satan's influence behind bad decisions and outcomes. The notion that Satan works to destroy relationships is an elementary point for most. Stirring up spousal jealousy, cultivating and prolonging conflicts between siblings, and attempting to impact parent-child relationships are tactics in every human experience. It is not surprising to know that

Satan influences our politics in destructive ways and pit males against females.

He muddles some people's minds to see the color of a person's skin as a defining characteristic of their being. In other instances, he is very subtle in his method. He will cultivate relationships that provide a false sense of security and satisfaction by influencing people to do whatever they choose, with whomever they prefer, for as long as their heart desires. He knows that if a person believes they are responsible for their happiness and satisfaction, God is an afterthought, if at all.

But as the saying goes, "Knowledge is power." Awareness of how these forces manifest is critical to averting them and circumventing insurmountability arising from these issues in relationships and one's spiritual journey. These forces are apparent in the following ways:

The Absence of Critical Thinking in Spiritual Contexts

Members of specific faith communities view critical thinking as a humanistic threat to faith and religion. The essential part of thinking that encourages a person to avoid accepting arguments and conclusions is one of Satan's practical tools and the principal argument of those who oppose the concept.[24] Because of thoughts such as this one, conservative people of faith believe critical thinking creates precedence for believing the erroneous notion that God does not exist or is the basis for altering the Bible. But critical thinking is not evil. It tells people how to think as opposed to what to think. Most people use critical thinking as a tool every day in various contexts. How one uses this tool predicates whether it lends itself to something antithetical to God and His word.

The word critical derives from the Greek word kritikos, which means discernment, the capacity to judge, and refers to decision-making.[25] Critical thinking uses tools to assess the correctness or incorrectness of an argument or disagreement by testing the issues, evidence, or dynamics making up a particular position. Scripture encourages us to think critically about what we hear and not accept or believe everything. There is evidence of this concept, i.e.

I John 4:1

> Beloved, do not believe every spirit, but test the spirits to see whether they are of God...

The word "test" derives from the Greek word dokimazete, which means to scrutinize through a process that "salvages the good and discards that which is useless,"[26] which is what critical thinking does. In addition, the Holy Text uses this same word and its meaning when encouraging self-analysis.[27] Critical thinking in this chapter refers to a process in which parties in conflict assess the integrity of the issues (including everyone's motivations), make inquiries, and separate components contributing to disruption and insurmountability.

Most times, during the heat of conflict, people are not thinking critically but with their emotions. Executing major decisions during emotional moments is not wise. The word emotion, which has the word "motion" within, originates in Latin and means to lead out. How a person feels at any moment directs their path. Our emotions lead us by the nose, and many people follow their feelings wherever they lead, which is not always a good outcome.

This does not mean that people should live as stones, without emotions. We must recognize emotions for what they are and are not. Sometimes, a person's review of the outcome is not the outcome but their feelings projected onto the situation. The only way to decipher these and make those distinctions is to think critically during and after an event.

An individual may need to pause before responding. Emotions need to settle before the mind can think clearly and effectively. The length of the pause depends on the parties involved and the nature and severity of the issue. Once the mind settles, you can think critically about the problems. How does this look? Remember, critical thinking separates good from evil. It helps decide what is effective and productive and what elements contradict favorable outcomes. You do this by making inquiries, to which the answers offer definitions, goals, and direction. In addition, you are looking for answers that clarify the injuries and integral details of healing and reconciliation. You want to know how to make this right. This process is not usually used during indifference, disruption, and conflict. When people do not make the right approach, insurmountability is pervasive and becomes an accepted stalemate, even among people of faith.

Inability To Deal with Conflict

Some people in and out of the Faith struggle to deal with conflicts in any context. These either run from or seek to avoid them. This is likely due, in part, to the notion that conflict is terrible, unbecoming, and a host of other negative connotations. But, conflict may be beneficial and productive. Sometimes, conflict generates growth, maturity, and opportunities that do not exist otherwise. Some people respond to conflicts based on how they manifest themselves in childhood or their home environment. If a person's history includes painful and diminishing conflicts, they are less likely to see the experience as something they will engage in. The potential for conflict exists in every context because the nature of people is such that friction and disruption are unavoidable sometimes. Although conflict is a natural part of the human experience, many people do not know how to handle it. There are various conflicts, such as interpersonal (with others) and intrapersonal (within self), including the potential dichotomy between soul and spirit.[28]

Faith communities must include more curricula (biblical and otherwise) featuring conflict management, critical thinking, and problem-solving for modern-day issues and relationships. How do we help a family with a teenager on the verge of suicide because of peer conflicts and bullying?

How do you aid the members experiencing serious disputes at work or home? Often, resolution principles derived from the social sciences are biblical, i.e., Robert Fisher and William Ury (1981)[29] developed and introduced the Interest-Based Relational Approach (IBA) to conflict resolution. This approach suggests separating the parties involved in the conflict and their emotions from the issues to lead to a resolution. IBA helps develop mutual respect, understanding, and cooperation. This is what Romans 12:9-

21 teaches. Conflict resolution and management involves eclectic solutions that enable every person and group.

Peace is the mantra for those surrendering their lives to God.

Note:

> If possible, so far as it depends on you, be at peace with all men.
>
> Romans 12:18 NASB

> Blessed are the peacemakers, for they shall be called the sons of God.
>
> Matthew 5:8 NASB

Peace is devoid of conflict, tranquility of soul, and spatial dimensions in which happiness is uninterrupted. The origin of peace is internal and can move with the individual wherever they go. When individuals within a space are at peace, that environment becomes tranquil. However, most find it challenging to experience this kind of peace. Spiritual immaturity, egos, self-actualization, or personality flaws obscure the knowledge and skills necessary for resolution.

Irrespective of the disruption, conflict management, and resolution require mutual respect between persons. [30] Judgment, arrogance, and demeaning postures often torpedo resolution well before parties can experience it. Mutual respect is a safeguard and almost guarantees that whatever solutions derived from the process are inclusive of all parties. In addition, there must be a sense of commitment to the process in a way that nurtures benevolent love, honors good, and perpetuates mutual resignation. Selfishness, entitlement, and invisibility threaten this process and avert resolution.

People who refuse to implement these strategies or cannot because of spiritual immaturity or emotional challenges risk living in and out of conflict across various contexts. Mismanaging conflict not only exaggerates issues but also makes that which is private public for those outside the dynamic. Some conflicts and disruptions between parties should never reach the light of day. Consider Matthew 18:15-17,

> [15] "If your brother sins, go and show him his fault in private; if he listens to you, you have won your brother. [16] But if he does not listen *to you*, take one or two more with you, so that by the mouth of two or three witnesses every fact may be confirmed. [17] If he refuses to listen to them, tell it to the church; if he refuses to listen even to the church, let him be to you as a Gentile and a tax collector."

The first sentence of these instructions is where interpersonal conflicts should croak. When this does not happen, one or more of the following is in play:

- One or more of the parties involved do not have the proper skill set to bring a resolution.
- Dishonesty and denial of fact.
- Ineffective communication between parties,
- Spiritual immaturity,
- The issue(s) and impact are so severe that it is perceived as insurmountable.

When people commit to a resolution, they will find a way, make the sacrifices necessary for resolution, and approach the process with integrity and transparency.

Devoid of Discernment and Godly Wisdom

Discernment and Godly wisdom interconnect and function as the spiritual application of critical thinking processes. One source defines discernment as perception and the ability to garner spiritual direction and understanding.[31] Discernment is the strategic application of divine wisdom in critical contexts. It is curious about the appropriateness of methodologies used in a situation and seeks resolution without focusing on blame. It asks how we fix this. What do you need to move forward?

It involves understanding the issues in ways that generate impartial conclusions. It's wisdom in action.[32]

Godly wisdom is golden. We must diligently seek it while living for Him and attempting to resolve conflict. This wisdom is distinctive from all others and accessible through the Spirit of God. When wisdom is absent during indifference, disruption, and conflict, these become breeding grounds for insurmountability, leading to irreconcilable differences.

The Absence of Reward

The other force working against effective resolution to conflict and insurmountability is disincentives created by a reward vacuum. It may sound paradoxical, but disincentives can become incentives not to perform a particular act or make specific decisions. Why? Operant Conditioning (OC). OC is learning in which behavior increases or becomes consistent when it has a positive reinforcer, by an outcome a person likes, or desires or the behavior diminishes if some form of punishment follows it. [33] If the proposal for a resolution to the conflict or perceived insurmountability is not rewarding or interferes with behaviors within the conflict, the reward or response is a disincentive; it becomes an incentive not to embrace or accept the proposal. People will resign themselves to a stalemate when a resolution does not occur.

Fear and Challenges of Otherness

Otherness is one of those terms, concepts, and realities that frighten the heart and take people's breath in or out of the faith. Most often, they hold an automatic assumption and calculation that recognizing otherness is sacrilegious or endorses something contradictory to one's values. In the quest to define, become, and belong are expectations of similarity. Many people manufacture the dichotomy they live in by trying to assimilate and stay distinctive simultaneously. Otherness is the "quality or fact of being different." [34] Definitions of otherness beyond this foundational one are contextual. It is a concept embedded in subaltern studies.[35] Although not stipulated here, otherness recognizes and defines the trauma of those affected. In sociological contexts, otherness is the construct that gives individuals and groups their identities.[36] How does a man decide he is rich, except poverty is set in contrast?

When one exists, it defines the other or gives it existence. Evil exists because there is a sovereign God and Creator, the epitome and totality of righteousness and holiness. He is so supreme in His being that everything is to the left of Him. His holiness is so matchless that everything else is less than Him. He has an inherent predisposition for evil and failure. Because of the One, the other exists.

An "Other Sociologist," Zygmunt Bauman (1991), writing about how otherness establishes identities in society, states:

> "In dichotomies crucial for the practice and the vision of social order, the differentiating power hides as a rule behind one of the opposition members. The second member is the other of the first, the opposite (degraded, suppressed, exiled) side of the first and its creation. Thus, the abnormality is the other of the norm... Women are the other of men. Stranger the other of the native, enemy the other of friend "them" the other of "us"..."[37]

Dispelling fears and navigating challenges of otherness does not indicate sanctioning behaviors or lifestyles antithetical to

Scripture. It calls to recognize otherness as a deterrent to resolution, reconciliation, and surmountable outcomes. Change happens within relational contexts. Creating spatial orientations (meaning no communication or interaction) in response to otherness does little to change one's life in need. Otherness expands beyond controversial issues such as homosexuality, transsexualism, etc., but it includes race and gender issues and other lifestyle choices that are different and problematic to others.

These forces are cyclical and contradict processes leading to resolution. To improve the quality of relationships, we must understand the dynamics that make up good relationships and the forces seeking their demise. Given that insurmountability is contextual, situational, and finite in most cases, influential variables likely contribute to its formation and work against resolution. Considering these, people must admit absolutes. Some experiences cannot happen within or outside proper relationships, and the God who created relationships determines these.

Sometimes, people must be open and resigned to the notion that resolution may be out of reach for several reasons. The rising conflict between the Apostle Paul and Barnabas ended with a consensus that they should go their own way.[38]

We see this play out repeatedly in marriage and other relational contexts. When differences are so severe that they are irreconcilable, the fallout from no agreement between the parties and the unwillingness of one or more to do what is correct or best for their circumstance are likely culprits.

Selfishness and self-interest create indifference to healing, resolution, and recovery. However, no problem is insurmountable when all parties commit to a resolution, are clear about the issues, and work tandemly. Indifference to resolution, disruption, and painful conflict do not have to become irreconcilable.

In Philippians 4:1-4 Paul notes the intense conflict between two women in the church. The situation is so contentious that he calls Euodia and Syntyche by name. His encouragement is to "live in harmony." The phrase derives from the Greek word Phroneo, which means giving thought, thinking, or considering. The message is for each of them to think about and consider the other—consideration of the different moves people closer to resolving conflict.

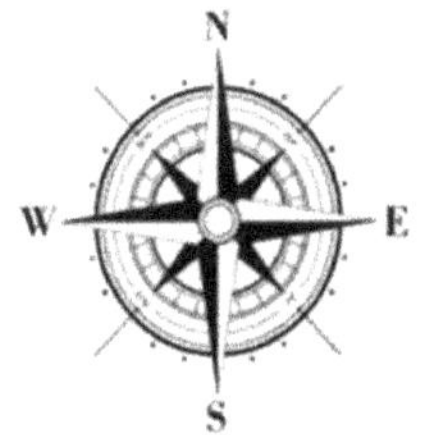

THE GUIDE POST

Seven Steps to Resolving Conflict In Relationships

1. Identify the nature and dynamics creating conflict between you and others (s). Additionally, not only look for God in the situation but identify Satan as well. Assess how much of your personality contributes to the impasse and creates a barrier to resolution.

2. Separate emotions generated by the conflict from the conflict and the person(s) involved. This will prevent pain and feelings from obscuring your view and analysis of the issues.

3. Petition to God for tranquility and wisdom regarding the situation. (James 1:5) Pray for strength to be the peacemaker. (Rom. 12:18)

4. Focusing on the tenets of resolution that promote peace and harmony, fairness, and impartiality, resolve

the issues as quickly as possible. (Eph. 4:26, 27; 5:15-17; Matt. 5:23-26)

5. Make harmony with God and the parties involved in the goal. (Amos 3:3; I Cor. 1:9-10; Phil. 4:1-4; 1 Peter 3:8-11)

6. Understand yourself and the other party(s) style and triggers. Additionally, recognize any value attached to or associated with the one you are against.

7. Make decisions that protect you, your family, and your environment.

Chapter Notes and References

[1] Irreconcilable differences retrieved from: https://www.merriam-webster.com/dictionary/irreconcilable%20differences

[2] Something existing only within a prescribed set of circumstances or events

[3] Refers to the limitedness of a thing held within a boundary or parameter; does not have the capacity to exist indefinitely.

[4] The emotional space between individuals or groups and the measures used to determine such positions, attitudinal approach, psychological orientation, or fences

[5] Romans 2:11-16; Acts 10:34

[6] Philippians 2:12

[7] See Philippians 2:12-13; Romans 7:14-25; Ch. 14; I Corinthians 3:10-17; 11:28, to name a few.

[8] Retrieved from: https://www.etymonline.com/word/perceive

[9] See note 9. Spatial orientations play out through moments in which we choose not to speak, interact, fellowship, or have anything to do with a person because of an infraction or our perception of their lifestyle and behaviors

[10] Based on Deut. 24:4, there is a theological debate regarding whether a person can remarry the one he/she has put away. How the woman is defiled is the question at the heart of much debate.

[11] Meaning fixed; unmovable or unchanging

[12] In the context of this chapter, it means constant change by activity, progression, or the propensity of

[13] Genesis 1:1-28; Ezk. 18:4; Col. 1:15-17

[14] Acts 17:28-29 King James Version

[15] https://www.dictionary.com/browse/de-

[16] Complete Biblical Library (1989) Vol. 7 Corinthians pg. 521

[17] Ibid

[18] An immoral woman of the Old Testament whose story and life is recorded in I Kings Chapter 16 and subsequent chapters.

[19] The simultaneous existence of mutually exclusive or opposite desires or response tendencies. David G. Benner (1985)
Encyclopedia of Psychology

[20] A therapist's governing approach philosophy to treatment is usually tailored to the client.

[21] Emotional, as used here, is not representative of psychosis necessarily. It depicts general worry or anxiety can, under certain circumstances, become a diagnosis of sorts, i.e., Generalized Anxiety Disorder Axis I 300.02 DSM V

[22] Singular concertation on something or someone creating an inability to see a problem from a new perspective; an impediment to
Problem-solving. David G. Myers (2008) Exploring psychology 7th Edition. Pg. 425

[23] Point action refers to an event or action that is not continuous, i.e., I dropped the book. The action has ended. I am not dropping the book because it has been dropped. To drop the book again requires that the book be picked up and dropped again. It cannot be continuous.

[24] Ibid, Myers

[25] Ibid, McGraw-Hill pg. 4

[26] Complete Biblical Library (1986) Vol. 12 pg. 160

[27] II Corinthians 13:5

[28] See Chapter 6

[29] As presented on the Mind Tools website (2018) Retrieved from https://www.mindtools.com/pages/article/newLDR_81.htm

[30] Romans 12:16

[31] Retrieved from: www.dictionary.com

[32] Proverbs 14:33

[33] Ibid, Myer pg. 232

[34] Retrieved from: www.dictionary.com

[35] Inferior people, groups, or positions determined by either race, class, gender, sexual orientation, ethnicity, or religion. In critical theory and postcolonialism, the term subaltern designates the populations that are socially, politically, and geographically outside of the hegemonic power structure of the colony and the colonial homeland.

[36] Dr Zuleyka Zevallos (2018) What is Otherness? Retrieved from: https://othersociologist.com/otherness-resources/

[37] Bauman, Zygmunt (1991) Modernity and Ambivalence Polity Press. Retrieved from: https://othersociologist.com/otherness-resources/

[38] Acts 15:3-16:10

Breach of Sanity

Racism is beyond common sense and has no place in our society. –Morrissey

Several years ago, I moved to Nashville, Tennessee, to attend a Bible school then situated at and operated by David Lipscomb College. I was an Assistant Manager for a local grocery store chain. This store was on the corner of Dickerson Rd. and Broadmoor Dr., a populated area. Three grocery stores were positioned in proximity to each other. The neighborhood was in a constant hustle and bustle throughout the week.

Employees trickle out the door one Friday evening as the day's business ends. I locked the door behind them, finished my accounting duties, and placed the money in the safe. The silence of the store magnifies the ticking sound of my watch; then I notice it's midnight. Preparing to leave, I realized I did not drive that day. Given the time, I call home to tell my folks not to get out of bed just for me. I will walk home instead. It was a summer night. It was a pleasant night. As I make my way down Dickerson Rd., the sounds of horns and cars fade into the background. The intermitting rhythm of my shoes striking the sidewalk lures me into deep thought and walking unconsciously. Halfway home, the sounds of an accelerating engine, loud music, and people screaming out interrupt my thoughts. Three Caucasian males in a pickup truck zoom past me. In the distance, I see their brake lights. They turned around and zoomed again past me, screaming out of the window. I look back over my shoulder and see the brake lights again. They turn around again. At this point, I am concerned. I know who I am, and I know where I am.

This time, as they zoom by, they scream out N-I-G-E-R!! Then they hurled three full, opened, bigmouth cans of beer at me. I wouldn't say I like beer... I wouldn't say I like the smell, either. The cans strike me in my face, chest, and right shoulder. There is beer everywhere! As they speed off, their laughter fades into the distance. I remember being angry and mumbling, “You darn idiots! These people are insane!” I have a few more minutes left to reach home. I am nervous now. I hope and pray that a cop does not take interest in me and stop me. A Black man on foot, drenched in alcohol, will paint the wrong picture, and with beer all over me, I will have a losing argument. However, under God's watchful eye, I made it... When I got home, I went straight to shower. My face, chest, and shoulder are bruised.

Embarrassed, I carried on as if nothing had happened, which was easy because everyone was asleep.

A Brief Encounter

In this same city, a preacher and his family are in the check-out lane at one of the local grocery stores. They are standing behind a Caucasian female and her son. While they wait patiently, the little boy turns around and spits into the face of the preacher's wife. The preacher and his family say it took everything to keep from reacting negatively. In addition, they note that their struggle with this issue protracted well beyond the event.

Mayhem at the Market

On Friday, my routine shift at work was the only thing on the agenda that day. But this Friday turned out differently than any other. Typically, I head out to work just a few minutes from the house. Upon approach, there is a lot of commotion and activity a few hundred feet across the road. One of our competitors was in a tumultuous strike and employee protest. The traffic is heavy; there are people everywhere, it is busy! We were extra busy because the other store's regular customers shopped at our store during the strike at theirs, which meant we were experiencing triple the volume of business that day. Mr. C (the senior store manager) and I supervised 30-plus employees during our shift. The store's ten check-out lanes are running full throttle. The volume of business was so high that we pulled overflowing cash drawers every 30 to 40 minutes. I am caught up in the hustle and bustle of things (approving checks, managing employee needs, maintaining customer satisfaction, replenishing inventory). Time moves on, and the sun sets for the evening. Looking out over the store, everything is in order... the operations are at cruising altitude. Mr. C and I take a breather and a quick chat. I prop against the office wall while Mr. C stands in the doorway.

Back then, store business offices were two-dimensional (only floors and walls) and positioned at the center-front part of the store or left or right from the entrance. In addition, they were elevated for an optimal view of the entire store. A short wall divided the space between our office and the express check-out. The computer system for the cash registers, phone, and fax machine was in between the two. While chatting, Mr. C decided that I should leave for the day. I replied, “Are you sure?” He said, " Yeah, I got it. You go home and rest. We will do this dance again tomorrow.” We chuckled. Unbeknown to us, while engrossed in managing the store and chatting, something sinister was developing across the road. I gathered my things and headed home.

The streets are still busy. As I turn out of the parking lot to access Dickerson Rd., a sports car darts in front of me, cutting me off from accessing our parking lot. It irritated me briefly, but I continued the short drive home.

Something catastrophic happened at work during the brief time between leaving the store and sitting down to eat a late dinner. Do you remember the sports car? It belonged to an African American male from a well-to-do family close to the store. It turns out that when he darted in front of me, he was coming from the store across the street, where he was harassing those taking part in the strike. One striker saw the man drive across to our parking lot.

He walked across the road to the young man’s car and sliced all four of his tires in retaliation for his harassment. After the young man comes out of our store, he realizes he sliced and cut his tires. He goes back into our store and asks for management.

Given I have already left the store, Mr. C. is the only authority to respond to him. He tells the young man that the store is not responsible for his tires. Witnesses report that he was upset and demanded that Mr. C take money from the safe to reimburse him for the tires. Again, Mr. C. declined. The teenager leaves, but only to return. Before he returns, his mother arrives at the store to shop. She is unaware of what is transpiring. Meanwhile, I am home now, changing clothes and preparing dinner. I am unaware of what is going down right now.

The young man returns to the store. Witnesses report he steps in through the outdoors with a deer rifle in his hand. He aims at Mr. C., who is standing in the office. The young man's mother is at the register to check out her groceries at that precise moment. Hearing the gasps of people around her, she looks up and sees her son with the rifle raised and aimed. She screams out his name. It's too late; he pulls the trigger, and the shot rings out, creating total pandemonium and panic. When the shot rang out, a teenage cashier sat at the computer between the office and the express check-out. She is on break and the phone the moment tragedy breaks out. The bullet travels through the thin, semi-walled office, striking Mr. C. in the neck! The impact blows the back of his neck out! He dies instantly. His body falls out through the office door, trapping the young cashier sitting in the corner on her break. Co-workers report she freaks out as she sees Mr. C's mangled body lying in front of her.

As this chaos unfolds, I pull up to the table. My plate is in front of me; the food is hot and ready. I give thanks for the food, and as soon as I raise the fork to my mouth, the phone rings. It is one of the courtesy clerks— "bagboys." Coworkers know him as a prankster, a joker of sorts. So, when he stated someone shot Mr. C., I did not believe him.

I replied, "Boy, stop playing around... I'm trying to eat." He spent a few seconds trying to convince me, but I was not buying it. There was a brief silence. Then another voice was on the phone, a paramedic: "Sir, you better get down here. There's been a shooting!"

I dropped my fork, scrambled for clothes to throw on, and then took off! As I race to the store, there are a million thoughts in my head, seemingly... I just left the store a little while ago... I knew someone shot Mr. C, but who else? How many shots? Why did this happen? Upon arrival, First Responders verified who I was and allowed me to enter the store. I look over at the office, and blood is still everywhere.

I look closer and notice two things: Mr. C's bloody handprint on a yellow pipe. He may have attempted to grab the pipe in the defense or while falling out of the office. But the second thing I noticed gave me pause and numbed me. The bullet's entry point is where I was leaning against the wall, chatting with Mr. C. earlier that day. Realizing that through Mr. C.'s gut notion to send me home first, God's providence spared my life. I teared up...

However, we are still in crisis mode. My emotions are short-lived. The police directed me to the other side of the store, where they huddled all the employees. As you can imagine, they are shaken up. Young and still "wet behind the ears myself," I take all the knowledge and experience I have up to that point and try to console, heal, and direct those traumatized by this horrific event. Meanwhile, the word is the gunman has escaped the scene. A search ensues. Authorities apprehended him at a nearby gym, where he took several hostages. After a short period, he surrenders to the police. In the weeks and months ahead, reports circulated that the gunman pleaded "insanity" in court regarding the crimes he committed that day.

An Insane Analysis

Three different narratives, three different outcomes, but one theme governing behavior–insanity. I am conscious that cultural nuances play into and shape discussions about racial bias. I do not intend to tackle such a vast and complex subject here. However, the debate is like a funnel; the starting point is broad but narrow as it moves to the bottom or end. The discussion culminates with an analysis and a question. The racist behaviors of the three men in the truck, the little boy in the check-out lane, and the criminal behavior of the young man in the store are borne out of a similar matrix. The word insanity captures the three incidences narrated above. What does it mean to be insane? Do we surmise it is relative, contextual, and determined, in part, by situational matrix? [1] Do we find it embedded in behavioral outcomes, or is it the by-product of distorted thinking? To appreciate its value and significance, let us define what it is not. It is neither rational, reasonable, customary, nor a mind or thought process categorized as healthy. These describe and define sanity. The technical definition of insanity is more of a legal term than medical or psychological. [2] When used in Forensic Psychiatry or Forensic Psychology contexts, it refers to a person with a psychological disorder or inability to know or understand the inappropriateness of criminal behaviors. [3]

One source identifies insanity as "extreme foolishness or irrationality. [4] The word sanity is derived from a Latin word that means healthy. This sharpens insanity as something unhealthy at its core.

The title of this chapter derives from an exegetical study of Romans chapter 12. Several years ago, I developed a series of lessons for a particular faith community interested in the teachings of the book of Romans. In Romans 12:3, the Apostle Paul encourages rational and humble thinking about the gifts that God has given each of us and that we should not think we are better than others because of our gifts. The Greek word he uses for the English word "think" has significant connotations and relevance to the subject. The word is phronein, which means "to be beside oneself or out of one's mind." [5] Sophronein means to be in one's right mind. The tenor and message of the verse is humility, and elevated thoughts of self indicate a deranged thought process. As stated in Wuest, Robertson notes that the concept of "conceit" used in the verse "is treated as a species of insanity." [6] It is a superiority complex of sorts. [7] The belief that one is superior and the other inferior solely based on skin color breaches sanity. A faulty thought process that renders a person insane. It is crazy thinking.

What is racism?

Racism is "prejudice, discrimination, or antagonism directed against someone of a different race based on the belief that one's race is superior." [8] This is crazy thinking. It is a breach of sanity, a cognitive defect. Racism develops through defective cognitive processing predisposed by an individual's schematic development. Chapter One mentions that the schema is a mental framework that organizes and interprets information. Life experiences and the environment in which one lives programs it. It is known that familial systems, cultural beliefs, and nuances shape our thinking and act as a filter for new information and experiences. In addition, associative learning of which fear conditioning is the most effective, helps formulate racial bias.[9]

For example, Abernathy and Stevens (2016) note that "many implicit themes in today's environment suggest minorities=fear." [10] Öhman & Mineka (2001) note that fear conditioning is the most vital type. [11] This defective concept not only exists in America but manifests globally. For example, s*some* countries in South Asia see Black people (males) as inferior, poor, and dangerous. Some view them as people to avoid. Given that these perceptions develop within the context of culture and family, they feel justified in the hatred and repudiation of any interaction with Black people. However, not every Asian family member buys into these perceptions. However, given common loyalty to the family, they are unlikely to make those differences public.

For instance, an African American male enters a relationship with an Asian woman. The relationship is secret because the woman's family opposes this kind of interaction with this group. At some point during their relationship, she becomes pregnant. She stays away from her family throughout the pregnancy. When it was time to deliver the baby, she checked into the hospital, gave birth, and then disappeared, never found again. The woman knew well that her family would reject her, the boyfriend, and the child. Given that Asian families are close, she could not bring herself to dishonor the family or offend them. –Author's file.

A person's attitude toward race (children) is cultivated by "being absorbed into social norms around them." [12] In this context, a person may be unaware of the wrongness or inappropriateness of such familial attitudes, caste systems, and cultural beliefs perpetuating racism. Thoughts of racism in America develop within the confines of the American culture. However, the tenets of some foreign cultures are a testament to the reality that racism is not only an American sin but a global dilemma.

For instance, in India, directors of a class musical deny a child as a practical, valuable participant because of the dark color of her skin; a man's family overlooks a woman as a candidate for marriage because of the shade of her skin. In

Greece, the Albanians, who fled to Greece after the collapse of the Albanian Communist Regime, are subjects of racist treatment. [13] Americans and Canadians oppressed Native American Indians. [14]

The steep and ongoing conflict between Jews and Palestinians in the Middle East, the violent treatment of Asian communities living in the UK, and the intentional clash of other populations around the world give rise to the reality that race and prejudice are a global dilemma. In another example, the terrorist attacks in the U.S. on 9/11 stimulated acts of racism. Research shows various forms of implicit anti-Islam prejudice and discrimination increased by 83%, and overt acts of discrimination toward Muslim persons increased by 76%.[15] These unfortunate experiences and the reality of racism provoke thoughts and contra-up questions as to the origin and rationale for such behavior. Prejudice questions are interwoven with questions about relations between individuals and groups.

Several theorists have proposed that tendencies toward racism and racial prejudice are the "evolutionary by-product of adaptive survival strategies that allowed early humans to distinguish between friend and foe. A process through which programs the human brain to rely on physical markers to assess the threat of competing tribes and clans."[16] Abernethy and Stevens (2016) note, "When certain races are seen as bad, we want to disassociate ourselves from them."[17]

Even if we surmise that "adaptive survival strategies" are the premise for such distorted behavior today, historical narratives and modern-day realities shed light on the inhumanity and destruction of racism, a reality that should prompt modification of such behaviors across cultures. When the deluded and defective thinking of racism assumes power, it creates a destructive cocktail that manifests in various contexts. In segments of the U.S., for example, they lace the immigration debate with insane thoughts and perceptions about those who they see as "the other." These mental constructs create and enact laws and regulations that judge, separate, and oppress those impacted. This does not circumvent indispensable legalities about proper citizenship or residency in foreign places. Indeed, people cannot stroll into and occupy a foreign land without meeting the prerequisites delineated by that country.

The racist mind must not use legal structures as apparatuses and mediums to enact distorted hatred. Given the fact that racial constructs form within legal structures, familial belief systems, and cultural traditions, many hold such beliefs and practices in tandem with acceptable behaviors. There is no contradiction in their minds or being.

An educated, law-abiding, decent person can hold racial bias as something synonymous with his being. This group will deny racial bias based on two assumptions: one, that racism is wrong. They must disassociate the behavior. Two, their behaviors are not biased but are consistent with family and cultural values.

It is noteworthy that this discussion takes exception to extreme hate groups whose behaviors are born out of sheer hatred and wickedness and whose souls have been disturbed and disintegrated by the act itself. The hearts of those perpetuating this level of evil are empty and ungodly at their core. This discussion focuses on those whose racial bias develops within systems in which protectionism and personal advancement are the catalysts for such behaviors. Humans are the by-product of their socialization. We become what socializes us. Groups socialized to think or believe that minority groups are dangerous and less likely to be successful in life, and families tend not to associate with this population.

People identify with and connect to groups they are conditioned to believe is the best avenue for a successful family to acquire power, wealth, and happiness. However, this ideology is contextual and situational. Although living under the auspice of white privilege, not every white person embodies the characteristics necessary for producing the expected outcome. Sometimes, the white population is like the minority from which they seek to disassociate. Foreign cultures sometimes understand the concept of white privilege better than whites. These hold negative views of nonwhites and believe they are problematic and incalculable to preferred outcomes.

People subscribing to the laws of God and, in effect, living out their lives in faith-based communities around the world are likely not surprised by the behaviors of those who either do not have a relationship with God or are not practicing faith. There is the expectation that those not living for God live for themselves. The probability of embodying principles against God's word and will is exponential among this population. They are likely subject to many behavioral outcomes that negatively affect the individual and the community. If this is the life of the world, how do we process racial bias within the context of faith-based communities whom God summons out of the world? How can ministry be effective in diverse communities? The following narrative challenges this issue and brings these questions front and center.

It is mid-week in a city sprawled and nestled against a seductive, breathtaking, and picturesque mountainous range. Tyre, a newcomer to the area, begins his day in typical fashion: prayer, coffee, and conversation with family. There are two significant events on his calendar on this day. One is a get-together with an ordination committee at the regional offices of a prominent denomination in the city. Tyre, a person of color, is responding to a referral by a family member to the denomination because of his pastoral experience and their need for exceptional ministers to serve ailing congregations in the area. Tyre received his ordination several years prior but sought ordination recognition through this denominational body. The process recognizes prior or existing training and experience of those seeking to serve or affiliate with the denomination. Tyre submitted theological papers, a resume, and references for consideration and recognition. The final step in the process was to meet with the committee, which was an interview. The committee contacts him for final instructions and meeting date, place, and time.

On the day of the meeting, unbeknownst to Tyre, the committee had already decided about him and his inquiry about serving in a ministerial capacity. Upon entering the room, several people, most Caucasian, were sitting around a long table, except for one African American female. The committee's greeting was very dull, he reports. It is noteworthy that besides his pastoral background, Tyre is in an investigative profession, a fact taken for granted by the committee. As a specialized investigator, Tyre can step into a space and quickly size up the environment. As they engage him, he notices two people sitting around the table not bother speaking or raising their heads to acknowledge his presence. One of the two remained glued to their laptop the entire time.

After a while, this person breaks the silence by asking Tyre questions about the school he graduated from. As he makes those inquiries, he never once lifts his head to make eye contact. Tyre reports he realized the man was looking up the school during the meeting. He does not seem to like where Tyre trained and becomes dismissive of him. As the meeting progresses, the environment turns adversarial, an obvious fact for a person whose training helps him decipher an interview from an interrogation. Tyre reports that the committee chair is a Caucasian female. She fires off rapid questions, and before Tyre can complete answers to the questions, she moves on to the next question in a very dismissive and demeaning way. Now, Tyre realizes that he is in a hostile environment. He surmises that the committee had concluded before the meeting began. As such, he is bewildered over why he was invited and not given due process.

One of the committee members realizes that the atmosphere is unbecoming. He tries to pivot by raising different questions in a more welcoming manner. But the chair cuts him off and redirects questioning to what she considers more interesting. While Tyre is responding to the chair's questions, she cuts off the meeting, saying, "I think we've heard enough. Thank you for coming."

He pushes back from the table and thanks the committee for the invitation. As he moves toward the exit, he extends his arm to shake the chair's hand and thank her for the invitation. The chair responds by coughing into her hands, and she states, " Oh, you don't want to shake my hand. Thank you for coming." She closes the door behind Tyre.

Now, what Tyre is not aware of during this process is that this committee has a history of treating women and people of color differently during their ordination process. Upon the knowledge of this, Tyre believes this explains (in part at least) the committee's unprofessional and unbecoming treatment of him during the process. Tyre writes a letter to the committee's office, withdrawing from the process and demanding accountability and action that ensures no one else has similar experiences. Tyre provides an excerpt from that letter.

He notes:

"... Although I rejected the department's ordination process, I am interested in procedural changes to prevent others from racial and negative experiences within ordination and ministry. I am interested in how the department processes transparency, forgiveness, and ecumenicalism, how its current ordination process reconciles with the denomination's commitment to inclusiveness, and the differentiation of ordination recognition from regular ordination processes. Disclosing this information will be helpful..."

Racism is a Problematic State of Being

Racial bias playing out within faith-based contexts creates an immediate paradox. It is a disgraceful act opposed to moral values and goes against these principles.
Namely, unfair and often inaccurate judgment, hatred, unforgiveness, and conceit, any of which help form attitudes that are problematic, destructive, and defy the order given to those surrendering their lives to God through Christ. There are biblical mandates directing how one should treat other people. Two of the most popular are

"You shall love your neighbor as yourself."[18]

> "In everything, therefore, treat people the same way you want them to treat you, for this is the Law and the Prophets."[19]

Old Testament scripture condemns this judgment, partiality, and hatred.[20] There are other issues with racism, such as the disregard for God as the Creator. It evokes love for God while hating others whom God has created, dishonoring His creative genius. A faith that reaches up to God must reach out to others. It is a horizontal connection to others in behavior, conversation, attitude, and moments of distress and despair, as support, guidance, love, and concern. If God intended or wanted one color or race to be and represent humanity, it would be so. Given that this is not true, it indicates there was no such plan in the mind of God for the earthly realm. Notwithstanding, there will be no distinctions in the heavenly or spiritual, which accentuates God's original agenda.[21]

Second, God created humans with the inherent capacity to adapt to the revolving environment to which we may be exposed. For instance, the dark African is such because of his geographical proximity to the equator. Science suggests that the need for solar protection and vitamin D predicates skin pigmentation changes.[22] Humans living near the equator have dark skin as added protection from the sun's rays. [23] Conversely, those living furthest from the equator (say Greenland) have fairer skin. A person's ethnicity or nationality means nothing to God. Those perpetuating this malignancy become something God is not, and he opposes. Note Acts 10: 34-35

> "[34] Opening his mouth, Peter said: "I most certainly understand *now* that God is not one to show partiality,[35] but in every nation, the man who fears Him and does what is right is welcome to Him."

James 2:1-9 is a section speaking about partiality and discriminatory practices. Three significant points are worthy of discussion here.

- The direct command prohibiting one from holding their faith in tandem with partial thinking and behavior. The New American Standard Bible (NASB) calls it an "attitude of personal favoritism."[24]
- This validates that this issue is a matter of thought... as noted above, it is a faulty thought process. Attitude in psychology is a constitution or matrix of emotions, beliefs, perceptions developed within a culture and familial systems, and other life experiences. The message of the verse is that we should not combine the essentials of righteousness with racial bias and

> discriminatory practices, whether the context is racial or not. It means, "Stop trying to maintain your faith"[25] with the practice of partiality. [26] These are not compatible. "Holding respect of persons is inconsistent with the first principles of Christianity."[27]

This must include faith-based community support of individuals and groups whose ideology and behavior are racial and, in effect, contradictory to holy principles we hold dear. It is both impractical and dubious for faith-based communities or individual members to throw support behind political candidates, community leaders, or groups whose being, focus, and modus operandi stroke and fan flames of racial bias for sordid gain. Those choosing to uphold this mantra and enact its dynamics violate holy principles and, in effect, sin. Note James 2:9

> "But if you show partiality, you are committing sin and are legally convicted as transgressors." NASB

- Given that racial bias and prejudice are the offspring of distorted thinking and hatred, its prevailing component is hardwired into a person's being, which makes change difficult but possible. When the Holy Mandate uses the word hate in this context, it refers to one whose spirit finds another person repulsive (including hatred toward another without cause) and intense animosity toward another. [28] It is hatred on steroids. One scholar notes a disdain "in which a person desires no relationship or amiable reconciliation." [29] Hatred is not always manifest through a "fire and brimstone" response and approach to people and circumstances. Sometimes, it is subtle and unassuming and influences decision-making aimed at the devaluation and demise of another; often, the basis is superficial.

Returning to Sanity

A man is on a routine business trip to a city 20 to 30 miles from his current address. He travels down the main road connecting the two cities. It is a popular trek for anyone navigating between the two places. People living in these two areas know of the ever-present dynamics of this route. Most travelers know that there are crime risks when traveling down this road. These risks are more significant for specific groups or individuals traveling through this area. As life would have it, thugs ambush, rob, and beat the man. His circumstance is critical. Injured, he falls to the ground, paralyzed by his condition. Another commuter comes upon him and sees his distress, but he also notices what kind of person he appears to be. He recognized distinguishing characteristics, those things about the man that made him different, that made him “the other.” The commuter is mindful of the things on his to-do list, which compels him to move on. In his mind, he is more critical, has responsibilities, and is nothing like this man. He stays clear of the situation and moves past the man without interacting with him. The victim, still suffering from his injuries, remains on the side of the road; given that the road is widespread and the main one between these two cities, another commuter happens upon him. Perhaps the man’s moans, signs of bleeding, or the fact that he is down alerts him to his trouble and the need for help. However, as his eyes survey the situation, his mind directs his feet to move, ensuring no direct contact with the man. The commuter, more concerned about his agenda, moves on, leaving the man helpless and in agony.

Time trickles by... and another stranger comes around the bend and sees him with different eyes. It is a view that causes one to feel. This stranger had eyes capable of perception and analysis, compassion and conviction, reflection and resolve. He moves closer. Influenced by the man’s condition and inner spirit, he provides critical components necessary for resolution. Moving the man out of his circumstances places him in healing and recovery. There is no objection or fear of using personal resources. He does this with care and benevolent love toward a stranger. Ensuring the man's recovery is adequate, he plans to follow up.

Who do you think these characters are? A better question might be, which of these characters do you identify with? How will you react when your journey through life brings you to an intersection with someone or a situation that requires you to dig deep and respond? Do you have the perception of seeing things? Will you be concerned about the resources, time, and effort needed to respond? What influences your decision-making in situations like the one described? Do people have to meet specific criteria or qualify for your help? If so, what rules and dynamics make up these criteria? Do you allow divine ordinances such as, "... while we have the opportunity, let us do good to all people..." or "... to one who knows the right thing to do and does not do it, to him it is a sin." to guide your decision-making?

The traveler's story is the parable of the Good Samaritan Jesus discussed in Luke 10:30-37, in which He teaches the fundamental concept of a neighbor. Jesus challenges a young lawyer's perception of righteousness by showing that absolute righteousness includes loving one's neighbor as one loves self. To justify his version of righteousness, the lawyer asks, who is my neighbor?

It is a question highlighting the pandemic and kaleidoscopic nature of discrimination across cultures and geographical boundaries. Jewish sects such as the Pharisees sought to narrow the answer to the question to limit groups of people. Powerful tenants of the 21st century aim to redefine their neighborhood to include the right to exclusivity as a part of the definition, relaxing expectations of accountability and responsibility to the wholeness and dignity of humanity. It leisurely and delicately codifies "the other" as extinct.

Jesus, conscious of this malignancy in His day and its tentacles into the generations to come, reconstitutes the concept of neighbor to its rightful and divine place. In delivering this concept, He selects the Greek word *plēsion* for neighbor, which reaches beyond the standard idea of proximity and likeness to a profound twofold connotation.

- First, it refers to someone not defined by societal restrictions. [30] In this way, the word refers to all people. Joseph H. Thayer (1977) notes this is "any other man irrespective of race or religion with whom we live or whom we chance to meet." [31] It is the "fellowman" or fellow human" not the Caucasian,

Black, Asian, Hispanic, etc.. It is the "fellow man." Jesus avoids identifying a particular person by including every human.

- Second, the meaning moves beyond that of people to a specific practice or behavior. It is neighborly to enact love toward another ("fellowman") without prerequisites for compassion and interaction. Zodhiates (1977) states:

  "... he who is outwardly near us should be the object of our concern although there are no ties of kindred or nation between us."[32]

A paradigm shift is necessary for any of us to appreciate this teaching. Those conditioned by racial bias and other forms of prejudice must be seen with new eyes. Notice that the Samaritan approaches the man after he "sees" him. The word saw, as used in verse 33, refers to perception, realization, and knowledge because of visualization.[33] In other words, this is knowledge and perception developed from surveying the individual's issues and circumstances causing injury and agony. The visual is not that of the individual's ethnicity, religion, or other, but of seeing the current condition with the end in mind. This is one reason

Jesus talks about love as fulfilling the whole Law. Love toward God and fellow humans ensures the right thing happens in every circumstance. It sees things differently.

Now, understanding what racial bias and prejudice look like and what it is in spiritual and psychological contexts, do you surmise that practicing faith and racial bias is something tenable? Do your thoughts and behavior toward "the other" align with God's call to love the neighbor? It is impracticable for genuine faith and racism to coexist; it is one or the other. A person cannot practice both, period. Racism is an old-fashioned, unique form of insanity that is destructive to the community. Although we now live in one of the most educated and advanced societies ever known to humanity, the ignorance and stupidity of racism and prejudice pervasively contaminate communities. There are far too many who have lost their minds in this area. There is an ever-pressing necessity to return to sanity. However, this is impossible without shifting thinking to include analyzing and identifying racial bias and prejudice as abusive because it perpetuates unmerited practices and exacts improper behavior aimed at causing injury. In addition, people of faith must see such acts as dishonoring God as Creator and an impediment to the call to holiness and authentic service. Suppose we ever overcome this malignancy. In that case, people of faith must lead the charge by ensuring that services to and interaction with communities have five essential elements embedded in them.

For example,

- Love- There must be love, for it covers a multitude of sins and ensures the well-being of the whole person (I Jo. 4: 8).

- Wisdom- Assess individuals based on their souls' quality and value (Ja. 2: 9).

- Discernment- Eyes of understanding; the ability to survey circumstances and situations and differentiate the person from these (Luke 10:33).

- Resolve action designed to meet people at their actual point of need (Luke 10:34).

- Review- Follow-up, ensuring the person emerges from their circumstance (Luke 10:35).

As noted earlier, there must be a paradigm shift in the minds and attitudes of those practicing racial bias or any other form of prejudice as the basis or standard for judgment and decision-making. The attitude of the individual must adjust to people of faith. Again, "attitude" defines one's perception or viewpoint, disposition, and mental approach to circumstances or people. It is a snapshot of one's mental construct; it reflects the experiences composing our thoughts and emotions and creates frameworks through which we process every other experience. We typically associate the phrase "attitude adjustment with a mental approach or response to a situation or person, which needs modification to establish understanding and resolution.

This adjustment should change the competition dynamics between individuals and communities and build up people. In racial contexts, people compete in negative ways, which proves harmful to society, ultimately. Notably, Romans 12:10 highlights competition as likely more productive and heartfelt than any other. Society teaches that competition is good, sometimes, especially in business and economics. We know this as a "competitive advantage." Michael E. Porter (1990) chronicles an article featuring the competitive advantage of nations. [34] Porter notes that the prosperity of countries, for example, is created, not inherited, through the evolving pressure and challenge of its people. The article's tenor suggests the nature of competition is such that it fosters the creation and assimilation of knowledge, spurs innovation, and champions strategic collaborations and alliances, as well as traits that will bode well between groups and individuals. Paul's competitive concept in this verse is strikingly different, but it creates alliance and collaboration. In addition, it is a competition to improve individuals and the community. He states:

> 10 "Be devoted to one another in brotherly love; *give preference* to one another in honor; " NASB

"Give preference" refers to "outdo one another in showing honor."[35] The Greek word for preference means to lead the way; go before and refers to that within which one excels. [36] Change in this context likely resolves unnecessary conflict between races and people. It can cause the Asian woman to see the African American male differently or satiate fiery disputes between communities. It will motivate governments to respect and celebrate differences between cultures, alter the appraisal of women in ways that restore glory, and celebrate their uniqueness. This adjustment restores homage and tribute to God as Creator, in whose image every man is born. The faith community must lead the way. Now, as the thoughts and voices of this discussion mute, as the dust settles and the fog of curiosity lifts, can you see your reflection? If so, who do you see?

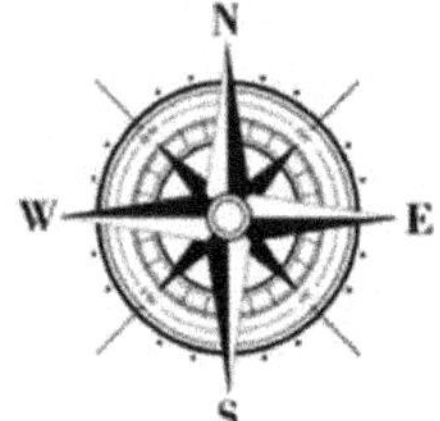

THE GUIDE POST

Seven Steps to Resolving Racial Bias

1. Acknowledge that racism, racial bias, prejudice, and discrimination are incompatible with Scripture (Leviticus 19:15-18; Deuteronomy 1:17; Matthew 7:12Luke 10:30-37; James 2:1-9; Acts 10: 34-35; Romans 12:1-10).

2. Adjust your attitude toward people to see them as a part of God's creation and honor God (Genesis 1:27; Romans 12:10).

3. Pray for and exercise Godly wisdom as delineated in James 4:17, i.e., pure, peaceable, gentle, reasonable, merciful, good, committed, and not hypocritical.

4. Spiritual discernment is used to assess the individual appropriately. Examples: (Gen. 41:33-41; Deut. 1:13; I

Kings 3:1-28; II Chron. 2:12; Prov. 14:33; 1:21; 18:15; Luke 10:38-42; 23:13-16).

5. Differentiate the circumstance or issue for the individual. (Luke 10:33-34)
6. See racism for what it is: an act of abuse that injures Spiritually, psychologically, physically, and financially.
7. Eliminate the spirit of competition that devalues others and the self.

CHAPTER NOTES AND REFERENCES

[1] Set of circumstances or state of affairs; an environment or material in which something develops.

[2] Durand, V. Mark, and Barlow, H. David (2010) Essentials of Abnormal Psychology 5th Edition, G-8

[3] Ibid

[4] Retrieved from www.dictionary.com

[5] Zodhiates, Spiros (1992) The Complete Word Study Dictionary New Testament. Pg., 1454, 5426, and 5426 under 3912 Pg. 1115

[6] Ibid

[7] A feeling of superiority or exaggerated self-importance, often accompanied by excessive aggressiveness, arrogance, etc. which are compensation for feelings of inferiority.

[8] Retrieved from www.dictionary.com

[9] The understanding that certain events occur together. Myers, G. David (2008) Exploring Psychology Pg. G-1

[10] Ibid, pg. 10

[11] Ibid

[12] Ibid

[13] Demalija, Rifat (Sep-Dec. 2016) Migration and Social Transformation. the Case of Albania and Greece European Journal of Multidisciplinary Studies. Vol. 3 Nr-1. Retrieved from: http://journals.euser.org/files/articles/ejms_sep_dec_16/Rifat.pdf

[14] PM to apologize for Canada's treatment of Native Americans. The Guardian. Retrieved from: https://www.theguardian.com/world/2008/jun/12/canada.usa

[15] Utsey, Shawn O.; Ponterotto, Joseph G.; Porter, Jerlym S. (2008) Journal of Counseling and Development. Retrieved from: https://www.questia.com/read/1G1-180861162/prejudice-and-racism-year-2008-still-going-strong

[16] Joseph G. Ponterotto, Shawn O. Utsey, Paul B. Pedersen (2006) Preventing Prejudice: A Guide for Counselors, Educators, and Parents. Sage Publications

[17] Ibid Abernethy and Stevens Pg. 17

[18] Matthew 19:19

[19] Matthew 7:12

[20] Leviticus 19:15-18; Deuteronomy 1:17; Acts 10:34

[21] See Galatians 3:28

[22] University of Oslo. Department of Physics: Why Skin Colors Differ. Retrieved from: https://www.mn.uio.no/fysikk/english/research/news-and-events/news/2011/why-skin-colours-differ.html

[23] Jeff Verkouille, Human (Dec. 25, 2016) Why are the people in Africa black? Retrieved from: https://www.quora.com/Why-are-the-people-in-Africa-black

---

24 James 2:1

25 The Complete Biblical Library (1986) Vol. 9 Hebrew-James pg. 207

26 Ibid

27 The Pulpit Commentary Vol. XXI Section: James pg. 32

28 Zodhiates, Spiros Key Word Study Bible. Lexical Aids to the Old Testament pg. 1787, 8130

29 The Complete Biblical Library (2000) The Old Testament Hebrew-English Dictionary Pg. 61 : 7983

30 Ibid

31 Thayer, Joseph H. (1977) Greek-English Lexicon of the New Testament Pg. 518:4139

32 Ibid, Lexical Aids to the New Testament Pg. 1868:4139

33 Ibid, (TCBL) Vol. 12 pg. 244

34 Porter, Michael E. (Mar.-April, 1990) The Competitive Advantage of Nations Harvard Business Review. Retrieved from: https://hbr.org/1990/03/the-competitive-advantage-of-nations

35 New American Standard Bible (2003) Updated Edition. Lockman Foundation Pg. 1151

36 Ibid[5] Zodhiates, Pg. 1219; 4285:proegeomai

5

Wanting More in the Land of Plenty

"Wealth consists not in having great possessions but having few wants."

–Epictetus

During one of the nation's dark economic periods, the Jaxis family found themselves behind the eight-ball, which was an unusual position and predicament to be in for "Mrs. J." Her history includes a prior marriage in which the family lived in a seven-bedroom home and an Olympic size pool in a well-to-do neighborhood: the family-owned a Range Rover, a Jaguar, and a Mercedes. The total annual household income surpasses 300,000, most of which was earned by her husband. Mrs. J is a practicing Christian, while her former husband is not. He believes in God but does not identify with anybody or live out Godly principles. He works excessively and provides a luxurious lifestyle for Mrs. J and the kids. This is important to Mrs. J because she believes money is so significant that she places it next to God. In addition, she considers her essence or being entitles her to the best lifestyle possible. Shopping at discount centers for jeans and other items is a mortal sin in her mind. Her clothes and those of the family are from high-end stores at the mall. Mrs. J enjoys the leisure luxury provides. For instance, she enjoys rounding off her day lounging by the family's indoor pool. But she believes she is down-to-earth and is a good person because she teaches Sunday school every week; she takes care of her body by eating right and jogging every morning before work. She involves herself with humanitarian projects, professional clubs, associations, and her children's extra-curricular activities. She is experiencing and living her perception of what a good life should be.

Accompanying this perceived life of luxury was the revolving nightmare of physical abuse, which contributed to the demise of the marriage and the separation of the family. She loses her bid for the house in the divorce proceedings. Her ex-husband's attorney outmaneuvered her attorney during these legal proceedings, which Mrs. J has been angry about for years. Following her divorce, Mrs. J moved into an apartment complex across town. The reality that her ex-husband still holds the keys to the family home while she now lives in an apartment disgruntles her. Complicating matters (in her mind, at least) is the fact she works in the corporate world, in which there is an ever-pressing need to perform, to be, and to belong. She does not like coworkers knowing the details of her situation. She does not want them to know she no longer lives in that luxurious neighborhood but an apartment in a modest community. She is rushing to move out of her apartment and neighborhood. Mrs. J attempts to buy a home on her own in the same neighborhood as the earlier home. One home is next door to her ex-husband, and the other is three streets away. Both attempts failed.

Mrs. J may seem comfortable to most people, but her past influences her outlook on life. As far as she is concerned, she is not doing well. Hunted by her new reality, buying a home in a better neighborhood inundates her thoughts nowadays. This is her latest mission, which she wanted to do yesterday. Behind the scenes so far is Mr. Jaxis, a person she met and dated during this transition. Although she finds him attractive, she does not see him as marriage material.

His inquiries about marriage on two occasions lead her to dodge and decline the offer. He is bewildered by why he is good enough to date but not well enough for her to marry. One year after her dreaded move into an apartment, she buys

a home, not in the neighborhood she prefers but a new home. There is a false sense of satisfaction. Her mind is now set on the next place, a bigger house in a better neighborhood.
She learns that her company is in trouble, and her job is now in danger.

This new revelation sparks a new level of stress and concern. The house is still new; she does not know how to manage it in the short run should the company close and she loses her job. In retrospect, the apartment, although not ideal, is much more manageable under such circumstances, but per her decision, that ship has sailed. Nervous now, she brainstorms and concludes that Mr. Jaxis' income (although meager compared to her previous marriage) can be helpful under the circumstances. Knowing he is interested in marriage, she proposes to him. Surprised, he pauses and stares... and says, "You realize what you are asking me, right? Look, you know I want this more than anything, but don't do this, and then two years later, talk divorce."[1] They marry, hence the reference "Mrs. J." He moves in, and Mrs. J has a new life and family. They live in a modest neighborhood and home with three bedrooms, two cars, and two pets. Their joint income is north of 150,000.00, most of which she makes. Although her life is decent and free from abuse, she is not happy. The house is on the wrong side of town, the Mercedes is not as new as it used to be, and she loses her job.

Irrespective of her prior experience as a victim of abuse, she contemplates going back to her previous husband for the lifestyle she once enjoyed. In addition, she is itching to get back into the corporate world but finds it more difficult than usual. Meanwhile, Mr. J struggles to keep up with her wealthy profile and demands. As expected, just over two years into the marriage, their financial rollercoaster rips into the relationship. Mrs. J begins talking about divorce. But this time, she is in control. The house has her name on it. After finding another job, she is under the conviction she can handle things on her own. She sees Mr. J as an expendable asset. She wants more but does not see her husband to that end. He attempts to fight back for the marriage, but his pockets are not deep enough. Mrs. J asks him to leave.

Any seasoned Christian or person of faith, analytical student of Scripture, or mental health professional will surmise that the tenants of this narrative have several red flags and revolving issues of concern. Although there is more to the narrative, the information presented here highlights the focal points of this chapter. To want something implies an existing deficit, and acquiring the missing elements or experience is critical to recovery, wholeness, and success.

However, the word 'wanting,' as used in the chapter, indicates coveting more resources and experiences to a perceived end. In this vein, one's status is irrelevant and incalculable.

It reflects actual or perceptional dissatisfaction and the engine driving this person's decision-making. In a theological context, it is the fallout from the vacancy of contentment and fulfillment codified through authentic spiritual dynamics. Psychological contexts see 'wanting' as the by-product of self-actualization portrayed as a constellation of personal beliefs and value systems, desire, will, directed behavior, and responsibility, which, in effect, aim to maintain and enhance the human experience. In this context, this chapter extends beyond just the concept of money to other resources, categories, and areas used to develop and enhance life, i.e., sex, admiration, and power. But money and power are chief among these three examples.

The Money

First, in this chapter, let us dismiss frequent misperceptions about God's view of money and the general concept of 'possessions.' Too often, people who are confused about God portray Him as a "killjoy" uninterested and not vested in man's happiness and success. People who do not have a relationship with Him but have money or pursue it are among those who hold such a flawed philosophy.

The misguided concept that man is the sole author of his success and blessings gives birth to such statements.

It is a humanistic view that dismisses God as cause and draws a paradoxical conclusion in which man is both cause and effect of his being or its quality. God's love and good nature stimulate concern about every creature He makes. [2] He is both instrumental and vital to our success. [3] When Jesus states, "... I came that you might have life abundantly,"[4] He is not referring to the physical body's life per se, but a particular quality of life. The Greek word used for "abundantly" means something in superabundance, much or remarkable, extraordinary, and profuse. [5] Thayer shows this as something "super-added, over and above, more than necessary." [6] For instance, during one of his blissful moments, King David describes the quality of his life as a cup running over the top.[7]

Many are led to believe that we write our destiny by attending elite universities or developing and harnessing skill sets coveted in the society in which we live. Others think they're independent and need no one for anything; they pull themselves up with their bootstrap. This group frowns on others who must ask for help or depend on sources other than themselves. Although that sounds independent and worthy of celebration to an extent, God authors the building blocks that make any of these attainable. A person's financial genius, scientific mind, and exceptional skill sets develop and mature through external sources. It may be the loan somebody gave you, the credit extended, and gifts from grandparents to help you start adult life well. In other instances, the hiring executive gave you an opportunity and those countless moments and interactions with key people, which translates as iron sharpening iron.

These gifts are not by-products of the so-called "evolutionary process" but that God determines, codifies, and disburses to His creation. As Creator, He is the author of the very breath a person breathes. Money and other similar resources are among the plethora of blessings God graciously provides, a fact that should fill us with humility and gratitude.

God does not oppose the acquisition of money or possessions; if this were the case, He would not have blessed Solomon with wealth, for example. [8] He opposes money possessing the person. God's objection is an individual making money their god, their cure-all. Enormous amounts of money or assets can cause individuals to see themselves as valuable people and independent of God. He wants confidence developed not through the power of the purse but through a personal relationship with Him. He finds the arrogance and perceived invisibility that significant amounts of money generate repulsive. In addition, God antagonizes using money and power to oppress and enact evil, such as human trafficking and prejudice, whether racial or gender specific. He stands in opposition to people depending more on their possessions than they do on Him. The pursuit of wealth and possessions is not evil. The questions are relative here: Why and to what end or purpose does one pursue wealth, power, and possessions? In His infinite wisdom, He keenly knows that money and possessions can reconstitute a person in destructive ways to that individual and their community. Money in significant amounts generates an unhealthy preoccupation and fixation, which, in effect, becomes the essence of that individual's decision-making process. Jesus states, "You cannot serve God and wealth."[9] God is always aware of the outcome in the beginning. He summons us away from the problems and snares money produces and proliferates.

When Jesus stipulates abandoning possessions as a prerequisite for discipleship, He is not demanding a vow of poverty. Nor is He suggesting that to be Christian, godly, and holy, a person cannot have or own things in this life. [10] God is aware of our need for mundane things to survive and live.[11] The warning Jesus gives to the rich in Luke 6:24 is to those who are followers and believers in Him but have selfish dispositions. [12] The verse suggests that those who pursue wealth and comfort to the point they worship it and are defined by it will get all they seek. They will gain it. They are receiving luxury and comfort in total now. There will be no more to come. This is the travesty of this reality. They may have it all now and be comfortable with the world's standard, but the day will dawn when it fades in death, and the comfort experienced here and now may not be available later in eternity. Given that Jesus gave this message to people who were followers of Him, it indicates that those identifying with Him were wealthy. This underscores the importance of balance and stewardship in our lives, making us feel responsible and accountable.

The point is that one can have money but not allow the funds to own you. In Matthew 19:16-26, a wealthy young ruler has eternality on his mind. He questions Jesus about the best route to that blissful experience. Jesus points to the common commandments to which most are accustomed: do not commit adultery, do not steal, and honor your parents. The rich man (as many will say today) "Well, I have done all of those things; what else?" Here, Jesus reaches into the depth of the man's soul and being; He broaches the essence of his spirit when He suggests that the man sell his possessions. Jesus knew the rich man's possessions possessed him, not the proper order. The man leaves in stitches because he is wealthy. It is one's attitude about wealth, power, and possession that is problematic, so much so Jesus states, "It is hard for a rich man to enter the kingdom of God."[13] Again, not because of wealth itself, but the attitude and greed it generates. It is not that one must live in poverty to be holy. The point Jesus makes to the rich man and the rest of the world is that the abundance of one's possessions does not determine the substance and value of life. [14] Many live and seek the latter to identify with and see it as life itself.

Jesus shows here that wealth and possessions must be appropriately prioritized and categorized. These things can exist in a person's life. Still, they must stay in their proper place and be accompanied by an appropriate attitude if they expect to keep an effective relationship with God through Jesus Christ. The call is more indicative of separation than depletion of assets. Zodhiates states:

> "The meaning of the phrase does not give up" in Lk. 14:33 does not mean reckless abandonment of one's belongings, but the proper categorization of them to carry out their intended purpose."

The desire for more expands beyond money and other tangible objects to include pleasures of all types and across the spectrum. Sometimes, it's intercourse, drugs, and in other instances, it is praise, power, etc. The dynamics and process are the same regardless of the nature and venue of the desire.

The Cause

Avarice or covetousness, self-indulgence, egocentricity, and the oppression these inflict develop within an individual over time. What causes an individual to evolve into such a person? What dynamics make up Mrs. J's mindset and need for more, for example? Why are some people this way and others not? Do we surmise that the origin is environmental or communal? Is it the result of flawed parenting? Is it psychological or spiritual?

Do we think exposure, whether too much too soon or too little too late, is the medium for such ideological approaches to life? There are likely several variables one can point to as the culprit. But, when this issue is prevalent among people of faith, the first perceptible cause is a vacancy of contentment. One might decide this applies to anyone, including people of faith. For instance, notice Hebrews 13:5,

> "[5]Make sure that your character is free from the love of money, being content with what you have; for He has said, I WILL NEVER DESERT YOU, NOR WILL I EVER FORSAKE YOU", [6]so that we confidently say, The Lord is My Helper, I WILL NOT BE AFRIAD." NASB

There is significant material here for digestion. First, the summons to abandon this lifestyle or behavior is not baseless or a derivative of an empty concept. The lifestyle noted here is a direct fallout from the absence of contentment in the life of a Christian, for example.

An individual's character[15] must be free of the love of money. This lifestyle is often identifiable by a set of excessive behaviors, i.e., the unnecessary purchase of an automobile priced in the millions or 2 billion dollars for a private residence is the excess to which this passage points. This concept concerns a person's mind, given that emotion and thought drive behavior. To fall into this category, one must not make a multi-million or billion-dollar purchase. A person can be insolvent and still struggle with the love of money. Why? It is more one's mental approach and the excess and dissatisfaction it perpetuates than the dollar itself. Failure to understand and exercise contentment is at the heart of the issue.

Although the love of money sounds harmless, it carries debilitating and destructive tendencies. The emphasis of the appeal is on the "love" of money, not money itself. Vincent (as stated in Wuest) notes:

> "It is not the possession of riches, but the love of them that leads men into temptations."[16]

When the Hebrew writer refers to character, it refers to the summation of distinctive structures and mannerisms that make the individual, or the "stuff," or dynamics that make a person who they are. In this light, the hortatory in verse 5 is for one to certify the absence of any form of the love of money in their being or as a method with which one engages in life. "It degrades the soul itself until, oblivious of its high calling, looking sharply upon material or perishable possessions"[17] to an end. For instance, Jesus gives a parable of a rich man whose perception of his wealth leads him to operate and process independently. [18] There is no parable with as many personal pronouns (I, me, and mine) as this passage. After surveying his wealth, Luke 12:17 states, "And he reasoned to himself..." The English translation loses some significance in this verse. It means that he kept "revolving" the matter in his head by asking himself questions regarding his wealth, i.e., what should I do about having more than I can handle or can accommodate? He plays the abundance of his wealth in his head and gives no thought to anyone else. The implication is that he chooses the direction he wants and does not consider God a critical part of his analysis. He did not give in any measure recognition to God for the blessings that are a privilege to receive. Barclay notes, "The rich fool was aggressively self-centered."[19]

One of the most unwitting moves or decisions a businessperson, investor, or other person of wealth can make is losing it in death after living well in this life and making no provisions or investments for life after this one.

The Apostle Paul expands the discussion and warning about the absence of contentment and the fallout of such- "love of money." I Timothy 6:6-10, within which the point is much more potent in its exegetical context:

> [6] "But godliness *is* a means of significant gain when accompanied by contentment.
> [7] For we have brought nothing into the world, so we cannot take anything out of it either. [8] If we have food and covering, we shall be content with these. [9] But those who want to get rich fall into temptation and a snare and many foolish and harmful desires, which plunge men into ruin and destruction. [10] For the love of money is a root of all sorts of evil, and some by longing for it have wandered away from the faith and pierced themselves with many griefs." NASB

Here, Paul contributes "longing for it" as one dynamic leading to an individual's fall. Temptation and snares are the mediums through which this spiritual tackle unfolds. To capture the meaning and impact of the word snare, Thayer notes that the word here indicates a "bird caught, entangled," and unable to fly. The word implies trapping someone in unsuspecting situations with lethal or life-altering consequences.[20]

However, what is noteworthy here is that temptation is the genesis of the dynamics in play, leading a man to a steep fall. This kind of temptation is only effective when there is a desire or something already lodged within a person's heart[21]. If a fish does not like worms, he will never bite and never contact the hook hidden under the bait. However, bait the hook with something this fish likes, which will draw the fish to it. The fish will investigate it, nibble, and then bite. When a person has money in their mind and heart in unhealthy ways, Satan will see he gets it or dangle the proverbial carrot of promise but never allow a person to bite, proving he is the father of lies. The love of money causes people and groups to pursue things harmful to themselves and their communities. An unhealthy desire and love for it will send you over the cliff into the abyss of depression. Given how it engulfs a man's soul to a destructive end, Jesus notes it is hard for a rich man to enter the Kingdom; no wonder Scripture warns against chasing it, which can be lethal to a man's soul.

Contentment

As noted above, a heart without contentment is the catalyst that sets up this inevitable calamity. There is good reason for the call to contentment. The word itself has powerful connotations. When people are not content, they wander, searching for solutions, fixes, and balm for their ailing situations. Their mind wanders because nothing satisfies the heart, which, most times, is the by-product of conflating needs and wants. In addition, it is the consequence of a person's failure to include God in their calculation to resolve an issue. But understand that the call to contentment is not to surrender progression, improvement, or advancement in life. As stated in the Pulpit Commentary, Ward Beecher notes:

> "It is not to be the content of indifference, indolence, unambitious stupidity, but the content of industrious fidelity."[22]

Regarding the Scripture condemning the pursuit of riches, Wuest states:

> "... what is here condemned in not an ambition to excel in some lawful department of human activity, which though it brings an increase in riches, develops

> character, but having a single eye to the accumulation of money by any means."[23]

The words content and contentment, as used in the epistle of Hebrews and I Timothy, refer to an inward satisfaction, "to possessed unfailing strength," which suffices and determines when enough is enough. However, the word suggests satisfaction from adequate resources that meet the original need.

For instance, if $5000 meets the need, do not become too ambitious; occupying and obsessing over $15,000 is the underlying concept. If the initial need is unmet, pursuing a financial resolution to the issue is not adverse. If a family determines that $1 million is necessary for retirement and that is a genuine number, pursue it. However, once this goal is achieved, do not obsess about more or fall in love with money and wealth. Another example of this concept of contentment is in the book of Exodus 25:1-2, in which God instructs Moses to have the people bring an offering to Him to finance the temple's construction. In Exodus 36:6, the people were offering more than was necessary. Moses issues a proclamation halting any further contributions by the people. This is a difficult concept to grasp for people living today and even more challenging for those in the business of making money. Accumulating as much as one can is the mantra of the 21st century. Doing the opposite or anything opposed to this is likely seen as insanity.

But that is the world's view or philosophy. In Philippians 4:11, Paul states, "... I have learned to be content in whatever circumstance I am." Here, Paul's sufficiency is not in self but in God through Christ. His relationship with Christ gives him a level of insurance beyond human capacity. Godliness produces contentment. There are two key reasons contentment is sufficient. The first is cloaked in Paul's warning about the love of money, within which verse 7 is paramount. Reread it:

> 7 "For we have brought nothing into the world, so we cannot take anything out of it either."

Evoking this truth within the context of the discussion regarding covetousness is significant. The subliminal message here is that one of the main reasons for contentment is that a man enters the world already wholly. His hands are empty because his soul is full. He lacks nothing. Fill a glass to its rim; it leaves no room for anything else. God has already given man everything he needs for success. Note:

> "seeing that His divine power has granted us everything pertaining to life and godliness, through the true knowledge of Him who called us by His own glory and excellence." (II Peter 1:3)

All necessary elements for developing worth are available already. A person enters the world empty-handed, suggesting nothing else can add to their stature or improve their worth. A man already is! His most important asset is immaterial and internal; God has planted and ordained. Therefore, an insolvent man is rich when he taps into the inheritance provided through Jesus Christ. [24] His task as he sojourns and tabernacles on earth is to find and align with the treasure already in him –the Spirit of God. A person's acknowledgment of God and relationship with Him through Christ qualify for the rich inheritance to be claimed later, on the other side of eternity. The world cannot give us anything to make us better before God.

Because it has nothing of value that adds to man's core being, that improves his nature, God mandates he leaves this world empty-handed. A man can accumulate as much power and wealth as the world can offer. But death forces him to forsake everything, rendering it inefficient for the next world. It does nothing to improve him or change his circumstances in the next life. He leaves with the sum of his being; if he were wise, he would have invested in his soul and spirit for the afterlife. Therefore, Paul is pontificating that godliness plus contentment equals a significant profit. One dynamic instrument in contentment is the presence and realization of man's internal value system. The second is much more profound, the power that correlates with trust. It is not just trust in anything or anyone but God. Hebrews 13:5- 6 gives an apparent reason for trust at such profound levels. Reread the verse:

> "[5]Make sure that your character is free from the love of money, being content with what you have; for He Himself has said, "I WILL NEVER DESERT YOU, NOR WILL I EVER FORSAKE YOU", [6]so that we confidently say, The Lord is My Helper, I WILL NOT BE AFRIAD." NASB

When a person "covets" or loves money in the manner stipulated in this verse, one stretches out to touch, grasp, or desire something, as defined by the Greek word for covet. Stretching causes something to lose shape and sometimes strength. People do not have to elongate or protract their hearts in unhealthy ways because they have access to a power greater than anything the world offers. The Hebrew writer sets up the second reason for being content by recalling God's promise.

Note:

> "I WILL NEVER DESERT YOU, NOR WILL I EVER FORSAKE YOU."

First, note that the statement is in caps, emphasizing importance. Second, the words are from God, which He made years ago, as documented in Deuteronomy 31:6, 8, and Joshua 1:5. Third, the stern emphasis of the statement in Greek is absent from the English translation. This verse is a triple negative in Greek. Triple negatives translate positively in English. The text states:

> "I WILL NEVER, I WILL NEVER, I WILL NEVER DESERT YOU, NOR WILL I EVER FORSAKE YOU,"

It is equivalent to someone saying, "I will never do that..." A powerful statement certifying a fact. Fourth, the Greek structure of the statement heightens God's use of the terms "NEVER DESERT" and "EVER FORSAKE." First, the term "DESERT or LEAVE" is not the term showing one going away, which is "lipo," but the word "anemia," which indicates something sinking into another, to relax or loosen, which unintendedly sure-up that adage "let go and let God!"

Do you remember that old test of confidence many of us tried with friends in school? A person would stand before his friend and then let go, falling backward, trusting that his friend would catch him and not allow him to fall. If I can create a visual of this verse, that illustration is it. Contentment has profound levels of trust, in which a person can let go and collapse into the loving arms of the Creator.

Besides the word "desert or leave," God uses the word "forsake." This word is a compound word of three Greek words constituting a powerful meaning. When God says, "I WILL NEVER EVER FORSAKE," He means that He will not leave you in "hostile circumstances," He will not let you down, He will not let you suffocate under your situation, HE WILL RESCUE! God is saying, "I got your back!"

Given that we are already complete and valuable and have access to a matchless love, infinite resource, and power unsurpassed, abandon the chase for more; give up your anxiety, let go, and collapse into the powerful arms of God. We must all evolve to where each one can say, "I do not need more because I have plenty, and trust that when my circumstances become hostile, God will step in and give what is necessary for that moment. I believe He will not abandon me or leave me in a crisis. I can loosen my grip on materials that cannot help me when I cross over. By the power of the Holy Spirit, I will let go and fall back into the arms of a caring Creator. I do not fear the outcome. I am content!"

Self-actualization

However, a noted philosopher, Immanuel Kant, once stated, "Give a man everything he wants, and at that moment, everything is not everything." [25] In addition, "We've been raised to compete, to want more! More! More! It is a way of life. It's about greed."[26] What makes a person want more? One reason is living without contentment. The second reason is what we know in psychology as self-actualization—a phrase surfacing strategically in this book. Here, I will broaden its introduction but reserve the details for the following chapter, The Cain Complex, which explains concepts of the self in more detail.

Self-actualization is the overarching drive and motivation for an individual's actions or behavior. It is a theoretical construct coined by Kurt Goldstein. [27] As mentioned earlier in the book, Abraham Maslow (as stated in Myers 2008) defines self-actualization as "the ultimate psychological need that arises after basic physical and psychological needs are met and they achieve self-esteem; the motivation to fulfill one's potential."[28] In the broader scope of things, Maslow suggests that once something meets physical needs, there is an awareness of safety and protection that follows, followed by the love of self and others, all of which are pretexts for self-esteem. When a person experiences self-esteem, self-actualization begins.

Self-actualization is a concept innate to humans. Man has within him a drive, innovation, and desire to climb higher and do more to maximize his potential. In this context, the push and pull, scratching and climbing upward, is natural to the human experience and, in effect, explains the basic tendency to want more. However, this natural process becomes problematic at those points in which society redefines concepts of the self. Society concludes that a person is near worthless without degrees, modes of transportation, residence in elite zip codes, membership, and social interaction with people and groups. They (society) determine that they are elite or significant. In addition, society's version of the best self mandates that such a one is rich, influential, educated, or appears to be above average in certain areas or capacities.

Man is hostage to his definition and prerequisite for good living. The ever-pressing need to be and belong causes him to covet, chase, and accumulate things that can never satisfy his soul. Money, power, possession, and pleasure are like drugs in that each of these is addictive, causing a person to want more and more. The more a person accumulates, the greater his power, the more options he has, and the higher society will elevate him. Some surmise that the natural component of self-actualization gives a person license to pursue as much as their heart desires. This is a flawed concept. Sexual desire is a natural experience. However, in Scriptural contexts, this does not give a person license to fulfill such desires with anyone, anywhere, and in any context. God, having created and ordained it in the first place, mandates how and in what context a person should satisfy their sexual desires. As we know, or should, sexual desire is only problematic or sinful when it unfolds in inappropriate contexts. Innate aspects of humanness do not trump divine order or permit a person to live and behave in ways harmful to self and the community. Those things innate to humans operate in tandem with divine order when used. When or where these fail, emotion is often in the driver's seat instead of the Spirit. People of faith must always allow the Spirit to walk ahead to direct and counsel along life's journey. Doing this will keep a lot of us out of the ditch.

Although much of this chapter focuses on excessive wealth or the like, it is noteworthy to highlight that the desire for more is cognitive. It is possible to experience it at any economic level or context independent of money and sex. When we understand desire and contentment, it is easy to see how the issue surfaces in various contexts. Our task is to balance those innate to us with God's call to live, honoring Him as the Creator of all things.

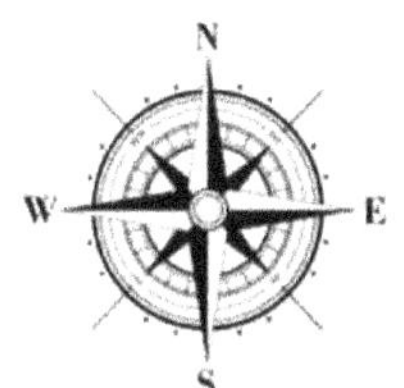

THE GUIDE POST

Critical Steps to Contentment

1. Seek and pray for divine wisdom regarding issues requiring contentment. (James 1:5)

2. Survey and decipher needs from wants or when the resources become excessive. (Luke 12:15-21)

3. Remember, contentment has less to do with settling for less than but more to do with trusting God for the rest of deliverance from/out of hostile situations. (Hebrews 13:5-6)

CHAPTER FIVE NOTES AND REFERENCES

---

[1] Author's file

[2] Matthew 6:25-34; I Peter 5:7

[3] James 1:17; Philippians 4:13

[4] John 10:10

[5] Complete Biblical Library (1991) Vol. 15 Greek-English Dictionary Pg., 164: perissos (3916)

[6] Thayer, Joseph H. (1977) Thayer Greek-English Lexicon of the New Testament. Pg., 505 perossos (4053)

[7] Psalm 23:5

[8] I Kings 3:13

[9] Luke 16:13

[10] Luke 14:33

[11] Matthew 6:32; Luke 12:1-12

[12] Luke 6:24

[13] Matthew 19:24

[14] Luke 12:15

[15] From the Greek word (Τϱόπος -tropos) , which is indicative of a particular method, a state of being, or a set of behaviors.

[16] Wuest, Kenneth (1973) Wuest's Word Studies in the Greek New Testament Pg., 95

[17] The Pulpit Commentary Hebrews Vol. XXI, pg. 408

[18] Luke 12:13-21

[19] Barclay, William (1975) the Gospel of Luke Pg., 164

[20] The Complete Biblical Library Greek- English Dictionary (1991) Vol. 15 Pg. 20 (3666)

[21] James 1:13-15

[22] The Pulpit Commentary Vol. 21, Pg. 408

[23] Ibid, Wuest Pg. 95

[24] Ephesians 1:7, 14, 18

[25] Kant, Immanuel 17th century philosopher Retrieved from: https://quotefancy.com/quote/831982/Immanuel-Kant-Give-a-man-everything-he-wants-and-at-that-moment-everything-is-not

[26] Duncan, Sandy Retrieved from https://www.brainyquote.com/quotes/sandy_duncan_381849?src=t_greed

[27] Benner, David G. (1985) Baker Encyclopedia of Psychology Pg. 1036

[28] Maslow, Abraham (as stated in Myers)

6

The Cain Complex

A Dichotomy of the Self

When Cain exits his mother's womb, he is unaware that during gestation, he likely inherited the neurological patterns and behavioral tendencies of his parents, Adam and Eve. By entering a sinful world, it predisposes him and makes him vulnerable to sinful forces. He is the evolutionary by-product of the fallenness of his parents, who inadvertently forfeited the pristine condition in which God created them. Cain, Abel, and the rest of humanity will never in this age know or experience the unadulterated body, mind, soul, and environment experienced by the first two humans post-creation. Cain's parents' exposure to sin altered their inner self. It reconstituted their perception, thought processes, and knowledge in ways that severed their prior relationship with the Creator and ushered in death as an inevitable consequence. Topographical changes took place following their fall.

Despite being marked with thorns, the rose's intricate beauty, alluring fragrance, and the unsettling presence of a slithering creature inhaling dust from the cursed ground are vivid reminders of humanity's fallen condition. Although the world transformed following man's fall, parts of it remain remarkably impressive even today. It is conceivable that the world was breathtaking before Adam and Eve's sin. Cain carries within him a nature that is prone to sin and error and inherits a cursed ground. Yet, there is a glimmer of hope, a potential for redemption and growth, even in this fallen state. Scholars estimate that the events of Genesis chapter 4 occur 196 years after creation. Although this may not be an absolute fact, the world has likely evolved as Cain and Abel matures. The stark contrast between how Cain and Abel develop and their parents is evident. As far as we can discern, God created Adam and Eve as mature humans or adults. In this way, they are exempt from the standard development of the self between infancy and adulthood. As this chapter will introduce, the self requires an object for development. In their context, God is the only object they measure 'self.' This underscores the need for object relations in every phase of life. As we will see, self-objects or objects concerning the self help define the self, provide clarity of person, direction, etc. In this context, Adam and Eve had the best example, model, and directive possible for humans in front of them. Through his encounters with God and the objects within his environment, Adam knows who he is, his place in God's creation, and the image that gives him being. Facing a complex task, he is to model the essence of his Creator yet remain a creature. Cain inherits this same complex and challenge. Destined to be like his Creator, man's paradox and difficulty are that as a creature, he is not an exact duplicate of God but made on the order of the Creator.[1] The act of creation destines man to bear the image of an uncreated God.[2] When the creature functions within the created order, he resembles God. Man's capacity for ingenuity is innate. The Creator endows man with gifts and talents reflective of Him. When the creature exercises intelligence through God-given talents, gifts, and those communicable attributes instilled in him, he becomes like his Creator. He bears the image of God. The shadow of God becomes visible as he functions in the capacity in which God creates him.

Adam and Eve failed at this attempt. The image of God is not only leadership, language and love, liberty and immortality, but intelligence and creativity, holiness, and living in oneness with God while honoring Him through the environment. These attributes are catalysts distinguishing humans from the rest of creation. God created all things, but only one aspect of His creation He forms in His image and likeness, man. The purpose of our lives is to glorify God by mirroring divine attributes in human form. Our task is to put God on display, to allow His shadow to move with us for others to see and glorify. Sin and disobedience are inevitable when the self does not merge with the image in which God creates it. Romans 3:23 captures the fallenness of humanity by noting 'all have sinned...' and by doing so, man has missed his mark, glorifying God through mind and body. Hence, the rest of the verse states, '... and come short of the glory of God.' When people live in disobedience and unholiness, they do not project or live in the shadow of His glory or reflect the image of God. The creature must reflect the essence of his Creator, not only for glorifying Him but as a prerequisite for a relationship with Him; note: 'Be ye holy, because I am holy.'[3]

Cain's parent's inexperience, weakness, gullibility, and an inward desire to expand, excel, and know more ignited a flame they could not control and caused them to miss the mark– the image of God. In addition, their issues are compounded by phantom forces seeking their demise. As noted, the effects of this devastation cascade across humanity. Cain's inner self develops and forms through objects within his environment that are flawed and failed by the strategic seduction of phantom forces undermining the union between the creature and the Creator.

Cain's intrinsic nature becomes the catalytic agent for his estranged relationship with God. Forces within his external environment make demands on his internal qualities, which, in effect, causes him to struggle to keep an equilibrium between the two. The daunting task before Cain and the rest of humanity is learning to reconcile who we are with the image and likeness of God. But how does a person reconcile the dynamics of the self with the image and likeness in which God creates and expects us to live? This is the Cain complex. This is Cain's challenge. His challenge becomes humanity's dilemma in that,

- one, the human architecture that defines him defines us;

- two, whether conscious of it or not, God tasks every person with conforming the inner self to His image and likeness.

In this context, the challenge Cain faces is characteristic of the human experience, the extraordinarily complex task of modeling the essence of the Creator while remaining characteristically human. The development of the self predicates how we navigate this challenge. Through biological and spiritual mediums, Cain's error embeds into the human attempt to live within the domain where he finds himself post-creation and fall. When left to human ingenuity, it is a disastrous shot at conforming to the image and likeness of the Creator. Given the Hebrew definition of the words image and likeness presented in Genesis and noted in chapter one, God sculpts a shadow of Himself when God creates man. However, within this framework, man has individuality, choice, will, and capacity, which is essential to developing the self in ways that reflect the image and likeness of the Creator and lend themselves to a meaningful experience with Him.

The Self

Given the ongoing reference to "the self" throughout this book, those unfamiliar with the social sciences are likely asking what a self is. There is likely the tendency to dismiss the word and concept as something irrelevant to faith and religion or ignore the disciplines in which many believe these concepts arise. People of faith surmise they are unessential because these disciplines are not biblical (which is an inaccurate assumption). Such a move is a critical error in understanding the human experience situated in spiritual paradigms. It is not that biblical concepts of human behavior are derived from social science; rather, behaviors matriculated in social science have biblical roots. For instance, as noted in chapter one, the word psychology derives from pusuche, the Greek New Testament word from which the English word soul translates.

The research findings of the pioneers of social science are not substitutes for biblical concepts and mandates. They affirm and assert what God has already validated in His word. In this context, separating the physical body's mechanics from spiritual paradigms is unnecessary and unproductive. Remember, God created the body as part of the medium through which we respond to Him.

God never designed the human experience to unfold independently of the divine agenda. Humanity's intricate task is to sustain the equilibrium between its spiritual and psychic domains to foster a harmonious relationship between its ambitious drive, creative abilities, and spiritual yearnings. Too often, people treat the human body as something separate from the call to a covenantal relationship with God or view it in limited contexts.

For instance, we have cornered the market in protests to fornication, adultery, homosexuality and transgender activities, and behaviors borne out of substance abuse.

These are tangible or perceptible evidence of lifestyles incompatible with the Holy Scripture. The unseen aspects of humanness are more challenging and dismissed by people of faith, i.e., the inner self. Many people are only sometimes conscious that forces driving behavior are internal. Concepts of the self are not things we should fear as some foreign doctrine of sorts. The Scripture has already validated man's inner self. [4]

We must embrace the concept as relevant to human experience in divine contexts. First, we must acknowledge the complex nature of the topic and the difficulty comprehending this concept in psychological and spiritual paradigms. R. L. Timpe notes the self as “the most puzzling of all concepts; in some ways the most mysterious of all entities with which human beings deal."[5] In addition, Carl Jung notes that the self is a significant and problematic archetype to understand. [6] There are various theories and positions on the authenticity of selfhood and its function across multiple contexts. However, this chapter will not explore every theory and position.

Instead, this chapter asserts the self's existence and application in multiple paradigms. In clinical contexts, the self is the axis of the psychological universe. It comprises the sum of our inner experiences of which we are aware. It is the core of one's being or an entity so connected and intertwined that by the time a person reaches adulthood, it is inseparable, which, in effect, becomes the essence of a person's identity. The self is not a dwarf living inside a person; it becomes and is the person. It refers to the way individuals experience him or herself and to the conditions that make these experiences possible. [7] Erez Banai, Mario Mikulincer, and Phillip Shaver (2005) explain the self as "the essence of a person's psychological being and comprises sensations, feelings, thoughts, and attitudes toward oneself and the world." [8] Heinz Kohut developed a psychological development theory based on the self's construct. [9] Kohut defined the self as the "center of initiative and a recipient of impressions."[10] Kohut notes that the self is a psychic configuration available to introspection and empathy, whose experiences are made possible through a core or nuclear self. He sees the self as that specific inner part of a person that fulfills the derivatives of the grandiose-exhibitionistic self and the part of a person that focuses on values and ideals that originate from the idealized parent image.[11, 12] Scholars also view the self as the quantity of all psychical entities with an unidentified integrating function. E. Jacobson's (1954) perception, like Kohut's, shows that the self develops through interpersonal exchanges and mediates between the individual and the object world.[13]

The self develops through stages between infancy and adulthood and has many components, such as self-consciousness, self-esteem, self-perception, and self-actualization. Roy Baumeister and Brad Bushman (2011) note that selfhood originates at the "interface between the inner biological processes of the human body and the sociocultural network to which the person belongs."[14] What I believe Baumeister and Bushman describe here is one marker of maturity in which the self realizes its existence and meaning as defined by sociocultural and spiritual paradigms. Jung saw the self as the collective unification of individuals' conscious and unconscious aspects.

He saw it as central to a person's existence, the whole psyche of an individual. He believed that the self could exist outside of time and space. As stated in chapter one, Jung references the self as the image of God within the psyche.[15]

In spiritual paradigms, or within a Christian faith framework, the self is significant because we believe the human/divine encounter is personable and relational.

Logically, there is a medium through which this dynamic and collaboration play out. The self is accountable to the One who created it and does not exist autonomously. As Chapter One explains, God created man as a social being to interact with his environment and Creator.

In this vein, the soul and selfhood collapse into one being for one ultimate purpose. It is of necessity that the soul or selfhood exist beyond the body in the afterlife. During a person's life, experiences and the cognition or thoughts and emotions generated by them become the sum of their being. Humans are the sum of their thoughts and feelings. Again, Proverbs 23:7 is relevant here and states: "For as he thinks in his heart, so he is."

C.S. Evans notes that the self is an artifact of activities created by various objective processes. [16] The distinct architecture of man's existence, i.e., mind, body, soul, and spirit, clearly indicates the Creator's intentions to synchronize, live in communion, and collaborate with His creation. God certifies this outcome by creating man in His image after His likeness. [17]

In the way a child resembles biological parents, humans resemble their Creator in that each has within them evidence of His uncreated nature, intelligence, innovation, breath, or spirit, the capacity for love, kindness, forgiveness, and those other communicable attributes.

Far beyond the automatic intake of oxygen and expulsion of carbon dioxide, the rise and fall of a person's chest is evidence that he is a breathing creature, a "self" and an immaterial presence linking him to his Creator. [18] As noted, Jung identifies the self as the image of God, which this author does not find implausible. Because when God creates man in his image and likeness, the framework and infrastructure for him to evolve as a relational creature is inherent. God did not create the self for itself but for His will. Contrary to human behavior in the 21st century, our existence is not the means to our end. The fallout from the "me decade" raised a generation of people who believe life is self-oriented and that every goal targets this outcome. [19] Nowadays, most people see living for someone other than themselves as a crazy, old-fashioned idea. In this context, some view service as a bad word, a redundant concept. Those seeking benefits from such a concept are viewed as less than. We see this play out in political arenas where one party believes each person is responsible for themselves and, therefore, should seek their end. These do not see the exploitation of others to accomplish this goal as nefarious behavior but the survival of the fittest by any means necessary. Conversely, the other side channels a help everybody mantra, which can be detrimental if implemented recklessly and without regard to the larger society. There must be a balance of both for either to work.

However, given that we are affectionate interpersonal beings made in the image and likeness of God, every relational experience exists within the God paradigm, including those developing within our communal and political arenas. Our relationship with each other does not exist in a vacuum or is independent of God's governance. For instance, several scriptures govern rules of engagement within social and relational contexts[20], i.e., marriage. [21] A man is to love his wife like Christ loves the church. [22] God expects us to treat others lovingly because what is innate to Him lives in us post-creation, i.e., note:

> "Beloved, if God so loved us, we also ought to love one another."[23]

God is love. [24] Love did not derive from humans. It is not an emotion we created and defined. Sarcastically, love is not a derivative of two tadpoles in a pond discovering affection between them, which evolved. Instead, the essence of love is divine. We know or understand love because He loved us first. [25] The DNA of love is innate, an active ingredient or element of the infrastructure placed in Adam and Eve, and passed on to humanity via secondary reproduction. Although this infrastructure is present as "the self," it must develop, cultivate, and mature in ways that deepen the relationship with God and other people. Since this dynamic is innate, humans seek relationships naturally. There is a natural tendency to love and live in relationships with others. Most often, when this does not happen, it is the fallout of spiritual and psychological injury. People are forever seeking companionship and connection, wanting to love and receive love. Psychologists refer to this as human bonding or attachment. [26] Love is not optional but necessary for human and spiritual development. [27] For instance, John Bowlby (1907-1990) was a psychoanalyst who developed a theory of attachment, suggesting that through a biological order, we are born into the world "pre-programmed" to form attachments with others as a survival mechanism. [28] Bowlby comes across the fingerprint of the Creator, whose intention and will is that His creatures live in association with Him and others. Bowlby's research highlights the negative consequences of a vacancy of love and proper attachment during pivotal periods of development. [29]

When the self develops and functions according to design, it naturally enacts behaviors that emphasize its purpose.

In addition, the self gravitates to selective thinking, activities, and behaviors that validate the quality of the individual and the Creator's mission.

Self Object Relations

The term self-object refers to the experience an individual has from another person's inner experience of the individual as if the individual had experienced it himself. [30] A wife suffering a significant loss is an example. Her husband embraces her to console and encourage her. Within this dynamic, the husband connects with the wife's emotions, and the wife, through feeling a sense of support and temporary relief, allows herself to connect with her husband's feelings about her circumstance. In this scenario, there is an interaction that causes each person to embrace the other's thoughts and emotions; the husband feels the pain and frustration of the wife, and the wife seizes the thoughts and soothing spirit of her husband as if they were her own. We must have self-objects, for without them, the self is subject to fragmentation and unable to sustain strength and support for goals, ideals, and values.

This is partly why it was not good for man to be alone. [31] When God says something is not good, we cannot make it otherwise. Humans are socially interactive beings by nature. "Human life now and in the future is irreducibly social."[32]

The fact that the self needs an object to develop is logical. How do we know that right is right, except there is a left to measure or compare it? His body and mind started functioning instantly when God created Adam and breathed life into him. Only through God (his object) did he learn that he was a created being and what this means in the grand scheme of humanity, which must have included his responsibility as a human and the first man. God is the object by which his inner self develops or matures. The relationship with the primary object, which in Adam's case is God, helps prepare the self for interaction with the rest of the world.

The self begins developing in infancy, around age two, when its fragmentations are consolidated into a psychological configuration, which Kohut calls the grandiose self. [33] At this stage, there is the natural and ever-present tendency for the child to display exhibitionism and idealization of perceived caregivers or self-objects. The self develops when the child's innate potential and the parent's expectations are exchanged during critical moments. There must be object relation and participation. However, during development, the child must experience a proper separation of the self from primary objects; failure to do so cultivates an unhealthy sense of grandiosity.

What is grandiosity? It is the attitudinal presentation of imposing greatness and pompousness born out of the narcissistic nature of the self, which the grandiose self regulates through proper nurturing. Scholars believe narcissism, the triad of vanity, exhibitionism, and arrogant ingratitude, is innate. [34] For instance, Kohut did not see narcissism as a pathological condition only but as an ordinary presence in the developmental process that assists in the alliance between self-identity, worth, definition, solidity, and actualization of an individual's inherent talents and assimilated skills. [35] Narcissism carries with it self-centeredness, emotional isolation, and manipulativeness. E. Becker (1973) situates narcissism within humanity's inextricable exertion to cope with existential anxiety and that deep within man is an operative level of narcissism inseparable from self-esteem. In addition, Becker points out narcissism with the first humans.[36]

The self is ambitious and presents as grandiose, perfect, and powerful, always attempting to solidify its place and demanding acknowledgment. As we can see, this is part of Cain's problem. Self-ambition and grandiosity are evident in some people's perception of others as inferior in style, intellect, status, performance, and looks.

During its beginning stages, the self expresses vanity and grandiose images. These images are formulated out of desires not responsive to realistic judgment. The individual believes they can accomplish anything or cross boundaries that protect them.

It is essential that the self is aware of its limitations and that they are not the object or the parent or God. This was likely Lucifer's issue. Recognizing God as Father and Creator, Lucifer did not acknowledge his limitation as an angel and, in effect, did not separate or differentiate the creature from the Creator. For instance, a child with successful parents must realize that he/she is not the father or mother, in effect, does not have wealth or power, etc. When children do not separate from their primary object in this way, they develop a grandiose attitude, an elevated perception of self, an inaccurate sense of entitlement, and a distorted view of the world. It is important to note that the nature of the self keeps its structure into maturity or adulthood unless the self has experienced a psychical injury that alters its original state. One can identify how the self was formed fundamentally in its mature stage or adulthood. This is one method in which clinicians can identify psychological injury or the onset of disorders that started during childhood development, i.e., attachment disorders.

If we surmise that the self is the spirit or soul and infrastructure of our being, Kohut's model suggests that there is an element of narcissism at birth, [37] which contributes to the grandiose self. In his view, this early narcissism moves toward a "cohesive self-structure" that lends to self-creativity and actualization. Man has within him the drive to move upward, to rise, climb, and innovate. I believe this inner drive is designed for a man to move toward his Creator, to rise to become one with Him, who is God of all. The natural tendency to be great, develop, and expand the self reflects the image and likeness in which he has been created.

The Human Dilemma

Considering the former findings and discussion, we must at least adjust our view of Cain or view him through this lens. We see Cain's issues as humanity's dilemma. His brief encounter with God represents the challenge of being human while trying to live in the image and likeness of God. First, as Adam and Eve raise Cain, they become his primary self-objects and become flawed and outcasts through disobedience.

By the time Cain matures, several competing objects are likely tugging and influencing Cain's personality and attitude. An analysis of Cain's approach to God and his response in the aftermath gives us insight into his mindset and the construct of his version of the self. The Genesis account does not elaborate on whether Adam and Cain experienced a healthy relationship, nor does it offer information on how successful Adam and Eve were in modeling God's image after their fall. Adam and Eve's problem is situated in their abandonment of the domain in which God created them and their venture into a world right for God, in that only God knew that evil existed by His being. God is the zenith of righteousness and holiness. Nothing and no one equals God's absolute holiness and righteousness. God can't create anything or anyone more powerful or equal to His being. Everything else is the opposite and less than He is. This explains how Lucifer, the archangel, had within him the propensity for evil while living in God's holy domain.

But because humans are made in the likeness of the Creator, each carries within them a self that is characteristic of God and which seeks to expand to greatness or at least resembles his creator in some form. For instance, a man is intelligent or has the capacity for intelligence because the Creator is a supremely intelligent being. The self that lives in every creature wants to know and experience something more remarkable.

It is certain that every person, irrespective of where they are in life, wants to be greater than they are now.

Lucifer, intrigued by God's greatness, wanted to be Him. Adam and Eve noted the exact attributes. Satan's tease that Eve would become like God, knowing good and evil, appealed to Eve and Adam afterward. They left their lane and, as a result, failed to fulfill God's intentions for them. Interestingly, this desire in Lucifer also existed in Adam and Eve and now exists in Cain. As noted in chapter one, when Lucifer approaches Eve, he knows what lurks deep within created beings: the desire to be more, to be greater, to be powerful, to be like God.

He knows that they are also created and, as such, have limited capacity, and, made on the order of their Creator, they have the capacity for intelligence, thought, communication, and emotions. Satan takes this knowledge and experience to woo Eve into the consciousness of her innermost desire and traps her and Adam. What makes an angel, a couple, and a son think and behave similarly?

Critical analysis points to an infrastructure that potentially exists in angels and humans. Each one has a spirit from God that gives them identity and is adaptive, personable, and capable of cognition, intelligence, and communication. This solidifies that the self is innate, created by God within the individual. The self is an infrastructure for created beings to develop into the image of God.

The quality of the environment and primary self-objects predicate the quality and success of the human self's development. As mentioned, there is a natural assumption that Cain's parents are the primary objects for his self's development. This is important because the self-object must give affirmation, idealization, strength, and cohesiveness for proper growth. [38] It's like the body's need for air and water. By the time we see Cain in Genesis chapter 4, his identity and self have formed. He is who presents in the narrative. He presents in three ways that encapsulate the human experience. These three dynamics will strain the relationship between the creature and the Creator. They are potent contributors to the difficulties people of faith experience within the human-divine encounter.

Self-actualization and Self-righteousness

The first thing we notice about Cain's issue, indicative of the human experience, is self-actualization. Chapter 5 defines self-actualization as the overarching drive and motivation for an individual's actions or behavior. It is "the motivation to fulfill one's potential."[39] Once a person satisfies their basic needs, an inner drive to maximize one's gifts, talents, and knowledge to their ultimate potential develops. Self-actualization is innate. As noted, Kohut sees self-actualization as a by-product of the narcissistic-grandiose self, which he believes a person has traces of at birth. [40] Humans are always trekking upwards. There is always a mission and motivation to climb higher, achieve more, and become something greater than one may currently be. A person has a job but wants a better one. They acquire the position they have always coveted but now want a promotion. It is the drive that causes people who have plenty to want more.

In addition, self-actualization, because it is born out of narcissistic-grandiose tendencies, contains traces of pride and arrogance. It causes a person always to be impressed with themselves through the gifts, talents, and skills they bring to the table. When there is a "disorder of the self," it

collapses into total narcissism, which a person cannot escape on their own.
Banai, Mikulincer and Shaver notes

> "People with a disordered self become focused on their deficiencies, extremely vulnerable to criticism and failure, and overwhelmed by negative emotions, pessimistic thoughts, and feelings of alienation and loneliness."[41]

These become fixated on imaginations of perfection and the acquisition of power. In addition, they embellish accomplishments, skills, and gifts. They get angry quickly and are saddened by those who do not view them as they see themselves. In spiritual paradigms, self-actualization is kin to self-righteousness, in which a person's faith centers on them. They measure themselves by themselves and justify themselves while condemning others. They are right by their standards and rules.
It is "narrow-mindedly moralistic."[42] When Cain approaches God with his sacrifice, he has the characteristics of self-actualization and self-righteousness.[43] In one sense, Cain is human; he's one of us. His offer is a human response to a holy God. However, the issue is that God must have

instructed Adam, Eve, and their children to approach and worship him. [44] Whether Cain received these instructions from God or through his parents is unknown.

The text infers instructions regarding one's approach and worship of God. We know God's character and attributes are such that He is just in His administration, meaning He would not have condemned Cain before teaching him what to do. Self-actualization and self-righteousness will make a person "dull of hearing," a phrase taken from Hebrews 5:11. There, it refers to "no push" to be sluggish in comprehending and accepting the New Testament truth. [45]

I use it here as emblematic of a self-righteous person's challenge to move out of their thought process and accept something other and more significant than they are. Cain is a master tiller of the ground, attributes derived from his father, Adam, who received the skill from the hand of God. [46]

Humanity's first son is so impressed with the work of his hands and has a penetrating desire to elevate that he ignores God's instructions and gives God what he wants Him to have instead. He was expecting to impress God as much as he was with himself. Self-actualization will cause a man to see himself in unrealistic ways. Not only does it appear that Cain ignores God's instructions, but he does not consider that God curses the ground from which his offering originates. [47] A person should never approach God with a cursed offering. He is a Holy God. There is no blessing or praise for anything that is cursed. Darkness cannot produce light, nor can a bitter fountain produce sweet water. Cain's approach is flawed from the beginning. But Cain, like so many living today, is impressed with who he is; they offer God what they think he should have instead of what he demands. There are similarities between people today and the Cain of yesterday in that there lies deep within most people's desires to elevate, become, do more, impress, and expect others to see and affirm them the way they see themselves. It's called humanness. Cain's desire to be more was not out of human order. But he did not allow the Spirit to temper his thirst and, in effect, capitulate to the command of God. When disorder of the self exists, self-actualization morphs into self-righteousness, unhealthy narcissism, and grandiosity. We cannot know whether Cain's self-objects (parents and other influences) harmed his internal being, the self.

What is clear is that by the time he matures, his inner being alters in ways unbecoming of God's call on his life. We do not know who Cain's most significant influence was, but I John 3:12 regards him as "the child of the evil one."

The need to affirm the self is innate and necessary for proper development. [48] The disorder of the self creates levels of narcissism and grandiosity that covet recognition and affirmation. If they do not receive it, anger and depression will overtake such a person. This is clear in Cain's next move. After God rejects Cain's worship and offering, he becomes mad. Why? Because he is impressive and reasonable in his mind, dare you reject the work of my hands. But he can't say this to a Holy God with immense power. He sulks. He's frustrated. God sees him as he is... and asks, "Why are you angry?" "Why has your countenance fallen?"[49] Remember, when God asks questions, He is not searching for answers; He knows all.

His interaction with Cain is now strategic and designed for a reflective analysis of self. We know that something is wrong with Cain and his offering, as God's next question shows. "If thou doest well, shalt thou not be accepted?"[50] (KJV) When a person experiences rejection after self-actualizing, it shatters them into pieces, creates doubt, and reduces confidence in their abilities.

Anger and depression or sadness perpetuate the individual, which leads to withdrawal from the environment in which the person seeks affirmation. These are those who quit attending a church or community; they will change jobs if possible.

Self-Elevation

Chapter 4 notes that elevated thoughts of self are a breach of sanity, yet it seems natural to think and feel one resembles one's parents or has the same abilities. In spiritual paradigms, the creature teeters on the threshold of greatness because he is from Greatness.

There is a natural tendency to rise or elevate at any opportunity. Cain approached God with a sense of arrogance and perceived greatness. The Creator rejects both Cain and his offering. Such rejection and failure send Cain into anger and sadness.

But this mood and attitude is short-lived because the grandiose self demands they find another way to rise. So, what does Cain do? He lures his brother into a field and kills him because he believes his brother is better than he is. Abel, likely because of his spiritual success, was about to take the leadership, and Cain opposes and kills him. In Cain's mind, killing Able ensures his position over him.

When attempting to elevate, a person must allow humility and obedience to lead the way. Cain did not humble himself under God's instructions and antidote to his dilemma. Note that God pointed out the issue with Cain. He states:

> "... And if you do not do well, sin is crouching at the door; its desire is for you, but you must master it." Genesis 4:7

God points out that the problem and the antidote lie within Cain, stressing that He has given man what he needs to succeed. Thousands of years later, humanity's problems and antidote are the same; they lie deep within the individual. The problem is a disordered self, a sinful soul. The antidote is the Holy Spirit, accessible through Christ and living within the individual.

The Dichotomy

The complex task of modeling God while remaining human requires a split, separation, or dichotomy of the self. Separation is an essential part of wholeness and healthiness in spiritual paradigms. Constant exposure to a fallen universe subjects the self to experiences and forces that taint and alter the inner being in ways counterintuitive to a relationship with God. The concept of separation is thematic throughout the Holy Scripture. God has always required those who seek Him to adjust in ways that emphasize holiness and communion with Him.

When Adam and Eve sinned, God included separation as part of the fallout from their transgression. God sends them out of the Garden of Eden and out of His presence. [51] Isaiah 59:1-2 teaches us that sin separates the creature and the Creator. The very nature of the church is such that it is considered separated, distinguished from the world and any entity therein, hence its Greek name Ecclesia, which means the called out.[52, 53] The sanctification process necessitates that the comer separates the mind and body from those things that defile a person. Christians are summonsed out of and away from people, situations, and things naturally contrary to what is holy.[54] Purification requires separation.

For instance, sanctification, as noted in I Thessalonians 4:3-7, results from separation from immoral behaviors. [55] However, in Ephesians 4:22-32 Paul not only speaks about behavior (which is the effect or outcome of a state of being) but calls upon the dichotomy of the innermost part of an individual. He calls it “the old self and the new self.”[56]

There is recognition of the necessity for a split or separation of the innermost part of a person to affect healing, restoration, and salvation. It is the prerequisite for a relationship with a holy God. This separation renders the old self dormant as opposed to vacating the body. The old self must die regarding its operations and activities, [57] a disconnect of sorts. The word death, as used in the New Testament, means separation, the soul from the body.

Separating from the old self indicates a capitulation to standards that immobilizes the old self's attitudinal approach to life and behavioral outcomes. The further we separate from the old self and forage its desires, it weakens, becoming inconsequential in the life of the Christian. Starvation will always lead to death if left unchecked. But the lurking question is, can what we crucify live again? Can a person reunite with a life and person once separated? If so, how? What are the dynamics contributing to such a restoration? When the holy text speaks of the old self in contrast to the new self, it does not refer to "new" as quantity or another; it speaks of something qualitatively new.

The old refers to a former lifestyle and thought patterns that were unholy and hostile to God. In this context, the new self is born out of the changing quality of the self instead of installing another being.

Take, for instance, two automobiles. One is new, meaning it is right off the lot, undriven or used. Every aspect of the auto is new. But the second is refurbished, meaning the old car's parts are replaced or rebuilt to function like new ones. Many refer to the old car as "like new" because the quality of the vehicle has improved.

It is not another but a different one because of its quality. Conversely, if the newness mentioned here regards quality and not another, the old self is present but sleeping, dead, and powerless. Furthermore, salvation does not mean one can return to environments, thought patterns, and behaviors that comprise the essence of the old self. Such a move will resuscitate and resurrect that old nature. [58] It is enough that upon the dichotomy of the self and its subsequent revival and redemption, the old self will not separate and die without a fight. Satan knows this. He leads people into temptation, which is only successful by appealing to desires already present deep within the individual. [59] Many scriptures establish man's fleshly nature as a part of his being, an undercurrent of sorts. Some passages warn and counsel against behaviors indicative of the old self. [60] As noted earlier, "COME OUT FROM AMONG THEIR MIDST AND BE SEPARATE" II Corinthians 6:17.

The new self is the by-product of the Holy Spirit's advent, presence, and power, the framework for which God installs in man in the beginning. [61] Cain's failure to dichotomize his inner self contributes to his failure. He approaches God and attempts to worship Him in a state unfit for a holy God and, in his self-righteousness, offers a cursed sacrifice. As paradoxical as it sounds, there must be a split or separation of the self to experience wholeness and oneness with God. As mentioned, Cain represents humanity, among whom people of faith attempt to live life meaningfully. Cain's struggle with humanness is relatable in that every human surrendering their life to God fumbles periodically. As with Cain, many people are caught up in their self-righteousness. Unrealized by many people of faith, self-righteousness is dangerous. This is Paul's argument to the church at Rome in Romans 2:1-5. A covenant relationship with God causes separation of the self for a new or qualitative self with whom God can commune. So, we find chatter in the New Testament about the old self and the new self. The dichotomy of the self requires three things.

- A sacrificial attitude. [62] A willingness to surrender things, people, and lifestyles to a covenant relationship with a loving Savior.
- Self-denial. Note: "... If anyone wishes to come after Me, he must deny himself, and take up his cross daily and follow Me." Luke 9:23: The denial feature in this verse means to disown, abstain, and separate. [63] God has always required a sacrifice, an essential component of a relationship with Him. But before one can deny oneself, one must know oneself.

  Find yourself, then lose it. Our inability to constantly navigate the terrains of life and align with God's

> purpose for us forces the inner man to emerge with new ideas of self-gratification and new agendas, which forces us to lose sight of our identity in God and abandon the path He has laid before us. Finding oneself is best during moments of solitude, meditation, and prayer. Introspective analysis can be very productive for the individual. In solitude, the human soul finds most of itself and enjoys frequent interviews with God. Personal time with God is an opportunity for growth or development. It is a space ripe for honesty and transparency. It is an opportunity to reflect upon the condition of the soul. [64] Anyone who tries to deceive or conceal their problems from God is not acting wisely.[65]

The story of Jacob in Genesis 32:24-30 comes to mind here as an example of how the self impedes one's relationship with God. This was an allegorical description of an inner conflict within Jacob. Noted in this narrative about Jacob are several subtle points we should understand. The first is the form in which the antagonist assumes that, on the outside, he appears to be a man. The confrontation was a subtle message to Jacob about self. Jacob was a shrewd businessman, self-centered and dishonest. God said the problem is with self; the issue is within you. Many scholars believe that the man with whom Jacob wrestled was God himself. The creature and his Creator confront each other. God could have taken any other form to communicate with Jacob, but he appeared before him as a man and wrestled with him. This is a subliminal message to Jacob that he was wrestling with himself. It is his inner self that is standing in his way. Whenever Deity confronts man, his imperfections, sins, and struggles expose him to God's righteousness and show man's true self.[66]

> People's propensity to egotistical motives obscures God's call to a meaningful relationship and man's subsequent obligation to "fear God and keep His commandments."[67] This form and capacity of the self must be dichotomized, split off, and separate.

- The third requirement is commitment and devotion to God. One cannot not be devoted to God with divided allegiance. The self must capitulate to the will of God.[68] Devotion embodies consecration and consideration of the other. It requires offering up the whole self.[69] Giving oneself wholly and entirely to God implies trust for all things.
-

Walking with God is a relationship. The contrast between Cain's self and his inner being and the fact that it enslaved him to a disordered self predicates his inability to have a meaningful relationship with God. Oneness with God is the highest merger a man can experience, with the greatest blessings and honor. Although self-actualization is natural, there are inherent risks of being self-righteous and capitulating to distorted thoughts in which man sees himself as his antidote.

His problem is that he thinks of himself more highly than he should. The security of a person's identity can only be known and realized through Jesus Christ.

CHAPTER NOTES AND REFERENCES

[1] God is a divine singularity and utterly sovereign. There is no other being before, after, or equal to Him. He alone is God.
[2] Dietrich Bonhoeffer in V. Norskov Olsen, 1988. Man, The Image of God, the divine design-the human distortion (Review and Herald Publishing Association Washington, DC Hagerstown, MD).
[3] Leviticus 11:44; 19:2; 20:7; I Peter 1:15-16
[4] Genesis 1:26-27; See chapter one, in which the soul is mentioned 82 times, which includes concepts of the self.
[5] Evans, C.S. As stated in Baker Encyclopedia of Psychology (1985) David G. Benner, Editor Pg. 1032
[6] Carl G. Jung (1875-1961) was a renowned Swiss psychiatrist and psychoanalyst
[7] Gary F. Greif, 2000 The Tragedy of the Self, Individual and Social Disintegration viewed through the Self Psychology of Heinz Kohut (University Press of America)
[8] Banai, Erez, Mikulincer, Mario and Shaver, Phillip R. (2005) Vol. 22, No. 2, 224-260. Pg. 225
[9] Heinz Kohut, 1971. The analysis of self. International University Press. New York
[10] Kohut, H. 1977. The Restoration of the Self. (International Universities Press, New York)
[11] Kohut, H. 1978. The Search of the Self. Vol. 3. (International Universities Press, Madison, Connecticut)
[12] An unconscious, idealized image of someone, like a parent, that influences individual behavior. www.dictionary.com
[13] Jacobson, E. 1954a The Self and the Object World. Psychoanalytic Study of the Child 9: 75-127
[14] Baumeister, Roy F., and Brad J. Bushman. "The Self." Social Psychology and Human Nature. 2nd ed. Belmont, CA: Cengage Learning, 2011. 57–96. Print.
[15] Encyclopedia of Psychology and Religion (2014) Retrieved from www.link.springer.com/referenceworkentry/
[16] Evans, C.S. as stated in Baker Encyclopedia of Psychology (1985) pg. 1036
[17] Genesis 1: 26, 27
[18] John 4:24
[19] A term coined by author Tom Wolfe that captures the sentiments or attitudes of individualism over communitarianism. For additional information, see Wolfe, Tom (1976) The Me Decade
[20] Luke 10: 30-37; Romans 12:9-10; I John 4:7
[21] Ephesians 5:22-33; 6:1-4; I Corinthians 7:1-ff; I Peter 3:1-8

[22] Eph. 5:25
[23] I John 4:11
[24] I John 4:8
[25] I John 4:19
[26] Emotional connection and intimacy between individuals and groups that are cultivated through attraction, dependence during significant periods of life. The attachment fades in the absence of the influencing object. See Baker, Robert (2003) The Social Work Dictionary 5th Edition; Feldman, Robert (2013) Understanding Psychology 11th Edition.

[27] Raghunathan, Raj (June 8, 2014) The Need to Love via Psychology Today. Retrieved from www.psychologytoday.com/us/blog/sapient-nature/201401/the-need-love
[28] As stated by McLeod, Saul (2007) on the Simply Psychology website in Bowlby's Attachment Theory. Retrieved from: www.simplypsychology.org/bowlby.html
[29] Ibid
[30] Ibid, G. Grief
[31] Genesis 2:18
[32] Micks, Marianne H. (1982) Our search for identity (Fortress Press, Philadelphia)
[33] Kohut, H. 1971. The Analysis of the Self. (International Universities Press, New York)
[34] Kohut, H. (1978b). Forms and transformations of narcissism. In P. Ornstein (Ed.), *The search for* KOHUT'S SELF PSYCHOLOGY 257 *The self* (Vol. 1, pp. 427–460). New York: International Universities Press. (Original work published 1966)
[35] Ibid, Banai Pg. 225
[36] Becker, E. 1973 The denial of death. (New York: Free Press)
[37] Ibid, Kohut (1971)
[38] Ibid, Kohut (1971)
[39] See notes 37 and 38 in the chapter titled: Wanting More in the Land of Plenty
[40] Ibid, Kohut
[41] Ibid
[42] Retrieved from: www.merriam-webster.com
[43] Genesis Chapter 4
[44] Although another topic, this validates that man does determine how to approach or worship God rather these processes are divinely elucidated and inspired.
[45] Wuest's Word Studies. Pg. 104
[46] Genesis 2:15

[47] Genesis 3:17
[48] Ibid, Kohut
[49] Genesis 4:5-6
[50] Genesis 4:7
[51] Genesis 3:23,24
[52] Zohdiates, Spiros (1984) Lexical Aids to the New Testament in Key Study Bible, pg.1830
[53] I Peter 2:9
[54] II Corinthians 6:14-17
[55] Ibid, Zodhiates pg. 1796
[56] Ephesians 4:22-24
[57] Romans 6:6; Galatians 5:24
[58] Romans 6:2
[59] James 1:13-15
[60] SEE: Romans 7:12-25; Eph. 4:22; Galatians 5:17-21 to name a few...
[61] Galatians 5:22-23
[62] Romans 12:1-2
[63] Strong's Greek Translation 533
[64] Hebrews 4:12
[65] Hebrews 4:13
[66] John 4:1-ff
[67] Ecclesiastes 12: 13-14
[68] Matthew 6:33
[69] Deuteronomy 6:5; I Corinthians 6:20

7

The Hook and Hang-up of Humanism

Precarious Substitution of Human Thought as Divine Truth

Have you ever considered Adam's first breath to be of divine origin? As God's spirit circulates his respiratory system, it must have jump-started everything necessary for life. Most people's appraisal of the creation does not appreciate the immaculate condition of Adam and the world after God finished creation. As noted, Adam is not the by-product of secondary reproduction. When a child is born, they have traits from their parent's DNA. Their body contour resembles their parents, nose, eyes, hair texture, and skin pigmentation. They inherit personality traits and some physical and mental flaws of their parents.

Given this, can you imagine Adam's appearance? Does he resemble God? If so, how? God is a Spirit. [1] There are no physical characteristics. What, then, is the color of Adam's skin pigmentation? The proposed geographical location of Eden may give us clues or provoke thought. [2] Do we surmise that the color of his skin is irrelevant? Adam, crafted by the hand of God, is perfect. [3] There are no defects in his body, no aches, pains, or diseases. He is not a victim of abuse. He is not depressed, bipolar, or show any other psychological ills. No social ills are influencing him. In addition, he is in an environment tailored for him, enhancing his being and posing no threats. There is no greenhouse effect and no unsanitary conditions in the neighborhood. Crime is not yet rampant in his world, and sin is a foreign concept.

At the onset of consciousness, the neurons in his brain fire, igniting networks from which thought derives. As his mind processes the Creator in front of him and the surrounding environment, he has no prior experience from which he can draw because he has never been, yet he is thinking and processing. In addition, he is not only a thinking creature but can convert thought into language and behavior. Consider Adam's unique intelligence and knowledge base, which is not a product of secondary reproduction like ours. His beginning is likely not as void as we may think. Adam's initial intelligence and knowledge base are from God, which makes him exceptional. As secondary reproduction starts, we develop and expand this intelligence and its capacity. Since this genesis, man has been and is a thinking creature. Throughout history, the world has experienced and, to some degree, is the by-product of great thinkers and minds. Aristotle, Marie Curie, Galileo Galilei, and Saul of Tarsus, aka Paul the Apostle, are unique individuals shaping and influencing the world.[4] Man is the offspring of his Creator and can increase and expand knowledge, wisdom, and talent. But, as time progresses, he is distant from Adam and the intelligence and skill sets implanted in him by the Creator. Time and distance alter how man sees the origin of his intelligence. In man's mind, his accomplishments are the by-product of his being, his mind. In this context, Adam is too distant to relate; God is not visible, therefore absent and not calculable. This ideology and man's innate need to self-actualize create a dangerous cocktail. It is harmful because it causes man to ignore and drift further away from the Creator and His purpose within the human experience. It is dangerous because it strips God of honor and praise for Him as Creator. In this disposition, man is a means to his end; he is the one for whom he is waiting. In his mind, he is the antidote to all his dilemmas and challenges. He measures himself and the world around him against himself.

In the recesses of his knowledge and wisdom, he determines what is wrong and right, acceptable or worthy of rejection. It is human thinking.

Humanism

When broaching the subject of humanism, we must acknowledge, identify, and differentiate its associated classifications. However, I will only elaborate on a few to prevent the chapter from becoming too complex. There are four types or categories of humanism. One is *scientific Humanism*, which includes behaviorism. [5] Second, *philosophical humanism* is structured against four principles: science, human progress and reasoning, and the self-sufficiency of man. Existentialism is a crucial part. The bedrock principle of contemporary philosophical humanism denies God exists or anything supernatural. [6] The third category is *psychological humanism*, known as psychoanalytic humanism. The fourth, *theological Humanism,* embodies theistic and Christian ideologies. The category highlighted in this chapter and the most problematic for the people of God is philosophical humanism.

In this context, humanism refers to a doctrine, attitude, or philosophy that rejects supernaturalism and stresses an individual's dignity, worth, and capacity for self-realization through reason. It asserts that the nature of the universe depicted by modern science makes any supernatural or cosmic guarantees of human values unacceptable. [7] Humanism not only makes no room for divine revelation but, of necessity, excludes it, which, in effect, places more significance on human reasoning than divine truth. Humanist beliefs stress human beings' potential value and goodness, emphasize everyday human needs, and seek rational ways of solving human problems. They use critical reasoning, irrefutable evidence, scientific methods, and other tenets of critical thinking to resolve human challenges and tragedy in place of the dynamics of faith and trust in an unseen God.

It is an attitudinal approach and thought process that elevates against the knowledge and power of God, [8] entrapping those who buy into it—characteristics of humanism point to man as its author and the antidote to life-challenging situations. Most people championing humanism are young adults and educated individuals of various backgrounds. We now live in a world that is so smart that many are educated beyond their intelligence. But man believes and behaves as if he teeters on the threshold of divine greatness. There are no boundaries, no feat beyond his reach. Where actual boundaries exist, scientific reasoning and philosophical rhetoric become the mask behind which his finite mind fleeces, producing a perpetual mirage of boundless intelligence. His humanness becomes his fate.

It is noteworthy to differentiate humanism from other ideologies:

- Secularism is the "indifference to or rejection or exclusion of religion and religious considerations." Secularism does not consider religion or God as a factor in human affairs. [9]
- Atheism is "the disbelief in the existence of deity." Atheism denies God, which renders religion irrelevant. [10]

- Agnosticism holds that one cannot know whether God exists or not. Such a view does not consider God to be of any concern for how people live their lives.

Complex systems of thought inundate the 21st century and aim at dismantling the things of God. Phantom forces have advanced in ways that strike the core of the inner man, rendering him wayward and convincing him that the things of God are of little to no significance to life and circumstance. Today's advanced thinking challenges the status quo, including those things God has set in motion through His word. Contemporary thought and philosophical reasoning contribute[11] to a fallacious logic that leads men deeper into themselves and further away from God. Capitulating to his distorted sense of wisdom, the human sees God as something obsolete and sees himself as the only one who can measure his status and determine his outcome. People see humanism as a more "meaningful and dignified life."[12]

Humanism is not a 21st-century phenomenon but has roots in ancient history. The historical analysis of humanism originates in the 13th and 14th centuries within the confines of northern Italy. [13] During this period, people knew it as humanismus, at the heart of which was an intellectual and philosophical prism of the human experience. The word encapsulates wholesome, attractive characteristics, such as kindness, mercy, and wisdom, to name a few. The concept embodies Western ideology, method, and beliefs that make man central to his being, the answer to his dilemma and destiny. As time progresses, this systematic inquiry advances to England and Europe. As humanism continued to thrive, it became very influential and defined an era known as the Renaissance. However, the tenets of humanism were vibrant and palpable in Greek philosophy during the early Christian era. Intellect and individualism became the mantra of the time. As did Adam and Eve, people living during this era were unaware that fusing human intellect and knowledge with the self-actualizing person within potentially obscure perception can lead to demise.

These are those to whom the Apostle Paul notes their "speculations" or reasonings (which stem from self-deliberations) procreate intellectual arrogance that dishonors and repudiates God as God and is situated against the things of God. [14] Much later, the philosophical aspect of the concept became both a license and a crutch for men to lean toward the distorted idea that the grandeur of intellectualism and the maximization of human potential will eclipse the darkness of the "dark ages."

The institutional approach to humanism is sophisticated and striking. Degree programs featuring elements of humanism embody characteristics that many consider valuable to society, such as freedom, self-determination, equality, diversity, and dignity. [15] These see individuals and institutions objecting to humanism as controlling forces, castrating liberty from those who seek to embrace the recesses of their deliberations. Church and religion are among those who oppose humanism. Many view it as controlling, antiquated in thought, and indifferent to self-realization. However, if you position the Christian faith and other religions parallel to humanism, you will note similar attributes and concepts.

We acknowledge the distinction between these philosophies in their origins, development, and results. For example, while humanism emphasizes equality and human dignity as fundamental principles, it reflects biblical teachings about leading a righteous and spiritually enriched life. We observe the disparities between the two regarding their origins and consequences. The humanistic view holds that these awareness, development, and exercise principles are human. It suggests that man can solely determine the need for such principles and how to realize them. In this context, the outcome is a more meaningful life. People celebrate humanism, which affirms the tenor of Paul's point: "They worshipped and served the creature more than the Creator."[16]

Christianity embodies the same principles but views them as a by-product of the spirit of God. It asserts that all aspects of goodness, love, and benevolence originate from God and that humans' ability to harness and effect a change in the lives of others is indebted to the spirit of God placed in them during creation. In this context, the outcome is a human, made to the order or likeness of his Creator. [17]

The central and most fundamental component of humanism is existential freedom and self-determination. The emphasis is on humanness or human capacity. It postulates that one has the liberty to do and believe what one chooses and, in effect, manufacture and govern one's destiny. This is one of several attractive qualities and tenets of the thought. People enjoy individual freedom and making their own choices. The concept of freedom did not originate with humanists. God has always given man free will.

He is created as a free moral agent. As such, he has choice and capacity. The notion of free moral agency is noted in Romans 1:24, 26 & 28, in which Paul evokes the phrase "God gave them up or over" to their lusts, degrading passions, and depraved minds, in which they reject God as God. This suggests that God did not force His will on those who were disobedient to Him but allowed them to pursue the desires of their hearts, which would later become their destruction.

God does not force His will on the rest of humanity but influences His creation through love, relationship, and holiness. Remember, humans have the capacity for relationships, knowledge, reason, and communication. God did not program us to be good and obedient creatures. He places His Spirit in man at creation as a medium for a relationship with Him. He has always given man the capacity and option to choose. Notwithstanding, what is critically noteworthy is man's inability to come to God the Son without being drawn by the power of God the Father.[18] However, since the beginning, He notes that our choices, decisions, and behaviors have consequences.[19]

Second, humanism channels behavioral characteristics and attitudinal approaches that most people define as good, i.e., exhibiting fairness and equality, diversity and dignity, and encouraging self-realization. Many consider these attributes regal acts of a decent human being.

Because these and similar characteristics are noble and harmless and identified as elements of a meaningful life, there may be pressure to embrace the idea. Humanists view the denial or subjugation of such hygienic concepts as controlling and collective control of church and religion.

In addition, the commonality and popularity of humanistic thought in the 21st century render any other notion in opposition to it antiquated. For Christians, the repercussions for such positions are feelings of awkwardness and fear of being exiled from significant groups, such as family, work, and other community affiliations. This presents a challenge in that the desire to be, become, and belong is innate. Depending upon a person's spiritual maturity and strength, such a response by humanists is likely seen as threatening to the quality of a person's being and antagonistic to their assimilation to groups they feel are essential. This feeling is expected exponentially if humanistic concepts dominate groups they are already a part of and believe are significant. Overwhelming feelings and motivation to adjust are likely sequential.

These are prone to adjusting their disposition to align with the tenor and thought of the groups they identify. It is a shift that is often faint yet implemented. People dislike being considered strange, outdated, or identified with concepts others interpret as weird. In contemporary environments in which almost anything and everything goes, moderate and conservative concepts and behaviors are easy to locate. The repudiation and rejection of such ideas are apparent in some of these environments yet covert and inconspicuous in others. However, association and connection between people on opposite sides are limited. Socialization between opposing groups of people is often limited because of perceived incompatibility. For instance, although the opposing group or individual may appreciate who you are, they are likely to restrict contact and association instead of the fact that your thoughts do not always align with theirs.

Sometimes, this response impacts people of faith, who assimilate to gratify the inherent need to be, belong, and become. As social beings, we gravitate toward connection and association with others. The brain is wired to connect to other human beings. [20] Remember, God designed the human body for relationship and connection with Him and other creatures he has made. So, it is logical that humans are predisposed to socialization and the need for the other. In this context, many people of faith will evoke scriptures that teach about the dangers of association or friendship with ungodly people. [21]

The argument is that Christians should not concern themselves about associating with non-Christians.

Although this bodes well, the desire is often not to associate with "sinners" as much as the innate desire to socialize and connect with other human beings. Attempting to circumvent this issue, Christians resort to homeschooling or attending Christian schools and participating only in Christian-sponsored events to protect them from such exposure. However, the fact is that if we live in a fallen world, we are subject to exposure to people and situations that challenge our attitudinal and behavioral approach to life.

As humans, an ongoing need for acceptance and identity exists. Whether wrong or right, one tends to adjust to one's outlook on life for a meaningful relationship. What does this look like? Let's take homosexuality, which in contemporary times many people view as acceptable, a decision belonging to those electing to embrace such behaviors. In this line of thought, this population sees any objection to the lifestyle as antiquated thinking. It is old-fashioned thinking, which is the principle of collective control of groups. The humanist's view holds that man can decipher these decisions on his own and, in effect, determine the rightness of a thing. They believe principles of a transcendent God are neither applicable nor necessary. Moderate or conservative people of faith hold that these views are erroneous, contradictory, and counterintuitive to the divine order. But when people of faith are in environments in which humanism dominates, they feel sheepish, outcast, and sometimes ill-treated. Fearing alienation, they circumvent this outcome by softening their stance and disposition by either remaining silent about their position or changing their views to accommodate the view that dominates the group. Here, the precarious substitution of humanism as divine truth is evident and problematic.

It does not limit this to individuals but includes groups and institutions. Over the past two decades, we have witnessed some (not all) prominent denominations, churches, and other religious entities converse and deduce that they must alter any doctrinal stance against homosexuality and, in effect, accept and allow both the presence and practice of such behavior within the confines of faith. Inaugurating such a notion is incautious and manufactured outside the parameters of Holy scripture because these conclusions are incompatible and incalculable.[22] When these institutions draw such codas, they buy into the humanist's narrative, in which man has the capacity and, therefore, can determine what is best for him without interjection or interference of a transcendent God. If churches embrace this ideology, why identify as a church if you are not called out?

The Hook

What drives individuals and groups to make the cognitive shifts and spiritual adjustments discussed here? A brief, limited deconstruction of the core elements of humanism sheds light on three critical dynamics that may explain such actions. Namely, self-actualization, existentialism, and fear of self-alienation. These form powerful constituents, and this author dubs the hook of humanism in that they appeal to the innate needs and desires of the individual. Most people gravitate to things they believe or think will enhance their being or life experience. Intentional or not, humanism plays this reality like a fiddle. Like a baited fishhook, hygienic tenants of humanism camouflage its dangers.

As noted in earlier chapters, self-actualization[23] is the innate desire to maximize one's potential. Humanism encourages individuals to elevate themselves by looking inward and celebrating their gifts, talents, and capacities without considering their divine origin. It suggests that these alone are adequate for life's most challenging questions and situations.

The second critical dynamic, and likely the most dangerous, is existentialism. This philosophical dogma asserts an individual is a free, responsible executor of their evolution and improvement through acts of the will determined by that individual. [24] It is self-discovery and meaningfulness orchestrated through free will, choice, and responsibility independent of rule, law, or any governing entity. [25] There is something about freedom that is euphoric, which gives a person flight and permission they may not have otherwise.

What is freedom?

Is anyone free? If so, who determines the essence and authenticity of such freedom? Absolute freedom suggests that one's decisions are not accountable or subjected to another and that such a person is immune from behavioral outcomes. From Adam and Eve to the modern day, the annals of history prove liberty without wisdom and discernment has destructive consequences.

Humans enter the world as free beings, free agents. Liberty is characteristic of the human experience. It does not belong to others to give or withhold. It is God-ordained. But one must hold freedom and wisdom in tandem. This is the tenor behind Paul's message to the church at Corinth, which held that people could do anything they pleased. The Apostle notes that "all things are lawful to me, but not all things are expedient." [26] Just because you can does not always translate; you should. Wisdom and spiritual discernment will help individuals navigate situations conscientiously and against the backdrop of the Holy Scripture.

Even though God teaches Adam and Eve how to navigate the Garden of Eden, they can enact or ignore such instructions. As we know, Eve exercised her free will and decided within herself to behave counterintuitively to divine order. When confronted with an alternative to divine instruction or guidance, she did not consult with her husband or the Creator but, by her own will, choice, and responsibility, decided to self-actualize without exercising wisdom. The consequences of such an unwise move ripple across humanity still. The error had nothing to do with the fact she is female but human instead.

Understand that this does not endorse collective control or the denial of free thought. As stated, freedom is intrinsic to the human experience. However, behavior has consequences, whether experienced in this life or the future. A man's liberty is not a license to injure or not a means by which he should defy and elevate above the Creator. The fact is that people enjoy freedom, the power of choice, and denial across every sector of life. Humanism offers and gravitates to that part of the individual. Sometimes, this proves problematic. It is narrow thinking, if left unchecked, that helps form the narcissistic self. It constructs a quasi-intelligence that places God in a therapeutic chair for analysis and interrogation. [27]

The third dynamic comprising "the hook of humanism" is the fear of self-alienation. Although this may sound like something one does to themselves, self-alienation is a by-product and effect of underdeveloped or broken relationships. As noted earlier in the book, man's disobedience ruptured relationships and generated alienation in multiple areas. The first example is the alienation generated between God and man. [28] Second, within man himself, [29] his relationship with others[30] and the environment. [31] Guinness (1973) categorizes these as "theological, psychological, sociological and ecological." [32]

What is alienation? Hammes regards it as estrangement. It's more than just a personal experience. It's a societal issue, a reflection of the disharmony and divisiveness that can be generated by a loss of value and personal significance. This experience within an individual is the fallout from rejection by critical groups for which an individual has an affinity and needs to be connected. The rejection is experienced as devaluation of their person, leaving a sense of meaninglessness. This societal impact of alienation is a pressing concern that needs our attention.

Although written several decades ago, W.G. Cole's (1966) reflection and analysis of society then resembles the issues and tenor of people today, most notably the seemingly unending need for fulfillment. [33] Rollo May (1967) notes that the breakdown of societal values has produced a hollowed man subsequently. I believe this hollowness motivates an ongoing inquest and rummage for fulfillment through others and, in some cases, other things. Scientists, scholars, and others believe this emptiness is the basis for pathology and maladaptive behaviors. In addition, it may suggest that the absence of significance or meaningfulness is a critical factor contributing to aggressive, violent behavior. [34]

Sometimes, fear of this outcome or experience influences religious people to adjust their faith, beliefs, and worldview for acceptance and a sense of value defined by those they hold significant. In this context, other people determine one's self-value. This arrests and subjects an individual's appraisal of self-worth and, in effect, produces a species of vulnerability by which one is hostage. Need-based relationships are always vulnerable to collapse by missing critical components defining that relationship. It echoes Dr. Larry Crabb's (1992) view of spirit oneness within the context of marriage. In chapter two of his book (The Marriage Builder), he notes that constructing relationships based on fulfilling a need empowers a person to crush you at any moment by withholding what you need. He argues that the Lord satisfies our needs. Couples entering a relationship or marriage in this context experience a profound one-ness. [35] This does not nullify self-object relations and our need for the other. As mentioned, we are social beings with the infrastructure to interact and affirm one another. Eve's presence affirmed Adam's being. However, this is a small component of what gives a person value. We are valuable because of the Spirit of God living in us. In this context, self-worth is independent of the other. The "I am because you are" mantra has its limitations. For instance, if God is in me, even though you are not, I am still. However, the fear of not being viewed as less-than and worthless causes people to assimilate into critical groups, even if it compromises their value system. Humanism provides a pseudo sense of value, and given that humans need to become and belong to connections that provide value, it is easy to view humanism as acceptable.

The Hang-up

The innocent traits of humanism are dangerous for those who embrace them. This dangerousness is exponential for the people of God. Celebrating human capacity is central to its precepts. Although natural to both seek and give affirmation of the other, such affirmation and celebration must never elevate the creature above the Creator. If we digest humanism as stipulated in its manifesto, not only is God diminished, but He also does not exist. [36] Such a move will leave man without a covering, sacrifice, arbitration, and an intercessor in the Court of Glory. [37, 38]

People of faith entering humanistic domains do so without intentional efforts to compromise core beliefs.

As mentioned, the shift is most often subtle and undetected. But people of faith who embrace humanism create a complex paradox. Given humanism's mantra and Christianity's core principles (for example), coexistence is impossible.

"Christian Humanism" is an oxymoron, a paradox that collapses truth with principles antithetical to its existence. Truth originates through Christ, God Himself, a notion humanists not only find objectionable but repudiate His very existence. This concept's proponents allege contiguity between the archaic principles of Renaissance humanists and contemporary Christian thought.

But it is an oxymoron given that at the core of humanism is man, not God, hence the word human in humanism. While acknowledging that "Christian Humanism" is an oxymoron, the principles of humanism used to authenticate the so-called human dignity, individual liberty, and happiness are vital to humanistic concepts. Those who embrace the idea of "Christian Humanism" note that these characteristics as components of philosophical humanism are compatible with Christ's teaching. They then believe these are worthy of embracing in humanistic contexts.

The tenets of humanism draw parallels and similarities between the principal teachings of Jesus Christ, which do not originate with man. Human dignity, goodness, and liberty originate from God through the Holy Spirit. For instance, the Holy Scripture identifies wholesome characteristics as by-products of the Spirit. [39] Love and joy, peace and patience, kindness, goodness, and faithfulness are among these. [40] Various societies and cultures worldwide understand and accept that these are moral attributes and are the right thing for any of us to do. When humans embrace and enact these, they are derivative of the Spirit of God in a person. The humanists' narrative suggests that man's capacity is so great that even these attributes originate from him. Nothing about the flesh or humanness is worthy of glory and celebration independent of the Creator. [41] This is the hang-up of humanism, celebrating man or human capacity in ways that challenge and deny God as Creator. This contest and repudiation are not always visible. But most often subtle and hidden because it masquerades as knowledge, intelligence, and human capacity. Humanistic concepts will make people believe they may challenge and interrogate God about divine precepts, directives, and commandments. It converts tenets of critical thinking as the basis for believing that humans know more about humanness than the One who created the human. In addition, it will cause a person to question whether such a supernatural being even exists. It postulates the knowledge of God as a silly notion by concluding He does not exist and is redundant, in that man has the capacity for will and reason to resolve life's dilemmas. They believe a transcendent God is not necessary. It is elevated thinking on their part. This is what Scripture condemns and notes as problematic in II Corinthians 10:3-6

> [3] For though we walk in the flesh, we do not war according to the flesh, [4] for the weapons of our warfare are not of the flesh, but divinely powerful for the destruction of fortresses. [5] We are destroying speculations and every lofty thing raised against the

> knowledge of God, and we are taking every thought captive to the obedience of Christ, and we are ready to punish all disobedience, whenever your obedience is complete. (NASB)

Four critical phrases within this passage showcase both the issues and their resolutions. But first, consider the tenor of the passage. These vital phases manifest within the Apostle Paul's defense of himself and his ministry. The passage asserts that although we are indigenous to and engulfed by the human experience, it (humanness) is not the prism or utility and the weapon tackling life's inescapable battle. Humanness is the problem. If humanness is a critical part of our dilemma, it is insufficient for resolution. This reality demands a weapon far beyond human capacity. Phantom forces pressed against the human experience invert humanness and bind it to humanity, creating a matrix impossible to break. [42]

As Paul infers, humans live in a body limited to that reality. But not our humanness or the body with which we wage war against evil. God equips his people with powerful spiritual weapons when used promptly and effectively. Appreciating this begins with a proper understanding of the elements and consequences of spiritual warfare, which this verse captures in the four critical phrases:

- **Destruction of fortresses-** human wisdom, reasoning, and arguments that enclose an individual behind strong walls between human experience and divine reality. Thayer (1977) suggests that this refers to human wisdom and reasonings used to "fortify one's opinion" against his opponent, which, in the passage's context, is the reality of a God. Satan uses human wisdom and reasoning to create strongholds that sever dependence on God and deny His existence. This fortress of thought can become so strong and impossible to escape without divine power. [43]
- **Demolishing speculations or imaginations-** refers to antagonistic thought or thinking still lodged in a person's mind and not yet executed, hence the King James translation imaginations. They calculate their thoughts for destructive purposes. In the passage's context, it refers to antagonism toward God and His word precisely.
- **Knowledge of God-** is a significant point to note here. It refers to experiential knowledge, knowing, or knowledge derived from a relationship or direct participation with the object known. It is distinctive from propositional knowledge, information gleaned

from textbooks or manuals. Humanistic thought suggests that experiential knowledge is impossible because God does not exist. They believe that even if He did, such knowledge could not transcend human capacity and experience. It gives meaning to the question: do you know the Lord?

- **Casting or pulling down-** refers to demolition specific to buildings and walls. It is the wrecking ball for destruction instead of a jackhammer. In context, "the weapons" God supplies his people with a capacity that destroys fortresses of thought imprisoning and rising against His being. Such an arsenal includes divine wisdom, prayer, spiritual guidance and discernment, the Word of God, and salvation through the vicarious sacrifice of Jesus Christ.

What is evident in these is the power of the mind or thinking in human terms and reasoning. Satan has always targeted the mind and the brain because they influence behavior. He aims to expose an individual to situations, information, substances, and experiences that will alter how a person thinks and behaves. When we see life through human perspectives, things will change across life's spectrum.

People of faith are vulnerable to these changes when they abandon the spiritual realm of our existence and depend on the human experience. Worship and bible study become obsolete, and human reasoning evolves as the compass by which one navigates life.

Self-actualization and optimization become the goals of life. In this context, man becomes less dependent on God and more on his capacity. God fades out as a critical part of man's calculus. He embraces life without consideration of the will of God for his life. He chooses his mate, profession, and destiny independent of God. Human reasoning becomes the approach and solution to life's dilemmas. Premium education or training, a lovely home in an elite zip code, a fine car, pleasures at will, and a stellar retirement package become his Heaven. Acquiring these creates a level of comfort that obscures necessary thoughts and concerns about the afterlife. A pseudo sense of security engulfs him.

As Chapter 5 indicates, it is not that the pursuit and possession of these are wrong; it's how a man arrives here and his attitude when he accomplishes his goals. When people measure themselves against themselves and, in effect, conclude that by their hand, they live and succeed, God is irrelevant. Like the rich man in Luke 12:13-21, he does not include God as a critical component or central factor for resolving life's challenges.

When people are so impressed with their intellect and philosophy that they elevate human capacity beyond its proper place, they are hooked on humanism. Only a foolish person will trade in his Creator for his humanness.

Chapter Notes and References

[1] John 4:24

[2] Christian archaeologists propose that the Garden of Eden was situated in Southeast Iraq. Retrieved from: www https://www.express.co.uk/news/science/815423/Garden-of-Eden-adam-and-eve-noahs-ark-bible. There are opposing reports and narratives regarding the location of the Garden of Eden. At best, we are uncertain of its original location.
Given the massive flood in Noah's day, the topography would have been drastically altered, likely destroying evidence
pinpointing its location. However, what is certain is that it existed according to the Word of God.

[3] Perfect in the sense that Adam meets God's design and goal in that moment and is free of defilement, temporarily.

[4] Aristotle was an ancient Greek philosopher who, in addition to Plato, was dubbed the "Father of Western Philosophy. Source: Wikipedia. Marie Curie was a French-Polish physicist and chemist who pioneered radioactivity. Source: Ibid. Galileo Galilei was an Italian astronomer, physicist, and engineer. Saul is a divinely appointed man through whom God authors 13 of the 26 New Testament writings. Paul's spiritual life and mind have influenced many people since the New Testament era.

[5]. This approach to psychology was coined by Joh Watson in 1913. It is based on quantitative factors and analysis.

[6] As Hammes, John (1978) noted in Human Destiny, pg. 20. Our Sunday Visitor, Inc.

[7] Merriam-Webster Dictionary. Retrieved from: https://www.merriam-webster.com/dictionary/humanism

[8] II Corinthians 10:4-5

[9] Webster Dictionary

[10] Ibid

[11]

[12] Humanism and Humanity in the 21st Century. Revised Research Programme 2010-2014.
University of Humanistic Studies

[13] Retrieved from: www.britnnica.com/topic/humanism

[14] Romans 1:21, 22; II Corinthians 10:5

[15] Ibid

[16] Romans 1:25

[17] Genesis 1:26-27

[18] Jo. 6:44. This is a verse that reflects the Sovereignty of God over His creation and a notion with which many modern-day Christians struggle.

[19] Romans 6:23

[20] Why we are Wired to Connect (October 22, 2013) Scientific American. Retrieved from: www.scientificamerican/article/why-we-are-wired-to-connect/

[21] Deuteronomy 13:6-9; James 4:4

[22] Leviticus 18:22; 20:13; Romans 1:24-27; I Corinthians 6:9

[23] See Chapter 1, note 97; Chapter 5, pg. 13; chapter 6, pg. 5

[24]Retrieved from www.dictionary.com

[25] Existentialism as defined by All About Philosophy. Retrieved from: www.allaboutphilosophy.org 2018

[26] I Corinthians 6:12; 10:23

[27] See Romans 1:18-32

[28] Genesis 3:24

[29] Romans 6:5-14; 7:12-25

[30] Genesis 4:8

[31] Genesis 3:17

[32] As noted by Hammes, John in Human Destiny (1978) pg., 6

[33] Cole (as cited in Hammes, 1978)

[34] Rollo May (1969, 1972) as cited in Hammes, 1978

[35] Crabb, Larry (1992) The Marriage Builder Chapter 2. Pg., 25

[36]; The Humanist, 1973

[37] Romans 8:26-27; Hebrews 9:22; 10:19-22; I John 2:1-2

[38] II Corinthians 5:10

[39] Galatians 5:22-23

[40] Ibid

[41] Romans 7:18; 8:8; I Corinthians 1:31

[42] In this context, this refers to self-actualization, desire, and pride, specifically.

[43] Thayer Greek-English Lexicon of the New Testament pg. 471, line item 3794

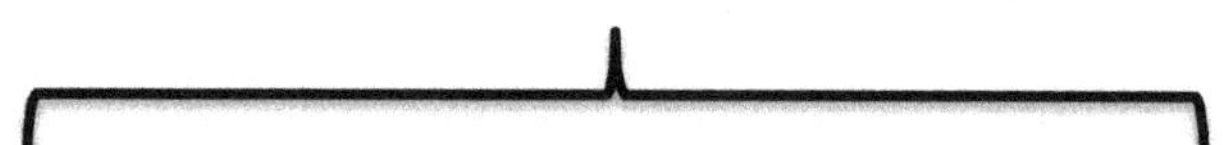

This chapter discusses conventional themes regarding the sacredness of marriage and the impact of emotional abuse and infidelity on the institution. It highlights the biblical perspective on adultery and its psychological consequences. In addition, it features the lives of those who have unconventionally remained married after these experiences. The story of King David and Bathsheba is used as an example to demonstrate that adultery (although a severe sin) is not an unpardonable sin. The narratives that unfold in this chapter are authentic. However, fictitious names are used to preserve the identity and privacy of those involved.

8

LICENSE TO LEAVE BUT CHOOSING TO STAY

EMOTIONAL ABUSE AND INFIDELITY IN MARRIAGE

Marriage is an honorable and holy institution created and ordained by divine ingenuity and wisdom. It is a unique multidimensional union of a man and a woman that aims at their happiness and glorifies God as Creator. After his creation, man will learn and develop a variety of relationships. But of all the terrestrial relationships known to man, no other is so intricate and intertwined that those living within are one. This exquisite and powerful symmetry is so sacred that it requires caution and deliberation, discretion, prayer, and reverence to God before entering. Kindred spirits and anatomical differences, matchless love, trust, effective communication, and unwavering devotion (to the institution God ordained) create a symphony of satisfaction that honors God as Creator. As mentioned earlier, Dr. Larry Crabb (1982), a noted psychologist, in his book, The Marriage Builder,[1] highlights the power and beauty of marriage when couples live as one in submission to God. Such an act moves marriage from manipulation to ministry and back to the original blueprint, creating an institution worthy of honor. But in a fallen world, this prodigious institution is under threat. The tenants of humanness (abuse, selfishness, pride, lust, and adultery) are the kryptonite that weakens and destroys what God has codified as essential to the human experience. The unintended consequence is a perpetual merry-go-round in which those who are in marriage want out, and those who are unmarried seek the benefits of the institution without ever exchanging vows. Although not the leading cause for divorce, adultery or infidelity is the most destructive to the marriage union because it not only severs, it destroys.

Notwithstanding, this does not launch another theological exposé of the marriage, divorce, and remarriage doctrine. Erroneous assumptions, opposing schools of thought, and thousands of years of protracted debate avert consensus, even among those in the church and denominations practicing in the 21st century. Irrespective of the current theological ambiance, there is unanimity that adultery is biblical and legal grounds for ending a marriage.

Scripturally, what lies at the heart of adultery is a breach of the covenant between those living before God as husband and wife. A married individual engaging in sexual activity with someone other than their spouse is one medium causing this rupture. If we surmise that what is at the heart of adultery is the breach of covenant, are there other means by which the marriage covenant is severed?

In most societies, a version of this mandate (Do not commit adultery) serves as a guide for those living in holy matrimony. [2] Antiquity reminds us that although infidelity appears commonplace in the 21st century, it has harassed and assassinated marriages and individuals throughout human existence. As far back as 4004 BCE (the period of Genesis) until now, adultery remains an effective satanic tool aimed at dismantling families and promoting disobedience to God. The Journal of Pastoral Care, Leadership Magazine, and Christianity Today conducted surveys in which a significant number of ministers and lay members acknowledge intercourse outside of their marriage and exhibit inappropriate behavior. [3]

The Janus Report's research on sexual behavior highlights that "more than one-third of men and more than one-quarter of women admit having had at least one extramarital sexual experience, but extramarital affairs account for fewer than one-quarter of divorces." [4] Not every act of adultery is probably knowable or recorded, even within divorce proceedings. Irrespective of the number of cases, Christians and other religious groups understand the behavior as incompatible with the will of God. There is an elevated comfort with ostracizing and judging those guilty of such an act. The way some faith communities address adultery, divorce, and remarriage wreaks havoc and more confusion in the lives of those affected by it.

Understand, the mere acknowledgment of such does not minimize the sacredness of the God-ordained union or the seriousness of adultery whenever and by whoever commits it. But there is scriptural precedence that adultery is not an unpardonable sin, as identified by some. Among several vital people guilty of adultery in the bible, King David stands out among them. Although David had over ten wives simultaneously, it was his sexual contact and relationship with Bathsheba that would bring great condemnation and consequence to his life. Why Bathsheba and not the others? First, note that it was common for men to have multiple wives during that period, a debate and subject for another writing. However, those in leadership (such as a king) could not have numerous wives for fear that they would turn the king in the wrong direction.[5] Second, and more to the point, Bathsheba was the wife of another man during the moment King David had sexual intercourse with her.

In addition, David's sin of adultery caused more problems, such as deception, illegitimate impregnation, and accessory to murder (and in this case) marriage to Bathsheba.

In II Samuel 12:13, God's grace and mercy towers over David's sinful monstrosity. God forgives David of the sin of adultery and the other transgressions that followed. Although God forgives him, the consequences of his sins come to fruition in his life. God's mercy restores King David (II Samuel 19:8-ff; I Kings 1:29). Second, Jesus' encounter with the Samaritan woman in John 4:7-ff and the unknown woman caught in adultery in John 8:1-11 shows mercy and forgiveness, in that the penalty for such a transgression was death. After the Apostle Paul encourages condemnation and repudiation of the one who had sexual intercourse with his father's wife (his stepmother), he encourages the church to forgive and reaffirm their love for such an individual (I Cor. 5:1-5; II Cor. 2:5-8). The modern-day church must learn to be as forgiving as she is holy.

Toxicity and Discrimination in Spiritual Discernment

Had David, the two women Jesus encounters, and the brother at Corinth committed their sins in our time among Christians today, the faith community would destroy them (metaphorically), label and sear them by their sins. There is a natural tendency and expectation for faith communities to condemn (as it should) the one guilty of such an offense. In the wake of such condemnation by the offender's family and church, they often feel forced to leave their home and spiritual family, too. The heinousness of the sin, the injury it causes, and the common inability to manage such transgressions in a way that minimizes more damage to the family and the church predicates this seemingly indispensable departure.

Because faith communities condemn such behavior (and we must), divorce recovery programs (for those who have them) drift toward healing the innocent party (which they should). Unfortunately, these programs place less attention on healing and restoring the one guilty of adultery. Most of the time, the guilty party is no longer around; they have moved out of the home and no longer attend services and programs offered by the congregation the family attends. Whether intentional or not, sometimes the environment in these places becomes too toxic for the guilty party. Open knowledge of the affair and their family's destruction invite treatment and judgment difficult for anyone to navigate. For example, several years ago, a church hired a 33-year-old preacher to replace the prior minister (hereafter dubbed Chuck), who was caught up in an adulterous relationship with a congregant. Upon the new preacher's arrival and installation, he learns that not only Chuck has this issue, but a former minister (hereafter dubbed Maximus) attending the congregation is in a similar predicament. Members circulate allegations of adultery during his first marriage.

After this, several members were disturbed by Maximus's marriage again and his participation in the worship service by administering communion, ushering, reading scripture, and offering prayer. His tenor was such that they felt he should go somewhere else or stay seated and silent should he become a part of their church. The existing leadership should have discussed the issue more adequately and saw no harm in allowing him to participate.

The new preacher reports that what stood out to him was the contrast between how the congregation responded to the two ministers. What was the difference, he wondered? They allege that both men committed the same sin, adultery. Compelled to manage this issue right out the gate, the new preacher conducts interviews and meetings with the parties involved in each case and attends a conference hosted by another church regarding Maximus' affair. The minister learns that Chuck is much younger than Maximus and that his adulterous relationship ended without destroying his marriage, at least on the surface. His wife and the husband of the woman with whom he had an affair chose not to divorce but extend forgiveness and continue their membership at the congregation they were attending.

Although this likely created tension and awkwardness, the move is an enormous act of courage and forgiveness by those impacted by the affairs. However, there were members disheartened by Minister Chuck's behavior. Overall, the congregation displays similar acts of forgiveness by remaining prayerful and welcoming toward Chuck and the parties involved in his case. But their response to Maximus is diametrical. Why? The new preacher notes that upon his arrival, there was more "fan-fair" over the case with Maximus than Chuck, to the extent that the preacher thought the offense surrounding Maximus was much more recent.

After attending meetings and interviewing key people regarding the issue, the preacher learned that the affair occurred almost 40 years before that time! "I almost fell out of my chair when I heard this!"[6] He says. "In addition, there *appeared* to be no smoking gun. The allegation hinges on the fact that Maximus' office phone was busy for over one hour during the time the alleged mistress was visiting, suggesting that the phone was off the hook for sexual purposes."

Maximus has always denied having the affair as alleged. However, during a private meeting with the new minister, he confesses that while he did not have sexual intercourse with the alleged woman, he allowed her to "use her hand to stimulate him to climax."[7] The minister informs him that the Greek definition of the word fornication includes behavior, as he describes it.[8] The sexual behavior is biblically unlawful in this context.[9] He states that Maximus looked stunned, followed by several minutes of silence. He soon breaks his silence by confessing on the spot and requesting prayer. The preacher prays for him and then discloses the confession to the congregation the following Sunday. In addition, the minister reminds the church that it is biblical to forgive him and adds that it is obligated to forgive and restore him at some point.[10]

However, the preacher still needed to understand why they treated the men differently after committing the same sin. The church likely took her cue from those closest to Chuck and Maximus. This approach influences how the congregation responds and treats each person—for example, given that Bro. Chuck's wife did not divorce him; there appears to be less agitation and repulsion toward his behavior. As best as can be determined, this was not in response to Chuck but to his wife, who evoked sympathy from those who cared about her. There were those invested in ensuring she received support in her decision, even if it meant that her husband (Chuck) remained in her family and the church.

The same approach is probably taken with Chuck's mistress and her husband, who, too, decides to forgive and stay.

It is worth noting again that the church requested that Chuck resign behind his affair, which one can interpret as the church's direct response to his behavior. What is untold is the silent suffering of the spouses who remained in their marriages after infidelity. There is plenty of help and consolation for the injuries caused by the affair and plenty of theological support in condemning their spouses' behavior.

But there was little support and knowledge about remaining married after such tragedies. In fairness, the new preacher reports that neither family expressed much interest in ongoing sessions to address the fallout from their issues. Perhaps the fact that the parties saw each other every week created ongoing reminders of the issue week in and week out, making taking part in more discussions taxing.

As with any couple continuing a damaged relationship without spiritual and therapeutic intervention, time exposes vulnerabilities contributing to the demise of the marriage. Chuck's mistress and her husband later divorced. The mistress's husband states that "she did it again with someone else; she did not stop fooling around."[11] Chuck and his wife would later leave the congregation and the state. Unfortunately, allegations about Chuck having two additional affairs surface and circulate. This author does not know whether his wife remained in the marriage behind more allegations. As for Maximus' case, again, the church appears to take its cue from the first wife violated by his sexually inappropriate behavior. She elects to leave and scolds him for his behavior, encouraging others to do the same. Although his wife suspected impropriety, she and the church were unaware of the details Maximus disclosed to the new preacher. But their suspicion was strong enough to draw conclusions and condemn him. Because Maximus's first wife's response differs from Chuck's wife, the church's response to Chuck differs from their response to him.

As noted above, Maximus is guilty of violating the marriage covenant. But if he repents (like any other sin), God will forgive him. Maximus and his second wife experience ridicule and condemnation as they move on. For over forty years, they float from congregation to congregation, nomads in a kingdom of priests and saints.

Well before this book was published, Maximus departed this life. What is interesting about this narrative is that the one condemned the most and treated more harshly turns out to be the one more consistent in demonstrating the fruits of repentance.[12] Unlike Chuck and his mistress, there were no more allegations about Maximus having an affair or misbehaving during his second marriage.

Suppose we surmise that the adjudication of adultery severs or destroys the original union of a man and woman enthroned in the bonds of holy matrimony and that a person guilty of such is ripe for harsh treatment, condemnation, and rejection. In that case, the verdict of the innocent party does not and cannot ratify or eradicate the guilt of the one causing the breach. God (through the work of Christ[13]) and only God can justify individuals. [14]

However, notwithstanding Chuck's wife's decision to stay in the marriage, is he not still guilty of adultery? From this perspective, at what point does Chuck become an adulterer? Does he become guilty at the moment his wife divorces him or whenever he has sexual intercourse with someone other than his wife? Given that the latter predicates condemnation in this case, how long is he an adulterer? What is the consequence of such an act, and for how long?

We note the church's error in their decision to follow cues given by the innocent spouses in each case, which influenced how they treated those guilty of adultery. For those of us called by and obey God, scripture must always catalyze decision-making. Although both men are worthy of condemnation, they are eligible for forgiveness and restoration. Some of the details of this situation are unorthodox. Most often, people condemn, dismiss, and search for known perpetrators of adultery by their failure; that's the norm... that's the tradition among most churches and communities. Irrespective of what they do, their adultery becomes a point of reference from now on. We see this even with King David. It has been thousands of years, yet most Christians referring to David remember his sinful act with Bathsheba first and jettison almost all other aspects of his life, the acts of God.

In most cases, the structure of ministry is such that it is easy to condemn people guilty of adultery and offer support to the innocent party. Most often, people condemn and banish those who are flawed, fallen, and unbecoming. However, our task or commission as Christians includes loving and forgiving everyone, the good, the bad, and the ugly

(Luke 17:4; Romans 12: 14-21). We have cornered the market with excellent divorce recovery programs that more often help innocent Christians deal with everyday struggles associated with divorce and help them decipher the best ways to move forward in rebuilding their lives, often including remarriage.

Choosing to Stay

But what happens if the innocent party stays even though scripture gives them license to leave? What are the common problems or struggles in such cases? How do you minister and counsel people trying to save their marriage after adultery? How will the church, the family, and the community view the spouse as guilty of breaching the marriage covenant? Answers to these questions were notably absent in the church and leadership presented. Although they were trying to support the two spouses who stayed in marriage after infidelity, they did not know how nor what to do with those guilty of breaching the marriage covenant in that context.

Arguably, drafting and delivering adequate responses to infrequent unorthodoxy requires that the church (especially her local leaders) thoroughly appreciate the daunting dynamics behind the scenes of those living in the church and the community. The church's failure to do this efficiently contributes to the data constructing Pew Research Center's report, America's Changing Religious Landscape. [15] Too often, there is a "cookie-cutter approach" to ministry in which the church treats people and every situation equally. This dismisses how issues confronting members and the community evolve and that these are not always traditional or identical but atypical now and then.

The rest of this chapter focuses on three couples who are Christians and God believers and whose situations are atypical. As horrific as their stories are, each couple has a spouse who chooses not to pursue a divorce, opting to stay in the marriage, but does so at a high cost.

It would be insensitive and immature for anyone to surmise that their plight and suffering are solely theirs because of the decision to try to save their marriages. There are Christians who sometimes find themselves in unorthodox situations. Given the unorthodoxy, many still need help to navigate their situations without compromising their faith. Subsequently, their ad hoc approach to these unique circumstances becomes the agency through which they attempt to mitigate their struggle. Although denominational and non-denominational churches now understand the value of adjusting ministry to meet the community's demand (i.e., divorce recovery programs), many remain too inadequate to minister in unorthodox situations, a fact highlighted in this book's introduction. For the record, "adjusting ministry" does not refer to changing the word of God to accommodate others; such a maneuver is sinful.[16]

However, the church's discriminating ambiguity cloaks details essential to understanding the struggle of those caught up in unorthodox situations, which, in effect, obscures how to minister to this population.

For instance, a Christian woman attending a church in the southern part of the United States approaches an elder about the domestic violence she is experiencing at home. She has a divorce on her mind, and she is uncertain what to do.

Instead of trying to understand the horrific details of her suffering, the elder does not engage in the details of her situation and dismisses her by saying, "Well, you picked him! Sister, you must ask God to help you live with that... you can't divorce your husband for that... What he is doing may be wrong, but not adultery."[17]–Author's file.

Had she approached him about her husband committing adultery, the elder would have likely endorsed her thoughts about divorce, given common teaching and interpretation of Matthew 19:9. It would have been an easy decision. If what lies at the heart of adultery is a breach of covenant, domestic violence may be subject to debate in this context, in that such violence cannot enact the positive dynamics of marriage as God intended and not the harmony codified by Him in such relationships. It is indisputable that such treatment of women is included in the catalyst prompting Moses (God's man) to regulate certificates of divorce, [18] to which Jesus alludes in Matthew 19: 8,

> "... Because of your hardness of heart, Moses permitted you to divorce your wives..."

The Elder's statement to the young woman shows a vacancy of spiritual wisdom and discernment, inadequate leadership, and inefficient ministry to this woman's issue, which is challenging to her if no one else. You will see a similar difficulty in the lives of the following three families, whose details are anecdotes from clinical and pastoral notes, direct conversations, journals, and observations. As in the introduction, certain sections of this book are written anonymously to preserve confidentiality and obscure some geographical locations. This chapter is included in that approach.

As you survey their situations, ask yourself: What would I do if I were in this predicament? How would I respond if someone disclosed daunting details about their life and struggle? How do I minister or counsel someone whose situation is unheard of or unorthodox? What does God expect of me upon knowing such a problem exists with my neighbor, brother, or sister in the faith?

The narrative about this first couple, hereafter referred to as Jonathan (pronounced: R-Kee-Lee-US) and Ruth (pronounced: Del-Fee-A), is likely the most horrific and heartbreaking of the three featured in the rest of this chapter, not solely because of the details, but how they play out and the impact they have on them. Their unfortunate experience fosters disintegration, displacement, and decentering for each of them, but for different reasons and ways.

Disintegration

For clarity, disintegration is the complete shattering of the inner self, disfiguring one's core being, and sifting of the soul in ways that alter identity.[19] Subsequently, disintegration in this context is similar to Luci's approach to the term in an article written for the Journal of Analytical Psychology entitled Disintegration of the Self and the Regeneration of 'Psychic Skin' in Treating Traumatized Refugees. [20] Luci sees disintegration not only as "deep somato-psychic dissociation but a loss of intrapsychic[21] and interpersonal space."[22] Disintegration causes ideas and internal conflicts that create injury and a feeling of lostness within the mind or psyche of the individual, which influence how one forms and processes distance for social dynamics and interaction with others.

What happened to Jonathan and Ruthis traumatic because they both experience disintegration. Trauma is not limited to physical injury but includes injury to one's psyche and soul precipitated by sudden and unanticipated events or situations, manifest by emotional numbness, withdrawal, vulnerability, depression, anxiety, and fear in which one or all these inferiorly changes an individual, creating dissonance between them and God. [23]

In his article, Disintegration of the Self-Structure Caused by Severe Trauma, Vito Zepinic encapsulates this same idea. He states:

> "Severe trauma affects all structures of the self–one's image of the body; the internalized images of others; one's values and ideals–and leads to a sense that the self-coherence and self-continuity are invaded, assaulted, and systematically broken down... leads to de-centering of the self (at-worst), loss of groundlessness and a sense of sameness, self-discontinuity and ego fragility, leaving scars on one's

> 'inner agency' of the psyche, and fragmentation of the ego-identity resulting in proneness to dissociation."[24]

Goran Simic (2016), in his book Disintegration of the Soul, associates this process with the "inexpressible suffering" of an individual. [25] Rick Spinos (in an article entitled: Disintegration of Character) identifies this process as the point in which one

> "... suffers a constant weakening, becoming ever more acceptable to collapse where the structure itself can be broken, like a bone that can be broken, producing permanent damage, or a healing process that takes much longer."[26]

Romans 7:24 delineates the spiritual equivalent in Paul's description of the fallout and effects of sin when it dominates one's life. He states:

> "O Wretched man that I am! Who shall deliver me from the body of this death?"[KJV]

Wretched (ταλαιπωρέω – talaipōreō in Greek) implies one exhausted and expended from hard labor. Dr. Olu Shabazz describes wretchedness as "beaten beyond the point of recognition." [27] It reflects the breakdown of an individual. The words "body of this death" are a throwback to ancient custom in which authorities bind a criminal to the rotting corpse of his victim to carry until he perished of contamination from the decomposing cadaver. [28] The picture is that of devastation, death, and despair.

Displacement and Decenteredness

Disintegration will always give way to displacement and decenteredness. There are multiple contexts and approaches to defining displacement, i.e., social, psychological, and spiritual. When used traditionally, it is a social reference to refugees, homeless persons, and people displaced by disaster. Mahalingam (2006) notes that a displaced person is also decentered in this context. In addition, she states that "displacement and decentering are spatial orientations relative to a place called home."[29] In this context, one idea behind the word is physical, which refers to the forced removal of a person from an environment associated with home. However, in this chapter, displacement and decentering embrace all of the above with greater emphasis on the spiritual effects. In this way, the trauma of sin forces the soul out of its spiritual matrix, decentering its moral compass, which obscures the soul's appraisal of life and dismantles the pillars upon which spiritual discernment rests. [30]

When a person experiences this devastation and spiritual decomposition, the soul is now foreign to the Spirit living within, turning off its capacity for introspective analysis. The anchor that once centered the soul in its rightful place severs from the force of daunting desire, rebellion, and short-sightedness, creating moral deficiency and dissonance that is too problematic to recover without adequate help.

In this first case, you learn much more than adultery, but phantom forces altering the lives of people. Jonathan's narrative picks up at the point in which he has confirmed (in his mind, at least) that Ruth is engaged in a supernumerary amount of sexual activity outside their union, which he shares with their counselor and documents in his journal.

Both Jonathan and Ruth find themselves in this condition. The story itself is unorthodox (to a degree) in that narratives like this one are accustomed to men. Here, they flip the script. Although women can and have disregarded divine precepts for marriage, most often, they are victims of such behavior. [31] As noted above, Jonathan and Ruth are disintegrated for different reasons. Jonathan is such because of the dramatic revelation and impact of his wife's flagrant and pervasive infidelity, and Ruth because of succumbing to inappropriate sexual desire and sustained mind-blowing sexual encounters over a protracted period.

Jonathan and Ruth are a power couple who have never recognized or learned how to use this power. Both of whom are educated professionals respected in their fields. Their family, church, and community view them as a great couple. This is not one of those couples in which, when you see them, you wonder, how did that happen? They are stunning. Jonathan stands nearly six feet tall, is very muscular, is known for his good looks and eloquent speech, is devoted to serving the church, and is an expert in his professional discipline. Ruth is foreign-born and raised and has striking features. The natural smoothness of her skin, silky hair, unique shaped brows, and light accent point out she is from another country. She is not only more beautiful than her husband, but she has multiple graduate degrees, and she is likely more educated. Her community reveres her for her intellect and professional work. In addition, she is known as a Christian from a devoted family.

Jonathan's suspicion that Ruth is having sexual intercourse and outercourse behind his back for quite some time is the impetus for the couple's participation in Christian counseling.[32] Although suspicious that she is having intercourse with another man, he stumbles upon evidence that suggests a covert practice of solitary pleasure. Ruth's uncharacteristic behaviors, inquiries, and evolving interests in intercourse compound Jonathan's suspicion.

Initially, Jonathan gives her the benefit of the doubt and surmises that her frequent acts of solitary pleasure may be the extent of the forbidden sexual activity captivating her.

But, as time progresses and more compelling evidence discloses, a much more daunting picture emerges, unveiling that she has had intercourse with several people over an extended period. Jonathan's suspicion includes at least five men, but he has only confirmed three, all married. Ruth denies all sexual activity outside of her marriage, including activity in solitary, and refuses to discuss Jonathan's allegations or answer questions about suspicious and unbecoming behavior, odd comments, and questions she has raised about sex out of context. He states, "She has the admit to nothing and deny everything approach to the issue." - Author's File.

This is a sensitive issue for Jonathan because he had a similar experience in his prior marriage in which his spouse had multiple affairs. He has the unfortunate experience of knowing the signs of an affair, how they play out, and the ultimate impact on the lives involved.

Conversely, Ruth is a novice in relationships. Although in her late thirties, she has never dated or married, she was a virgin before marrying Jonathan, which in his mind made Ruth a rare find in this American culture, a diamond in the rough. Ruth has no history of relationships from which she can draw. Her choices today, then, are not from the experiences of yesterday. Curiosity and desire drive her decision-making. Jonathan's heartbreak is exponential because he hand-picked Ruth to avoid what he has experienced in prior relationships. Ruth's purity, conservative upbringing, modest approach to life, and profound religious values were necessary to foster a successful marriage. Ruth's personality and faith were such that Jonathan felt that even if she did not live according to her religious beliefs, the culturally conservative principles guiding her would not compromise the integrity of their marriage. He describes this as an "extra layer of protection against adultery and divorce." The two made a solid front against Satan's tactics, in his mind at least.

But he finds out too late that Satan has found his way in to wreak havoc in their marriage. Jonathan learns that his wife's place of employment, professional conferences, and his intermittent absence from home become venues for his wife's intimate playground. He notes that several times a week, he would find evidence of intercourse during his absence. Jonathan identifies Ruth as 'hyper-sexual' and says that she was engaged in the activity so extensively that she began to have problems with her body for a while.

The husband reports that her behavior continued for approximately eleven years.

The level of trauma in this narrative is so conspicuous that one does not need a graduate degree in psychology to appreciate the psychological upheaval and injury or a Master of Divinity degree to measure the spiritual impact. This is a classic case and optimal performance of Satan's sifter. [33]

As noted in chapter one, Satan's cunningness or craftiness is epic; the tentacles of his devices reach into the heart of an individual; his attacks are brutal and aimed at a complete annihilation of one's core being, disrupting any harmony and symmetry between the individual and God.

What is likely unseen or hidden in Jonathan is an inflated and illogical sense of self, which contributes to his loss of value of self. The impact of Ruth's infidelity and the actualization of a collapsed sense of self defeats him. Teetering on the threshold of greatness, he now finds himself crouched in pain and agony; losing his spiritual balance, he tips over into a free-fall. His intellect, professionalism, and stature crumble under the weight of his circumstances, altering his identity. Weeping under clouds of doubt, he questions the things God has solidified in him. Unbeknownst to him, he has shipwrecked his faith. The way forward is foggy and obscured, which perpetuates fear and hesitation that was not present otherwise. Once known and held as confident (and, in some people's view, cocky), his voice is now weak, and his eyes do not contact people he encounters. Vitality has abandoned him. He's self-conscious. He hides his credentials now because he is too embarrassed to tout who he is because of who he has become. Self-analysis makes him wonder how one with such accomplishments or experience can unwittingly and unwisely subject himself to such failure and emotional abuse.

Although, in this particular case, the wife (Ruth) appears to be Satan's target (or do we surmise that Ruth is merely a subject of the target, in that Jonathan may have been Satan's target the entire time?) regardless of one's approach or analysis, what is clear is that with one stone Satan shatters multiple lives and successfully disrupts the relationship between the couple and their relationship with God.

We note Ruth's hidden struggle in succumbing to sexual curiosity and her incapacity to appraise and appreciate the beauty of chastity as ordained by God. Wikipedia defines chastity as the absence of sexual conduct of a person deemed praiseworthy and virtuous according to the moral standards and guidelines of their culture, civilization, or religion.[34] Other connotations suggest chastity as purity of mind and body manifest in sexual abstinence in singleness and fidelity in marriage. [35] "All major religions, i.e. Christianity, Muslims, Buddhists, Hindus and Confucianists," channel this concept into the hearts of their followers. [36] This sentiment and perception is biblical and is likely the origin of others. There are many people, among those who do not subscribe to faith and religion, that find infidelity inappropriate behavior in marriage.

But pressed against the push of modernity, this concept capitulates to broad acceptance of casual sex before marriage and its mere pleasure, aka "fun-dating." The sanctity of the body and the exquisite symmetry of sex in marriage is the furthest concept in the minds of most people, especially youth and young adults, which nowadays are those under the age of 55.

Abstinence before her 30s and before marriage made Ruth uniquely pure and priceless in the throngs of an oriented, sexually consuming society. Stunning, brilliant, young, religious, and undefiled, she harnessed a rare gift and power, making her a superwoman of sorts, which Ruth either misapprehends or is foreign to her psyche. Considering Jonathan's vivid description of her, she does not recognize that her foreign accent, the sway of her hips, silk-like hair, smooth skin, and brows angled in a way that creates a piercing exotic look were all reasons to glorify God's handy work[37], which in effect is reserved for and accentuated in the bonds holy of matrimony. [38]

Unfortunately, and like so many people, curiosity and desire became kryptonite for this superwoman in that it led her astray, destroying her family and herself. It is the same as the Apostle Paul's concern with the Corinthians as noted in II Corinthians 11:2-3 in which he states:

> "For I am jealous for you with a godly jealousy; for I betrothed you to one husband so that to Christ I might present you as a **pure** (Greek -hagnotes, meaning chaste or chastity[39]) virgin.
>
> But I am afraid that, as the serpent deceived Eve by his craftiness, your minds will be led astray from the simplicity and purity (or chastity) of devotion to Christ." NASB

What Paul alludes to here and what Jesus describes in Luke 22:31 became Ruth's reality, sifting by "an inward agitation," which was, in her case, sexual desire. When Kenneth Wuest translates Luke 22:31 from Greek, he identifies "inward agitation" as the mechanism and medium by which Satan sifts the soul. [40] The word agitation has an interesting etymology. First coined in 1547, it referred to a persistent and sustained effort to arouse emotion, an irregular, rapid, and violent movement back and forth.[41] During the 1560s, mental tossing back and forth emerged as another connotation of the word. [42]

With these definitions in tow, this author surmises that despite Ruth's ghastly behavior, Jonathan is Satan's target, making Ruth the subject or a means to an end. But, this does not dismiss Satan's interest in Ruth's demise, for he knew that through one, he could destroy both. Jonathan is chief between the two. How do we know? Satan's approach to Adam and Eve is indicative that he is not ignorant of the divine order of marriage and family. [43] Second, the level and intensity of the attack speak to the depth of Jonathan's strength. For example, consider Luke 11:21-22 for clarity, which states:

> "When a strong man, fully armed, guards his own house, his possessions are undisturbed. But when someone stronger than he attacks him and overpowers him, he takes away from him all his armor on which he had relied and distributes his plunder."
> NSAB

When Satan attacks, he does so from a place of knowledge, wisdom, and strength. He is never reckless in his pursuit but is strategic in the ambush and assassination of the hearts of men. Satan keenly knows that he should underestimate Jonathan's capacity and experience. He is a warrior for the King and very devoted to God. Satan knows God has gifted Jonathan in many areas, making him a formidable opponent. But he knows of his weaknesses, the areas within him that are void of knowledge and wisdom and still maturing. He knows Jonathan's need for a devout woman, how much stock he places in such a person, and his intermitting misplaced self-perception. Having studied Jonathan, Satan binds him with the thing that agitates him inwardly: his wife and erroneous view of self.

The intensity and complexity of an individual's temptation, trial, or hardship are symptomatic of either that person's inner strength, the severity of their entanglement in unscrupulous behavior, and the mindset that both proceed and follow such behaviors. Note: II Corinthians 10: 12-13, in which he states:

> [12]"Therefore let him who thinks he stands take heed that he does not fall. [13]No temptation has overtaken you but such as is common to man; and God is faithful, **who will not allow you to be tempted beyond what you are able,** but with the temptation will provide the way of escape also, so that you will be able to endure it." (Emphasis is my own)

In one sense, we could surmise that God is (as he was about Job) aware of Jonathan's limits, which is where his breaking point is. [44] Here, a novice or critic may question why God allows horrific hardships. Given our finite limitations, God's manner and reasons for doing or allowing things are often beyond our comprehension. His ways and thoughts are much higher than ours. [45] What Satan wants to use to eradicate Jonathan is also used to prune and purify the soul from the destructive nature of sin and ungodliness. [46] What is meant for death is used in resuscitation and life. The soul needs only to give themselves to the hand and will of God. Rebellion will only intensify the hardship until the person experiences spiritual renewal. There is an example of this concept in I Corinthians 5:5, in which the Apostle Paul addresses complacency in the church at Corinth following the revelation of a man having sexual intercourse with his father's wife (his step-mother) in which he states:

> "I have decided to deliver such a one to Satan for the destruction of his flesh so that his spirit may be saved in the day of the Lord Jesus." NASB

Jonathan is in a similar predicament. It appears God grants permission for an all-out assault on his life. Remember, Ruth's infidelity is not Jonathan's sole challenge. His finances (manifest through the loss of his career), family (as noted in his marriage), faith (which is apparent by lurking doubt in his mind), and health issues are components of a quadrilateral assault on his person, rendering him disintegrated. Having his life turned upside down, Jonathan falls to his knees in anguish, staring at the daunting revelation that he is not as great as he imagined but incomplete, wounded, and the treasure in which he places so much stock now pierces his heart. Jonathan's recovery is arduous and protracted. It is unclear whether his marriage will survive.

The remaining two narratives are brief when compared to Jonathan and Ruth. However, the impact (at least for those involved) is significant. The first features a pastor and his wife, in which the wife is a victim of deception, a deception some might find cruel and usual. The narrative begins with the couple's courtship, in which they determined that sexual intercourse would not happen before marriage. This is a natural course of action between two people who have given their lives to God. This likely sounds antiquated, but the fact of the matter is that God never intended men and women to explore sex outside of marriage and with good cause.

However, what looked wholesome, proper, and holy were, in fact, tea leaves of a hidden struggle. The reason the pastor emphasizes remaining celibate during courtship is because he is sexually impotent. They date for an extended period, and at no time during the courtship does he disclose his severe issue. There has been little to no progress, even in the age of Viagra. Perhaps there is a surgical remedy, but this seems out of reach.

A few years into the marriage, his wife finds out that his struggle with impotence existed well before their marriage. She feels duped or tricked into what is now a fraudulent covenant. Given that the pastor cannot experience sexual intimacy, he does not know how to be intimate but is very insensitive toward his wife. This does not suggest that intimacy is only practical through intercourse but extends to other aspects that generate closeness and oneness between two people. The dishonest and immature way in which this pastor deals with his issue in marriage has an indirect impact, making his struggle now hers, although experienced differently. One could surmise that it intensifies her battle because she is not only embattled by sexual urges from no legitimate sexual opportunity but devaluation matriculated through the pastor's decision to deceive her about his sexual capacity and motivation for celibacy during courtship. She is embarrassed, stressed out, and has low self-esteem.

What should she do? The conservatives would say she has no grounds for divorce because the husband has not committed adultery. Has he not? Is adultery limited to sexual intercourse? Is not the breach of covenant the central element of adultery? What is a covenant within the context of marriage by God's design?

Although the word covenant evokes a legal contract, marriage is much more than a contractual agreement between two people; it is not a business deal within which terms of profit and property are elucidated and negotiated. This is one flaw in the foundation upon which many marriages develop. These are important but should not be the sole purpose of entering a marriage. One way to expand our appreciation of the marriage covenant is to acknowledge its architect and see it in its purest form. The fact that it is God-ordained is indisputable. Second, and more importantly, the covenant of marriage includes God and so is naturally trichotomous and holy. This position contras questions about what God had in His mind about marriage, outlined in the inaugural passages describing the institution. God never leaves anything that has to do with Him solely in the hands of men. Directions and expectations are always outlined for us to follow and embrace. Subsequently, the covenant of marriage is a binding vow two people make and enter before God and includes roles defined by God.

Given this approach, do we surmise there is no covenant between the pastor and his wife? The wife did not know and could not make an informed decision about entering marriage under these circumstances.

But learning the truth, she is attempting to stay married for now. Even with what appears to be an admirable decision, it does not mitigate the fallout from this situation. Divorce dances in her mind, and her sexual cravings give way to thoughts of an affair. Satan sends someone to ensure she falls, but she has not taken the bait. Other sexual outlets become more and more appealing, but still, she chooses not to embrace them. She has a growing aversion to her husband and feels conflicted because she is experiencing such emotions. To make matters worse, the pastor has more issues complicating their marriage. She suffers and struggles. The people around her (family, work, and church) do not know what is happening behind the scenes. The stress and hurt from this situation exacerbate her health issues.

It is only a matter of time before she breaks. Given no transparency, integrity, or spiritual and psychological intervention, this marriage will likely end.

The final narrative features a couple in which the wife (dubbed Salunia) is a devoted Christian who considers herself a prayer warrior. She believes in passages like Matthew 21:22; James 5:15-16, which states:

> 22"And all things you ask in prayer, believing, you shall receive."

> 15"and the **prayer offered in faith will restore the one who is sick**, and the Lord will raise him up, and if he has committed sins, they will be forgiven him.
> 16Therefore confess your sins to one another, and pray for one another, so that you may be healed. **The effective prayer of a righteous man can accomplish much**." NASB (Emphasis is mine)

Additionally, she believes profoundly in I Peter 3:1-2, which states:

> [1]In the same way, you wives, be submissive to your own husbands so that even if any of them are disobedient to the word, **they may be won without a word by the behavior of their wives**, [2]as they observe your chaste and respectful behavior." (Emphasis mine)

She reports that her husband is engaged in multiple affairs, is an alcoholic, and is verbally abusive. She states he engages other women and comes home at 3 or 4 in the morning if he decides to go home. On multiple occasions, she screams, "I'm leaving!" but sex and insufficient income draw her back into the relationship. She feels her predicament holds her hostage. She elects not to disclose her marital issues to the pastor of her church but seeks counsel from a pastor unaffiliated with her and the church she attends. Shrouded by faithful church attendance and public displays of devotion, the malignancy in her marriage and the anguish she experiences hides her home life. She discloses to the pastor that she has been praying that God will change her husband, stop him, and make him behave.

But (in her mind, at least) God does not answer. God's silence confuses her. Why does He not respond to my crisis? She continues to suffer under the emotional abuse of her husband. She feels abandoned by both God and her husband. Shipwrecked by her circumstances, her faith staggers, and depression seeps into her soul. On one occasion, she contacts the pastor at 1:30 am, and she is distraught... he's at it again... the late nights and assassination of her character and person deepen her depression and agitate her wounds. The pastor senses she is on the verge of collapse. He attempts to snatch her from the brink and brings her back to stability by reminding her that God (although silent) knows her circumstances and is in total control. She is no different from many others who see prayer as a medium to fulfill a wish list when prayer is relational and embodies faith, trust, and dependence on God as Father and Creator. It must acknowledge the Holiness of God. [47]

Salunia's inability to keep these essential components and the purpose of prayer central exacerbates her suffering. Finding treasure in trials is difficult, but a silver lining or blessing often waits for discovery. As the pastor's wife mentioned above, Salunia's husband's sins are impactful and become her trial to muddle through and emerge stronger, wiser, and closer to God. The sins and mistakes of one can and will often impact those around them, especially those closest to the individual. When an earthquake strikes, the property and people closest to the epicenter will sustain the most damage. But trials or hardships do not happen in a vacuum or are without purpose, a principle we remember well. These unwanted difficulties have a way of strengthening and increasing wisdom. But only if one sees it through or allows it to mature in ways that increase understanding, knowledge, and value. This is what James alludes to in James 1:2-4, in which he states:

> 2"Consider it all joy, my brethren, when you encounter
> various trials. 3knowing that the testing of your faith
> produces endurance. 4And let endurance have its
> perfect result, so that you may be perfect and
> complete, lacking in nothing."

Chapter Two suggests how one processes under duress and approach impediment predicates the keys to surviving trials or suffering. Perseverance or endurance, in this context, involves one's ability to not crack up under pressure. Trials allow every child of God to show why we believe what we believe and why we trust and depend upon the omniscience and omnipotence of God. Those who can hold on through the trial, meaning not succumbing to spiritual dysfunctionality and, most times, complete emotional upheaval, will experience renewal and healing. Again, James alludes to this principle. He states:

> [12]"Blessed is the man who perseveres under trial..." (James 1:12)

Salunia's confidence in the power of prayer influences her decision to remain in her marriage. She plots to leave while her husband works, fearing how he might react to her departure. This creates concern at once. The more she reveals her experience, the more traits consistent with domestic violence emerge. She is emphatic over the fact that her husband has never hit her, but she does not know that he would not under certain circumstances.

A closer analysis of Salunia and her situation reveals another issue likely hidden from her or that she will likely deny: her failure to trust God fully. Inefficacy of trust in God creates paralysis from which she cannot escape. This failure is at the heart of some of her challenges and their resolution. Failure to trust God produces fear and indecision, i.e., her inability to leave an abusive marriage in fear of the lack of sex and financial adequacy. This does not minimize clinical impressions, which may surmise that her failure to leave the relationship may be associated with a "trauma bonding."[48] In some aspects, her choice to stay in the relationship is admirable but is diminished by her failure to turn the matter over to God and trust in His power and deliverance. Last reported, Salunia was planning to move but never did and continues to live with her husband, whose behaviors continue.

Summary

Central to every marriage with problems is the failure to enact divine essentials for the institution. As a sacred institution, marriage is flawless regarding the objectives God ordained during its inaugural year. It is not marriage but the people in them that create conflicts and grievances and fall south of what God intends for the institution. Marriage is not the by-product of humanistic ingenuity but divine objectives and accomplishment. Reverence for the institution, the God who ordained it, and living in oneness with each other remains a tried-and-true principle that leads to marital success. When those living in the bonds of holy matrimony do not honor God and live selfishly instead of harmoniously, in contrast instead of in tandem with each other, they lose sight of the purpose of marriage and create cracks within it that lead to collapse and destruction, which varnishes not only the sacredness of the institution but those attempting to live in it. Failed marriages most often fall from underpinning forces or stressors that impact people individually or as a unit, creating an inability to navigate these without exacting added injury.

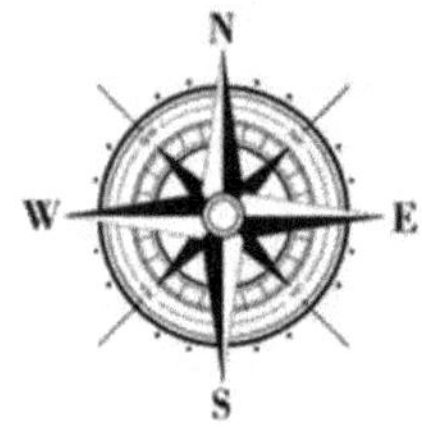

THE GUIDE POST

Seven Steps to Repairing Breach of the Covenant of Marriage

1. Acknowledge the breach and any subsequent damages.
   Denial of fact will only breed contempt, bitterness, callousness, and pride for the person guilty of such an act. (Ps. 38:18; 51:1-19)
2. Introspective analysis of self,* (which includes a spiritual
   component, Rom. 7:14-25; 12:1-21; 13:13-14) and determination of precursors[49] that lend themselves to and form behaviors that breach the covenant of marriage, i.e.

   - Perpetuating precursors- invading and ongoing attitudes, emotions, and behaviors (i.e., feelings about unresolved marital conflicts, drugs, alcoholism, and unbridled lust) masked by attempting to act or respond to daily responsibilities and interests typically.

- Precipitating precursors- childhood or pre-marriage experiences that shape how a person feels, processes, and acts within the context of marriage (i.e., any trauma, domestic violence, or abuse during adolescence and before marriage).
- Predisposing precursors- thought processes, including thoughts devoid of godliness, as well as the emotions and risky behaviors from them. These are triggers of conditions that breach the covenant of marriage (i.e., watching pornography, solitary pleasure, anger, and hostility that lead to isolation) *Depending upon the complexity of the situation, this may require clinical and pastoral expertise.

3. Begin or restore a covenant relationship with God, as this is critical to proper evaluation not only of self but also the damages imposed on others by inappropriate behavior. Adequate assessment of these ensures identifying essentials necessary for reconciliation. (Ps. 51:10; II Cor. 5:17-19).

4. Establish or renew patterns of behaviors that reconnect areas of the relationship damaged by the initial onslaught. Revisiting tried and true methods or behaviors that contribute to the security and soundness of the relationship is of utmost value here. (Jer. 6:16; Rev. 2:5; Eph. 4:31-32; 5: 22-33).
5. Appraise your relationship by identifying dynamics and issues that give rise to thought processes generating behaviors that violate covenantal relationships.

6. Implement any or all clinical and spiritual strategies to modify behaviors that contribute to breaching the marriage covenant. These must include an extended prayer life, meditation, and reflection upon holy mandates and derivatives that support thoughts and behaviors solidifying the marriage covenant.

7. Seek professional counseling (pastoral and clinical) to ensure the preceding steps are understood and executed properly and promptly.

It is highly likely that any marriage experiencing adultery will change fundamentally and will never be the same, even after reconciliation. However, in some cases, issues such as those delineated in this chapter can be managed with time-limited measures and pastoral and therapeutic methods to relieve emotional and spiritual conflict that breaches the marriage covenant. As such, self-awareness and control are maximized, which increases the probability of marital and spiritual success. This requires constant leadership of the Holy Spirit, motivation, and structure directed toward greater self-discovery and impulse control.

Chapter Eight Notes and References

[1] Lawrence J. Crabb, Jr. (1982) The Marriage Builder: A Blueprint for Couples and Counselors. Zondervan Press

[2] Exodus 20:14

[3] As documented on Bible.org/adultery

[4] Janus, Samuel E. and Janus, Cynthia L. (1993) The Janus Report Sexual Behavior. John Wiley & Sons, Inc.

[5] Deuteronomy 17:14-17

[6] 33-year-old Gospel Preacher

[7] Solitary pleasure can occur in solitary or in tandem with another person. See chapter 11 for more details.

[8] See notes from chapter 11

[9] Ibid

[10] Matthew 18:15-20; Gal. 6:1-2

[11] 32-year-old Christian husband

[12] Luke 3:8

[13] Romans 4:25; 5:1

[14] The Greek words Dikaioo[1344] and Dikaiosis[1347] are in mind here. Both refer to the process by which one is made righteous by removing the guilt associated with their offense and their being. As such, it is a process that only God can enact, not man. Because the process requires the work of one who is not guilty of anything to justify another. Although justification is a legal term, it should not be confused with modern legal processes in which one is set free from condemnation if he/she complete a checklist of requirements. The declaration of righteousness is a sole act of divinity. Zodhiates Lexical Aids to the New Testament in the King James Hebrew/Greek Study Bible. (1984) AMG Publishers

[15] Study by Pew Research Center (Released May 12, 2015) www.pewresearch.org

[16] Galatians 1:6-9

[17] An elder of a church

[18] Deuteronomy 24:1-5

[19] The inner-self comprising both spiritual and psychological paradigms

[20] M. Luci. Journal of Analytical Psychology. 2017 Apr;62(2):227-246. doi: 10.1111/1468-5922.12304.
https://www.ncbi.nlm.nih.gov/pubmed/28321873

[21] Ideas, conflicts pertaining to impulses or other phenomena that is psychological and arises or occurs within the mind or psyche. Retrieved from: www.psychologydictionary.org/intrapsychic/

[22] Ibid, Abstract

[23] Baker, Robert (2003) The Social Work Dictionary 5th Edition NASW Press

[24] Zepinic, Vito. Psychology and Behavioral Sciences. Volume 5, Issue 4, August 2016, a reputable journal in the field of psychology.

A reputable journal in the field of psychology.

Pages: 83-92 Disintegration of the Self-Structure Caused by Severe Trauma.

http://article.sciencepublishinggroup.com/html/10.11648.j.pbs.20160504.12.html

[25] Simic, Goran (2016) Disintegration of the Soul. Google Books

[26] Spinos, Rick (2017) Disintegration of Character. https://soulaid2.com/2017/04/26/the-disintegration-of-character/

[27] Dr. Olu Shabazz, Minister of the Harlem Church of Christ New York

[28] Complete Biblical Library. The Book of Romans

[29] Ibid, 65

[30] Eph. 4:18;

[31] Divine precepts are specific commands by God

[32] Sexual outercourse is a technical term referring to the practice of solitary pleasure, which usually stimulates the body outside or on top of sensitive areas.

[33] Luke 22:31

[34] Wikipedia

[35] New World Encyclopedia. (2017 Feb. 7) Chastity Retrieved from www.neworldencyclopedia.org/entry/chastity

[36] Ibid

[37] Psalm 139:13-16[A]; I Corinthians 6:19-20

[38] Genesis 2:23-24

[39] Complete Biblical Library Greek-English Dictionary Vol. Alpha-Gamma, 1-1131, pg. 58

[40] Wuest, Kenneth S. (1961) The New Testament, An Expanded Translation. Pg. 197

[41] Merriam-Webster Dictionary. Retrieved from https://www.merriam-webster.com/dictionary/agitation

[42] www.etymology.org

[43] Gen. 2:20-25; I Corinthians 11:3, 7-10; I Peter 3:7

[44] Job 1:6-22

[45] Isaiah 55:8-11

[46] James 1:12-16; I Corinthians 3:10-15;

[47] Matthew 6:9-16; Luke 11:1-4

[48] An unhealthy attachment to destructive relationships. See The Recovery Expert, Dr. Sharie Stines for additional Reading. https://pro.psychcentral.com/recovery expert/2015

[49] Precursors as reflected in the Glossary of Terms used in the Management of Sexual Offenders (1999) Center for Sex Offender Management, pg. 16

9

HELD HOSTAGE BY A MOMENT IN TIME

The Hidden Struggle with Forgiveness

Humans do not always grasp and appreciate concepts about the induction of time as space and experience lodged between the two poles of eternity. [1] We must exercise caution not to limit our perception of time to scientific and philosophical interpretations. Many view time as an abstract dimension, a construct within which unforgettable moments of life happen. This view reduces time to fleeting pleasures, opportunities, treasures, and accomplishments. Time is a revolving season of failure, hurt, and disappointment for some people. These convoluted perceptions of time obscure and augment the conciliatory opportunity for which God designed it– the opportunity to live in joy and harmony with a Holy, loving Creator. Our tenure and sojourn here are to reach up to and build a relationship with God. [2] An authentic relationship with God necessitates a relationship with others. Faith that reaches up will reach out to others. Time is a God-given gift for life. It does not restrict the Creator, who rules over time. But for humans, life on Earth is swift, provisional, and climatic. [3] The finality of death stresses how precious and invaluable time is. It is a reminder of the dawn and evolution of sin into humanity and the infinity of salvation through Christ Jesus.

HOSTAGE

The value of moments that make up our days, months, and years measures the impact and brevity of human experience. Depending upon their impression, the realization of the inevitableness of death often leaves people thirsting for or running from these memorable experiences. For instance, while love and success cause one to gravitate toward the source, abuse and emotional loss are impressionable moments that will wound the heart, creating a paralysis by which a person is a hostage. This concept of being held 'hostage' by experiences and emotions is powerful, evoking empathy and engagement from the audience. In addition, these experiences become the catalyst for decision-making and the prism[4] through which we view other aspects of life.

The word hostage is likely familiar to the average person. In this chapter, the meaning reaches beyond the idea of holding someone as security from a threat until one reconciles specific stipulations. Here, it indicates the manipulative demands imposed by the captor, which can be a person, circumstance, experience (traumatic or otherwise), and an overwhelmingly intense desire. It is a revocation of liberty, not physically but mentally or emotionally; paralysis of the inner spirit in effect. It points to injury inflicted by offense and betrayal borne out of unscrupulous behaviors, experiences that challenge the act of forgiveness.

Have you ever experienced this? Have you ever experienced something so impactful and impressionable that it consumes your thoughts, alters your state of being, and hinders you? It may come as no surprise that people have these experiences, including people of faith. For instance, a Christian couple succumbs under unique circumstances, pressuring their marriage and entering divorce.

THE ASSAULT

During the first several years into the divorce, they are amicable and co-parent with their child's best interests at heart. But at some point, the mother decides she wants full custody of the child. Her motives are not pure. Full custody means she will have sole decision-making and enjoy any monetary remuneration associated with such outcomes. She realizes that a court of law must find legitimate reasons to adjudicate her request. In her mind, the problem is that her ex-husband is a model parent to their child. There are no reasons for stripping him of joint custody. Notwithstanding, the mother researches reasons a court will award full custody to a parent. After her findings, she realizes she cannot attribute these to the father.

She is adamant about winning full custody of their child. Later, she enacts a sophisticated, diabolical plot protracted over several years. Unbeknown to the parties, the mother has a timeline by which she operates. In the run-up to the target date, she pieces together and paints a negative picture and narrative of the father to present to the court.

Although divorced for years now, the mother runs a background check on the father, as far back as his youth, hoping to find something nefarious enough to suggest altering the current custody arrangement. She gathers credit information and other financial information. Unsatisfied with these, she takes a darker approach by fabricating child abuse by the father. She exploits various circumstances surrounding the child and creates reasons for doctor visits. The father shows that the child's medical records reveal an excessive number of visits to the pediatrician in which the mother is the accompanying parent. In addition, during almost every visit, the mother alleges that the child's presenting issues are the by-product of abuse by the father. The medical community finds her assertions baseless and does not corroborate them. She continues to assault the father's character by making similar claims to law enforcement and the Human Service Department. The father reports he received several visits from law enforcement, the Fire Department, and several calls from social workers regarding the mother's allegation. He notes that on one occasion, the visit by law enforcement regarded his new wife, whom the former wife alleges is also being abused by him.

Extending her assault, the mother meets with and persuades medical staff and school administrators to embed negative, unrelated information about the father in the child's records. The father notes that in his mind, her goal was whoever reads the child's medical and school records would also view disparaging information on him. The aim was to place the father in the most negative light possible. The father's relationship with the child's medical and school community members was good-natured and professional, which he reports the mother envied. As if this was not enough, the zenith of her assault against the father's character came after an argument between the two, in which the mother (as it was determined) fabricated and alleged that the father sought to harm her physically.

Later, she petitioned the court to issue a temporary restraining order, which, in effect, barred the father from any contact with the child, which was the mother's goal the whole time.

With this advancement, their issues now stand before a court of law. During the proceedings, the mother takes one more epic jab at the father by alleging that he tried to kill her. In addition, in her closing argument, she requests that she make decisions in education, health, religion, and other activities, that the father only visits once a week for half the day, and that the court order him to pay child support. I include details of this narrative here to broaden your appreciation of both individuals' challenges. It is easy to craft a headline that reads, "Two Christians locked in a Bitter Custody Battle," a testament to how these things usually circulate. Likely, ultra-conservative people of faith will not entertain the details of their circumstances beyond the condemnation of divorce. This is an unproductive move in the grand scheme of spiritual accountability. Although the headline is correct in this case, what does it tell you? How do you know what your prayers or concerns should be about? How do you minister to them without knowledge of the details? Divorce and custody battles are commonplace in the 21st century. But the notion that a segment of the faith community bands together solely for corroboration and coagulation through judgment but gives little attention to the fallen in the aftermath is also common. But what is the final analysis if we review and discern the issues in this narrative? How could we restore wholeness to people shredded by their circumstances? At first glance, the narrative focuses on the mother's issues. However, the father faces many challenges during and after these proceedings. The mother's dishonesty, deception, and the duplicitous allegations raised throughout court proceedings have a significant impact on his psyche. Not only has war erupted between them, but one rages within him. The reality of his circumstance ruffles his tranquil spirit and mannerisms. He is angry in ways that cannot be healthy for anyone.

His anger deepens and intensifies with every blow and turn of the case. He is struggling with the fact that he is Christian; he should temper his response as kind and forgiving while trusting in the power of God throughout the experience. Nevertheless, for the first time in his life and Christian experience, he finds these moral attributes challenging to execute. The two-year span of his circumstance unsettles his spirit. His mind is stressed out, and unhealthy thoughts and emotions inundate his soul. During one discussion, he states:

> "May God forgive me... I'm not too fond of the sight of this woman. Sometimes, I think she is Satan in a woman's body. I wouldn't say I like some thoughts I have... I've had visions of sticking this woman in a wood chipper alive! She is the epitome of evil!"[5]

It is likely at this moment, his injury generate emotions that drive words and illicit thoughts, a fact clear through the process of time generated. Several years have passed without incident. Although it takes time to get through court proceedings, the father emerges victorious. Not only did he win the battle, but the mother abandoned the child, never to be seen or heard from again. In his mind, this validates the mother's malicious intent. He is grateful and relieved by the outcome. But a different picture and story emerges underground. During the period in which this mayhem unfolds, the father suffers on multiple fronts. The situation has taken him hostage. His blood pressure skyrockets, likely because of his ongoing anger and the stress of his situation. He experiences chest pains, insomnia, weight gain, and is angry at the world. He stops attending church for about two years and spirals into depression. Although the case is over, he is struggling with forgiveness, which dismantles him piece by piece.

One night, he experiences a nightmare in which he is sitting in a chair handcuffed and over 1000 cuts to his body, including two significant deep cuts in his back, which indicates betrayal. The image is terrifying and hard to grasp. He believes dreams are important messages from God. The Scripture teaches us that sometimes dreams and visions are methods by which God sends messages for directives and decision-making regarding life's circumstances. For instance, we find the first record of such in Genesis 20:3-7, in which it states,

> "God came to Abimelech in a dream by night and said to him..."

In addition, sometimes dreams are manifestations of the will of God, [6] and in other experiences, they are disclosures of future events. [7] Given that he has collapsed and capitulated to the demands of his emotions, he interprets the dream as a message, a compass indicating that he is not only wounded but has also lost his way. He prays several times a day now. He works his way back... he returns to the church and is conscientious about softening his emotions and response to people and various situations. He permits himself to forgive the mother, who, in his mind, is enemy number one.

What is forgiveness?

It sounds weird for a person of faith to struggle with forgiveness, or does it? In one aspect, working with forgiveness is second nature. How can one who has been forgiven struggle with forgiving? Isn't forgiveness the bedrock and hallmark of faith, such as Christianity? The chief purpose for Jesus entering the world was to pay the penalty for humanity's transgression and, in effect, offer pardon, forgiveness, and reconciliation. [8] There are explicit directives in Scripture about forgiveness, each pointing to the fact that we should forgive others since God has forgiven us. [9, 10]

Although the narrative featured above highlights the struggle of forgiveness individually, we know that this struggle happens within institutions, communities, groups, and entire societies. Forgiveness is a process that includes self-analysis, divine precepts, and consideration of the other. It partitions and dismisses the fault (s) of a person or party, restoring the rights and privileges of the wrongdoer. It must also include terminating any anger or resentment in response to the offending event.

Most people identify as a forgiving individual. People recognize the act of forgiveness as an admiral or moral attribute worthy of embracing. Most people identify with good things because it is distinguishing; it makes the self look and feel good. But mundane challenges test the strength and essence of forgiveness. Challenge and conflict help decide whether a person or group has the capacity for forgiveness. For instance, when a pastor or politician, a lawyer or judge, a professional teacher or neighbor commits a sin or a crime, forgiveness is selective and challenging, even among Christians. This plays out even in more familiar places, such as the workplace. In both secular and spiritual contexts, the expeditiousness and degree to which people forgive (if at all) is selective. More often, the identity and reputation of the guilty person, the offense, and its impact predicates forgiveness. From where does this criterion evolve? Do we surmise that a community or a society decides the criteria for forgiveness and demand eligibility? If so, does a community (secular or spiritual) hold the right to adjust and alter the requirements or eligibility? Are we to believe that impossible issues annul the act of forgiveness?

Answers to these questions and similar ones are in the primordial [11] definition of the term and concept of forgiveness.

"Primordial definition" to differentiate any connotations and concepts derived from individual perception and cultural contexts from those cultivated through divine mandates. But before defining these, it is essential to note that the construct of forgiveness, as seen in Christianity, differs from those of other major world religions. This unique opportunity is too often taken for granted by practitioners of Christianity. Although religions offer ritualistic practices as appeasement for sins, they do not provide explicit avenues for a personal relationship with the divine entity for achieving full personhood [12] through the act of forgiveness. The opportunity for full personhood in and through the sacred act of forgiveness is not unique to Christianity. Still, it is the linchpin to the entire divine-human story.

Genuine appreciation of this experience demands knowledge of critical dimensional aspects regarding forgiveness, one of which (as noted above) is the human response. The human response is not limited to a perception of God's act of forgiveness but includes perceptions of forgiveness borne out of personal conflict and offense. We can surmise that forgiveness is unknown or unrealized for some, independent of individual offense and betrayal. The second dimensional aspect, and likely the most significant, is what I dub the God-factor of forgiveness, meaning the divine purpose for conceptualizing and extending forgiveness. Given that forgiveness originates with God, [13] any proper analysis of the subject independent of Scripture limits defining characteristics. Defining forgiveness within Scriptural contexts is correct and displays the Creator's initial purpose for such an act.

One of the critical elements in recognizing the Scriptural framework for forgiveness is realizing that forgiveness is born out of offense, betrayal, transgression, sin, and violation. However, more significant for us to understand and accentuate is who a man's transgressions violate. You may think this needs no explanation, but it does. It is not just the name by which we identify the Creator, but His being that humanity's sins offend. Violation of his holy attributes always demands penalty and punishment. [14] This is another example of why understanding God is essential. He is not just God and Creator but a sacred, loving God and sovereign Creator. God's goodness and loving nature are too often taken for granted, even by those who claim kinship with Him. They minimize His holiness because of His love and goodness. Some religious people see the holiness of God so elementary they do not discuss or teach it. In their purview, His holiness is secondary to other things about Him that they have come to know.

This position is foolish and dangerous. Too many people of faith are unappreciative of God's quality and power, as evidenced by their apathetic approach and response to Him who sits on the highest throne.

It is essential to identify forgiveness as an innate attribute of God. [15] He is the epitome of love and forgiving by nature. It is always important to give close attention to how God describes Himself. God identifies Himself by name and attributes as He passes in front of Moses during another meeting with him on Mount Sinai. Embedded in the list of divine traits is the word "forgives." He identifies Himself as the one who forgives. [16] When God forgives, He completely forgives and restores. [17] However, two prerequisites are inescapable before doing so: 1) a substitutionary atoning death for the sinner. [18] Why? Death is the immediate consequence of sin. [19] Again, Genesis 2:17 and Hebrews 9:22 (NASB)

> "but from the tree of the knowledge of good and evil, you shall not eat, for the day that you eat from it, you shall surely die."
>
> "...all things are cleansed with blood; without shedding blood, there is no forgiveness."

Not only is death demanded, but the substitution must be pure or undefiled to qualify as an atoning act. Therefore, salvation does not and cannot hinge on another man.

Sin and transgression defile humans. God becomes a holy man in the person of Christ and the sole substitutionary atoning death for sinful humanity. The crucifixion, death, and subsequent resurrection of Jesus Christ is the only acceptable sacrificial atonement accepted by God, period.

2) the sinner must adjust their mindset to include repentance and faith. [20]

When we embrace and enact these, God's forgiveness follows. God selects the Hebrew word nāsā' to convey forgiveness and encapsulate its significant impact. This word sets up three semantical [21] concepts worthy of dissemination and application and, in effect, composes a profound realization of forgiveness. The first meaning of nāsā' is "to lift." This part of the forgiveness process takes the heavy weight of sin, guilt, and wrongs of the offender. The weight is mental and spiritual, which, if left unattended, will press a person's mind and soul into the ground, paralyzing the individual under it. We must remove the weight of sin and error.

Second is the act of carrying or bearing the sins of the sinner. [22] This weight is lifted, and another person carries it away. This is likely the most beautiful point of the semantic triad, which Old Testament symbolism captures. The scapegoat featured in Leviticus 16 symbolizes this and is a prototype of Christ regarding its role.

In verses 21-22, the people's sins symbolically transfer to the scapegoat and send them away from those guilty of sin, transgression, and iniquity. Even more impressive is sin's destination: 1) the wilderness, as defined in Chapter Two,[23] is a paradoxical experience and place. But here, it suggests that dimension is "a barren, dry place unconducive for long-term residence," often devoid of adequate substance for life. It is where things go to die. In Scripture, the wilderness and dessert are considered a place outside God's blessings. The blessings of God always rest within the land or place He designates and the preconditions for them.

2) in solitary (g^e^zērāh in Hebrew), a word significant, if not greater than the word wilderness. This word is a derivative of the Hebrew phrase gāzar, which means to cut, to decide. [24] The Hebrew text uses it about a land or area designated for

separation, where two critical survival elements are vacant – water and occupants. In this vein, destructive forces work in solitary confinement. Although several tentacles to "solitary confinement" exist, I use it here for a targeted discussion. The central aspect of solitary confinement relevant to any context is its potential destructiveness. For instance, when prisoners are in solitary confinement over an extended period, they meet the worst form of abuse and, more to the point, experience detrimental psychological and physical effects. [25, 26]

The tenor in which Leviticus 16:22 uses the word solitary suggests that forgiveness removes sin from a person (and the community it impacts) to a place where it cannot survive and, in effect, is unattainable. Cancer is inside and, in effect, killing the body is of no consequence when extracted and separated from it. Separation from the contaminants of sin breeds life and is the highlight. The separation stressed here is kin to the concept of death, which in Greek is "Thanatos" and means separation. Here, it is the death of sin and not the sinner. [27] The sinner and the community must understand that separating from sin is significant, and neither should continue to embrace and rehash these matters.

There is a reason God uses the scapegoat as a symbolic mechanism of atonement. The message targets both the sinner and the community. The sinner must (via authentic repentance) release the sin to the scapegoat (who is today Jesus Christ), and the community must allow the scapegoat to carry the sin away. Through forgiveness, the sin goes and is no longer present in the forgiver's mind. When sin is carried away to its place of solitary, one cannot find it, neither should he search for it. When individuals or communities continue to rehash the sin and impeach a repentant sinner, they create destructive conditions for that individual and the community.

Such posture forces the parties involved into what this author dubs "spiritual psychosis," an enduring loss of contact with the reality of forgiveness and fixation on something that is no longer present or available. When people do this, they invert the process of forgiveness and spiritual accountability, [28]ensuring the malignancy lives on, destroying the individual and those who cannot let go.

3) The final semantic dimension is nāsā's concept of taking away or pardoning sin and transgression. The ideology behind "taking away" sin differs from carrying it away. Here, "taking away" sin only belongs to God. It is a divine attribute. [29] It implies justification, not only the removal of sin but its guilt. Only God can justify a man. Neither the local congregation of the church nor its leadership or pastoral

tenants can justify anyone for their sins. Religious entities and members must avoid decision-making suggesting the authority to explain, pardon, or "take away" sin. It is the sole act of God.

These are the components of forgiveness as ordained by God: substitutionary atonement that lifts, then carries away sin into a solitary wilderness, in effect beyond reach, and the guilt from such sin taken away by God Himself. However, the sinner's acknowledgment of fact and repentance toward God predicates forgiveness. How we forgive others influences the Father's forgiveness of us. [30] God's extension of grace, mercy, and forgiveness to us mandates we extend the same to others. [31] In this context, forgiveness is not optional but mandatory. The practice of forgiveness is one critical trait of a godly person. [32]

The dimension of forgiveness God expects of people is the ability to release those guilty of sins from their errors. This is the father's struggle featured in the narrative above, along with many others. Some faith communities have poor ratings for releasing the sins of others and allowing sinners or offenders the opportunity to show "fruits of repentance."[33] This does not mean we should gloss over or ignore sin. Holiness necessitates repudiation, discipline, correction, and instruction where and when proper. [34]

But these are time-limited. Restoration is a critical part of the forgiveness process. [35] A person (irrespective of their error) should be able to show change or repentance. [36] This is not always the case. For example, the leadership of a mid-size congregation discovers that one of their members, who collects and counts the Sunday offering, has helped himself to envelopes of cash placed in the collection plate. Upon discovery, the leadership confronts him and removes him from his post—an intense debate between leadership members about the practicability and wisdom of disclosing this issue to the congregation.

Some leaders held that the matter should stay between the leadership and the one guilty of the transgression if he makes restitution. [37] However, others believe that shame and Exposure are excellent tools for chastisement and learning and that the church's awareness of the issue is a medium to that end. But there was no consensus. Later, the majority held that they should say nothing until there was a consensus among them. However, one among them is adamant about exposing the brother to the church. The following Sunday, without permission or consensus from the others, while making an unrelated announcement to the church, he seizes the moment and discloses to the church what has happened.

As you might imagine, this did not play out well. Given that the church was unprepared for such information, it caused an automatic reaction, which included anger toward the leadership for what the congregation notes as improper supervision and management. In addition, it created an atmosphere of mistrust and doubt about future collections. It takes months before the church is back to normal. Meanwhile, as this mayhem unfolds, someone is missing. The brother whose behavior set these events in motion is absent. It does not appear that anyone within the church has reached out to him, including leadership members.

Initially, he stepped away out of guilt and embarrassment, not only of the sinful act but added questions that will probably follow, such as, what's compelling you to make money in the first place? Where is your family, and why have they not helped? However, his reason for staying away for as long as he has is his perception of the church during this issue. In his mind, no one cares, sentiments evident by no calls, visits, letters, or other outreach.

Riddled with guilt, he makes his way back to the church. After the minister extends the invitation, he stands before the congregation, confesses, acknowledges his error, and solicits the church's forgiveness, prayers, and guidance. The congregation does what it always does, and it responds ceremonially. As time progresses, the brother attempts to get back into participating in the worship service and other activities at church. But he notices they reject his attempts to serve and take part meaningfully. In addition, they overlook him as a willing participant in the church's activities. Detecting cold shoulders, he leaves the congregation to attend another one on the other side of town. But he learns that news about his past issue has traveled, and they, too, are pessimistic about allowing him to participate in the activities of the church. He is welcome to attend either congregation, but they are reluctant about his participation beyond that of a lay member.

The behavior of those around the one guilty of this sin begs the question of whether he is forgiven. Why do they struggle with letting what happened go if the brother he has repented? Could it be that they do not know or are uncertain that he has repented? If so, how can he show repentance? What likely sickens and paralyzes this congregation and the father featured in the initial narrative is the inability to navigate the process of forgiveness. Forgiveness is a strategy and process that must center on divine objectives throughout. The psychology of forgiveness highlights the process and features additional age-old questions, such as how many times must a person forgive? Do I forgive those who have not apologized? I address interrogatories like these and the strategy and process of forgiveness in the final sections of this chapter.

The Psychology and Process of Forgiveness

What goes on in the mind of those who find themselves challenged to forgive someone who wronged them, especially if the offense causes injury? Although this final section of this chapter includes the "psychology of forgiveness," there is limited literature on the science of forgiveness. Regardless, forgiveness is inescapable and weaves into the human tapestry. It is one medium through which theology and psychology intersect with the public square. In this chapter, the psychology of forgiveness focuses on mental or cognitive processes (and the emotions and behavior generated by them) that occur during the preamble, validation, [38] and execution [39] stages of forgiveness.

This concept rests on what I consider to be two fault lines[40] within the process of forgiveness, mainly if it occurs within spiritual paradigms. I show these as analogical [41] and interpersonal. They qualify as fault lines because if someone leaves either of them unresolved, it will create issues of seismic proportions and ramifications.

During forgiveness, the forgiver induces analogy as a critical part of the preamble. The preamble here resembles the legal definition, which refers to an introduction or declaration of the purpose and justification for a rule or act. [42] In this context, this is a significant part of developing other steps leading to decisions about forgiveness. It is within the preamble stage that the analogical fault line emerges. Analogy refers to comparing and processing information cognitively about behavior and its communal interpretation. When a person realizes objectionable behavior, there is an immediate comparison (which we do subconsciously) between the one guilty of the behavior and the innocent called upon to enact forgiveness.

Analogy is a core part of analogical fault lines. It begins with an analysis of the wrongdoer, i.e., the person's history, position, and reputation, the nature of the sin or offense, and the impact and relationship with the person, if any.

Later (if not simultaneously), the one petitioned to forgive takes a silent inventory of self to assess similarities between them and the wrongdoer. They review their past sins in this context. People who have experienced similar sins or errors are more likely to extend forgiveness to others, but this does not always happen.

Sometimes, when the forgiver determines that they are innocent of the offense the wrongdoer has committed, they highlight the dissimilarity between them. As noted, one aspect of self-appraisal is whether the individuals see themselves as similar or dissimilar to the one they consider the other. Sometimes, this plays out in unhealthy ways. For instance, note the Pharisee in Luke 18:11,

> "The Pharisee stood and prayed to himself: God, I thank You that I am not like other people: swindlers, unjust, adulterers, or even like this tax collector." NASB

If dissimilarities between the wrongdoer and the forgiver filter through love and are guided by the Spirit of God, a healthy symbolic substitution or exchange occurs. [43] The forgiver becomes empathetic toward the wrongdoer. This does not mean there is no repudiation and condemnation of the wrong; rather, the forgiver understands the need for forgiveness and restoration. In addition, this substitution or exchange causes the forgiver to contemplate earlier scenarios in which someone forgave them. This way, empathy alters the type and tenor of questions raised in these contexts, i.e., What if it was I? How do I want others to respond? God calls upon Christians to express empathy[44] within the context of the restoration process.

But if narcissistic tendencies [45] stoke the realization of dissimilarities between the wrongdoer and the forgiver, devaluation, elevation, and judgment will follow. This will create divisive issues of seismic proportions and ramifications, which will appear and feel impossible for those involved. However, there is a natural evolution of the self in which people differentiate, mesh, and differentiate again daily across various contexts. We use the other to help define or bring clarity to self. In this context, noting differences and dissimilarities between persons is more definitive about self than devaluating others.

However, if a person is self-serving, they are more inclined to seize the event as an opportunity to elevate themselves by evaluating the wrongdoer.

Remember, devaluation reduces a person's worth or importance, which can then become a currency of hate and ill-treatment of the other. If this spirit is dominant, forgiveness is difficult to achieve.

The second fault line within the process of forgiveness is interpersonal, which the validation stage of forgiveness highlights. Forgiveness in this context is much more challenging because the offense is direct and personal. When a person becomes a victim of wrong, their cognitive process differs from those with no personal impact. This will vary depending on the offense. Violations committed by those held in high esteem or with whom the victim has a close relationship are likely more impactful. These offenses are matters of trust, explicit needs, equitableness, and devaluation, to name a few. Injury experienced through any of these is exponential when an existing agreement or expectation between parties, such as in a marriage or an employer-employee relationship, or kinship between siblings. Like analogical fault lines, any violations or conflicts within this category of unresolved relationships will cause a seismic shift that will crack even the foundations upon which these rest.

How victims process sin within this category will improve our understanding of their challenge to forgive fault. When people are victims of sin or are on the receiving end of objectionable behavior, whether the perpetrator is a person or group, there is a sense of loss and worthlessness. This experience is exponential when the victim deems a person or group significant. J.M. Brandsma (1985) identifies this experience as a loss the victim processes as a diminishment of the self, feelings of inadequacy, and vulnerability. In addition, he notes that the psychical response is automatic, which is expressed typically in anger and protects the victim from more injury. [46]

We know that in some instances, people's injuries are too severe to be angry in the immediate aftermath. However, anger will follow and is more likely expressed as a defense (protection) instead of an offensive maneuver (attack). Anger creates spatial orientations conducive to protection and healing. Although anger in these cases is a defense mechanism, it manifests in unattractive ways and can be spiritually lethal not only for the perpetrator but also for the victim. It heightens this reality if the victim does not process healthy emotions. This is where following the leadership of the Holy Spirit is critical to survival. As mentioned, anger can disrupt an individual's spiritual equilibrium, Satan's aim. [47,48]

Besides feelings of inadequacy and diminished capacity, there is a sense of betrayal. This experience intensifies when the guilty party is one the victim holds dear and values.

It is the 'I can't believe you did this' response to the perpetrator. Betrayal is one of the most painful encounters in human experience, out of which eroding trust and dysphoria evolve. When a victim is petitioned to forgive disloyalty, one of the leading questions in their mind is, how do I know they will not do this again? This question is paramount if the perpetrator has shown little evidence of change and transparency.

Most times, the victim wants to forgive the one who injured them in this way but remains skeptical, most often. They hide behind their anger and the act of betrayal itself. Nightmares and imaginations of further injury create hesitation within not only contextual relationships but also developing new ones. Their disposition hardens, and their expectation of the other rises as they look for tangible evidence of change and recommitment. New relationships seek proof of commitment and loyalty before extending reciprocity.

There is another kind of interpersonal fault line that challenges the act of forgiveness, of which the terminology is likely familiar. The context in which I use these may appear unorthodox, but it is notably evident. These are what I call emotional theft and rape. I note a compelling description of emotional theft in the words of a person betrayed by a close family member. They state:

> "It is painful enough that this person entered my home and took from me what was mine to claim and experience. But that the one closest would assist by capitulating to their desires is unconscionable. It is as if they aided and abetted the theft of my peace, joy, and happiness... and as if they conspired to assassinate my relationship."[49]

There is a sense of depletion behind injuries like the one in our example. People are often unaware of the real hurt and consequences behind their decisions and subsequent behaviors. When people experience injury to this degree, forgiveness is distant and in the background of the unbearable emotions of the experience. Resolution (if possible) is always significant because God ordained and defined these relationships to orchestrate His will and as essential elements to the human experience.[50] But another level of injury that most often impedes resolution- is emotional rape.

The term rape here does not refer to sexual assault or in any other customary use. It indicates the pomace left of grapes after the juice expresses or emanates,[51] which in this context reflects something crushed to "a pulpy mass."[52] Sometimes, the blow to the person and relationship is so devastating it crushes, making reconciliation appear impossible. People experiencing hurt do not see forgiveness as a choice, if ever. Those who can offer forgiveness do so after an extended period in which healing has evolved or one who has surrendered to God and the Holy Spirit. Regardless, those around and who minister to people in this context must know the emotional and physical impact of injury.

Attempting to counsel and minister without recognizing and appreciating such hurt is likely unproductive.

Restoration

There is one more aspect to the process of forgiveness-restoration. This aspect is often separated from the act of forgiveness when it should be a critical component. Restoration cannot happen without forgiveness. In too many instances, faith communities do a poor job of restoring even if they forgive the wrongdoer. The issue of taking money out of the collection plate is a good example. This is much more widespread among church leaders and members of the clergy. When a community does not restore the fallen, it gives up an opportunity to show the love of God and the act of forgiveness to onlookers. Again, there is a need to repudiate, call out, and separate from what is wrong and is not under dispute here or what to do when a person refuses to repent and end objectionable behavior. As noted, there is Scriptural evidence for this. However, just as there are commands to maintain the church's purity and discipline the wrongdoer, there are commands to love, forgive, and restore. There must be a strategic balance between the two, lacking in too many faith communities.

But in one instance, there was such a case. Several years ago, the regional office of a denominational church contacted me about one of their minister's adulterous behavior. The contact person was familiar with my ministerial history and my work in forensic mental health. After explaining why he was calling, I remember him highlighting that after disciplining the minister, which included removing him from the pulpit until further notice, the church felt obligated to offer or help him find a way back into good fellowship and service. They saw my services as a tool to that end. I administered a clinical interview and issued a specific assessment, which included risk and recidivism components.

Initially, I saw this as an odd request, not because of the nature of it, but the fact that churches were not known to do this, at least during that time. However, to their credit, they could find the value of not only disciplinary action but also enacting forgiveness, which led to restoration. One of the major deterrents to restoration is the fear that the wrongdoer will relapse and commit the same offense and that such behavior will be much worse. In its authentic form, forgiveness will move a person from the emotions generated by the initial issue or offense to critical thinking and spiritual discernment. As I understood it, they were not looking to substitute the sanctifying work of the Holy Spirit but rather a tool to help measure change and predict future complications. Judging from the conversation, it seems there was a genuine concern about restoring the minister to their perception of the specialty and sacredness of the call to ministry and the utilization of God-given gifts and talents to that end. Even today, churches do not appreciate the value of creating pathways that ensure fallen leaders (or lay members) have a way back to good standing, fellowship, and resume service in the kingdom. We praise the confession (and we should) as a critical indicator of a changed heart and attitude. [53] But in some communities, people conflate confession with reporting. Many are caught up in the narrative of the sin rather than the condition of the sinner's heart. In this context, the wrongdoer comes up short of complete restoration.

In other instances, some surmise that there are situations in which a person should not re-assume responsibilities involved in the issue, nor can they do so. For example, some believe that the church accountant found fudging the books (repentant or not) should not serve as the accountant after that and is unlikely to be recommended to other congregations or organizations. What is the premise or core principles used to arrive at such conclusions? Is it perception and influence? Is it upholding moral standards? Or do we conclude that the blood of Christ is only adequate for sins committed before baptism? Have we decided that forgiveness is possible without restoration or that restoration does not include continuing responsibilities before a person falls? If so, how is that determined, and by whom? If we find a person is a thief, an adulterer, dishonest, or one with violent tendencies, how long are they? What are the criteria for relabeling? These questions underscore the need for clear principles in restoration and forgiveness.

For instance, when a minister or other "high-profile" people within faith communities show objectionable behavior, they are removed from their position or leave voluntarily. Regardless, the issue often strains the relationship between the outgoing minister and the church. Given the few opportunities to resolve these issues after the minister leaves, the perceptions of all the parties involved are most often seared by the circumstance. Each person sees and processes the issue and the person by the perceptions and emotions formed during the conflict or issue. This underscores the detrimental effects of ineffective restorative processes on faith communities and organizations.

It is rare for these communities to work out and work through the issues before the minister's departure.

This author believes faith communities should work through the issues, forgive, and restore the individual before departure. In most cases, clergy move on to the subsequent work (if possible) without resolving the problems and in ways that ensure healing for everyone. Authentic, effective restoration will accomplish this.

Judging how these things play out at the local level, it is not inconceivable that segments of the faith community do not entirely understand biblical restoration. Teaching about restoration has been too shallow over the years. Significant attention is given to the nature of the sin, but insufficient attention is given to the individual's well-being overall. People only view the wrongdoer through a prism of their sins.

Authentic biblical restoration encompasses the necessary components for the wrongdoer's sins and the community's sanctification. Galatians 6:1-2 is the classic text that gives us a kaleidoscopic view of the restoration process. First, the principles of restoration delineated in this passage develop within the context of the discussion in chapter five about life in the Spirit. Paul details the fruits of the Spirit, five of which are instrumental to the restoration process.

Love and peace, patience and kindness, faithfulness and gentleness are among these. Paul opens chapter six by continuing the discussion in chapter 5, which, in a broader contextual view, points to the absence of an intellectual understanding of the work and power of the Holy Spirit. The Galatian Christians, who were taken away from grace by the inaccurate teaching Judaizers, were vulnerable to legalism and attempted to obey Christian ethics and the legal tenets of the Mosaic law independent of the presence and power of the Holy Spirit. Any Christian trying to follow and obey God through the capacity of the flesh is susceptible to failure. In the Book of Galatians, Paul writes it alarming (hence the word "overtaken") that they were sinning through their human-fleshly attempts to be obedient. It's like trying to be spiritual without the Spirit –it is nonsensical.

However, irrespective of the Galatians' sins, the restoration process outlined in the text is significant and pertinent to this discussion. Given that God inspires these, the essentials involved in the restoration process are immutable and germane to every sin or context in which a person falls from grace. Notwithstanding, we may tailor the technique or proportional to the type of sin or error committed, i.e., methods used to restore a person guilty of adultery may differ from those used for one guilty of theft. However, the essentials of restoration are the same in both instances.

What are the essentials or fundamentals of restoration?

The strategic choice of terms delineating this process underscores the divine nature of restoration. The Holy Spirit, as the chief change agent, plays a pivotal role in this process, convicting the sinner. The psychological, spiritual mechanics, and practical details of the indispensable soul adjustment are not the by-product of humanistic ingenuity. This thinking and perception is problematic. Such an approach lends itself to the superiority complex commonly associated with and that which distorts the restoration process. Galatians 5:25 and 6:4, Paul discourages superior thinking at the expense of the heresy of others. When superior attitudes are unchecked in this context, it leads to judgment, complicating restoration.

The Scripture mandates that those involved in the restoration process are spiritual, meaning they are a part of and led by the Holy Spirit. The fruits of the Spirit noted above will dominate attitudes toward wrongdoers and the restoration process. Accompanying their spirituality is crucial to keen discernment and maturity, which are both important to navigating the restoration process. Given the Scripture's mandate, anyone who is insufficient in this area should not involve themselves in any restorative processes.

Once the right people are involved and their attitudes are coordinated with the Spirit, the overarching aim becomes clear: to restore.

Restoration is a universal concept transcending disciplines, categories, contexts, and institutions. Each entity or group has its process for restoring order, relationship, or responsibility. Although this discussion unfolds within a spiritual paradigm, the tenets apply across multiple contexts. Notwithstanding, in spiritual contexts, the divine directives for restoration are not optional but mandatory. Given how significant issues unfold in faith communities, it's probable that not everyone has an intelligent understanding of what the word "restore" means. Likely, the average definition or interpretation of the word and the concept fall far short of its authentic meaning.

The word restore originates from the Greek word *katartizo*,[54] which captures the real essence of restoration. It is as follows:

- To repair,[55] like one would repair something broken, putting the pieces back into their proper place;
- Placing something back into its former good condition;[56] To fit something back into its proper place like a disjointed limb or bone.[57] To equip,

perfect, or complete something the way it was beforehand.[58]

In every etymological or lexical source, restore indicates returning something to its good condition, to its former place. In addition, the implication or inference is that the subject is improved by doing so, meaning the person moves from a disastrous state to one of stability, from brokenness to wholeness. In plain English, if the thief has repented of his sin when forgiveness extends, and the restoration process is implemented, the thief is no longer a thief and cannot and should not be addressed or treated as a thief. The permanent searing, labeling, and boycott of repentant people of faith is an incredulous act that abases the redeeming power of the blood of Christ and the regenerative work of the Holy Spirit.[59] Forgiveness must include restoration, and restoration must restore. This is the goal of the passage and the act itself.

Besides defining the goal and objectives of restoration, Paul describes the attitude, tenor, and the way they knead the wrongdoer during the process- by gentleness and meekness. When paramedics arrive at the scene of an emergency, they delicately treat injured victims with special care and attention. Their injuries dictate the appropriateness and quality of care the first responders deliver.

However, not everyone knows how to respond to an emergency in faith communities. Sometimes, people pay more attention to the sin than they do to the person, and the wrongdoer is roughed up during the restoration.

In ultra-liberal, educated faith communities, the sins of others are so privatized and personal that the community sees both the sin and the act of forgiveness as something private and something they should not involve themselves in. This creates a distance between the wrongdoer and the community. In addition, it minimizes the work and responsibility of the community to the one in need of restoration. Some see a private and individualistic approach to forgiveness as losing sight of the inner self and relations with the broader community. [60] Repentance is the wrongdoer's sole responsibility, but forgiveness is communal. Forgiveness is not just a personal act; it maintains relationships and preserves the community, emphasizing our shared responsibility in restoration.

When forgiveness mediates through the Holy Spirit, the community and the victim's attitude toward the wrongdoer is concerned about that individual's spiritual welfare. This means "bear one another's burdens" in Galatians 6:2. Love causes the community to reach out, minister, heal, and restore the sinner. All too often, judgment prohibits the practice of forgiveness. There are reasons Jesus discourages people from judging each other (Matthew 7:1-2). 1) Judgment belongs to Him. [61] 2) Judging causes division and separation. The word judge originates from the Greek word *krino*, which means to divide, separate, and decide. It means to pass a sentence or give one's opinion privately. [62] Given judging, it isn't easy to forgive and reach resolution and restoration with this sentiment. When judging infiltrates, it destroys any opportunity to achieve the goal. It deepens the divide and causes more injury to the one needing healing and restoration. We do not limit this reality to spiritual paradigms, but applies across various contexts. Judgment, repentance, forgiveness, and restoration are experiences in every context and people. Ruptured relationships are transparent everywhere we turn. The tenets of forgiveness and restoration are beneficial for everyone, everywhere.

Nowadays, it is common for siblings to live in ruptured relationships for extended periods, for the parent and child dynamic to strain relationships for years, for feuds to exist between families and individuals at church, or for conflict between co-workers to persist unremittingly. Irrespective of the context, forgiveness, and restoration are processes and tools that certify reconciliation and tranquility in a relationship and strengthen a community.

Love is the bridge between rupture and reconciliation, love not only of self but of the other. David Augsburger (1996) notes:

> "Love of self and love of other are not two separate loves, but two aspects of the same attitude of equal regard."[63]

When love is vacant, a person's calamity defines them and holds them hostage by the event and the emotions it generates. People must be empowered to surrender their trust in God's providence and promises. Note:

> "casting all your anxiety on Him because He cares for you."[64]

Learning how to surrender is a critical element in the forgiveness process. Protracted retention of pain, hatred, and the anxiety generated by tumultuous events will only lead to a state of bitterness and perpetual unhappiness. Bitterness is that thing or matter that has soured within the individual, making the entire person sick. [65] It is an unwise state of being. [66] However, the elephant in the room for many people is an interrogatory– how many times am I obligated to forgive, and for how long?

Peter raised this question with Jesus, as recorded in Matthew 18:22 and Luke 17:3- 4. What is the question behind the question? What was Peter and many others today asking?

This question suggests that the forgiver is looking for a moment to take off the gloves (so to speak) and cut off the wrongdoer. For others, is there a point that justifies the victim's retaliation or rejection of the request to forgive? When can the offender receive what they deserve?

First, when surveying answers to these questions through the passages in which the original questions emerge, Matthew suggests that not only is there an unlimited number of times to forgive, but it is unconditional. This is an incorrect interpretation and application of the text. Luke clarifies the issue by using the word repent as a condition for forgiveness. The wrongdoer's repentance of objectionable behavior, meaning that the individual is no longer involved or practicing any tenets of objectionable behaviors, predicates forgiveness.

There is always a demand for repentance and sacrifice. It is our love that should always remain unconditional.

The Phantoms of Forgiveness

There are unseen and untold truths about those who struggle with forgiveness. First, the thought, much less the practice of forgiveness, causes a person to relive the injuries associated with the offending event. The psychological impact of the entire process is challenging for most people.

Remember, I identified validation as essential to forgiveness. As a person seeks validation to forgive or not, they relive the details of the event, which causes emotions in them to recycle. Sometimes, this part of the process behaves and feels traumatic, which makes execution difficult.

The other unseen truth is that in certain circumstances (not all), people depend on an individual, a context, or experience for happiness. If we do not need something from specific experiences, contexts, or individuals, we are less likely to experience violation and injury by its absence. Oddly, forgiveness exposes our vulnerabilities, from which people hide or turn away. If forgiveness exposes hidden, embarrassing vulnerabilities, a person will choose not to forgive the wrongdoer. What I identify as dependent or dependency, Brandsma (1985) refers to as the "awareness of ownership of a need in the situation of violation." [67]

In addition, an inflated perception of self impedes the process and act of forgiveness. The arrogance that bleeds out of an inflated sense of self will see the process of forgiveness as something beneath them, stooping down to the offender. Forgiveness is difficult to enact and carry out when a person has this mindset. Surrendering oneself is vital to implementing forgiveness and healing from the injuries caused by the offending event.

A person must surrender to the power and work of the Holy Spirit. This will create a canal for love to flow and other aspects of the fruit of the Spirit that are significant to forgiveness and restoration. In Matthew 11:28-30, Jesus makes “the great exchange.” He beacons us to come and make an exchange. Give Him your heartache, injury, stubbornness, sins, failures, and improper attitudes, and He will exchange those for what He has– a burden that is not heavy, a yoke that is easy, and unparalleled rest from the toils of life. Let go, free yourself from the circumstance that has held you hostage long enough.

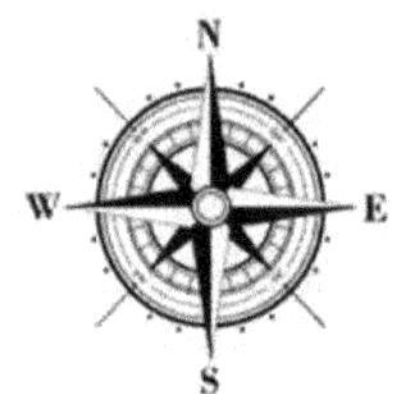

THE GUIDE POST

Steps to Forgiveness and Restoration

1. Surrender to the leadership of the Holy Spirit to navigate the spiritual paradigms of forgiveness.

2. Differentiate the offense or sin from the wrongdoer, then work to reduce negative emotions toward that individual.

3. Identify the need(s) that were violated by the wrongdoer.
4. Surrender the desire to punish and the demand for restitution. This does not mean that the wrongdoer should not or will not be punished or suffer consequences.
5. Alter your perception of the wrongdoer as a means to an end or need.
6. After releasing the sin, restore the individual, if possible.
7. Seek appropriate counseling to address emotional injury.

CHAPTER NOTES AND REFERENCES

[1] Eternity past is the period before Genesis 1:1. Subsequently, eternity future is the period following the Great Judgment in Revelation 20:11-15. The synopsis, then, is that time is the space and period between creation and the end of the world.

[2] Deuteronomy 6:5; Ecclesiastes 12: 13-14

[3] Ecclesiastes 3:1-10; James 4:14

[4] A medium that misrepresents whatever is seen through it.

[5] Author's file

[6] Genesis 28:11-22

[7] Genesis 37:5-10

[8] Matthew 9:1-7; Luke 19:10; Col. 1:13-14; 3:13; Rom. 4:25; Rom. 5:10; I Timothy 1:15; I Cor. 15:12-28

[9] Eph. 4:31,32; Col. 3:13; Lk. 17:3-4

[10] We must not confuse forgiveness with consequence. Forgiveness does not mean every The consequence of sin is mooted. For instance, a person can be forgiven for robbing a bank, but it does not mean he/she is not accountable to the law of the land, which may require incarceration as a penalty.

[11] Something existed at or since the beginning of time; first created or developed. See www.merriam-webster.com

[12] Capacity for and attributes like morality, consciousness, and reason; critical elements constituting the wholeness of a person, of which fellowship with divinity is essential.

[13] Exodus 34:7; John 3:16; Col. 2:13, 14

[14] Gen. 2:17, Rom. 1:18-32; I Pet. 1:16

[15] Exodus 34:7; Nehemiah 9:17; Daniel 9:9

[16] Ibid, Ex.

[17] Ps. 51:1-2; Is. 38:17; Heb. 10:17

[18] Leviticus 5; 17:11,14; Heb. 9:22

[19] Romans 6:23

[20] Ps. 51; Acts 2:37, 38; II Peter 3:9

[21] That which relates to or is developed out of the different meanings of words or symbols. Retrieved from: www.dictionary.com.

[22] Generally, this is the concept or idea behind Galatians 6:1-2 and Romans 15:1

[23] See page

[24] Complete Biblical Library: The Old Testament. Hebrew-English, Gimel-Zayin. 1996, pg. 91

[25] Haney, Craig (2017-11-03) Restricting the Use of Solitary Confinement. Annual Review of Criminology doi:10.1146/annurev-criminol-032317-092326. ISSN 2572-4568.

[26] American Journal of Public Health (March 2014) Solitary Confinement and Risk of Self-Harm Among Jail Inmates.

[27] Romans 6:6-7, 11-13

[28] Galatians 6:1-2

[29] Ex. 34:7; Numbers 14:18; Mic. 7:18; Romans 3:26; 5:1, 11

[30] Matthew 18:23-35; Luke 6:36,37

[31] Eph. 4:32

[32] Mark 11:25; Matthew 5:43-48

[33] Matthew 3:8

[34] II Thessalonians 3:6, 14; Rom.12:9; 16:17, 18; I Cor. 5:11, 13

[35] Galatians 6:1

[36] Thayer Greek-English Lexicon of the New Testament (1977) notes the Greek word for repentance means the following: "the change of mind of those who have begun to abhor their errors and misdeeds and have determined to enter upon a better course of life so that it embraces both a recognition of sin and sorrow for it and a hearty amendment, the tokens, and effects of which are good deeds." (#3341, pgs. 405, 406)

[37] Matthew 18:15,16

[38] The point at which the forgiver decides whether to forgive or not, as well as the primes for their decisions.

[39] The culmination of the process of forgiveness, in which the forgiver enacts what he or she deems valid. Where forgiving is granted, restoration is included automatically.

[40] A divisive issue or difference of opinion will likely have serious consequences. Retrieved from www.dictionary.com

[41] Comparison between two objects, or systems of objects that highlights respects in which are considered similar. Standard Encyclopedia of Philosophy. Retrieved from: www.plato.stanford.edu

[42] A clause at the beginning of a constitution or statute explanatory of the reasons for its enactment and the objects to be accomplished. The Law Dictionary. Retrieved from: www.lawdictionary.org; justification for stature or deed. Retrieved from www.dictionary.com

[43] I Peter 4:8

[44] See Galatians 6:1

[45] Vanity, exhibitionism, and arrogant ingratitude. See also: Kohut, H. (1978b). Forms and transformations of narcissism. In P. Ornstein (Ed.), *The search for* KOHUT'S SELF PSYCHOLOGY 257 *The self* (Vol. 1, pp. 427–460). New York: International Universities Press. (Original work published 1966)

[46] Brandma, M.J. (1982) Forgiveness: A dynamic, theological, and therapeutic analysis. Pastoral Psychology pgs. 40-50.

[47] James 1:19, 20; Eph. 4: 26-31

[48] See Chapter One

[49] Author's file

[50] Genesis 2:18

[51] Retrieved from: www.merrianwebster.com

[52] Ibid

[53] James 5:16

[54] Weust, Kenneth (1973) Weust's Word Studies from the Greek New Testament. Pg. 165

[55] Ibid

[56] Ibid

[57] Zodhiates, Spiros (1977) Lexical Aids to the New Testament in the New American Standard Key Word Study Bible. Pg.1846

[58] Ibid

[59] Eph. 4:23; Titus 3:5-7

[60] Jones, Gregory L. (1995) Embodying Forgiveness A Theological Analysis. William B. Eerdmans Publishing Company

[61] John 12:48; James 4:11-12

[62] Ibid, Zodhiates Pg. 1849

[63] Augsburger, W., David (1996) Helping People Forgive. Westminster John Knox Press. Pg. 46

[64] I Peter 5:7 New American Standard Bible. Lockman Foundation

[65] Hebrews 12:15; Eph. 4:31

[66] James 4:13-14

[67] Ibid

This chapter contains beneficial information for almost anyone, but it is not intended for novices or those who ignore the law of God as a way of life. Understanding this chapter's scholarly information and biblical teaching requires critical thinking, an open mind, spiritual maturity, and acceptance of God's word, essential to navigating life's challenges. Although significant efforts were made to sanitize the content of this chapter, some may still find it challenging in a Christian context. A symphony of biblical exegesis and medical and psychological science are used throughout the chapter, including language conventionally used in these disciplines.

— APOLLOS I

10

The Liquid Handcuff

The Snare and Sin of Solitary Pleasure

It was a beautiful spring day in the mile-high city.... blue skies, a warm sun, and the persistent wind dance set the tenor. After getting her family up and out the door, Rosetta embraces the day by running errands. Driving down Parker Rd., she opens the sunroof of her Mercedes to capture the spring breeze. As her hair flutters in the wind, the soft sound of contemporary jazz music thumbs in the background. Lost in thought now, Rosetta's mind slips back to an astonishing and compelling conversation she had with a girlfriend a few days ago.

Her friend had disclosed a recent experience with solitary pleasure. Rosetta reports that her friend raved about the frequency and intensity of the experience. "The experience is exhilarating, she says.... My husband does not know." - Author's File.

As Rosetta (a Christian) narrates the conversation in her head, it bewilders her because where she comes from, that kind of experience is inappropriate outside the context of marriage. Although the revelation stuns her, she is both confused and curious. She reaches her destination, closes the sunroof, and shuts off the engine. Sitting in that moment of silence, she begins to think and asks herself,

> "I wonder... what would happen if I tried it?? How different is it? What makes it irresistible? I am unsure if I want to do anything, but as I listen to her, the experience seems mind-blowing! I don't know; it does not seem right. But... gosh, she is so hyped over it... almost crazed, like... out of control in a way... I'm not sure if I like anything having that kind of control over me or my body... My husband and I are fine; maybe I should stay away from that... wow, don't know," - Author's File.

Historical Perceptions of Christianity Regarding Sexuality and Sexual Behavior

The notion that intercourse is one of the most powerful human experiences is likely undisputed. Irrespective of how humanity profligates and denigrates the individual experience, it is ordained by God as something exclusive, beautiful, and aimed at championing His agenda for life and marriage. In a Psychosocial context, this idea contradicts the narrative produced by today's public square and various theological frameworks, in which the discourse and commentary about intercourse and sexuality lead one to believe that man authored the experience; it is accessible to all and regulated by society at large.

The term psychosocial shows the intricate union between psychological factors and social conditioning. It is one of the paramount forces that influence and shape sexual attitudes and behaviors.[1] Sitcoms, soaps, reality TV, the "big screen," and today's music feature various forms of casual intercourse and present solitary pleasure and pornography as a standardized part of sexual development.[2] In addition, ideology suggesting more casual intercourse (if approached respectfully and exercised with minimal risks to others) "could be morally inferior but not sinful..." [3] is a notion that disregards God's teaching about intimate behavior and the context in which these behaviors should play out.[4] This proposal is complicit in the standardization of casual intercourse to a (perceived) better end.

The normalization of intercourse by any means, in any context with any person, creates a paradigm shift reconstituting society's attitude about sexual beliefs and practices. What many considered sinful, deviant, taboo, or inappropriate is now mainstream and approached with the question, why not? Some argue that sexual liberty is a significant part of the evolutionary process of community development and so is in concert with how society functions. Sociologists suggest that our communities and groups shape acceptable behavior and the rules we live by, determining what is deviant and what is not. It is a relative notion constructed by values, beliefs, and norms defined by groups and subcultures. Clinard & Meier (2008) states

> "...social groups create deviance by making the rules whose infraction creates deviance."[5]

Deviance results from violating norms, beliefs, and rules determined by society or subcultures. This definition is fluid and presents the attitudes and values of groups as the catalyst for norms they observe and sanctions imposed for violating these norms. In this writing, deviance is a departure from what is expected as defined biblically and socially.

However, there are differences within groups. Twenty-three-year-old, free-thinking college students attending classes on sexuality tout that the intercourse experience from solitary pleasure is "mind-blowing." They believe the practice is something to which it entitles them and that no one can deny such pleasure. The students are part of a larger, diversified group or community whose values and norms they find antiquated and hegemonic. In addition, the steep rise of others who not only hold the same ideology but indulge in such activity gives belief and acceptance and standardizes their behavior, which is not spiritually or theologically driven but socially constructed.

Some of the tenets of progressive theology hold that scripture is void of "definitive normative sexuality and intimate behavior" and that "there is no one universal binding form of intimate relationship or activity for all humans." In addition, they suggest that Christianity "does not and should not have one specific interpretative framework for sexuality"[6] and "the suggestion heterosexual attraction is normal, and the perceived perversion of homosexual attraction is unproven."[7]

In addition, they suggest that Christianity is "contaminated" by hegemony[8], is misogynistic, and is driven by patriarchal systems aimed at controlling others by promoting slavery, rape, and oppression.[9, 10]

These believe Christianity and the inherent teachings constituting it are insolvent and, in effect, incapable of being the sole source that governs humanity, including intimate behavior. Their suggestion that men contaminate Christianity (faith or religion predicated on the teachings of Jesus Christ as the Son of God and subsequent beliefs and practices), averting its power and goal, is a nonsensical conclusion. Contamination suggests that the substance (in this case, the word of God and principles of life derived from it) is polluted or poisoned and, therefore, can no longer perform its original task, which renders it inconsequential. Such distorted thinking is an insult to God and portrays Him as unjust and weak in His theocratic governance. It suggests He cannot preserve the purity and power of His truth, by which the world is judged.[11] The Apostle Paul's charge to Timothy and the Romans regarding the word of God is diametrical to this conclusion.

Paul states:

> *"All Scripture is inspired by God and profitable for doctrine, reproof, correction, and instruction in righteousness..."*[12] *"For whatever was written in*

earlier times was written for our instruction, so through perseverance and the encouragement of the Scriptures we might have hope."[13]

In addition, the Apostle Peter states:

"But know this first, that no prophecy of Scripture is a matter of one's own interpretation, for no prophecy was ever made by an act of human will, but men moved by the Holy Spirit spoke from God."[14]

In addition, it brands God as dishonest and questions His providence,[15] the perpetual act of preserving and governing creation, and His absolute superiority. [16] He can control the universe, the world, the affairs of nations, the life and destiny of men, and protect His people if he desires.[17] So, for God to state He has or will give us everything we need for life and godliness, but allowing elite men's fallacious acts to obscure these provisions renders Him unjust and incapable of preserving the tentacles of successful living and salvation.

This does not mean people do not manipulate and orchestrate Scripture for their agenda, nor does it dismiss that during the early republic, there were several attempts and agencies aimed at policing intercourse in society. [18] Throughout the annals of history, elite men have invested significant interest and energy in controlling vulnerable populations, i.e., first-century Romans developed intimate practices and narratives that gave more intimate freedom to "freeborn males" than their female counterparts, effectively preventing women's intimate activities. Opposition to such practices still saw intercourse as something that citizens should not pursue for mere pleasure.[19] Faith and religion have served as a conduit to this end, a conclusion tainted by the fraudulent use of religion and moral values to control society and women. But these facts do not upend biblical principles or the fact they originate from God. The sins, incompetence, and lack of morality of elite men do not nullify the principles upon which Christianity rests.

In the effort to evade hegemony and its contamination, many begin to reject the Christian rule over intimate behavior. Women saw such authority as a medium for cloaking the violations of white males and their perceived privileges. However, this freedom would lead to distancing believers from the God factor pertinent to sexuality. The Bible (if accepted as the Word of God) is and should be our natural law.[20] As such, it becomes the framework around which our lives and communities develop. We are conditioned to see natural law as something other than God's word. In her argument regarding the social construction of sexuality, Sands et al. (2000) state,

> "A natural law approach to sexuality is redeemable within a critical constructionist framework, but only with the sacrifice of the physicalism and the addition of a great deal of complex internal dialectic. One great advantage of a natural law approach is that it gives a theological basis for using the sciences as a central resource for constructing Christian sexual ethics, for biological and social science have become the primary methods for discerning divine intentions within an evolving, dynamic creation."[21]

Society lives at a different intersection when determining who should govern behavior. Individualism encroaches upon natural law, rendering it almost obsolete. Modern society's current construct condemns the notion of a standardized religious order and invites everyone to approach life from their own perspective. It inspires individuals to be who they choose to be in every situation.

Waskul (2003) states that:

> "In the highly individualistic culture of contemporary Western society, individuals are socialized to have a unique, unitary, paramount self. In other words, a

> personality, core, and stable set of personal characteristics are carried with them from place to place and situation to situation as a constant referent to who they are.[22]

Eastern societies encourage and expect their people to model beliefs and practices consistent with their way of life, family, faith, and principles regarding sexuality. When Easterners invoke too much individuality, their society views such behavior as rebellious and converting to Western ideology. Most often, Easterners who abandon all or part of their cultural heritage do so through individualism and not collective measures. However, this concept is changing as more Easterners (as a group) integrate and encourage individuality in their philosophical approach to life.

Society's paradigm for sexuality and intimate behavior suggests it (society) is the primary medium for determining normative intimate activity. People search the Internet and consult friends, sexologists, therapists, and other human service professionals for directives about intimate identity and practice.

Notably absent from this list are faith and religion, which some individualists see as an integral part of collective control, which they reject as the sole medium for governing life. Even Christians do not always solicit God (through meditation, prayer, and biblical study) or seek spiritual counsel (from those who legitimately called or held themselves out as pastors, ministers, or spiritual leaders) for directives about their intimate lives. This may be due (in part) to the notion that some view faith and organized religion as control mechanisms aimed at minimizing pleasure and controlling the desires of women, which is true in many colonized countries.[23]

In addition, too many reports of clergy members involved in sex scandals and inappropriate behaviors stifle trust in their ability to aid congregants and the community to navigate these rugged terrains, i.e., on June 29, 2017, CNN Breaking News features a high-ranking Catholic Church official charged with sexual assault in Australia.[24] Today, people seek alternative resources to guide them in these areas. Contemporary socialization, mental health professionals, and professors propagate that permitting oneself to explore sexuality, identity, curiosity, and desire is necessary for healthy erotic development, a notion constructed by man, not God.

People view the celebration of the individual (which is essential) as the premise for solutions to the most challenging questions about life in our time. Individualism demands that each person be free to resolve delicate dilemmas and reject mandates forged by perceived collective control. Although there is pressure and a tendency to individualism, people capitulate to sexual behaviors defined by the society in which they live.

Gudorf (2000) states:

> "As individuals, we make free intimate decisions, but we do so within a social nexus that has shaped our understanding of ourselves, others, and human sexuality itself, and those decisions we make involve social-sexual institutions such as marriage, heterosexual and homosexual cohabitation, and celibate religious communities."[25]

However, vast differences between groups obscure consensus about acceptable intimate behavior, creating tension between individualism and collective control. They view no consensus as permission to choreograph solitary solutions to intimate challenges and interests, which more often jettison God's call for exclusive, standardized, intimate behavior among Christians.

As Creator, the law of God is for humanity, in the sense that God wills everyone to experience salvation through Jesus Christ. [26] This divine order is exponential for those surrendering their lives to Him through Christ and who, by doing so, acknowledge man's fallen state and need for atonement. However, too many people of God are sheepish about enacting quantities of God's law that society views as old-fashioned, hegemonic, or misogynistic. Today, any faith that appears to micro-govern life is seen as unpopular, antiquated, politically incorrect, and theologically uninformed. There is a revolt among those seeking to modernize faith and religion. Their repudiation of collective control misguides and drives their fear of moral and ideological patriarchalism. [27] Mark Kann (2013), writing about moral patriarchalism, notes:

> "Moral patriarchalism was based on the premise that political authority belonged to the original generation of fathers beginning with the biblical Adam."[28]

In response to the ever-increasing control of intimate behavior, individuals and groups position themselves as far left from such authority as possible, creating an entirely different issue to confront and resolve. Sands et al. (2000) states:

> "The increasing resistance of white male hegemony contributes to society's pendulum from roles defined by them, including intimate roles. In attacking the legitimacy of traditional forms of patriarchal control,

> challenger groups also attacked the sacredness of the patriarchal, biblically legitimated ethic that had validated the elites. The sexual double standard, in which Christian sexual rules were normative for all subjugated groups but under which (white) male violations were largely invisible, was an early target."[29]

Christianity's attempt to ensure religious liberty has forced faith to extreme opposites, foraging concepts and conclusions that converse to and contradict God's holy mandate. However, this modern push to individualism makes this position seem normal, at least from a societal perspective. There is constant gravity between the faith in which the Christian seeks to live and the world around them.

There is ongoing pressure to assimilate into the world, which influences daily decision-making. Although scripture highlights requisites for differentiation between those who follow God and those who do not,[30] people of faith align their faith practice with the expectations of the world around them. For some, the view of peers as too different or antiquated in their approach to life is problematic. For example, when people of faith suggest that intercourse should be an exclusive act between a man and woman in the bonds of holy matrimony, others within their work, community, and sometimes their family see such a position as an old-fashioned thought process in today's environment.

People of faith who are serious about their walk with God and care about their standing in the community embrace a delicate dance to balance principles of faith with expectations of the surrounding environment. Sure, perhaps we should not concern ourselves with the world's view, which sounds good and is correct, but the power of influence between opposing groups is real and plays out in people's decision-making. What we think about and how we practice intercourse are chief among the plethora of issues caught up in the tug-of-war between faith and society.

The Presenting Issue

Solitary pleasure (aka, masturbation, onanism, or self-stimulation) is of utmost concern and exigent for some people of faith, both married and single (meaning those never married and divorcees). This chapter presents solitary pleasure and self-stimulation interchangeably. Solitary pleasure or self-stimulation is self-explanatory. However, masturbation (manipulating or stimulating one's self for pleasure) can happen in solitary or can involve another person, i.e., a husband or wife. Most often, solitary pleasure occurs in solitude, which is most people's view of the

practice. R. E. Butman (1985) states: "Solitary pleasure (also called autoeroticism) is any self-stimulation that produces erotic arousal.[31] The practice of solitary pleasure dishonors God as Creator and moves practitioners out of His will.
In addition, it creates a dynamic in singleness and marriage that makes relationships and intimacy challenging for many. But first, let's educate ourselves on the history of the practice in humanity.

History of Solitary Pleasure

Historical narratives about solitary pleasure are critical to understanding the context and details of this chapter. Irrespective of the current hypersexual era, the concept and practice of solitary pleasure is not a 21st-century phenomenon. The history of solitary pleasure dates back thousands of years across various cultures and Greek Mythology. Driel (2012) notes that the oldest known dildo, 30,000 years old, was found in Germany, and someone discovered another one dating back to 4,000 BC in Pakistan.[32] Religious Tolerance's website (2005) [33] lists references to solitary pleasure between the first and twentieth centuries. Although inconclusive, the site suggests that solitary pleasure may have originated among the Romans. One etymological view holds that the word derives from compound words, which include the Latin term "stuprare", which meant "to defile, commit a sexual wrong against."[34] Another Latin connotation suggests that the origin stems from compound words meaning masculinity and to move violently.[35] There are not many references to solitary pleasure in Roman literature.[36] However, the few references that exist place the practice within Roman culture.[37] Most of the historical data on self-stimulation places the behavior in negative contexts, which include moral issues and several physical or mental problems. Plato presents solitary pleasure in his writing during the fourth century BC (427-347) and in Hippocrates' work (460-375 BC), who believed solitary pleasure caused tuberculosis of the spine and that ejaculation weakens the body.[38]

The ambiance in the late 1500s was such that solitary pleasure was condemned. The practice of faith and theology during this era provided insights into the mind and behavior of the community it served. The church propagated teachings that denounced illicit intimate behaviors, which included solitary pleasure.

This wasn't easy because various religions and faith communities struggled to reach a consensus on intimate behavior. However, this was not a license for churches, denominations, and other faith communities today to ingratiate the often misguided desires of the masses and substitute God's demands by altering or relaxing intimate behavioral expectations.

Just as the divine call to holy standardized living is not a license for slavery or control and judgment over individuals and groups, human agency does not translate into liberty cart blanched. The tension between these opposing sides causes each of them to react in ways counterintuitive to Divine expectations.

Those who claim they are living for God can be rigid and judgmental toward others, and the opposing group lives for God with an anything-goes approach to faith and religion. Today's churches change and adapt to the bruised ego and emotions of the masses to increase the number of souls in the pews on Sunday. The face of the church revolutionizes into something unrecognizable scripturally. Any attempt to repackage God and salvation to accommodate the masses will lead to chaos and risk Divine repudiation.

God created humans as free moral agents. However, there is an ever-pressing expectation for man to hear and respond to the invitation to return to holiness and restore the human-divine relationship lost through sin in the Garden of Eden. As Lord of lords, King of kings, and the Sovereign Creator, God determines what life should look like concerning Him and extends perquisites for those willing to surrender their lives to Him through Jesus Christ. In this context, the commandments of God are a means of structure designed to restrain the agent and his or her decisions that defile and broaden the chasm between the creature and his Creator, i.e., although Adam and Eve were at liberty to live in Eden and eat, God implemented a rule (you shall not eat of the tree that is in the midst of the garden[39]) preserving purity of fellowship and harmony they experience with Him. God knew and, therefore, warned them that disobeying this rule would usher unfathomable consequences for them, their relationship with Him, and humanity at large. However, through satanic swagger and good-ole human gullibility, they determined that God did not know what He was talking about and that nothing adverse would happen should they eat. But we now know how the story ends.

Balancing divine expectations and human reality has been the ultimate challenge for faith and religion throughout the annals of history. The church (nor the society in which she operates) does not create the Law of God but teaches, leads, and assists congregants and the community in interpreting and applying holy mandates to human situations and everyday living. Intercourse is among the most significant dynamics of human life and behavior. It is so substantial in the eyes of God that two of the Ten Commandments fall into the parameter of intimate behavior.[40] In addition, there is a host of scriptures or commandments regulating intimate behavior. Culture, ethnicity, and other differences are factors or variables under consideration here.

However, religious diversity and historical change are not acquiescence to changing God's expectations regarding intimate behavior. If we understand God, He did not start conversations about salvation and holy living for man to finish. He did not determine or proclaim the need for salvation and behavioral adjustments, leaving it to humans to orchestrate. If this is our thinking and approach, we miss the mark. The contrasts and variations in faith and religion are the by-product of cultural influence and human ingenuity, not divine will and reasoning.

As time progressed, members of the clergy, medical professionals, philosophers, and other influential people weighed in on the polarizing subject, i.e., in 1595, Franciscan Benedicti, writing about solitary pleasure, states:

> *"Whoever engages in voluntary pollution outside of marriage, termed molalities by the theologians, sins against the natural order... Voluntary pollution procured while awake, either by touching, cogitation and delectation, locution or conversation with women*

> *or men, by reading immodest books, or by whatever other means, is a mortal sin."*[41]

In 1653, Pieter van Foreest published a medical compendium, which included information about hysteria, a common medical issue ascribed to women during that period. He characterized it as untamable emotions, irritability, and insomnia and ascribed it to women experiencing sexual frustration. The word hysteria originates from Greek and refers to the woman's uterus, unfairly making the disorder a female issue. [42] Erotic massages by male physicians became a treatment modality for the disorder. In addition, physicians during this period utilized the same procedure for widows, religious females, and young people as a means of chastity. Doctors did not recommend the service for young females, public women, and married women.[43] Samuel-Auguste Tissot (1728-1797), a Swiss doctor and writer of a six-volume work on mental disease, regarded solitary pleasure as criminal and noted a laundry list of physical ailments. He believed desensitizing nerve endings near the top of the male anatomy was an adequate medical response. He held that solitary pleasure includes intimate fantasy, which could cause a person's brain to shrivel up.[44] Tissot saw sperm as an exceptional, valuable liquid that should not be wasted to illicit intimate desire through solitary pleasure. Time would render some of Tissot's findings and position exaggerated and even outlandish. However, Tissot's positions profoundly influenced the movement against self-stimulation, which included persuading clergy and other professionals alike.

Count de Mirabeau (1749-1791) did not buy into the narrative concerning solitary pleasure but believed in the concept of toxicological issues borne out of unreleased sperm. He viewed self-stimulation as permissible. In the early 1800s, there was a powerful, fear-driven revolt against the practice of solitary pleasure among the French. Since the medical community saw self-stimulation as the origin of various illnesses, they enacted multiple efforts to curb the activity. The medical community, all of whom were male, floated the concept of penile amputation as an antidote to the issue. However, unwilling to convince themselves and the community that such an act was suitable, they turned to the female, who, in their mind, was an easy target.

Renowned surgeon and gynecologist Isaac Baker Brown first introduced cauterization as a treatment for self-stimulation. Given that there were those calling for clitoridectomy (complete removal of the clitoris), some physicians saw cauterization as a less harsh form of treatment. However, this was a matter of opinion. They often performed cauterization with red-hot iron, which desensitized the female anatomy and led to its removal.[45] It is a practice that is barbaric and inhumane in any society. The practice continued until 1905, at which time Sigmund Freud (a world-renowned psychoanalyst), in his Three Essays on the Theory of Sexuality, found the mutilation of women's bodies unconscionable.[46] As expected, the revolt against solitary pleasure included religious communities, i.e., the Catholic Church held that self-stimulation was nothing but disordered pleasure sought outside the normal process of intimate pleasure and antagonistic to procreation.[47] The Churches of Christ and other protestant churches throughout recent centuries have long held that any intercourse outside of marriage is sinful, even within marriages the church deemed illegitimate. Various theologians have contributed their studies and thoughts on the topic throughout the centuries. Thomas Aquinas (1225-1274) believed solitary pleasure was a crime and worse than having intercourse with one's mother.[48] In 1842, J. C. Debreyne, a Dutch monk, called for the removal of the clitoris for women who practiced solitary pleasure, arguing that the clitoris was not involved in procreation.[49]

Muslim theologians (contemporary and earlier) disagree on whether self-stimulation is a sin or (zina) in all circumstances. Although condemned, some held that it is permissive if it avoids fornication or adultery, which is the clandestine belief and practice of some members of the faith community. [50] In other circumstances, such as long-term isolation or to avoid homosexuality self-stimulation, the Koranic school of thought permits such practices.[51]

Taoism [52] sees self-stimulation as a loveless act without human connection and harmony of yin and yang. They agree with Tissot in their view that male sperm is a vital liquid that men should not waste through solitary pleasure.[53] Today's Asian cultures still believe sperm is a special liquid that should not be lost at all. Driel (2012) notes that Indian doctors see a significant number of men with Dhat Syndrome. The Indian Journal of Psychiatry defines Dhat Syndrome as related to semen loss and "is a culture-bound syndrome seen in the natives of the Indian subcontinent."[54] Those experiencing the issue are ridden with guilt and shame as they identify the problem with excessive solitary pleasure. [55] Many other theologians, philosophers, and scientists were pro and against self-stimulation—faith communities of old gravitated to science and research highlighting self-stimulation's dangers. Religious leaders believed medical science during this period made it easier to persuade the community and congregants not to engage or to abandon the behavior if such was the case.

However, the annals of faith and religion and the church's current methodological approach to this issue draw sharp criticism among non-religious people, modern philosophers, feminists, and Christians or believers who hold an ultra-liberal view about faith and God. Often, their view supports private interpretation and application of scripture if they accept scripture as the premise and guide for human intimate behavior. Contrary to the contemporary theology of feminists and liberal or progressive theologians, the Bible is, in fact, a direct guide for human behavior. God intended His Word and Law to be the basis upon which all others construct and enact.[56]

Evoking the Holy Bible as a guide for sexuality does not at all suggest that solitary pleasure is antiquated or limited to the popular concept, which suggests it is a "Western Obsession." The fact is that self-stimulation is a relevant issue and pervasive across various cultures and religions. The revolutionary advent of the Internet and the multiple social media platforms it supports are modern venues through which pornography, illicit intimate behavior, and solitary pleasure are accessible. One platform boasts over 2 billion users and another over 1 billion users spanning the globe.[57]

It is no surprise to find people of various ages, ethnic backgrounds, and religions engaged in such acts. From the senior citizen to the teenager behind their bedroom door, self-stimulation has become the antidote to loneliness and intimate desire. The Internet solidifies that solitary pleasure lives in almost every culture, from Moscow to Hong Kong to Papua New Guinea to Madagascar to Argentina to Mexico, U.S. and Canada to Greenland and Sweden.

As such, it has found its way into profoundly religious and conservative cultures. As a conservative culture with profound religious values manifest through Christianity, Islam, and Hinduism, India is a paradoxical phenomenon. Coveting "love marriage" is common, and they hold the efficacy of family in high regard. The culture demands and expects intimate purity of maidens pursuing matrimony and faithfulness thereafter. But the phantom of anxious eroticism veiled by ongoing mantras of chastity, faith, and devotion glimmers through erotic dance and movies. In a country with over a billion citizens, it promotes eroticism as a cultural seeking expression beyond the confines of marriage.

In this context, India, as a conservative society, does not differ from other places. The Kamasutra and modern

YouTube channels unveil hidden intimate behavior that includes self-stimulation. Vatsl Seth Cast—Ankur Sharma and Prashant Khandelwal Chief AD—Sandeep produces an Indian YouTube channel that features what they dub as "most interesting video content."

On April 6, 2016, the group published a video clip of one of their "entertainment hosts" conducting random interviews of women on the streets of India about self-stimulation. The host (a female) begins the interview and video by acknowledging that "Indian girls are very conservative." Then she asks if they engaged in solitary pleasure and how common it is. Those taking part in the interview (on camera at least) acknowledged that "solitary pleasure among Indian girls is very common, but no one talks about it, not even with their best friends and certainly not with family."[58] It is worth noting here that the phrase "Indian girls" is not limited to teenagers but includes all Indian females. The video interview continues by asking, "What would urge a girl to participate in solitary pleasure?"

Their answers ranged from "anything... if something arouses her, do it" to "lack of boyfriend," "sexual desire," "a nice guy, hot guy," and "horniness." When asked how often they think Indian women participated in solitary pleasure, their answers ranged from once a week to every day, with each act

lasting 20 to 30 minutes. Interviewees stated that pornography, intercourse toys, and images or fantasies of individuals of interest play a role in solitary pleasure.
They conclude that "it is not a sin" and that "everybody is doing it." Three of the participants said, "If an Indian girl says she's not masturbating, she is lying!" While that assessment is likely overly broad and not applicable to everyone in that culture, their response accentuates that in this conservative culture, behind their veil of chastity lies pervasive intimate desire and behavior as is in many other places.

An Indian woman (identifying as an unmarried Hindu) takes part in a U.S. court-ordered forensic-mental health treatment for driving under the influence of alcohol, aka DUI. The initial process for treatment requires that she take part in a clinical intake, which includes an interview and completing forms aimed at garnering information regarding all aspects of a client's background and current issues. Questionnaires used during clinical intake processes include a survey of the client's sexuality and behavior. As she reaches this section of the form, she pauses and asks, "Is this information necessary?" the therapist answers, "Yes." Complying with the therapeutic process, she completes this section of the form in which she discloses that she has solitary pleasures and has had intimate intercourse with twelve men over twelve months. Given her faith and culture, are the answers to these questions unusual, or are they?

Some may wonder why or how this information helps the therapist offer treatment specific to DUI in this case. Information derived from clinical intakes assists mental health and human service professionals in assessing relevant issues and informs decision-making about classification, treatment programs, and other therapeutic recommendations. In addition, such information helps decide causation and correlation, as most impaired functioning manifests or influences psychologically, biologically, and socially/culturally. A person's sexuality and behavior offer clues to their inner workings or issues, whether past or present. For instance, consider a 36-year-old Caucasian American in treatment for the same reasons as the Indian Hindu. The American identifies as an unmarried Christian. Taking part in the same intake process and answering the same questions as the Indian, she discloses that she has not had intercourse in seven years and does not identify her faith as the reason for not having intimate intercourse. Given that she identifies as a Christian, one may surmise that her abstinence is praiseworthy.

However, given other issues revealed on the form, pertinent variables such as the American culture (which is highly sexually charged), her abstinence raises additional questions regarding deeper issues. True to order, she discloses that she is a victim of sexual and physical abuse and exhibits characteristics consistent with impaired cognition. Regardless of the two women's cultural differences, without these details, it would obscure additional underlying issues, which, undetected, may minimize the internalization of their current treatment protocol, increasing the likelihood of recidivism or reoffending.

While India's sexual behavior seems clandestine, America and other places remain unashamedly overt. Mona Chalabi, a British data journalist, featured an article in the Times of India Life in which she highlights research regarding how often men and women have solitary pleasure. Indiana University's National Survey of Sexual Health and Behavior conducted the study, in which (NSSHB analyzed the frequency of solitary pleasure according to age. According to the article, "the NSSHB collected data from 5,865 Americans between the ages of 14 and 94 between March and May 2009."[59]

Their findings suggest men still have more sexual pleasure than women. "Only 7.9 percent of women between the ages of 25 and 29 have solitary pleasure two to three times a week whereas 23.4 percent of men do." According to the National Survey of Sexual Behavior, 84% of women aged 25-29 practice solitary pleasure.[60]

Chalabi notes "that women are less likely to try solitary pleasure," which shows those who do are that much more extraordinary.[61] However, given that the data collected in this study features Americans, it is unclear if Chalabi includes other global citizens in her analysis or summary. Regardless, a persistent taboo against women pleasuring themselves in contrast to their male counterparts still exists. Feminists and other groups see the taboo as another form of male dominance and control of women's intimate desires.

It is likely to have more discussion and studies about women engaged in solitary pleasure than men. Irrespective of the motivation for the taboo, women are increasingly involved in self-stimulation for intimate pleasure but fall short of men in terms of number and frequency.

In another case, (for example) a Caucasian evangelical Christian wife is in therapy for family issues. She identifies two presenting problems: 1) the revelation that her son is homosexual and 2) marital problems derived from the intimate desire and behavior of her and her husband.

The latter is relevant to this current discussion. She reports being "uncomfortable" with her husband's interactions with his daughter (her step-daughter).

> "He allows her to sit on his lap, and when she gets up, he is aroused. He claims it is normal. I'm afraid I have to disagree, and she should not be sitting in his lap; she is a 13-year-old now. But I am a step-mom with little power in this case. He took her on a trip and rented a room with one bed, meaning she had to sleep in the same bed with him. He says no foul here... I say it is inappropriate. Making matters worse, he is trying to make me look like a little girl, which you can imagine grosses me out!! This stuff has gone on for a few weeks now. I am turned off towards him. I have asked him to leave... until we figure out what to do.
>
> He needs help, or I will get a divorce.... And to add fuel to this fire, I am dying to have intercourse... the cravings are mounting; I need a resolution... and I need it fast! I don't know what to do. I don't want to cheat... I will not cheat. I feel trapped. But still don't want to be with him right now." –Author's file.

A person does not need a PhD to see that the issues paralyzing and suffocating this family are significant, complex, and multiphasic. To offer better insight into the wife's narrative, other background information is feasible, i.e., to save the marriage, the husband takes part in a psychosexual evaluation, a therapeutic measurement of an individual's sexual development, history, interests, sexual adjustment, and risk levels. The results suggest that the husband harbors inappropriate intimate tendencies, which require treatment. In addition, it legitimizes the wife's concerns and frustration.

Besides the husband's issues, the wife has an eight-year history as a victim of sexual abuse during her childhood. She has a rapacious sexual appetite, which she attempts to govern through marriage. It is not uncommon for those who have suffered extended sexual abuse in childhood to emerge in adulthood as "hyper-sexualized or sexually reactive." During one session, the wife discloses that she and her husband have intercourse 7 to 10 times during weekends.

The current issues between her and her husband threaten the life of the marriage, which is also the conduit for her sexual appetite. This creates extraordinary levels of stress on top of exceedingly tricky issues in her family. As her need for intercourse reaches critical mass, the subject of solitary pleasure surfaces as a temporary antidote to her situation. She says, "I have been thinking about doing it, but I'm unsure. I've thought about allowing him to come back home, but I can't deal with him the way he is. Don't know what to do!" At some juncture between sessions, she convinces herself to try self-stimulation. Returning to the session and responding to the therapist's inquiry, she states, "Oh my gosh, I don't need a man!" While that might garner praise from feminists or proponents of solitary pleasure, it is diametrical to what God codifies in Scripture.

What is interesting about solitary pleasure among people of faith is the injudicious notion it is permissible in abstinence, less sinful if practiced in singleness while waiting to find Mr. or Mrs. Right, and authorized if practiced in avoiding adultery. This appears more common with females than males. If single men are having intercourse, it is more likely with a person than in solitary, although research suggests men have more sexual pleasure than women. It is expected that some men not only seek women for pleasure but also solitary pleasure.

Give a man a choice between intercourse with a person and solitary pleasure; intercourse is more likely chosen.

The single Christian female takes a different approach, especially some African Americans who are often single. This is likely better understood using the attachment theory model,[62] which (Bowlby, as stated in Benner, 1985) explains as "the propensity of human beings to develop strong affectional bonds with significant others and to experience emotional distress when those ties are disrupted."[63] For this population, God is the substitute affectional male relationship. Many times, and unbeknown to them, there is an erotic spiritual relationship between them and God. He becomes the object of their attachment. This concept is not new. Plenty of authors and scholars have written and researched the idea. Rowatt and Kirkpatrick (2002) states

> "Research has shown that such individuals correlate inversely with loneliness, depression, and similar constructs."[64]

They further explain by suggesting that people with attachment issues "compensate for insecure relationships by becoming more religious."[65] In addition, these are more passionate about their faith and tout independence from male affection (because of their relationship with God) but constantly seek the male affection they claim they can live without. Granquist and Hagekull (as stated in Rowatt and Kirkpatrick, 2002) states,

> "Individuals who do not have a current love relationship partner, compared with individuals who do, were found to be more religiously active, to perceive a more personal relationship with God, and

> to experience a religiosity that is based on affect regulation."[66]

Among these are those (while holding allegiance to God) who use self-stimulation to reconcile sexual frustration. They convince themselves that their behavior is acceptable if their intimate experience does not involve another human being and is enacted in solitary. These see solitary pleasure as something better hidden and less sinful than intercourse with different individuals. Two factors contribute to this kind of rationale: 1) the erroneous perception and approach to solitary pleasure as a nonsexual act or intimate behavior that differs from that which Scripture teaches and regulates; 2) the fact they conduct it in solitude, therefore likely hidden from others. However, the truth is that in this context, solitary does not sanction or give permission. Solitary creates a pseudo-perception that the behavior is acceptable in singleness or during abstinence.

For example, a divorced Christian woman with two teenage children decides that following the divorce, she and her children should wear 'chastity rings" as a sign of abstinence and devotion to God. She wore the ring staunchly and demanded that her children keep theirs on. The mother scolded her children for any signs of being intimately active.

But her routine practice of solitary pleasure is largely hidden. Her experience emboldens her ability to be "chaste," at least her version of virtue. -Author's file

While taking part in a survey of over 4000 people on social media regarding solitary pleasure, a single Christian female, divorced for almost ten years, identifies herself as "a queen, diva, and a warrior waiting for the right person..." She is vocal on social media about her faith and commitment to God in singleness. However, the hidden power driving her singleness is not what most expect. She uses solitary pleasure to combat "humanness" while searching for Mr. Right. -Author's file

The problem with solitary pleasure for people of faith in singleness rests with the cognitive approach or mental disposition about the act in this context. Participants see and treat the act as if it is not intercourse because it is practiced in solitary. Neighbors do not see people leaving their homes; there isn't a revolving door of guys or girls coming in and out. They attend worship and bible study alone or with their children, skirting curiosity and questions about whether they are sexually active. People in their immediate community see them as chaste and devoted to God and His church. This reinforces their faulty disposition. In their minds, they are not violating Scripture because they are not having intercourse; they do not offend others by their behavior because it is practiced in solitary. As advocates of godliness, they emphatically reject anyone seeking intimate relations or companionship that includes intimate activity, which on the surface is emblematic of devotion and piety.

Experiencing intimate satisfaction in solitude, they become more selective or meticulous about the timing and person with whom they enter a relationship. Because they can satisfy themselves intimately, there is no rush to find Mr. or Mrs. Right. A checklist comprises evidence of a godly character, criminal background, credit history, financial status, current residence, and attractiveness as defining measures or qualifiers for entering an intimate relationship. This process is more prominent in women than in men. There is nothing wrong with this process; it's helpful as a disqualifier and information that may explain a person and increase the likelihood of success in a relationship.

However, theoretically, if we extract solitary pleasure from the equation, these are less likely to remain single for as long as some do. Given they differentiate solitary pleasure from fornication as defined by Scripture, they see no wrong or harm. These see the act as something that falls outside of divine regulation. Their entire approach to this topic and issue is the by-product of self-deception. Deception is an interesting word in both Latin and Greek. The early 15th century depicts the Latin version of the word as "deception, an act of misleading." The noun form defines the word as "ensnare, beguile." [67] One "ensnared by error." [68]

The Greek word "planao" is most often translated deceive in New Testament writing. It indicates causing one to stray or to be led astray; "lead away from the right way; to roam." [69] It is one thing to be the victim of deception or one who deceives. But self-deception is a different nexus of issues, more problematic and challenging to neutralize. The origin of self-deception complicates rehabilitation.

It comprises two significant factors. The first rests in one's inefficacy to understand God's core principles and attributes and the relationship codified by them. Some sins, evil, and errors humans commit stem from erroneous attitudes toward God or misunderstanding who He is. This is one reason misunderstanding God is configured in the Adam Complex and placed in chapter one.

An improper approach and attitude toward God is the genesis of evil and failure. If we do not understand Him, we cannot appreciate or observe the expectations and directives He gives. We will fumble our approach and stagger in our walk or life before Him.

The second factor nestles in the notion that deception requires intrigue and bewitchment. Intrigue is the most critical component and the most dangerous. Too many people of faith do not appreciate that the embryo of sin begins within and not externally. For instance, James 1:14 notes that a person experiences temptation when the diseased condition of humanity intersects and conflates with attraction and projected outcome. The etymology of the word attraction shows that, as early as the 1400s, it reflected a medical action in which someone drew a diseased matter to the surface. [70] Temptation only works when there is something diseased or flawed within the individual or something to which a person is interested and attracted. Otherwise, temptation has no power. You cannot tempt a weight-challenged person with food they dislike or have no interest in. But when there is an attraction and interest an individual risk bewitchment, the process that seduces and spellbinds the person by the projected outcome of the act. When a person is bewitched, they will talk and counsel themselves into approving what God has denied and will enact what their faith or values describe as sinful or inappropriate.

But not every person living a single life (never married, divorced, or widowed) gravitates to or practices solitary pleasure, which is noteworthy.

Holy Scripture and Solitary Pleasure

The practice of solitary pleasure remains contentious in today's public square. The words "sex" or "intercourse" are not a part of any empirical data appearing in the Holy Mandate, but the idea and palpability of intercourse are apparent. Many theologians, clergy, and lay members have debated what God had in his mind during the induction of intercourse. Many believe (at least those in conservative cultures[71]) that intercourse is for procreation, and so humans should not indulge in the act for mere pleasure. Throughout the annals of history, this teaching was directed more toward women than men.

Genesis 1:27-28 predicates their argument. Here, God commands Adam and Eve, "... be fruitful and multiply and fill the earth..." a teaching or principle that has found its way into the fabric of various religions, cultures, fables, and traditions worldwide. Some religious people argue we are created in the image of God and after His likeness and that God is a Spirit and neither male nor female.

It is convoluted reasoning hinting that humans should not be intimate beings outside of procreation. Intimate desire is discouraged even within the context of marriage for this population.

However, this one-dimensional approach obscures the richness of the teaching in this passage. Although the text channels procreation, it is significant to note that God's call to be fruitful and multiply expands beyond quantity to include duplicating His image and likeness, enhancing the quality of the individual while honoring God as Creator.

The corporeal process and neurological response (presented in more detail later in this chapter) to the intimate experience indicates God's endorsement of the pleasure associated with the act when humans experience it within the milieu in which He designed it. Here is an example of why misunderstanding God leads to an erroneous conclusion in life and behavior and contributes to unnecessary struggles. Remember, God is the sovereign Creator and is a perfect being; everything He does is intentional and not the byproduct of process. Suppose intercourse between a male and female is only for procreation. In that case, there is no need to command and restrict the practice to the context of marriage, and the biological processes of intercourse are meaningless and unnecessary, which is clearer after this chapter considers the psychological and neurological aspects of intercourse. In this context, it debunks the concept that intercourse is solely about procreation. Procreation is only one part of the multifaceted purpose and process. Other passages corroborate this point, i.e., in I Corinthians 7:1-9 the Apostle Paul writes to address concerns about intercourse and marriage.

The Bible states:

> *"Now concerning the things about which you wrote, it is good for a man not to touch a woman. [2] But because of immoralities, each man is to have his own wife, and each woman is to have her own husband. [3] The husband must fulfill his duty to his wife, and likewise also the wife to her husband. [4] The wife does not have authority over her own body, but the husband does; and likewise, also the husband does not have authority over his own body, but the wife does. [5] Stop depriving one another, except by agreement for a time, so that you may devote yourselves to prayer, and come together again so that Satan will not tempt you because of your lack of self-control. [6] But this I say by way of concession, not of command, [7] I wish that all men were even as I myself am. However, each*

man has his own gift from God, one in this manner, and another in that. [8] but I say to the unmarried and to widows that it is good for them if they remain even as I. 9 but if they do not have self-control, let them marry; for it is better to marry than to burn with passion."[72]

Here, the bible sheds light on the ideal construct in which we should experience intimate desire and intercourse, the obligatory nature of intercourse that exists between spouses, and the spiritual danger of the inability to govern one's intimate desire. [73] At no point in this passage does Paul identify procreation as the sole purpose for intercourse.

Intimate desire is at the heart of questions raised by the Corinthians. In response, the Apostle reemphasizes marriage as the venue through which we reconcile intimate desires.

That God only approves of intercourse in a marriage between a man and woman is consistent throughout Scripture, which is apparent by condemnation leverage against those who practice intercourse outside of marriage. God abhors intercourse with relatives, animals, and other sordid forms of intimacy. [74] In addition, the Corinthian passage directs spouses to engage each other to avoid sexual temptation or the fallout from boiling intimate desire.

In this framework, the text suggests that spouses engage each other routinely, except where there is an agreement to abstain for personal and spiritual development. The passage advises single people who cannot govern their intimate desires that marriage is the conduit to gratify these urges.

> Note: "*But I say to the unmarried and widows that it is good for them to remain even as I. But if they do not have self-control, let them marry, for it is better to marry than to burn with passion.*" [75]

At no point is solitary pleasure solidified as a proper means to temper intimate wishes, period. There is a misguided perception dancing in the mind of some theologians and Christians, who postulate that the bible does not discuss solitary pleasure and that the absence of a direct discussion warrants individual liberty about the practice. As Brenner (1985) cited, Johnson states: "Since the Bible says nothing directly about solitary pleasure, it is difficult to take a dogmatic stand." [76] But He acknowledges that the act of self-stimulation is a "solitary activity" and short of what God intended and that the Bible places high significance on sexuality as an essential part of the marital relationship.

In addition, he notes that self-stimulation distracts from the wholeness codified through relationships. [77]

Some believe that the sin of Onan in Genesis 38: 1-10 was about self-stimulation. Others hold that God took his life because of disobedience as opposed to the act of solitary pleasure. An appropriate analysis of the text will show that this was not solitary pleasure, indicated by the phrase "he went into his brother's wife." This suggests intercourse long enough to climax. Onan extracted himself to allow his sperm to fall on the ground, avoiding impregnation.

This passage does not reflect self-stimulation, which does not support the erroneous notion and conclusion that the Bible does not address the issue. In addition, the passage in Ezekiel chapter 16 is inundated with intimate references as God delineates His problems with His people. We can interpret a reference to solitary pleasure or self-stimulation in this passage, which Driel (2012) suggests cannot be interpreted in any other way.[78]

The Bible states:

> 15 "But you trusted in your beauty and played the harlot because of your fame, and you poured out your harlotries on every passer-by who might be *willing*. 16 You took some of your clothes, made for yourself high places of various colors and played the

> harlot on them, which should never come about nor happen. [17] You also took your beautiful jewels *made* of My gold and of My silver, which I had given you, and made for yourself male images that you might play the harlot with them."[79]

The first response to this verse is likely that it is an allegory as if it has no significance as such and no reference to solitary pleasure. An allegory is an emblematic representation of truth about human experience and behavior. [80] In literature, it is a method of teaching aimed at simplifying truth by using real examples drawn from human conduct. It is a method God, Christ (as God the Son), and the Apostle Paul used. The two famous allegories are the one by Jesus about the wheat and the tares in Matthew 13:24-30, 36-43, and Paul about Hagar and Sarah, Ishmael and Isaac in Galatians 4:21-31.

In every biblical instance, the allegory used in a passage integrates truth. No example of something false or fictional is used in an allegory to convey a truth or Godly principle. This concept is genuine in the passage found in Ezekiel. The unanimity and covenant of marriage and the mandate for faithfulness and intimacy are analogous to our covenant relationship with God. His use of the term harlotry is polysemic[81] in that, on the one hand, it refers to fornication, intimate promiscuity, and illicit intimate intercourse.

In other instances, it refers to illegal contact between Israel and other nations and their gods. [82] The over-arching message in this context is that in the same way in which a wife is unfaithful to her husband by inappropriate intimate intercourse and solitary pleasure, Israel is unfaithful to God by pursuing other nations and their gods. This passage condemns intimate intercourse out of context and solitary pleasure.

Although the word solitary pleasure does not appear in Scripture, it addresses the components and processes involved in the act in various places in Scripture, including I Corinthians 7:1-9. What are the components and methods of solitary pleasure? To what end? That solitary pleasure or self-stimulation intercourse, including desire and fantasy or lust, is indisputable. The Bible discusses and condemns any of them outside of the marital relationship. Solitary pleasure, like most things, is the sum of its parts. If the components and dynamics that make up the practice are condemned, then we conclude that Scripture condemns the act in totality. Analytical students of Scripture know well that any approach to Scripture must include an analysis of the historical context prompting the writing. For instance, Paul's argument leading up to I Corinthians 7 (the last nine verses of chapter six) emphasizes the proper use of the body, which is not for immorality but is sanctified for the Lord. We must treat the body as holy because of the indwelling of the Holy Spirit, a concept not often emphasized today. The premise predicting Paul's position is the fact God has purchased us.[83]

Paul is cognizant of the prevailing teaching of Gnosticism, which holds that knowledge is essential to salvation and that all material and flesh are evil. [84] This teaching directed many in their day to believe that one can do whatever he/she wants, given that the body and spirit are separate. This may explain some wild and sensual activities in Corinth.

In addition, Gnostic teaching influenced Jewish husbands to deny intercourse with their wives, except where it was in the husband's interest. This is the backdrop and the premise for the questions submitted to Paul within the context of the Corinthian letter. Paul, called and allowed to speak for God, begins chapter seven, addressing their concerns about prevailing issues of their time. In Paul's response are directives that talk to the components and dynamics of solitary pleasure and the series of behaviors that legitimize the intimate experience.

The first is the concept of "touch" (haptesthai in Greek), as presented in verse one: "It is good for a man not to <u>touch</u> a woman."[85] Here, the Greek grammatical structure places the word touch in the present infinitive mode, which means touch is a repeating, continuous action or behavior, i.e., caressing, fondling, or massaging the body. The word's etymology stems from "haptic" in Greek, which means to make an impact and to cling, kindle, or light a fire to something.[86] In Classical Greek, the word is a euphemism for intimate relations and " grasping an idea or concept."[87] The Septuagint[88] features the word with a similar connotation, i.e., the Lord instructed Abimelech to "not touch" (hepatoma) Sarah in Genesis 20:6.

In the New Testament (I Corinthians 7:1), the word touch means to handle something in a way that "exerts a modifying influence" upon an object or "oneself."; to touch for manipulating." Given the etymology of the word, its connotation, and the context here, this is an intimate touch that precipitates intimate activity for those involved. Hence, the phrase "but to avoid fornication" ..., implies that touching in this manner is or leads to intimate activity.

The body responds to stimuli, which is expected in this context. This is a deliberate touch aimed at stirring intimate arousal between a man and woman in holy matrimony. Beyond this context, Christians must avoid touching this way because of the potential outcome. The body's response to erotic stimuli is enormously powerful.

Crooks & Baur (1996) states:

> "Stimulation of the various skin surfaces is probably a more frequent source of human sexual arousal than any other type of sensory stimulus. The nerve endings that respond to touch are distributed unevenly throughout the body, which explains why certain areas are more sensitive than others. Those locations that are most responsive to tactile pleasuring are commonly referred to as the erogenous zones."[89]

Solitary pleasure incorporates touching one's body (whether by hand or object) to create or gratify intimate desire, often culminating in a climax. Drawing any other conclusion suggests that the act of solitary pleasure in and of self is not intercourse, intimate, or arousing, which then raises whether the androcentric model sexualizes and legitimizes the intimate experience. Are we only to believe that intercourse happens when a man enters a woman? When is intercourse intercourse?

At the heart of the androcentric model is a denial of clitoral stimulation (which science confirms as the most explosive and gratifying intimate experience for women) in favor of vaginal orgasmic production, which favors the male and may only be a perceptional concept at that. It is traditional and likely for men and women to experience satisfaction during androcentrism. In fact, given how God designed the body, we expect climax when the body functions by design. However, history notes that (in the 17th century, at least) 70 percent of women did not experience satisfaction through the androcentric model. [90]

Female intimate exasperation kindled speculation and theories about why this was happening. Did vocational demands impact men in the bedroom? Were there health issues that prevented males from performing? Was it because of the male's view, which held he was the only one eligible to experience pleasure? If one takes the latter explanation, then the woman's need for satisfaction was uncharacteristic, at least in the minds of men during that period. Suppose society surmises that males were seeking to control the desires of women by denying their intimate pleasure. In that case, men (during this period, at least) are complicit in the condition and the fallout from denying women a basic physical need within the context of marriage. As mentioned, the woman's condition during the 17th century gave birth to the medical concept of "hysteria." Medical doctors felt pressured to treat women suffering from intimate exasperation. [91] Physicians were hesitant to address the issue directly. In response to the demand for treatment, doctors developed a regimen that included massaging the female until satisfaction was achieved. To free themselves from what they viewed as dreadful work, the technological orgasm was born.

Medical doctors created devices and objects such as vibrators to aid women in hysterics and over their sexual frustration. Not that self-stimulation did not exist before this period, it only acknowledged devices as opposed to the hand for intimate pleasure in the 17th century. Driel (2012) notes that in Greece, doctors gave women dildos in their husband's extended absence to remedy or prevent hysteria.[92]

Women seeking intimate satisfaction during that period still sought male companionship or connection, the natural order. Most of the physicians between the 17th and 18th centuries were male, most of whom felt that self-stimulation "conflicted at a visceral level with the androcentric paradigm." [93]

Irrespective of the rationale for solitary pleasure, whether people explore the practice as an antidote for intimate dilemmas or pleasure, it is incumbent on Christians to ensure that their behavior aligns with what God deems appropriate. Again, whatever solutions we enact to solve life's problems cannot violate the principles and commandments of God. The sins of many do not justify the sins of one. Irrespective of circumstance, the principles of God never change.[94] It was never God's intention for men and women to compete with machines and devices for intimate pleasure. The physical and psychological dynamics of intimate climax indicate divine perception and purpose.

The second (and the critical part sanctioning the series of behaviors that establish intimate activity) is sexual desire. In this context, Jesus Christ defines desire in Matthew 5:28 as (epithumeo in Greek) an intense longing to have someone ultimately; fantasizing or envisioning intercourse with someone other than your spouse. This is the tenor behind the tenth commandment..." you shall not covet your neighbor's wife or his male servant or his female servant..."[95] and Paul's point in Romans 7:7, in which he quotes the Old Testament, "... you shall not covet". Neurobiology suggests that desire, internal motivation, or goal-directed behavior is anatomical or innate. It is my opinion that the anatomical presence of desire is innate and directed not only for pleasure but is also spiritual and aimed at God Himself. The Creator forms humans with an intrinsic longing for a relationship with Him.

However, in this chapter, sexual desire focuses on and always precedes eroticism. Besides other analyses, the reality of anatomical and spiritual views warrants investigation. Desire is a powerful emotion often underestimated and approached without consideration of fact.

As noted, desire was the catalyst of the fall of humanity in the Garden of Eden, from which we learn that desire, on the one hand, is a formidable dynamism fortifying the constituents or elements of the soul. When diametrical to divine purpose, it is a critical threat to the spiritual equilibrium between God and man, a symmetry not only developed by the atoning work of Christ but also sustained by the intrinsic, sanctifying mission of the Holy Spirit.

In an article entitled Neurobiology of Sexual Desire, published in NeuroQuantology (2013), neuroscientists Suck Won Kim, Carlos H. Schenck, Jon E. Grant, Gihyun Yoon, Peter Dosa, Brian L. Odlaug, Liana R.N. Schreiber, Thomas D. Hurwitz, James G. Pfausll K. states:

> "Sex drive is an intrinsic, natural phenomenon, for which there is a fundamental purpose for its existence; Desire does not exist in a vacuum; it is an intermediary process that propels a strategy into action."[96]

Spector, I., Carey, M., & Steinberg, L. (1996) suggest "that as a construct, sexual desire is primarily cognitive," an idea which affirms Christ's view of intimate desire as used in Matthew 5:28.

Helen S. Kaplan (1979), an Austrian-American psychologist, psychiatrist, and sexual therapist, defines intimate desire as follows:

> "... an appetite or drive produced by activating a specific neural system in the brain... is experienced as specific sensations which move the individual to seek out or become receptive to intimate experiences.... When this system is active, a person is "horny."[97]

In addition, as Kaplan elaborates on the neurophysiological processes of intimate desire, she highlights that it operates in concert with the brain's pain centers. If an intimate experience is unpleasant or "destructive," it will inhibit intimate desire, shutting down any pleasurable interpretation of the experience. Conversely, she notes that the bonding chemical of the brain, the connection, attraction, and receptiveness of a male, stimulates the intimate centers of the brain. When love is present, one's belief or infatuated emotions toward the individual, intimate desire, or libido are elevated. That individual's mere presence or thought functions like an aphrodisiac; smell, sight, sound, and the person's touch "are powerful stimuli to intimate desire." [98]

Sometimes (such as with Ruth in Chapter 8), a person can experience hypersexual desire or hypersexuality, aka Compulsive Sexual Behavior. In a discussion about the neural circuitry of intimate desire, Kim SW et al. (2013) state:

> "When these circuits are overheated, there are uncontrollable urges to engage in a behavior even if the behavior might bring about unbearable negative consequences subsequently (e.g., loss of money from gambling, divorce, etc.)." [99]

In addition, Kim notes that the brain learns to reinforce behaviors that bring about rewards. This crucial factor keeps people returning to behaviors they know they should not engage in. It is easy for any form of pleasure to become uncontrollable, hence the birth of hypersexuality.

The Mayo Clinic defines hypersexuality as "an obsession with intimate thoughts, urges or behaviors that may cause you distress or that negatively affects your health, job, relationships or other parts of your life; may involve a commonly enjoyable intimate experience (for example, self-stimulation) that becomes an obsession and becomes disruptive or harmful to you or others."[100]

The Mayo Clinic details the following criteria as evidence of one struggling with this issue, which is not limited to these:

- "Your intimate impulses are intense and feel as if they're beyond your control
- Even though you feel driven to do certain behaviors, you may or may not find the activity a source of pleasure or satisfaction
- You use compulsive intimate behavior as an escape from other problems, such as loneliness, depression, anxiety, or stress
- You continue to engage in intimate behaviors that have serious consequences, such as the potential for getting or giving someone else a sexually transmitted infection, the loss of meaningful relationships, trouble at work, or legal problems
- You have trouble establishing and maintaining emotional closeness, even if you're married or in a committed relationship."[101]

The neural pathway of sexual desire is the same as the pathway that makes up the self, our inner being, and the elements that make a person who they are.

It is where the executive function of the brain is located. It governs human strategy, identity, and decision-making. [102] We sift everything we think and do through the self, that inner being. A person is the sum of their desires, a concept captured in Proverbs 23:7: "For as he thinks within himself, so he is..." Kaplan (1979) draws the same conclusion, "sex circuits are extensively interconnected with those parts of the brain that analyze the complex experience and with the memory storage and retrieval... There is evidence that intimate desire is extremely sensitive to experimental factors that figure and shape the objects and activities that will and will not evoke our desires." [103]

In addition, desire risks stimulating the dialogical self (a psychological concept that captures the mind's ability to conceive various points of view within narratives, balanced with those held) whose latter end (in this context) compromises. [104] Consider the following examples for clarity;

1) In I Peter 2:2, the bible states:

"...like newborn babies, "desire" the pure milk of the word, so that by it you may grow in respect to salvation."

Here, desire for the word of God develops and fortifies our relationship with Him.

2) Conversely, the word desire used in Genesis chapter three disrupted the equilibrium between God, Adam, and Eve. In addition, the surge of the dialogical self is apparent.

The Bible states:

> "Now the serpent was craftier than any beast of the
> field which the LORD God had made. And he said to the
> woman, "Indeed, has God said, 'You shall not eat from
> any tree of the garden'?" 2 The woman said to the
> serpent, "From the fruit of the trees of the garden we
> may eat; 3 but from the fruit of the tree which is in the
> middle of the garden, God has said, 'You shall not eat
> from it or touch it, or you will die.'" 4 The serpent said
> to the woman, "You surely will not die! 5 For God
> knows that in the day you eat from it, your eyes will be
> opened, and you will be like God, knowing good and
> evil." 6 When the woman saw that the tree was good for
> food, and that it was a delight to the eyes, and that the
> tree was desirable to make *one* wise, she took from its
> fruit and ate; and she gave also to her husband with
> her, and he ate. 7 Then the eyes of both were opened,
> and they knew that they were naked, and they sewed

> fig leaves together and made themselves loin coverings."[105]

During Eve's encounter with Satan, her dialogical self emerges. She imagines various points and interpretations of God's instructions and her internal narrative. She contrasts her internal dialogue with her external conversation with Satan. Having permitted herself to see God's commands differently, she now longs for what God restricts.

This intrinsic dance between her internal dialogue (her thoughts and convictions) and the external dialogue with Satan (his deceptive viewpoints of God's commands and her thoughts about them) she compromises, which in effect breaches God's law and disturbs the equilibrium between them. Her eyes (the window to her mind and soul) cultivated desire that had a protracted and far-reaching effect, ushering death and dangerously changing relational dynamics between the creature and the Creator.

Since that moment, God has warned humans about mismanaging desire. Desire is a common emotion, but how it plays out or what we long for differentiates whether it is good or evil. Whenever desire appears in the bible, it is presented as lust, which includes not only intercourse but money, power, and other tangible things and experiences. In

Mark 7:21-22, Jesus highlights that this issue originates within a person's heart.
He states:

"[21] From within, out of the heart of men, proceed the evil
thoughts, fornications, thefts, murders, and adulteries,
[22] deeds of coveting *and* wickedness, *as well as* deceit,
sensuality, envy, slander, pride, *and* foolishness."

The Proverb writer cautions us to guard or protect the heart.

The Bible states:

> "Keep thy heart with all diligence, for out of it are the issues of life."[106]

And warning men of adultery, the Proverb writer states:

> "Do not lust in your heart after her beauty or let her captivate you with her eyes, for the prostitute reduces you to a loaf of bread, and the adulteress preys upon your very life. Can a man scoop fire into his lap without his clothes being burned? Can a man walk on hot coals without his feet being scorched? So is he who sleeps with another man's wife; no one who

> touches her will go unpunished. A man who commits adultery lacks judgment; whoever does so destroys himself."[107]

Most people view "desire" as distinct from the intimate act itself. However (and at the risk of sounding too conservative or narrow-minded), desire is a part of an intimate response or behavior. Kaplan (1979) was famous for her triphasic phenomenon view of human intimate response, which includes desire as a part of this process. [108] This is a reasonable concept because our emotions and thoughts originate from our mind, which influences intimate behavior, i.e., Crooks & Baur states:

"Sexual arousal can occur without any sensory stimulation; the process of fantasy can produce it, and some individuals may even reach orgasm during a fantasy."[109]

In addition, Kaplan (1979) states:

> "Erection and even orgasm may at times be achieved purely based on external stimuli and fantasy without any physical stimulation of the genitals."[110]

The ancient teaching of India held that there were eight forms of coitus[111] or "Maithuana," seven of which did not involve actual intercourse, which is as follows:

- "Samarana- merely thinking of it
- Kirtana- speaking of it
- Keli- dallying with it
- Prekshana- viewing it
- Guhyabhashna- secretly conversing
- Samkalpa- firmly willing to indulge in it
- Adhyavasaya- resolving to do it
- Kriyanishpatti- the actual act"

Each constitutes an intimate union (Maithuana) according to their ancient teaching. In addition, "various forms of contact or association within the two intercourses, without actual intimate intercourse, constituted adultery and is punishable."[112]

There are pastors and Christians who believe that we can have thoughts and even imagine having intercourse with others if we do not engage the person or the act. How is that determined?

This is dangerous territory. In addition, it ignores Romans 7:12-25, in which Paul lays out three critical points regarding the challenge to live for God.

1) The fact we are part flesh and part spirit is a perpetual human dilemma, in that these are in constant tension; 2) Evil and lust are Hell's devices aimed at the sensitivity of the "fleshly man," and 3) sin's impact can leave one unrecognizable and in need of heavenly deliverance through Jesus Christ. The passage captures our sensitivity to temptation, sin, and evil. We should stay as far away as possible from things that cause stumbling.[113]

As mentioned, Jesus points out that what is in us can condemn and defile us and that adultery originates from a man's heart (mind & soul), his inner being. Dancing with this temptation will lead to calamity. Again, will do well protecting our mind/hearts from things that cause us to sin."[114]

It encourages Christians to keep their minds renewed and concentrate on holy things.[115] Because history teaches that a person's ungoverned thoughts or desires will lead to transgression and chaos, Genesis chapter 34 describes what unbridled desire will lead an individual into and how it impacts those affected. Here Shechem sees Dinah and desires her, so he rapes her. After raping her, he continues to groom her to have her. Because marriages were arranged then, he approaches her father to strike a deal for her hand in marriage. But while there appears to be consensus around the agreement, Dinah's brothers are disturbed that their sister is now defiled and treated "as a harlot by Shechem."[116] Simeon and Levi (Dinah's brothers) kill him and others. In addition, David's thoughts and desires lead him to commit the 'fourth stage' of adultery, deception, cover-up, and accessory to murder. As best as determined, God forgives David of his sins. However, he suffered significant losses and consequences for his transgressions.[117]

Desire is a significant and intricate part of an intimate response and, if not bridled, can lend itself to dynamics that forge spiritual and moral failure as defined by God. Let's be clear: the phrase "if not bridled" is not capitulating or endorsing collective control aimed at the abjection of female desire as defined by Kristeva (as cited in a dissertation by Dondapati Allen, 2008)[118]

Speaking within the context of the Indian culture, Dr. Dondapati Allen states:

> "In a culture which adheres to the notion that deriving pleasure from intimate activity is prerogative of the male, the purely pleasurable expression of desire in women cannot be confined unless it is constructed as an undesired element that must be expelled- Kristeva calls this process abjection. Kristeva states that abjection is "something rejected from which one does

> not part." According to Kristeva, what is constructed as abject has only one quality: it is opposed to I. As such, it can be neither assimilated nor ejected from one's being, forever taunting and threatening to overflow the boundary."[119]

God's instructions about life and immorality are not gender specific. Direct commandments for men and women are prevalent in Scripture. However, the ordinances that govern intimate attitude and behavior are for every person submitting to the rule of Christ. Contrary to what feminists and progressive theologians think, the bible acknowledges the inappropriate way in which men treat women. This is evident in passages discussing intercourse and marriage—these passages take into consideration historical and cultural contexts about how men treat women. [120]

Everyone must accept the Scripture outlining human behavior. For example, Paul's statement in Romans 13: 13-14 about proper behavior, intimate promiscuity, and avoiding provisions to fulfill these lusts is not misogyny, and feminists or any other group should not view it as such; It is not a license for men to use against women while exempting themselves from the passage. It is a biblical Christian principle for living in Christ.

The Apostle Paul states, [13] "Let us behave properly as in the day, not in carousing and drunkenness, not in sexual promiscuity and sensuality, not in strife and jealousy. [14] But put on the Lord Jesus Christ and make no provision for the flesh regarding *its* lusts." Encouraging men and women to denounce and deny desire that contributes to intimate promiscuity and lust outside of marriage is not a joy-killing control mechanism aimed at teenagers and women. It is a Godly principle and command designed to jettison the flesh and its attitudes, thus synchronizing the mind, body, and soul with the Holy Spirit, certifying a living holy sacrifice to God. [121] In Matthew 5:27-28, Jesus captures how significant avoiding intimate desire out of context is for those living godly lives. In addition, His statement proves that intimate sin reaches beyond sensory stimulation- touch.

He states:

> "...but I say to you that everyone who looks at a woman with lust for her has already committed adultery with her in his heart."[122]

Wuest's (1961) states:

> "...Everyone who is looking at a woman to indulge his intimate passion for her already committed adultery with her in his heart."[123]

Here, Jesus emphasizes desire or lust as contributing to adultery. Most people view intercourse in one dimension, limiting it to sensory stimulation and intercourse. Here, Jesus finds that the act of intimate desire outside of marriage is so severe that it breaches relational boundaries and covenant. As mentioned in chapter 8, adultery is a breach of covenant between God and those living in holy matrimony. Jesus' statement in Matthew 5:27 is in harmony with this concept.

Another passage in the Bible sheds light on another problem with self-stimulation, one rarely (if ever) evoked in this argument. Romans 1:18-28 is a stinging indictment postured against the practice of homosexuality and other depraved acts of men. The passage is a complex and powerful passage worthy of analysis within the context of this chapter.

Total exegesis warrants more time and space here. But for the sake of this discussion, information pertinent to it is highlighted. The Apostle does not hold his tongue here. He unloads with both barrels to spotlight divine repulsion and irritation of humanity's repugnant and unrighteous behavior. He captures God's significance, sanctity, and sovereignty as Creator, not only of the universe but the human body and every creature that moves. One could use a few more words to capture the ambiance, tenor, and repudiation toward those who ignore God as Creator and embrace degradative behaviors in the highest form. After declaring that he is not ashamed of God's gospel and, in effect, does not fear the regal power of Rome, Paul pontificates the wrath of God against ungodliness (asebia in Greek), which refers to ungodlike, licentious, or immoral living. It connotes profound irreverence and disregard for God's law and person.

Next, he discloses the wrath of God against unrighteousness (adikia in Greek), which points to a person's improper attitude and conduct. [124] This is the backdrop of Paul's message in this passage. But how the people sinned against God stands out and illuminates the corrupt nature of solitary pleasure.

After God declares His identity and shows the awesomeness and eternality of His power through His created order (verse 19, 20), humanity places Him on trial to authenticate His Godhood based on their measure and criteria of a god. The

Creator does not meet their standard. They dismiss Him as God and Creator. Creating and worshipping their god, they violate and dishonor Him in the following ways:

- Not accepting Him as the Sovereign God and Creator, in effect eliminating God from His rightful place;
- Exchanging God for humanism and animals as the object of worship;
- Exchanging the natural intimate function or use of a man's body and that of a woman's;
- Embracing other degrading passions and behaviors in the most extremist way possible.

The passage unfolds three concepts capturing how solitary pleasure degrades—first, dishonoring the human body. Remember, one reason for the unfettered wrath of God is unfathomable irreverence and disregard for Him as Creator. As far as it concerns God, the human body is perfect within its sphere, meaning when it functions in the manner and context in which He designed it, it is perfect. Man is the climatic, crowning jewel of God's creation, which He declared superb. [125] The Hebrew word for good (tov) suggests that which fulfills expectation, which in this case- God's.

This underscores the reverence we should have for God's creation, including our own bodies.

It means that God met the objectives He had in mind for creating man; therefore, the creation is final. There is no need for an upgrade or changes to the original blueprint for humanity. Creation's functionality is satisfactory with God and did not need change or improvement then or now. [126]

The human body, an exquisite manifestation of God's creative power and intellect, is a holy vessel created for the human and divine will. [127] The body, as mentioned, is for the habitation or indwelling presence of the Holy Spirit, which, in effect, is a conduit for the union between the creature and the Creator. The Apostle Paul dubbed the body as a Temple of the Holy Spirit. This highlights the divine purpose of our bodies and the significance of our responsibility in using them.[128] It is incumbent on us to preserve and use it to ensure this outcome.[129] It signals accountability and responsibility regarding how we use the body. Although we can claim ownership of our body, it does not translate into using the body in any manner that dishonors it and the Creator.

Self-stimulation dishonors God as Creator and the divine purpose for which God created the body. In an exegesis of Romans 1: 18-32, Wuest describes the words honor and dishonors as follows:

> "Thus, to honor someone is to evaluate, respect, and love due to his character and position. To dishonor a person is to either put an incorrect appraisal upon his worth and treat him accordingly, or having rigorously evaluated his character, to refuse to treat him with the respect and deference his due."[130]

Those who engage in solitary pleasure will probably balk at this exegesis and theological summary. In addition, those who do not practice it but believe that people can do whatever they want will also disagree with this conclusion. However, both can only stake their position by jettisoning the context and meaning of this passage or the principles upon which it rests.

The audience to whom Paul is directing this message harbors desires that diminish the human body's sacrosanctity, dignity, and wholesomeness in its created order and use it in a manner that dishonors God. Self-stimulation falls into this category. It uses and manipulates the body in ways counterintuitive to natural order. The design of the human body suggests that the male and female must unite for intimate intercourse and pleasure. The process that makes intercourse is anomalous to the oneness of God. In fact, "oneness" is thematic throughout scripture. There is, but one God, God (Elohim) the Father, Son, and Holy Spirit are one; there is one hope, one Lord, one Faith, one Spirit, one Baptism[131], one body[132] (church), one sacrificial atonement for the sins of humanity and as noted, the relationship between husband and wife intertwines so they are one.[133] The body's design does not suggest solitary pleasure was under consideration during creation. Two facts about self-stimulation are indisputable,

1) It originates among men;
2) it is intimate behavior. The same biblical statute that governs natural or traditional forms of intimate desire and behavior delimits solitary pleasure. How is it different? What is the rationale for the distinction if so?

In addition, and the most damming is in Paul's emphasis on the moral trifecta of the words "natural, exchanged and function" in Romans 1:26, 27 (NASB). Here, the scripture detests not the freedom of choice but the dynamics of the behavior intrinsic to homosexuality. As mentioned, man is a free moral agent. People may accept or reject God's way. God will force none of us to do what is not in our hearts to fulfill. On two occasions in Romans 1: 18-32, the text states: "God gave them up," meaning He allowed them to pursue their degrading passions or desires of their heart, but not without consequence. Paul's point is that the condemnation (in this case) rests within this trifecta, which involves physical, mental, and spiritual processes of self-stimulation.

First, the word natural (phusis in Greek) refers to the constitutional element of something, nature's law, and order caused by something innate. [134] The heterosexual relationship is natural, made up by God as the sole means by which men and women procreate and experience intimate love and pleasure. The body functions in a manner that processes and stresses this divine aim—rejecting God as Creator eliminates filters that temper spiritual irrationality, producing self-indulgence that gives rise to sordid thinking and behavior. When minimizing God's sovereignty, humans always permit themselves to embrace their desires and perceptions, even if these are contrary and degrading to God. Humans will always rationalize their behavior.

Second is the word "exchanged" (metallasso in Greek) to convert to a different state. [135] The basic concept of "exchange" suggests altering something for something else, removing one thing for another. The third word in this trifecta is altering the human body's natural intimate function, naturally referring to its design and divine purpose. The word "function" or "us" (chassis in Greek) refers to that which something is used to do and how something is utilized; in context, it speaks to the wrong use of the body in intimate contexts.

The male is for the female, and the female is for the male. Altering this law and fact dishonors the body's purpose and the God who made it. It is irrefutable that self-stimulation (with the hand or dildo) alters the natural function of the human body and dishonors God as Creator. The act suggests that God's design for intercourse or the milieu and conduit for intimate desire and pleasure is immaterial and inadequate for human intimate experiences. It infers that God's design is flawed and that humans are more informed about their bodies than He is, jettisoning the fact that He made us.

There are indisputable facts that those who practice self-stimulation cannot ignore. intimate desire is the motivating factor; it is not relational; it does not honor God or champion the purpose for which He created intimate intercourse and is an effect void of the human exchange that strengthens a relationship. Man cannot glorify God through solitary pleasure.

PART

II

THEOLOGY OF THE SCIENCE

Solitary Pleasure within the Context of Marriage

Can a person living in the bonds of holy matrimony indulge in solitary pleasure? If so, what is the purpose of solitary pleasure in marriage? Do marital problems permit one or both spouses to embrace this behavior? Are there exceptional circumstances in which a spouse is exempt from the androcentric and divine model of sexuality, i.e., a spouse has a permanent medical condition that prevents him/her from intimate intercourse? Who determines the extent and duration of such exemptions? Can one spouse give the other permission to practice solitary pleasure? If a spouse does not disclose and is dishonest about practicing solitary pleasure, does the act itself constitute adultery? What are solitary pleasure's spiritual, emotional, and physical impacts in marriage?

The best answers to this series of questions are more straightforward when analyzed through the prism and dynamics of marriage as constructed by God, who is the architect of matrimony. Masculinity and femininity are the by-products of Divinity and reflect determinations essential to the heterosexual union. As such, the inherent challenges of Adam's brief life in solitary are inescapable. Contrary to modern thought, the woman is a direct response to Adam's challenges in solitary socially, physically, emotionally, and intellectually. [136] If one thinks critically here, one may ask why anyone would return to solitary as an antidote to that element of humanness God deems is only resolved through anatomical differentiation and heterosexuality. As mentioned earlier in the chapter, intercourse has multiple outcomes. There are four reasons God inaugurated intercourse in marriage; [137]

First, God set up oneness or union between male and female / husband and wife and synchronized their relationship with Him. The natural and distinctive design of the male and female body is such that intimate intercourse requires they come together so that they become one in the act itself (Gen. 2:24).

Second, pleasure. To cement the union between the male and female, in Genesis 1:28, the bible says, "God blessed them." Theoretical and theological frameworks suggest that blessing is a physical attribute that must include the anatomical nature of the male and female and the process and response to intimate desire. Although this text does not specify the way God blessed Adam and Eve, the declaration proceeds divine order to be "fruitful and multiply," a reference to procreation through intercourse. In addition, as noted in Genesis 1:27, it is indisputable that God created man and woman, including their homogeny and differences. The neurological circuitry connected to male and female anatomy not only affirms intimate pleasure but directs the solidification of the union between husband and wife. A thorough analysis and understanding of the process associated with climax affirms this. Science confirms the nature, purpose, and outcome of intercourse as designed by God. During the intimate climax, the human brain releases significant levels of a chemical known as "dopamine," aka "the feel-good chemical." [138] This chemical is the reason an individual craves climax again and again. In this context, the woman gains more through this experience, in that the male's climax only lasts 3 to 10 seconds and has a refractory period. During this interlude, he continues to experience pleasure but cannot climax. It can last anywhere from a few minutes to hours. However, the female experience is such that the climax lasts twice as long as a male (20 seconds or longer) and is not limited by a refractory period. This enables consecutive, multiple climaxes. Now, I highlight this not because of the pleasure of it but neuropsychological and spiritual outcomes. In most cases, these are more intense as the process continues and more dopamine is released.

But although the woman gains the most through this process, she is at greater risk for injury if she abuses the process.

The Journal of Neuroscience notes that dopamine released during climax is synonymous with a brain exposed to heroin. [139] In addition, the orbitofrontal cortex (the part of the brain that governs self-evaluation, reason, and control) shuts down, precipitating a loss of control during the event. [140] A person evokes behaviors, thoughts, and words they may not otherwise express. It turns fear and anxiety off, allowing the person sometimes to experience mind-blowing pleasure.

Mind-blowing (something that is so shocking, surprising, unexpected, or wonderful that your brain cannot comprehend it) is a natural neurological phenomenon and a concept explored in more detail in the next section of this chapter. [141] When females experience this, it shuts areas of their brain down during climax, rendering them more susceptible to neurological outcomes from such pleasure. [142] In addition, and significant to the point raised in this section, dopamine is released in tandem with oxytocin, aka the "bonding or love chemical." [143] It increases devotion, attachment, and conviction about and toward the intimate partner, a process dubbed here the "Oxy-factor."

This illustrates why two people (married or unmarried) having intercourse over time will bond or become closer. intimate climax ordinarily connects males and females and, by design, brings husbands and wives closer together during and after intercourse.

The third reason is procreation. Again, Genesis 1:28[b] clarifies that intercourse is the medium for procreation. As mentioned earlier, as we procreate, God expects us to duplicate His image and likeness in our children and family.

Fourth, interpersonal exhibition and experiential knowledge. There is a word in scripture that refers to intimate relations, i.e., Adam "knew" Eve, his wife..., (Genesis 4:1[KJV)]. "knew" originates from the Hebrew word "Yadha," which means to gain knowledge, discern, and know, not as an abstract but through conscious, personal, or direct experience. Chung Gwan Joo (2014) [144] calls this process communication. But Genesis 18:19 captures the authentic ambiance and weight of the word know or knew. God, regarding His relationship with Abraham, says:

> "For I know (Yadha) him, that he will command his children..."

When God knows something, He has comprehensive information at profound levels. Nothing is hidden from His eyes (Hebrews 4:13). This is the tenor behind the word "know" in Genesis 4:1: knowledge of an individual at personal and profound depths. Intercourse provides a space for interaction at personal and profound levels. It is a conduit for an experience at levels no one else is privy to, creating a unique bond between them. It reaches into one's core and conjures up emotions and language uniquely expressed in this context. It is a restricted dialogue designed to help closeness between a male and female within the context of marriage. Of all the relationships between humans, there are no others so close; they, too, are considered one.

The intimate experience builds trust and value because the act warrants the relaxation of barriers, a process innate to humans and designed to protect the individual's heart. The emotional, psychological, spiritual, and physical processes associated with intercourse expose participants to vulnerability and force them to collapse (figuratively) into the heart and emotional care of the one with whom they are engaged. The language, emotions, and anatomical outcomes associated with intercourse are so reflective, powerful, and compromising that people practice it in secrecy. Many enter the privacy of a bedroom and other spaces to cloak erotic exhibition. Because of the personal nature of intercourse, even couples licensed to engage in such pleasure are rightfully sheepish and private about the event.

The statement by Jesus in Matthew 5:27-28 and Paul's details about intercourse and marriage in I Corinthians chapter 7 are synchronized in that both passages place intimate desire within the context of marriage. Paul's details, however, beg the question of whether self-stimulation (as a form of solitary pleasure) is appropriate in marriage. As mentioned, it is indisputable that self-stimulation is, in fact, intercourse and that throughout the annals of scripture, intercourse that does not include a spouse is vehemently rejected as appropriate and subsequently condemned by God, i.e., Hebrews 13: 4 states:

> "Marriage is to be held in honor among all, and the marriage bed is to be undefiled: fornicators and adulterers God will judge."[145]

Notably, fornicators refer to those engaging in intimate activity outside of marriage, and adulterers (in this context) refer to married people having intimate intercourse with someone other than their spouse. As previously mentioned, contemporary therapists not only suggest that self-stimulation is healthy and acceptable but is permissible in marriage. [146] Remarkably, mental health professionals (except those who offer Christian counseling) do not consult or integrate Scripture as a part of their analysis or therapeutic recommendations. Subsequently, some of their advice falls outside of Godly principles. Irrespective of their talents and in-depth knowledge of mind, behavior, and personality, their consensus and recommendations do not trump holy mandates enacted by God.

However, some of their findings can and do affirm God, His creation, and the principles by which we should live. Rosetta's friend (introduced at the beginning of this chapter) and the evangelical Christian wife's (noted above) intimate behavior are incompatible within the course of marriage as defined by Scripture. The Apostle Paul's response to the church in Corinth is clear: a "no brainer" in that any intimate desire among married people is expected to play out or is fulfilled within the context of the marriage itself. The text mandates that each spouse engage the other to relieve intimate desire. The marriage relationship is, therefore, a conduit for intimate behavior, interests, or curiosity.

Although self-stimulation can lead to a robust and personal climax, it cannot fulfill the relational objectives established by God for the act of intercourse. Furthermore, it risks eliciting issues in the marriage, such as problems with emotional closeness (as indicated by the Mayo Clinic above) and anatomical changes that potentially complicate traditional forms of intercourse between spouses in that satisfaction dwindles or is altered. These issues are not limited to Western culture or practitioners of Christianity. Dr. Abu Ameenah Bilal Philips, Dean of the Islamic Online University, participates in a Q&A in which a question about solitary pleasure arises.[147] Dr. Philips responds by indicating that "there is no clear text"[148] regarding solitary pleasure.

As such, he is "hesitant to call it Haraam" (an Arabic term meaning "forbidden") but views solitary pleasure as "Makrooh" (an Arabic term indicating something that is disliked or hated.)

In Sharee'ah Law, it indicates that one is asked not to do, but not definitively).[149] He continues by stating that solitary pleasure is "not good."[150] "People cannot find fulfillment in normal husband and wife relations."[151] In addition, he notes many cases in which people have come to him complaining about this problem. Furthermore, Dr. Philips emphasizes that solitary pleasure was never given as an option for intimate desire.

CNN Health recently featured an article by Ian Kerner, a licensed "couples therapist" who suggests that "highly satisfying intercourse does not have to be limited to penetration," and going even further, he suggests that penetration doesn't have to be included at all.[152] Kerner highlights recent research (spearheaded by "Debby Herbenick, director of the Center for Sexual Health Promotion at Indiana University and in conjunction with a research fellow-intimate health educator at the Kinsey Institute") in which clitoral stimulation, which is at the heart of self-stimulation is the more prominent method for intimate satisfaction among women. "The internet-based survey held that only 18% of respondents reported climax during traditional intercourse." [153] However, the study (as detailed in the article) does not indicate what variables are considered or factored in their response, i.e., physical problems in which the distance between the clitoris and the vagina opening are too far apart to produce adequate orgasms[154] or emotional issues that dampen libido, whether those having difficulty achieving climax traditionally are among those who routinely practice self-stimulation and the frequency in which respondents self-stimulate, the effectiveness of communication between parties before, during and after intercourse, and relationship problems that skew intimate outcomes, potentially.

In addition, the article references a book entitled Becoming Cliterate: Why Orgasm Equality Matters—And How to Get it, written by Dr. Laurie Mintz, a therapist. The book suggests that humans have been thinking about intercourse wrong and that the traditional or androcentric model of sexuality (namely, a person's genitals) is insufficient in that "women do not orgasm this way," a concept that is likely disputed by other men and women for that matter. However, she suggests, "there is a pleasure gap between men and women."

In fairness, Dr. Mintz includes some of the variables under consideration regarding this issue, i.e., in chapter one of her book, she details issues associated with trauma as a deterrent to typical heterosexual outcomes. In addition, she cites the following statistics as a premise for some of her other conclusions:

- "50% of 18-35-year-old women say they have trouble reaching orgasm with a partner
- 64% of women vs. 91% of men said they had an orgasm at their last intimate encounter
- 55% of men vs. 4% of women say they usually reach orgasm during first-time hookup intercourse."[155]

However, as indicated earlier in this chapter, the findings regarding self-stimulation are indisputable. In most cases, clitoral stimulation produces a much more powerful orgasm or climax. In addition, Jesus and the Apostle Paul's extended sense determined the reality and dynamics of "outercourse" by indicating that humans can experience intercourse and intimate desire separately from the androcentric model.[156] Notably, neither Jesus nor the Apostle Paul suggests that intercourse or intimate desire is legitimate in solitary. Shifting the divine paradigm around human intimacy will usually obscure divine objectives and contribute to humanity's failure to live in and embrace the richness of heterosexual intercourse fully.

The research headed by Herbenick and Mintz's dynamics to becoming "cliterate" patterns pharmaceutical companies' ambitious quest to find Viagra for women, which notably failed initially. These companies focused on increasing blood flow to the woman's genitals to improve her intimate desire and experience. Their drugs had no effect, quickly signaling the difference between male and female processes for intimate desire. In the book A Billion Wicked Thoughts: What the World's Largest Experiment Reveals About Human Desire (2011), Sai Goddam and Ogi Ogas highlight research that unveils the dichotomy between psychological and physical arousal in women. As such, it is noted that what is happening in and to a woman's genital area is not always indicative of what is happening in her mind, i.e., a woman's body can respond naturally to intimate stimulation. Still, her mind can live in rebellion, simultaneously dampening the overall intimate response. The male's response to intimate cues or arousal accentuates differences between the intercourses, i.e., when a man has an erection, it is reflective of what is in his mind at the time of his erection. Women operate differently. The pathway to explosive climax in women does not have to scrap the God-ordained process for intimate desire. "Women need to feel psychologically aroused."[157]

In addition, Goddam and Ogas point to previous research in which women identified that the obstacle to climax is psychological, not biological. The explosive climax associated with clitoral stimulation is also probable through traditional forms of intercourse when female biological and psychological arousal operate in tandem.

It seems what is in error is not our view and expectation of the androcentric model of sexuality but rather the inability to grasp the beautiful symmetry and human exchange codified through heterosexuality.

Contemporary sexuality is self-centered and routinely proliferates competition between sexes, i.e., males obsessively seek intimate dominance by maintaining unprecedented intimate prowess. In addition, his subsequent, persistent search and conquer mission (meaning some men's quest to certify that his intimate performance is the one that is dubbed mind-blowing by females, even among those who are in a relationship with another man) is among a plethora of behaviors aimed at personal gratification. A Saturday visit to the barber shop (especially those serving minority communities) will provide a front-row seat to a classic kiss and tale as guys swap porno on their phones, detail intimate encounters with females (some of whom are mistresses), and salivate over what they would like to do to the one they have not conquered.

Conversely, females compulsively and persistently position themselves as equals to their counterparts and as those better suited to determine the intimate relationships of their choosing, even if they trample over natural order, religious expectations, and norms defined by their communities. Their competitive chase for status and supreme intimate experience risks minimizing or (in worse cases) severing the goal of a heterosexual relationship, which is of least concern to the one egotistically seeking her pleasure.

THEOLOGICAL ANALYSIS

Allowing self-stimulation in the context of marriage is to 1) see it as something other than what it is, intercourse, and 2) alter the Divine purpose of intercourse in marriage, as well as the antidote to the issues raised by Adam's solitude. God's perspective is such that self-stimulation is not optional. Subsequently, it is incumbent on humans to preserve the divine objectives of the heterosexual union. "What God has joined together, let no man put asunder" (Matthew 19:6).

Psychological and Anatomical Issues of Solitary Pleasure

There is an odd consensus among many therapists, other professionals, and laypeople that solitary pleasure is harmless and healthy for people to explore. It is strange because data suggests otherwise. Narratives regarding self-stimulation should include not only perceived rewards but also possible risks associated with the behavior.

The current approach to the issue parallels that of the alcohol and tobacco industries a few decades ago, which enticed the public to buy and use their products without disclosing potential risks. Today, the Surgeon General requires messaging on packages that warns users of potential hazards or the effects of long-term use of these products.

Fearing another religious effort to control people's intimate desire and behavior (especially women) are those who balk at the notion that self-stimulation has any adverse effects, maybe because they have engaged in the practice without harm or know of others who have, in their minds solidifies reasons for continuing the behavior. For this group, the notion that this behavior is risky and people criticize the practice fuels revolts against the ideology that lends itself to this conclusion. Most people believe they can do whatever they want with their bodies, including people of faith.

But this chapter has noted the spiritual complications solitary pleasures create. Any form of intimate behavior antithetical to God as Creator and the mandates He enacts is problematic. Irrespective of other problems with self-stimulation, behavior antithetical to God is enough reason to end such practices. However, humans look for ways to get as close to the cliff's edge as possible without falling. There is always a motivation to adjust the rules to one's preference, which is what humans do.

The degree to which solitary pleasure is harmful depends upon several variables, such as the strength or weakness of the person's body, the frequency and intensity of climax, and the way one practices such behavior.

Appreciating the notion and potential that self-stimulation has adverse effects requires one to understand the anatomical process for intimate climax. The average person likely gives no thought to this mechanism or process. Most people get into and drive their cars without a second thought to the mechanics until there is a change in its performance, or something goes wrong, causing the vehicle to stall. If things are working to their ultimate satisfaction, people ignore the details and mechanics of intimate climax, except to highlight details that produce extraordinary results.

Some of the ultra-conservative Christians will likely dub this as too much information or unnecessary and feel somewhat squeamish about addressing such details. However, obliviousness of the strategic design and function of the human body dissociates and obscures the Creator's agenda and projected outcome.

Here, our moral view of the body is significant, i.e., many Christians condemn smoking. Why? Many contrast the known effects of smoking to the traditional understanding or teaching of I Corinthians chapters 3: 16-17 and 6:12-20, in which the bible teaches that the human body is sacred and a temple for the indwelling Holy Spirit and that God will destroy the one who destroys the temple because God created the human body for divine purposes.

Reviewing the anatomical process associated with intimate climax is in concert with understanding solitary pleasure in this framework. The neuropsychological aspect of sexual arousal expands to include how intimate pleasure codes and wires the brain, impacting behavior and decision-making. Keep in mind that what is in reference here is an ongoing, intensive, intimate climax generated by self-stimulation. In this view, neuroplasticity is pertinent. Rizzo & Eslinger (2004), in their book Principles and Practice of Behavioral Neurology and Neuropsychology, define neuroplasticity as a "notion that in the absence of pathology, neurons have and keep the capacity for alteration and growth." [158] Neuroplasticity is a rewiring process through which the brain develops and reorganizes neural connections in reaction to new information gleaned through learning and experience. Neuroplasticity primarily aims to acclimate the brain to the latest data, chemistry, and experiences. When these definitions parallel the neural process of orgasm, it is easier to surmise how repetitive intensive climax and the behaviors associated with it can alter a person's mind, decision-making, and behavior in effect. Dr. Mark Richards (2015), in an online article on intercourse and solitary pleasure addiction, speaks about neurons and brain chemicals in this context. Note:

> "BDNF can mediate the neuroplasticity and influence learning, cognitive behavior, and memory. A chronic intimate over-stimulation will induce the over-release

> of BDNF, which will alter the brain and synaptic plasticity and lead to addictive behavior. The over-stimulation of certain nervous systems and functions as the dopaminergic, noradrenergic, and glutaminergic will modify the brain function and lead to addiction and psychological disorders."[159]

In addition, Dr. Richards notes that intimate addiction results from plasticity (rewiring) of the area of the brain that influences intimate response and that solitary pleasure increases levels of dopamine. Dopamine converts into a chemical in the brain that keeps one aroused, which leads to addiction. [160] Richards points to brain chemicals **prostaglandin E2** (ideal for learning and memory), **Oxytocin** (as mentioned, the chemical that creates bonding and attachment), **and norepinephrine** (a stress hormone affecting organs in the body) as essential chemicals at the heart of changing individuals when stimulated too often. [161] Dr. Richards emphasizes that too much prostaglandin E2 is harmful. In addition, he notes that excessive prostaglandin E2 leads to severe addiction and "discontinuation difficulties since the brain has already been wired." [162] Solitary pleasure burns excessive amounts of testosterone into dihydrotestosterone, which, according to Dr. Richards, causes baldness and prostate problems in men. [163]

These changes under review here are not the result of casual, moderate intimate encounters but intense, intimate pleasure. Not that married couples cannot experience or aim for mind-blowing intimate outcomes between them. Mind-blowing, a phrase and concept noted earlier in this chapter is worthy of elaboration. We commonly associate it with shocking and incomprehensible experiences with new, intensive, intimate experiences. It is more common with women in that during the climax, most of the brain shuts down, creating a deadening effect, ensuring that she experiences pleasure in its totality.

During a medical conference in Copenhagen, a series of experiments conducted by the University of Groningen in the Netherlands were interesting. [164] One of their experiments used brain scans to monitor men and women while stimulated sexually. They conclude that the woman's climax is a mind-blowing experience. However, judgment and reasoning are lost when this part of the brain deactivates. [165] Biological experiences shape how we feel, think, and behave subsequently. [166]

Sometimes, this mind-blowing experience can cause memory loss and has had adverse outcomes for women, i.e., the Journal of Emergency Medicine reports that a 54-year-old woman enters Georgetown University Hospital for sudden amnesia one hour after having intercourse with her husband. After assessing her, doctors decided that she was suffering from Transit Global Amnesia, a condition in which a person has sudden and brief memory loss. [167] According to Live Science, a mind-blowing climax can wipe your memory clean! [168] Intense intercourse can produce transit global amnesia, more likely among adults 50 and older.

The effects fade after a short while. The chase for mind-blowing climax through solitary pleasure has its risks because of what happens in the brain; women are more vulnerable.

The Oxy-factor with Dopamine

As mentioned, oxytocin is the chemical the brain releases during nurturing or erotic touching, hugging, and in large doses during climax. It operates in tandem with dopamine, the well-known 'feel-good chemical.' Oxytocin is released during parenting and facilitates attachment between parents and children. In a marital relationship, oxytocin and dopamine cause a husband and wife to desire one another, experience euphoria through intimate intercourse, and create a secure, happy, permanent bond with one another.

This powerful and beautiful process of oneness highlights the value of reserving such experiences for the one with whom you are in a covenant relationship.

If one interprets the anatomical and neurological differences between males and females, the female likely produces more oxytocin and dopamine than the male. In parental and marital contexts, we perceive women as more maternal or nurturing, caring or loving than men. Given God's purpose for the woman, was she created with more significant oxytocin levels? Are dopamine and oxytocin levels in females a fallout of the woman's role in the primer of sin? For example, consider this biblical phrase: "...your desire will be for your husband..." (Genesis 3:16) is the God-given response to the woman's behavior and one of three consequences of her disobedience.

The Hebrew word for desire mirrors characteristics associated with the collective effects of dopamine and oxytocin, i.e., to stretch out toward something, long for something or someone, and yearn. In Hebrew, it reflects strong attraction between men and women and is, therefore, essential to normative heterosexual attraction.

These functions function in concert with the union between husband and wife. However, too much oxytocin can be problematic. Given that the brain releases it during climax, it is present in large amounts during climax by solitary pleasure. There is a general misconception that the brain responds the same during coitus and self-stimulation because they lead to the same outcome. There is a significant amount of research to the contrary. One of which Brody and Kruger (2005) determine that hormone release during solitary pleasure is “400% higher concentrations”.[169]

In addition, they note that oxytocin activates prolactin in equal amounts. Prolactin is another hormone believed to be responsible for the satisfactory feeling one experiences following climax.

Prolactin creates this emotion by attempting to temper the effects of dopamine.[170] An excessive release of dopamine desensitizes the brain, which, in effect, elevates the need for more of the behavior producing such dopamine levels.[171] Herein lies the tentacles of the liquid handcuff. Like heroin addicts, excessive dopamine will hold a person hostage and in a perpetual chase to relive the explosive experience. In addition, based on principles of psychological conditioning, interviews, and counseling sessions with couples dealing with solitary pleasure and sexual addiction, this author believes that not only is the brain desensitized, but anatomical changes render the androcentric model of intercourse less effective in comparison.

This might account for complaints from spouses experiencing solitary pleasure in marriage in excess.

In most cases, solitary pleasure involves direct stimulation, which, when practiced excessively, conditions the body to respond quicker and more intensely to direct stimulation, in effect making indirect stimulation (traditional intercourse) potentially less productive comparatively. This impacts men and women in different ways, i.e., men who use solitary pleasure excessively not only experience the neurological issues noted above but also condition their anatomy to direct stimulation by something less conducive than the female for which it is designed.

The fallout from this experience is that when the male returns to traditional intercourse, he will experience over-stimulation, which causes him to experience climax much faster, which (as you can imagine) can lead to intimate frustration for the woman most times.

During a counseling session, a church member discloses that her husband's solitary pleasures are in the bathroom. When attempting to have traditional intercourse, he climaxes almost upon contact or shortly after, leaving her frustrated. –Author's file

This same process has the opposite impact on women. Excessive stimulation of the clitoris conditions the woman for the need for direct stimulation to have an orgasm sometimes. This does not mean that traditional intercourse is not pleasurable or does not produce a climax for them. Still, the conventional method becomes more difficult to achieve the same results and often requires much more effort, time, and intensity. A Christian husband (as a part of the therapeutic process for marital counseling) attends an individual session in which he discloses that his wife does not climax through traditional intercourse. [172]

Although he attributes this issue to her sexual behavior, he still feels inadequate as a man and is not sure how to move forward, giving her reluctance to end solitary pleasure.

Jonathan (in Chapter 8), after discovering his wife is having an affair and masturbating secretly, reports that encounters with her changed drastically. Frustration is not his only experience behind this revelation, but the psychological domino effect that further strained intimacy. His analysis of their situation attributes the changes in her body to excessive solitary pleasure and other intimate activities in which she is engaged. To the best of his knowledge, he believes there were no problems in this area before she began this series of intimate events. –Author's file

As mentioned, the anatomical changes that occur after excessive self-stimulation may contribute to the number of reports of intimate problems and dissatisfaction by spouses and partners of those who have solitary pleasure often—many report they cannot satisfy their spouses who practice solitary pleasure in their marriage. As previously mentioned, Dr. Abu Ameenah Bilal Philips alluded to several couples seeking counseling. [173]

Two other issues with excessive dopamine are worthy of mentioning here. 1) The brain can only produce so much dopamine at a time. [174] If the bulk of it expends during solitary pleasure or other intimate experiences, it is not accessible during other significant moments with family, friends, or other things people might enjoy. [175] This may explain why those engaged in an affair often lose interest or are less motivated to be intimate with their spouses. If they do, the experience is less rewarding than other intimate encounters with excessive dopamine release.

If merging dopamine and oxytocin promotes and sustains the relationship between males and females or, in this case, husband and wife, what happens when it is experienced significantly in solitude? One hypothesis suggests that excessive solitary pleasure and oxytocin contribute to a sociality or a predisposition to this behavior or personality.[176] Asociality refers to an individual indifferent to social interaction and often lacks sensitivity to social values and norms.[177] However, the preference for solitude or isolation for those addicted to self-stimulation may be motivated by the desire to create opportunities to continue the behavior as opposed to indifference to social interaction. Regardless, asociality can still develop as an unintended consequence.

2) The amount of brain stress associated with high doses of dopamine is physically taxing.[178] It will burn you out! We often attribute the person's fatigue to other factors like work, school, and family responsibilities, rendering them clueless to the possibility that their brain is over-stressed by high doses of dopamine.

In addition, dopamine is a precursor to stress hormones. Excessive amounts cause the adrenal glands to overproduce, putting the body in a perpetual flight-or-fight stage, which increases cortisol, heart rate, blood flow to muscles, and glucose, straining the body.[179]

The second anatomical issue after excessive solitary pleasure is pelvic floor dysfunction (PFD). It is a disorder associated with aging women, but as you will see, men can experience this as well. The pelvic floor functions like a hammock and comprises ligaments, muscles, and other connecting tissue designed to support organs, including the bladder, uterus, and rectum, by maintaining their anatomical position and functioning. [180] In addition, the urethra, vagina, and rectum are stationary by the work and strength of the pelvic floor. [181] This likely sounds like a bunch of medical science. However, the pelvic floor muscles' role in intimate response is significant in this chapter.

Sarit O. Aschkenazi and Roger P. Goldberg (2009), writing in an expert review of obstetrics and gynecology, note that "the pelvic diaphragm has a crucial role in intimate response... any insult to the pelvic floor might lead to denervation of the female erectile tissues with intimate dysfunction following." [182] Reviewing how the pelvic floor functions during intimate response will expand our appreciation of the research around pelvic pain associated with intense, intimate climax.

Drs. David Wise and Rodney Anderson chronicle the impact orgasm has on the pelvic floor in their book, A Headache in the Pelvis, A New Understanding, and Treatment for Chronic Pelvic Syndrome (6th Edition). They note that compulsive intimate activity causes the pelvic floor muscle to contract and relax during spasms commonly associated with orgasm. In addition, when pelvic issues are already present, orgasm intensifies the tone of the pelvic floor muscles, causing chronic pain for days at a time. [183] Dr. Jeannette Potts (a urologist and pelvic pain researcher) notes and identifies the orgasm as a "pleasure spasm." An increased pelvic floor contractions exacerbate the condition by tightening the muscles even more. [184] Each time the person breaches the threshold of normal pelvic floor functioning, their pain worsens, making their baseline always painful. [185]

According to Wise and Anderson, solitary pleasure deteriorates pelvic floor conditions because it overburdens the pelvic muscles. It is common for this population to experience pain or discomfort hours or days after the orgasmic event. Why? The orgasm produces muscular contractions of the pelvic muscles each second during the event. [186] Compelling already tightened pelvic muscles (whether the tension is from solitary pleasure or the natural process of aging) will hasten the deterioration of these muscles, leaving the victim in chronic discomfort even when they are not having intimate intercourse. However, anatomical issues associated with pelvic floor dysfunction are not confined to the intimate experience. Incontinence, chronic lower back pain, and pelvic organ prolapse (a medical condition that develops when the pelvic floor does not support the pelvic organs) are other problems connected to the disorder. [187] Those issues that play out in an intimate context have their origin in excessive solitary pleasure. Sometimes, solitary pleasure tempers the pain associated with these issues. But, this experience is short-lived in that the pain returns to greater degrees, making the quest for solitary pleasure as an antidote ineffectual.

This is likely what Jonathan (Chapter 8) alludes to about his wife, Ruth. Her unbridled intimate desire and curiosity contributed to excessive solitary pleasure and intercourse with multiple individuals. Jonathan believes that given her medical assessments and his knowledge of her intimate behavior, it is highly probable that these behaviors are the genesis of her pelvic issues. Jonathan notes that her problems surfaced in the aftermath of the pinnacle of her intimate escapades and that the correlation and timing are suspect at minimal. He believes that his wife has not told her doctors about her excessive intimate activity.

It is not likely that her behavior factors into her diagnosis or in treatment, he feels. In his mind, she is too embarrassed about her behavior to disclose such details to medical professionals and in a therapeutic context.

Regardless of the origin of her issues, it is a medical fact that solitary pleasure exacerbates such conditions, not to mention the marital and spiritual problems the behavior produces. Marnia Robinson (2009), in the book Cupid's Poisoned Arrow: From Habit to Harmony in Intimate Relationships, highlights that "compulsive solitary pleasure can trigger what we commonly call prostatitis, a chronic pelvic pain syndrome or pelvic floor dysfunction." [188]

Additional issues associated with self-stimulation are the effects of diminishing returns. The law of diminishing returns is a business concept in which profit levels or benefits fall below the money, resources, or energy invested. In the same way, too many successive intimate encounters will push the person across their threshold of pleasure, diminishing the intensity and effectiveness of the intimate encounter, known as being "sexed-out." There is a temporary effect in which there is no immediate interest or response to intimate overtures. Again, this is likely what Jonathan is referring to when he talks about his wife's issues. Her inability to climax and diminishing interest in him may be due to too many successive orgasms in other contexts. Excessive solitary pleasure can cause "sexual exhaustion," an experience more common with men than women. Sexual exhaustion is different from the diminishing effects of too much intercourse within a short period.

This has nothing to do with weaning interests. According to Dr. Richards, intimate exhaustion results from depleting the brain and nervous system's supply of dopamine. This is the fall-out and by-product of overactive intimate activity. [189] Fatigue, depression and mood swings, generalized anxiety, muscle weakness, headaches, weak erections, low libido, hair loss, ear buzzing and ringing, penile shrinkage, and excessive sweating characterize sexual exhaustion. [190]

Sexual exhaustion can happen to anyone engaged in excessive intimate activity at any age. Take, for example, in an open online forum, a 20-year-old male. The individual has been experiencing symptoms of sexual exhaustion since the age of 14. These symptoms include erectile dysfunction, lack of morning erections, shrinkage of the penis and testicles, semen leakage, watery ejaculation, eye floaters, brain fog, loss of motivation and concentration, chronic fatigue, insomnia, depression, hair loss, and premature ejaculation. He expresses frustration and concern about his inability to pursue relationships due to their sexual performance issues and is seeking help and guidance.[191]

Summary

It is indisputable that self-stimulation or solitary pleasure is an intimate behavior. It is subject to God's holy mandates regarding sexual morality. That the bible addresses all the dynamics and processes associated with solitary pleasure is indisputable. God sanctions one method of intimate behavior, the androcentric model (meaning traditional intimate intercourse between male and female), and in only one context, which is holy matrimony. This chapter produces enough evidence to debunk or push back on the erroneous notion that self-stimulation is not harmful or sinful for anyone.

The fact of the matter is that it can destroy relationships, alter the human body in counterintuitive ways, trample over God's commandments, and dishonor Him as Creator.

The neurological response to solitary pleasure is robust. Solitary pleasure, then, has an addictive quality. The orgasm and the obsessive pursuit of the experience is the liquid handcuff that enslaves, defiles, and dishonors. When God blessed humans with the extraordinary gift of intercourse, it was to aid the process of procreation and strengthen the union between man and woman codified through holy matrimony. Solitary pleasure does not and cannot facilitate this objective. The behavior is not social or relational and can neither develop nor sustain relationships between sexes.

It is incapable of reflecting the image of God. Driven by intimate desire, it breeds lust that the Word of God teaches to abandon upon entering a covenant relationship with Him through Jesus Christ. [192] Emotional profit and euphoric outcomes produced by intimate climax do not evoke freedom to indulge in intimate behaviors that jettison the beautiful symmetry between man and woman in marriage and the honor it gives to the Creator.

The notion that solitary pleasure is an intimate act is indisputable. The truth of the matter is that God only endorses intercourse within the context of marriage. This is the commandment and, therefore, ideal. However, so many indulge in a plethora of ways or contexts. Solitary pleasure as an intimate act falls within the parameters of fornication (porneia in Greek) as it's presented in Matthew 19:9. Here, Jesus uses the word in a way that answers questions about solitary pleasure in singleness and marriage without ever using the word. First, "porneia" is a term used to define intercourse outside the context of marriage[193, 194] whether the person is single or married. It also shows that the act (sex) is the exclusive right and privilege of those in holy matrimony. When an individual practices solitary pleasure in singleness (not married, i.e., those never married; divorced or widowed), it is intercourse, which outside of marriage is "porneia" fornication.

Because solitary pleasure happens in solitary, when it occurs within the context of marriage, it becomes fornication, which in this context is also adultery. God allows those who marry to have intercourse with the person with whom they share matrimony. Solitary pleasure upends the "one flesh or oneness" codified by God through the intimate union of the husband and wife. If we surmise that solitary pleasure is intercourse, one cannot draw any other.

conclusions than those delineated here. Not every person or couple engages in self-pleasure or commits adultery. Despite how society may distort the beauty and balance of intimate relationships, many instances demonstrate the goodness, purity, and unity of the intimate experience within marriage. Although bedrooms are private, the benefits from the work of the Holy Spirit in marriage and the neurological response to the intimate experience are visible in many marriages. We see it through their efficacy of oneness, honor, submission, respect, and love for God through each other. Individuals and couples honoring God with their bodies are commendable for their consistent surrender to the leadership and power of the Holy Spirit. Thank you for your devotion, counsel, and example. Honoring God through our bodies is an exceptional tribute to Him as the Creator. It acknowledges His agenda for our lives and the holiness living within. Maintaining equilibrium with Him in singleness and marriage is an admirable experience.

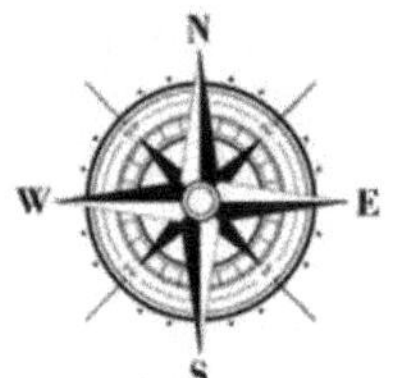

THE GUIDE POST

Ten Steps to Freedom from Solitary Pleasure

1. Terminate all intimate activity (including viewing intimate images) and commit to fasting for 30 days. If you are married, resume intimate activity with your spouse (only) at the end of the fast. This process will help you purify and reset.

2. Upon repentance, seek and completely surrender to the power and leadership of the Holy Spirit. He is a guide, comforter, and counselor who works, revolutionizes, and empowers individuals internally (Rom. 8:4-12, 26-27; Eph. 3:16, 20; Gal. 5:16-17).

3. Identify an accountability partner (preferably the same sex) with whom you can pray, call upon, and fellowship during challenging moments or episodes (Ja. 5:16-17; Gal. 6:2; Rom. 12:10).

4. Rewire your thoughts and neural pathways by consulting scripture (i.e., James 1:13-15; Ps.119:11) and replacing

intimate urges with other thoughts that disrupt intimate patterns. If married, engage your spouse each time you have the compulsion or urge to solitary pleasure (Phil. 4:8; I Cor. 7:2-5, 9; II Cor. 10:5).

5. Avoid (as much as is practical) situations or places that create opportunities and venues for solitary pleasure (Rom. 13:14; Eph. 4:27). Increasing church and community activities will help minimize these opportunities.

6. Identify triggers to self-stimulation and develop coping mechanisms for each trigger (I Thess. 5:8; I John 2:16). A therapist can assist you with this process.

7. List personal rewards of abstinence in singleness or monogamy in marriage. Contrast your list with the adverse outcomes of solitary pleasure.

8. "Exercise to consume the excessive testosterone elsewhere in the body, rather than burn it into DHT via solitary pleasure."[195]

9. Develop an issue-specific prayer strategy and cycle (Matt. 7:7; Eph. 6:18; II Thess. 5:17; Ja.1:5-6).

10. If solitary pleasure has evolved into an addiction, seek professional help through a licensed mental health professional with expertise in addictions. Dopamine and oxytocin are potent chemicals that require therapeutic strategy and extended methods designed to govern inappropriate intimate behavior, identify triggers, and reduce psychological conflict. Allow the therapist and your minister or elder to work harmoniously to establish achievable goals and alleviated spiritual conflict as well.

Chapter Ten Notes and References

[1] Robert Crooks & Karla Baur. Our Sexuality 1996 Brooks/Cole Publishing CO., pg. 7
[2] Kammeyer, W.C. Kenneth (2008) A Hypersexual Society, Sexual Discourse, Erotica and Pornography in America Today. Palgrave and Macmillan
[3] Sands, M. Kathleen, Brock Nakashima, Rita, Countryman, William L., Gudorf, E. Christine, Hunt, E. Mary, Jakobsen, R. Janet, et al. (2000) God Forbid. Oxford University Press (Pg. 55)
[4] Lev. 18:19-24; Rom. 13:13; I Cor. 6:9-11; 7:1-5; I Thess. 4:3; Heb. 13:4; I Peter 3:12; Rev. 2:20-22
[5] Clinard & Meier, 2008:4 (as stated in Becker, Howard S., 1963. Outsiders: Studies in the Sociology of Deviance
[6] Ibid Sands, pg. 54
[7] Ibid, Sands, pg. 48
[8] Dominance of one group over another. Typically refers to elite white men of old.
[9] Typically refers to a system of society or government controlled by men.
[10] Strongly discriminatory against women.
[11] John 12:48
[12] King James Bible. II Timothy 3:16 (Greek translation for inspiration of God or inspired by God is "God-breathed".
[13] New American Standard Bible. Romans 15:4
[14] Ibid. II Peter 1:20-21
[15] II Peter 1:3-ff
[16] Liberty Illustrated Bible Dictionary, 1986
[17] Ps. 103:19; Matt. 5:45; Ps. 66:7; Gal. 1:15; Lk. 1:52; Ps. 4:8;
[18]Kann, E. Mark. Taming Passion for the Public Good, Policing Sexual in the Early Republic. 2003
[19] Neel, Burton. (2012) Sexuality in Ancient Rome, Psychology Today Blog. www.psychologytoday.com/blog
[20] Static moral principles embodied as the foundation for human behavior.
[21] Ibid, Sands, pg.46, 47
[22] Waskul, Dennis. (2003) Self-Games and Body-Play. Peter Lang Publishing
[23] Allen, Dr. Anne Dondapati. Off The Menu. Chapter Ten: No Garlic Please, We are Indian Pg. 189
[24] www.cnn.com
[25] Ibid, pg. 44
[26] I Timothy 2:4
[27] "The premise that political authority belonged to the original generation of fathers, beginning with the biblical Adam." Language, symbols, and images of fatherhood extended to political authoritarians and the concept that "men had the natural authority to govern other men and all women." Kann, E. Mark. Taming Passion for the Public Good. Chapter

One, pg. 2-3

[28] Kann, E. Mark (2013) Taming Passion for the Public Good: Policing Sex in the Early Republic Pg. 2 New York University Press

[29] Ibid. Sands

[30] II Corinthians 6:14-18; I Peter 2:9

[31] Benner, G. David. (1985) Baker Encyclopedia of Psychology. Baker Book House pg. 687

[32] Driel, van Mels (2012) With The Hand. Reaktion Books Ltd. Pg. 62

[33] www.religioustolerance.org/masturba4.htm

[34] *Adams, J.N. (1982). The Latin Sexual Vocabulary. Johns Hopkins University Press*

[35]. Ibid, Pg. 1

[36] David S. Potter & Amy Richlin 2006 The Roman Empire, p. 351.

[37] Antonio Varone, *Erotica Pompeiana: Love Inscriptions on the Walls of Pompeii* («L'Erma» di Bretschneider, 2002), p. 95

[38] Ibid

[39] Genesis 2:16,17

[40] Exodus 20:14, 17

[41] Benedicti (as cited in Jean Stengers & Anne Van Neck, 2001). Solitary pleasure, the history of a great terror.

[42] Women and Hysteria in the History of Mental Health. Cecilia Tasca, Mariangela Rapetti, Mauro Giovanni Carta, and Bianca Fadda Clin Pract Epidemiol Ment Health. 2012; 8: 110–119. Published online 2012 Oct 19.

doi: 10.2174/1745017901208010110

[43] Ibid, Maines, p. 1

[44] Ibid, pg. 101

[45] Ibid, pg. 125, 126

[46] Freud, Sigmund (Vienna, 1926) Drei Abhandlungen zur sexual theorie, 6th Edition

[47] Catechism of the Catholic Church (1997) paragraph 2352

[48] As stated in Driel, van Mels, With The Hand (2012) pg. 158

[49] Ibid, 159

[50] Abdul-hawid van Bommel (Dutch Muslim) as stated in Driel (2012)

[51] Ibid, pg. 162

[52] A Chinese philosophy based on the writings of Lao-tzu (*fl.* 6th century BC), advocating humility and religious piety. www.dictionary.com

[53] Ibid

[54] Om Prakash, Sujit Kumar Kar, and T. S. Sathyanarayana Ra, 2014 Oct-Dec; 56(4): 377–382. Indian J Psychiatry.

[55] https://en.wikipedia.org/wiki/Dhat_syndrome

[56] The books of Exodus, Leviticus, Deuteronomy and II Peter 1: 3-11, 20-21; Romans 1:16-17; II Timothy 3:16-17

[57] Facebook News Room. www.newsroom.fb.com/company-info/ You Tube for Press. www.youtube/yt/about/press/
[58] Ibid
[59] Times of India Life ANI | Sep 5, 2014, 12.00 AM IST
[60] National Survey of Sexual Behavior, 2010
[61] Ibid
[62] Developed by J. Bowlby. The making and breaking of affectional bonds. British Journal of Psychiatry, 1977, 130(Mar. 201-210.
[63] Ibid, pg. 79
[64] Wade C. Rowatt and Lee A. Kirkpatrick, as stated in the Journal for the Scientific Study of Religion 41:4(2002) 637-651
[65] Ibid
[66] Ibid, 638
[67] www.etymonline.com/word/deception
[68] Pope, Charles (January 28, 2014) A Biblical teaching on the problem of (self) deception. Retrieved from: www.blog.adw.org
[69] Thayer, Greek-English Lexicon. Pg. 514, #4105
[70] www.etymonline.com/word/attraction
[71]. Ibid. Allen Pg. 187
[72] I Corinthians 7:1-9 NASB
[73]New American Standard Bible, Foundations Publications Pg. 1160. I Corinthians 7:1-5
[74] Gen. 4:1; Ex. 20:14; Prov. 5:15-23; 7:27; Deut. 5:18; 22:22-29; 23:17; 27:20-23; Numbers 5:11-31; Lev. 18:6-28;
20:13-16; Rom. 1:26-27; 13:13-14; I Cor. 5:1-5; 6:12-20; II Cor. 12:21; Heb. 13:4; Rev. 21:8
[75] I Corinthians 7:8-9 (As best as can be determined, the Apostle Paul was never married and led a single life style)
[76] Ibid, pg. 688
[77] Ibid
[78] Ibid, Driel
[79] Ezekiel 16:15-16
[80] Ibid, pg. 35
[81] Having more than one meaning; having multiple meanings. www.dictionary.com
[82] Zodhiates, Spiros. (1991) Lexical Aids to the New Testament in the Hebrew/Greek Study Bible. AMG Publishers, Pg. 1610
[83] The Complete Biblical Library. 1989 Romans | Corinthians (pg. 327) This is the ransom concept of atonement and salvation. During the time of this writing it was customary for a slave to save the price of his freedom and contribute to the Temple treasury to be purchased by the god. He is to live a life of service and devotion to that god.
[84] Nelson's Illustrated Bible Dictionary (1986) Thomas Nelson Publishers
[85] Ibid, verse one
[86] The Complete Biblical Library Greek-English Dictionary. (1990) pg. 414

[87] Ibid, 415

[88] A Koine Greek translation of the Hebrew text (Jewish), originated between 300-200 BC. www. septuagint.net

[89] Crooks, Robert and Baur, Karla (1996) Our Sexuality. Brooks/Cole Publishing Company pg. 139

[90] Ibid, pg. 5

[91] Ibid

[92] Ibid, 62

[93] Ibid, pg. 56

[94] Hebrews 1:12; 13:8; Ps. 90:2

[95] Exodus 20:17

[96] Suck Won Kim*, Carlos H. Schenck*, Jon E. Grant†, Gihyun Yoon*, Peter I. Dosa‡, Brian L. Odlaug§,
Liana R.N. Schreiber*, Thomas D. Hurwitz*, James G. Pfausll. Neurobiology Of Sexual Desire. NeuroQuantology
June 2013 | Volume 11 | Issue 2 | Page 332-359

[97] Kaplan, H. (1979). Disorders of Sexual Desire. New York: Brunner/Mazel

[98] Ibid

[99] Ibid, 335

[100] The Mayo Clinic http://www.mayoclinic.org/diseases-conditions/compulsive-sexual-behavior/basics/definition/con-20020126

[101] Ibid

[102] Ibid (Kim)

[103] Ibid, (Kaplan)

[104] The Dialogical self is a psychological concept that captures the mind's ability to conceive various points of view within narratives, one has internally balanced with those held externally. The dialogical self is at The heart of the Dialogical Self Theory (DST) was developed in the 90s by Dutch psychologist Hubert Hemans. www.onlinelibray.wiley.com

[105] Genesis 3:1-9. New American Standard Bible

[106] Proverbs 4:23

[107] Proverbs 6: 25-29, 32

[108] Ibid

[109] Ibid, pg. 136

[110] Ibid, pg. 13

[111] Ellis, Albert and Abarbanel, Albert (1973) The Encyclopedia of Sexual Behavior. Jason Aronson, Inc.

[112] Ibid, pg. 531

[113] Hebrews 12:1-2

[114] Proverbs 23:7. KJV

[115] Romans 12:2; Philippians 4:8

[116] Genesis 34:31

[117] II Samuel Chapter 11

[118] Allen Dondapati, Anne. (2008). The Abjection of Female Sexual Desire in Indian Christianity: A Pastoral Theological Analysis. University of Denver

[119] Ibid, pgs. 4-5
[120] Deuteronomy 24:1-5; Matthew 5:31,32; 19:1-9; I Corinthians 7:1-40
[121] Romans 12:1-2
[122] New American Standard Bible
[123] Wuest, S. Kenneth (1961) The New Testament: An Expanded Translation Wm. B. Erdmans Publishing Co. pg. 11
[124] The Complete Biblical Library Book of Romans, pg. 27
[125] Genesis 1:31
[126] Complete Biblical Library Hebrew –English Dictionary Heth-Yodh (2330-3625)
[127] Ps. 139:14
[128] I Corinthians 6:19
[129] I Corinthians 6:13
[130] Ibid, pg. 35
[131] Ephesians 4:4
[132] Colossians 1:18, 24
[133] Genesis 2:24
[134] Complete Biblical Library Greek English Dictionary; Spiros Zodhiates, Strong's
[135] Ibid, Zodhiates pg. 968 (3337)
[136] Genesis 2:18-24
[137] Chung Gwan Joo. (2014) Marriage and Sexuality in terms of Christian Theological Education in Procedia - Social and Behavioral Sciences 174 (2015) 3940 – 3947
[138] The Science of Orgasm. https://www.youtube.com/watch?v=hpc2NjUAtOY
[139] The Journal of Neuroscience. http://www.jneurosci.org/
[140] Ibid
[141] Your Dictionary. http://www.yourdictionary.com/mind-blowing
[142] Ibid, ASAP Science
[143] Ibid
[144] Ibid
[145] Hebrews 13:4
[146] Michael Ashworth (2016) Is It Normal to Solitary Pleasure When You're Married? https://psychcentral.com/lib/is-it-normal-to-masturbate-when-youre-married/

[147] YouTube https://www.youtube.com/watch?v=l4pamthypiY
[148] Ibid
[149] Ibid
[150] Ibid
[151] Ibid

[152] Ian Kerner, CNN. Intercourse isn't everything for most women, says study—try 'outercourse' http://www.cnn.com/2017/08/28/health/intercourse-outercourse-sex-kerner/?iid=ob_homepage

[153] Ibid
[154] Medical Daily website (2014) Clitoral Size, Distance from Vagina May Cause Women to Have Orgasm Troubles. Feb 22, 2014 04:22 PM By Anthony Rivas
[155] Ibid
[156] Ibid
[157] Ibid
[158] Rizzo, Matthew and Eslinger, J. Paul (2004) Principles and Practice of Behavioral Neurology and Neuropsychology. Saunders Publishing Company PhilaRutha, Pennsylvania.
[159] Ask Dr. Richards. (Feb. 4, 2015) http://cure-erectile-dysfunction.org/sex-solitary pleasure-addiction
[160] Ibid
[161] Ibid
[162] Ibid
[163] Ibid, http://cure-erectile-dysfunction.org/sexual-exhaustion-faqs
[164] James Meikel. (Monday 20 June 2005 20.35 EDT) Good Sex is really mind-blowing for women. The Guardian online https://www.theguardian.com/society/2005/jun/21/research.science
[165] Ibid
[166] John A. Johnson (October 20, 2016) Biology Determine Every Thought, Feeling and behavior.Psychology.www.psychologytoday.com/log/cuibono/201610/iology-determines-every-thought-feeling-and-behavior
[167] The Journal of Emergency Medicine | September 2011 Issue
[168] Mind-Blowing Sex Can Wipe Your Memory Clean. Stephanie Pappas, Live Science Contributor | October 11, 2011, 10:42 am ET. https://www.livescience.com/16488-sex-mind-blowing-amnesia.html
[169] Brody, Stuart, and Kruger, Tillman (2005), the post-orgasmic prolactin increase following intercourse is greater than following solitary pleasure and suggests greater satiety. Biol Psychol. 2006 Mar;71(3):312-5. Epub 2005 Aug 10. https://www.ncbi.nlm.nih.gov/pubmed/16095799
[170] Gammill, Justin (October 26, 201) According to Science, It's Time to Stop Masturbating So Much. www.iheartintelligence.com/2015/10/26/stop-masturbating/
[171] Ibid
[172] Web MD (September 20, 2017) http://www.webmd.boots.com/sex-relationships/guide/what-happens-to-body-during-sex
[173] Ibid
[174] Ibid, Gammil
[175] Ibid

[176] Solitary pleasure and Oxytocin
https://www.reddit.com/r/NoFap/comments/tlpko/solitary pleasure_and_oxytocin/

[177] Psychology Dictionary https://psychologydictionary.org/asocial/

[178] Ibid

[179] Ibid, Gammil

[180] Aschkenazi, O. Sarit, Goldberg, P. Roger, Expert Review of Obstetrics Gynecology. 2009;4(2):165-178. Female Sexual Function and the Pelvic Floor. www.medscape.com; www.expert-reviews.com

[181] Ibid

[182] Ibid, 166

[183] David Wise and Rodney Anderson. A Headache in the Pelvis, A New Understanding and Treatment for Chronic Pelvic Syndrome (6th Edition).

[184] Potts, Jeanette M.D. http://www.jeannettepotts.com/ and www.vistaurology.com

[185] Ibid

[186] Ibid

[187] Ibid, Expert Review of Obstetrics Gynecology

[188] Robinson, Marnia (2009) Cupid's Poisoned Arrow: From Habit to Harmony in Sexual Relationships. North Atlantic Books. Berkeley, California

[189] Ibid, http://cure-erectile-dysfunction.org/symptoms-sexual-exhaustion

[190] Ibid, Richards

[191] https://sexualreboot.com/topic/severe-sexual-exhaustion-please-help-me/

[192] Romans 13:13-14

[193] Complete Biblical Library Greek-English pg. 253; line item 4062

[194] Complete Biblical Library Vol. 2 Study of Matthew pg. 401

[195] Ibid, Dr. Richards

11

The Final Verdict

Facing Death and Fearing Finitude

Hebrews 9:27

A man does not die of love or his liver or even of old age; he dies of being a man.

-Miguel de Unamuno

April 18, 2018, I was given a vivid reminder of the uncertainty of life and the inevitable notion that there is something greater than all of us and that it is engineered by an even more incredible power, the Creator. Death, the king of terror, the equalizer and reconciler.[1] It is a paradoxical phenomenon in that it is an antidote and a problem, a Dreamweaver and a nightmare; it's punctual and disruptive. Its power can move slowly and catch and overpower the swiftest and strongest among us.

Death's presence and power are impressionable, neither partial nor prejudiced, taking the male and the female, father and son alike. It can strip wealthy people of their riches and usher a peasant into royalty. On that 18th day of April, my father's identity and life are under consideration before the God of the universe. As God sits on His throne, Dad's predicament and circumstances unfold before His eyes. He became ill suddenly, seemingly, and was hospitalized consequently. Upon this news and as things rapidly unfolded, I was in great distress because I knew it had started... the process that would later lead to his death. I knew he was in trouble and that there would be nothing I could do. Unknown to anyone but myself, God had revealed my father's death in a dream three weeks before. I was so disturbed by the dream that I contacted him the following morning to see how he was doing. There was no indication of anything concerning. But as the events unfolded on the 18th of April, that dream became evermore piercing.

The Dream

In the dream, the funeral home director, concerned about my father's reluctance to stay in his tomb, contacted me. I went to the funeral home and opened what looked like a tomb. Light pierced the darkness as I opened the stone-like door, revealing a neatly pressed, empty black suit. I closed the tomb and searched for my dad. The chapel doors swung open, and I saw him sitting a few pews into the chapel. (*What was unknown to me then was that the chapel in the dream was the same as the funeral home where his service was held.*) I sat next to him, and after a moment of silence, I nervously broke the silence by telling him that he needed to cooperate. He followed me back to his tomb, where men in white coats laid him down and dressed him in the suit. In the next part of the dream, he appeared as a decomposed body wearing an oxygen mask with a long tube attached, possibly indicating the ventilator he was on before he died. White smoke traveled through the tube to keep him unconscious. The dream abruptly ended at this point.

The Deception

The dying process is not always straightforward, quick, or even noticeable. We, like many other families in this predicament, were briefly deceived by "terminal lucidity" (aka "rallying") which is commonly associated with the dying process.[2] It is that brief period in which the patient's condition seems to improve; they begin to sound and act normally. People usually make specific requests when they know they are in this stage. However, in some instances (like my father) they can be clueless and begin talking about what they need to do or plan to do when they get out of the hospital, for example. Dad begins acting like his old self, joking and discussing what must be done. At one point, he sends a message through my sister, saying, "There is no need for me to come; I am ok." In addition, my brother sent a text message noting, "I think he is out of the woods, turning the corner." The update was so welcomed that I decided to drive instead of making an emergency flight home for me and my family. We left almost immediately. However, halfway through the trip, the phone rang, and the message was that things quickly declined, and he had died. There are no words to describe the impact of that moment adequately. I broke... It was like a sledgehammer slamming against a large window, shattering it into hundreds of pieces, like someone took the planet and dropped it on me. My body loses its strength and limps like a noodle. Helpless, anguished, broken, empty, and lost, I pull over and try to gather myself and continue the trek home to not only see my father's lifeless body but to embrace the reality that this is the last time. I stopped at a gas station near the interstate. Distracted by the news, I forgot that my cell phone was on my lap. It fell as I got out of the car, cracking the screen, which, oddly, became a symbol of my broken heart. After evaluating his life and the distress in which dad found himself, I had to accept that God makes an unforgettable and inevitable decision that Sandy J's time is up..."[3] What I had pictured in my mind after I got home was upended by this new reality.

During my tenure in ministry, I have placed many people in the ground, both young and older; written and delivered countless eulogies and have counseled and comforted grieving families; have pulled out the little black book and escorted families to the graveside and seen body after body placed in a grave. Individuals and families have sat in my office seeking guidance for dealing with depression, grief, and other emotional upheavals. I have delivered several messages about heaven and how death is the gateway to the rest of what God has in store for humanity. But even with this experience under my belt, the reality of death is a complicated phenomenon to grasp. My experience and knowledge do not exempt or nullify me from the typical emotional upheaval in such circumstances.

But the Spirit of God, the Comforter and Helper nestled in my soul, begin to heal my shattered heart.

Dancing Around the Inevitable

In 2016, America's annual healthcare expenditures increased by 4.3 percent to a whopping 3.3 trillion dollars.[4] This figure results from our effort and need for services to circumvent death by improving the quality of life, even in retirement. This mind-blowing number does not include billions of dollars spent annually on cosmetic procedures, products, and services. In the age of Botox, Viagra, superfoods, and modern exercise, humans can defy the aging process that leads to death, but these cannot substitute death itself. Death inescapably weaves into the human experience. Seemingly paradoxical, life begins with death in mind. Each moment of our existence marches us to an inevitable grave and irremediable end. Psychiatry professor William P. Wilson (1985) states:

> "Life is animate being, and once it begins, it inevitably leads to death. Death is a cessation of life, an irreversible state characterized by the cessation of all those processes that sustain life."[5]

All branches of science and physics fail to explain the reasons for this unending phenomenon. There is no mathematical equation for death as an inevitable experience or that describes and measures the world of the dead. Physicists cannot give us a kaleidoscopic view of the Unseen world (the world of the dead)or forecast that environment. Irrespective of their brilliance, the soul and the world that embodies it is immaterial. This knowledge is far beyond their reach and understanding, indicative of an entity being more remarkable and powerful than all their brilliance combined. It is a revelation that forces every scientist to their knees, if not in this life, then in the world that follows.

What is Death?

Why does evoking the word create panic or uncomfortable feelings for most people, including people of faith? Faith communities joyfully herald songs like “When We All Get to Heaven When the Roll Is Called Up, Yonder When the Saints Go Marching In, and This World Is Not My Home,” yet run from death like the plague and are despondent when it emerges. Why?

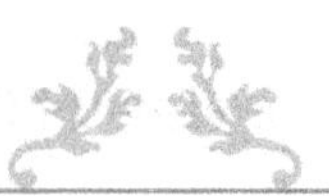

> "When one is afraid of death, when he doesn't look forward, he looks back, death petrifies him. He dies before his time, but when he's living on, looking forward to the great adventure that is ahead, then he lives."
> -Dr. Carl Jung

Humans love successful outcomes but never the process that leads to them. Coveting the benefits of marriage without ever exchanging vows, money without earning it, special skills without training for them, losing weight without going to the gym, and the benefits of Heaven without walking through the process that lends itself to that outcome.

When one surveys people about death, it appears that fear is the leading factor for both non-Christians and Christians struggling with the phenomenon. It is fear of the unknown. Kastenbaum and Aisenberg (1972) identify seven reasons we fear death.[6]

1. The end of all experiences.
2. Life after death.
3. What might happen to the body
4. No longer able to care for dependents
5. The grief that one's death will bring
6. The fact that one's plans will end
7. A painful death

We have little information regarding the soul during death and what transpires beyond it. True, we have heard similar stories of people around the world detailing "near-death experiences." They note peaceful out-of-body experiences, tunnels, and a beautiful light to which they are drawn. Additionally, each flat-line while receiving medical care or had experienced severe illness or accident.

However, Dr. Kevin Nelson, a neurologist (University of Kentucky) notes that "near-death experiences" are likely waking-dream experiences. As such, he identifies scientific or neurological processes that tender explanations for them. This, hypothetically, explains similarities between individuals' narratives about such events.

Dr. Nelson points to the robust activity of our visual system during dreaming to explain the bright light associated with "near-death experiences." The tunnel people see during these moments is likely produced by the eye: "When the retina does not get enough blood, our vision darkens from the edges to the center, creating a tunnel-like effect." But in every instance, the person experiencing the event is confident that they died and returned from t he d ead. Dr. Sanjay Gupta, a practicing neurosurgeon and chief medical correspondent for CNN, details similar narratives of people encountering near-death experiences in his book Cheating

Death.[7] If we surmise that the Scripture is correct (and we must, if we accept Scripture as a source from God, ultimately) it is then impossible for one to die and return to life, a fact explained in more detail later in this chapter.[8] Therefore, it is necessary to differentiate various forms of death. One can experience medical death and yet not die or experience actual death.

These confusing and convoluted implications underwrite the mysteriousness of death, which perpetuates fear in most humans. There are other notable factors contributing to people's fear of death, such as the finality of it. Knowing you will never see or interact with someone you love is disconcerting. Additionally, when death is imminent for some individuals or their loved ones, death anxiety (the inability to "discern the meaning of death")sets in, creating despair in the moment or during the process. How we discern the meaning of death is shaped by cultural values and definitions. In their book, Psychology of Death and Dying, Morgan and Morgan (2005)note and commentate on Robert Lifton and Eric Olson's (1975) psycho-historical analysis of cultural values and death in that they highlight Lifton and Olson's view that we live in an era in which our cultural symbols and values do not provide psychological meaning, which Lifton and Olson dubs psycho-historical dislocation. Morgan and Morgan note that the “effects of this dislocation are the intensification of death anxiety and the need to deny the reality of death itself.”[9] Such denial is sometimes cloaked in religion, which is evident in faith communities that hold that death is annihilation. There is nothing more afterward, or those who believe in reincarnation, which in effect skirts death as a reality.

However, before exploring further into the real meaning of death, it is worth noting that man was created to live, not die. First, let’s acknowledge that there are different types of deaths, i.e.,

- **physical death** (the complete and irreversible absence of life and the separation of the soul from the physical body),
- **medical death** (the point at which medical instruments and personnel can no longer detect signs of life. However, actual death may not have occurred)
- **spiritual death** (the fallout or consequences of violating God’s principles and commandments and separation from God, i.e., Genesis 2:17, “but from the tree of the knowledge of good and evil you shall not eat, for the in the day that you eat from it you will surely die). Notably, spiritual death includes and contributes to the necessity of physical death.[10]

Let's expand this monologue by interjecting other dimensions and concepts of death and their distinctions, namely "natural death and punitive death."[11] As noted above, we should understand and acknowledge that initially, man was created to live, not die. Among all the things God gave and prepared for him, death wasn't on the menu, yet God was ready for its eventuality.

God's work and creativity were not haphazard but intentional, purposeful, and directive. He created the world to support the human body and fulfill his will. The human body, a mind-blowing work of divine ingenuity, harnesses the capacity to develop, expand, and rejuvenate. Dr. Wilson notes:

> "...At maturity, the organism (body) can maintain its integrity by replacing cells that are injured and die..."[12]

H. Christopher (1875), in his book The Remedial System, notes the following:

> "Man was made to live forever. Though mortal as to his animal organism, yet it was designed that he should never die."[13]

There is biblical evidence for this notion. In Genesis chapter two, the Holy record notes that God created the Garden of Eden, within which were beautiful trees for food and, yes, the tree of life to sustain man's life beyond food's capacity. The tree's substance would ideally ward off diseases and likely prevent organ failure. It was to ensure man's body functioned optimally. This was man's support system, designed to preserve his life in the physical realm.

Even though man's soul lives forever, God decided to let humans live and enjoy physical paradise on earth without end. This is evident because the Tree of Life was not subject to the same restrictions as the Tree of Knowledge.[14] This meant Adam and Eve had unimpeded access to a source that sustains life. Christopher (1875) captures the significance of the Tree of Life in this manner:

> *Its virtues consisted in its powers to resist and prevent the wasting or disintegration of the body, and to renew and invigorate constantly the vital force, and thus perpetuate life by counteracting the tendency to decay and death in the same manner, but to a far greater extent, as the ordinary food does in man's extra Eden state... The tree of life, therefore, was designed to afford Adam a fruit that would give him immunity from*

> *disease and death just so long as he had access to it and would use it.*[15]

In this context, one surmises God's intention was for man to live, not die. However, two significant factors altered man's life expectancy, placing him on the trajectory of death.

First, the advent or irruption of sin in the Garden of Eden. Eden was stunning and, more importantly, a holy place, evident by God's presence in the garden.

He walked through the garden, note "They heard the sound of the Lord God walking in the garden in the cool of the day..." (Gen. 2:8) This simple point is significant in that wherever God is present, holiness must rule, i.e., when Moses climbs Horeb, "the mountain of God"[16] to see the Holy One, upon reaching the summit, God instructs him to remove his shoes because the ground upon which he stands is holy![17] Why? Was there something magical in the dirt? No! Simply, it was because God was present, and He is Holy. "By those who come near me I will be treated as holy, and before all the people I will be honored." (Leviticus 10:3)

How riveting and frightening it must have been for Adam and Eve to know and hear the God of the universe, the Creator, and the Holy of Holies walking towards them after they committed a significant error! God shows up asking questions. Whenever God asks questions, it is not because He is without knowledge. He is omniscient. He knows all. God's interrogation is designed to produce an introspective analysis of self, i.e., after Cain's offering to God is essentially rejected, God asks, "Why are you angry? And why has your countenance fallen?" (Gen.4:6) Those questions were designed for Cain to look deep within himself and find the flaw that caused his offering to be rejected. In his case, Cain was arrogant.

He was so impressed with himself, with the optimization and mastery of the gifts and talents God gave him, to the point that he wanted God to be as impressed with him as he was with himself. Hence, Cain gave God the work of his hands, and Abel gave God what He asked for or required.[18] Like Cain, Adam and Eve find themselves in deep trouble with the Creator; their bodies likely trembled like a leaf in the wind as they ducked behind a tree to hide from Him, who sees and knows everything. They must have felt a feeling of doom in their chests as they realized there was no escape from Him or the guilt of their transgressions.

It is noteworthy that Adam and Eve were clueless about their sins' natural effects and consequences. One may argue that God told them, "In the day that you eat from it, you will surely die." Eve (with Satan's assistance)only knew that when she ate it, she did not fall dead, making Satan's words seemingly true; and for Adam, all he knew was that his wife was still alive after having eaten from the forbidden tree. Christopher notes:

> "His mind became clouded, his purpose began to waver, and his wife continued to persuade. His love for her clouded his reason, warped his judgment, and obscured his perceptions. He remembered only that God threatened death, and yet Eve was still alive; so, he wavered, tottered, and fell!"[19]

They have no history, framework, or experience from which to draw to help them fundamentally navigate this challenge. Remember, as noted in chapter one, Adam and Eve were exempt from traditional developmental processes in that, as best as is determined, they were created as adults. Although flawless and pure immediately following their creation, they lack experience with life and the God who authored it.

God likely expected Adam and Eve to trust Him, who created them, and the world they were living in. Subliminally, it was as if God was saying, if I can command the world into existence and bring you to life from mere dust, then surely you can trust my word and obey my commands, even if you are devoid of wisdom. God was looking for devotion and trust in Him as God and Creator, to which they failed miserably. The eruption of sin and its effects c ascaded across the Garden of Eden and throughout humanity into the 21st century in which we now live. The special pristine place sanctified for man's communion with God and where all the things necessary for his survival were available is now contaminated. The once holy ground is now cursed, and[20] thorns and thistles mar the beauty of Eden. The environment has changed because of sin. Initially, it was a place fit for God, but there is no mention of His presence in the Garden beyond man's fall. However, before God leaves the garden, he expunges Adam and Eve from this holy place, creating separation not only between them and God but the tree that was given to sustain their lives.

Therefore, the **second** factor contributing to man's trajectory to death is physical and spiritual separation. As noted in chapter one of this book, after God creates man "of dust from the ground He breathed into his nostrils the breath of life and man became a living soul."[21] Note the point in which the text indicates there is life when God places something in man that he did not have after he was formed from the ground.

The soul and the spirit are of God ("all the souls are mine" Ezek. 18:4)and are the source of life in man and a conduit through which man converses and establishes relationships and fellowships with Him.

After sin's introduction into humanity and its escalation, the spirit's call to man and tenure in the human body is time-limited. In Genesis 6:3, The Lord says, "My Spirit shall not strive with man forever, because he also is flesh; nevertheless, his days shall be one hundred and twenty years." The theological variances associated with this verse suggest that 120 years is the maximum time a person can live on average. Moses lived 120 years, then he died[22]; others contend that this is about the 120 years before God sent the great flood to destroy life on earth.

Writing for the Telegraph, Sara Knapton chronicles an article in which she features scientific research that suggests that humans will unlikely live longer than 125 years, even with medical advances.[23] Irrespective of the position one holds, the Holy record affirms that life before the flood reached into the centuries, with Methuselah topping out at 969 years of age.[24] Can you imagine what their bodies must have been like? Their stamina and slow aging process would blow the minds of physicians today. Cosmetic services would go bankrupt in that era!

However, after the flood, their bodies changed or were significantly impacted by environmental changes, drastically reducing life expectancy, a fact that seems to breed life in Knapton's article. Some hold that the change was because the flood was so massive it tilted the earth's axis, exposing life to the more harmful rays of the sun and shortening man's life expectancy. Naturally, planetary scientists and physicists think such an idea is moronic. Any assertion that the earth's axis changed after the flood upends their physics and ultimately supports the existence of God as Creator, which is a fact they foolishly deny. However, according to Genesis chapter six, the flood is the fallout of pervasive evil and sin on earth.

It was a direct response from a Holy Creator to a wicked creature. As such, we reject erroneous notions such as the flood not happening, the result of an asteroid falling from space into a body of water displaced upon impact, or any other ridiculous explanation. Most people of faith believe unequivocally that this was an act of God!

The penalty for sin is death, i.e., "For the wages of sin is death..." (Rom. 6:23) In essence, sin produces separation, namely between God and man, i.e., "Behold, the Lord's hand is not so short that it cannot save; nor is His ear so dull that it cannot hear. But your iniquities have made a separation between you and your God, and your sins have hidden His face from you so that He does not hear..." (Isaiah 59:1-2, NASB)

Ezek. 18:4[b] "...The soul who sins will die" (Ezek. 18:4)and of course, the first teaching and warning ever given to humans "...for in the day that you eat from it, you will surely die." (Gen. 2:17) As previously noted, Adam and Eve were separated from God's presence after they sinned.

The concept of death as separation is a logical approach, given that it is diametrical to the initial process of life. Remember, God "breathes into man the breath of life," which we know as the soul.

It is a process of life that God automated. Job synchronizes life with "the breath of God in his nostrils (Job 27:3) Earlier, Job states that the life of everything is in the hand of God (Job 21:10) We now know that while in the womb, the infant uses its mother's placenta to breathe during development. However, the first breath is necessary to affirm lif e after exiting the womb. We are aware of the scenario in which the doctor holds the baby up and taps its bottom to stir a cry, fill the lungs with air, and, in effect, replace t he fluid in the lungs.[25] Medline Plus Medical encyclopedia is one of many resources that helps us understand that upon the first breath, the body experiences many physical reactions as it adapts to extrauterine life.[26] The breath of God has to be filled with enormous and mind-blowing capabilities. When God breathed into Adam's body, it came to life. His heart began to beat, carrying blood through the pristine vessels in his newly formed body; his chest rose as the respiratory system kicked in. As his retina floods with light, the neurons in his brain fire rapidly to comprehend the environment he finds himself and the immaculate being or Creator standing before him. He is in that moment, perfect!

There is another example of the fact that life does not exist apart from the breath of God. Namely, in Ezekiel chapter 37, the prophet is given a vision featuring the restoration and reanimation of Israel by the Spirit of God. To capture the point, Ezekiel is placed in a valley of dead men's bones. He is commanded to speak the word of God to restore them. Subsequently, the bones came together, and flesh covered them, and we can assume every other aspect of the human body (organs, vessels, etc.)was also in place. However, the text makes an exciting notation in verse 8. Although the flesh and bones came back together to form bodies, there was no life; "there was no breath in them." Then God tells Ezekiel to command "the breath" (wind/air)to breathe or blow on the bodies, "and they came to life..."[27]

Ironically and significantly, the Hebrew and Greek words for breath translate wind or spirit. As such, their connotation is indicative of the similarities between them. The soul, breath, and the wind are inanimate substances. The soul is only noticeable when the flesh embodies it; the wind can only be heard or felt; only when it is embodied by debris or some other tangible substance is it visible, i.e., we are only aware of whirlwinds when they are embodied by the dust of the ground, otherwise though they are audible and sensed they are invisible. An instructor at the former David Lipscomb University School of Preaching once told his class, “You haven’t seen me, just the house (body) I live in...” referring to his soul, the natural person.

Following this simple logic, if breath or wind is the medium through which the soul enters the body to establish life, then it is conceivable that a diametrical process will produce opposite results. In other words, if the body is only alive when the soul is present, then death is the separation of the soul from the human body. Hence, the Greek word Thanatos (which means separation) describes or names death. Interestingly, Thayer (1977) defines death as "...separation of the soul from the body by which life on earth is ended."[28]

The soul, in essence, is a being separate from the body and, therefore, exists outside the body, but the body cannot exist without such a being. The soul is immaterial. As such, it is eternal and can only be destroyed by its Creator -God, a fact to which Jesus Christ alludes in Matthew 10:28:

> "Do not fear those who kill the body but are unable to kill the soul; rather, fear Him who can destroy both soul and body in hell."

Physical death is, in fact, the separation of soul and body. Adam and Eve's expulsion from the Garden is viewed as spiritual death, separation from the immediate presence and fellowship of God. This separation leads to their physical death because they no longer have access to the Tree of Life, which was designed to sustain the body. Essentially and simply, it is cause and effect, the tentacles of which are far-reaching. Because sin entered the world, all flesh or all men must die. The Apostle Paul, writing to the church in Rome, notes that death is passed on to all men because of Adam. This is a convoluted concept for those who do not know or follow the Word of God.

It seems so unfair. Why should the rest of humans suffer for the failure of the initial two? Note Romans 5:12-14,

> "[12] Therefore, just as through one man sin entered into the world, and death through sin, and so death spread to all men because all sinned—[13] for until the Law sin was in the world, but sin is not imputed when there is no law. [14] Nevertheless, death reigned from Adam until Moses, even over those who had not sinned in the likeness of the offense of Adam, a type of Him who was to come."

A complete exegesis of this topic and passage is much more involved, convoluted, and protracted than what is outlined here. To temper and laser our focus on the subject and tenor of this chapter, the passage summarizes as follows:

Adam is seen as the "federal agent" of mankind or a type thereof. Sin entered the world by or through the agency of Adam. Interestingly, the Greek word for world in this text is "kosmos," translated as "cosmos," and refers to the world, meaning humanity. The concept of sin did not originate from Adam but from Lucifer, the Devil. Although, indeed, Eve was first deceived and, in effect, Satan's conduit to Adam (to whom God gives dominion, Gen. 1:26-28) they both become conduits through which sin enters the world. However, Adam, as the federal agent of the race, is identified as "the one" through whom sin enters and dies because of sin. All men die (even those who did not sin during Adam's time or beyond) because of Adam's sin. [29] God's government and justice demand that there is a penalty for sin, hence the phrase "thou shall surely die" or the soul that sins shall surely die." This phrase and the manner and context in which it is given is incredibly significant. The words "shall surely die" appears in several places in the Old Testament and as best as is determined from the original language refers to an immediate and violent death. In other words, the penalty for sin demanded an immediate and violent death! This is punitive death. Examples of this (which appears after the Law of Moses is instituted)are found in Leviticus 10:1-3, in which the sons of Aaron offered up to God a sacrifice he did not command. Subsequently, they were killed instantly! Additionally, throughout Leviticus and especially chapter 20, death was the penalty for immorality and other sins. Finally (and in rare form in the New Testament) in Acts chapter 5, Ananias and his wife Sapphira essentially died for lying to the Holy Spirit.[30]

Why did Adam and Eve and other humans who sinned behind them not experience such a death immediately? Two reasons: 1)Concerning 'other humans,' Paul points out that sin and death reigned from the time of Adam to Moses, during which there was no law. Subsequently, where there is no law, transgression is not imputed (Rom. 4:15; 5:13).

The Law was added because of men's sins (Gal. 3:19). This does not mean that evil did not exist or that there were no sins against God; it simply means they were not imputed, counted against those living during that period, temporarily. Punitive death was postponed until the substitute was ready.

Second, and more specific to Adam and Eve, is the fact that the love of God intervenes. The expulsion from the Garden of Eden was an act of holiness, righteous indignation, and love. Knowing the penalty that was due, God kicked the man out of the garden to save and restore him later. Careful analysis of God's response to Adam and Eve displays divine wisdom and intelligence manifest in the scarlet thread and scheme of redemption. It is the most significant upset and plot ever exposed to the minds of men. It is in Genesis 3:15 that God declares war and victory simultaneously. This single text becomes the cornerstone for the rest of the bible. After Satan's deception and man's fall, God states,

> "...And I will put enmity Between you and the woman, and between your seed and her seed; He shall bruise you on the head, and you shall bruise him on the heel." NASB

The seed of the woman is Christ. The bruising (or crushing, which is a more accurate translation) symbolizes the victory over Satan, sin, and death. “Shall bruise him on the heel” refers to Christ's crucifixion, the medium through which this victory is accomplished.

Satan, having duped Eve and toppled Adam, reclines over his temporary success, foolishly underestimating the power of the God who created him. He sees his demise in the beginning.

The Apostle Paul captures God’s scheme by referring to a first and second Adam, with the first Adam as a prototype or symbol of the second. The second Adam is Christ. Both figures have a dramatic, life-altering effect on humanity. The first Adam brings condemnation and death, t he second salvation and life. But more to the point and the question raised, the death penalty reprimanded and imposed on Adam and Eve is postponed for the second Adam (Christ)to bear and experience, not only for their sins but for all the sins in the world. In other words, Jesus Christ bears the penalty rightfully imposed upon Adam and Eve. Punitive death becomes the central focus of Christ’s mission on earth. He was born to die, born to be the substitute and sacrifice for the cosmos. As such, he is appropriately named Jesus, which means Savior of the world.

His death was not scheduled as any death, but a violent death, a harsh, cruel death. The type of death Christ experienced was necessary to appease the wrath of an angry God. Theological variances are surrounding whether the death of Christ satisfies God's wrath. However, to maintain the subject matter here, I will not engage the debate any further than the following texts:

> "Much more then, having now been justified by His blood, we shall be saved from the wrath of God through Him." Romans 5:9 NASB

Furthermore, the prophet Isaiah proclaims this same truth long before Romans was penned:

> "But the LORD was pleased to crush Him,
> putting *Him* to grief; If He would render Himself *as* a guilt offering, He will see *His* offspring,
> He will prolong *His* days, And the good pleasure of the LORD will prosper in His hand. [11] As a result of the anguish of His soul, He will see *it and* be satisfied; By His knowledge the Righteous One, My Servant, will justify the many, As He will bear their iniquities." Isaiah 53: 10-11,

> "and He Himself is the *propitiation* (satisfaction in the original language) for our sins; and not for ours only, but also for those of the whole world." I John 2:2 NASB

The need and manner of such death was imminent. Therefore, in Luke 9:22, Matthew 16:21, Mark 8:31, and 14:21-23 Jesus repeats the statement, "The Son of Man must die and suffer many things." The Holiness of God demands that a penalty, price, or debt be imposed for sin. It was a special penalty and debt that was only satisfied in a unique way and by a holy person. Christ paid this debt on the cross. Note Colossians 2:14:

> "having canceled out the certificate of debt consisting of decrees against us, which was hostile to us; and He has taken it out of the way, having nailed it to the cross."

The crucifixion was one of the most horrific forms of punishment and torture ever concocted by humans. Hanging was the term used in Jesus' day for crucifixion. The Romans of His day were the most barbaric of people. However, even they limited who was exposed to such horror. Their law was that Roman citizens guilty of punishment were exempt from

crucifixion a s a method by which s uch punishment was inflicted. Although Romans were known to be ruthless, it was the Phoenicians who devised crucifixion.
Several nations utilized this method of cruelty during that time, i.e., Assyria, Media, and Persia. Notably, Alexandra the Great ordered the crucifixion of 2000 people in Tyre.[31]

The Holy Scripture does not detail the gruesome way Jesus died. However, we understand these details through historical records about crucifixion generally and Christ's crucifixion specifically, i.e., Flavius Josephus (a Jewish historian writing during the time of Christ)chronicles the crucifixion of Christ in his records on April 3, AD 33.[32] Before the Romans crucified Christ, they beat or scourged him with thongs weighted with metal, which crushed and tore into the flesh of Jesus. As such, before Jesus was even nailed to the cross, his flesh was already ripped open. Mocking him, they made a crown of thorns and pressed it into his head for him to wear as King of the Jews. Behind this, He was forced to carry the beam (a tree)until he could not carry it further. Upon reaching the destination for the crucifixion, a 3-foot hole is dug out to place the cross into. The beams are laid out, and Jesus is forced to lay down on them. They drive spikes into feet and hands while he is already suffering from the wounds inflicted by the scourging and the crown of thorns.

All his ribs are visible when they stretch him out onto the beam. He hangs for six hours in scourging heat. There is a tiny seat fixed to t he cross, b ut it is insufficient for any comfort.

Every movement tears wounds already present. Given the position of his body, blood pools in His abdomen, causing pain you would not believe. At this point, not only is His body suffering, b ut His mind is in anguish a s well. His lips are severely cracked, and his throat is parched beyond belief. His vocal cords are so inflamed that they alter the sound and tone of His voice to raspy utterances. His joints are agonized and almost pulled out of the socket. They give Him vinegar to drink under such conditions. He gathers enough strength to utter a few words, among which were the most powerful words ever to pierce man's ears; it is finished! What is finished? The violent death is necessary for t he penalty of man's sins, the type of death required to appease the wrath of God, and the process for peace and reconciliation to a Holy, loving Creator.[33]

The Unseen World

Given that humans are made of flesh that is only animated and living by the indwelling presence of a soul, which is immaterial and eternal and separates from the body at death, what then happens to the soul? Death is the complete, irremediable separation of the soul from the body. We have some idea about what happens to the body because, in most cases, we attend funerals of family and friends and visually understand that the body is placed in the ground and ultimately returns to the dust from where it came. In other cases, this process is expedited by cremation. However, we don't see the soul, that part of the person that gives life and personality. Where did the soul go?

The blank stare you are probably experiencing now is not uncommon. Most people do not have an answer to such a question or find it too uncomfortable to contemplate. This is where many will flip the switch, turn the page, change the subject... and ignore the question. Why? Because of fear of the unknown. Information concerning the afterlife is limited at best. As such, ambiguity about death is seemingly inescapable.

As previously noted, several people claim they have experienced the afterlife only to return to this one, and people like those enumerated in the book The Afterlife Unveiled claim to have information about the afterlife by communicating with the dead via mediums.[34] While not privy to all the details and contexts of the situations contributing to their claims or their veracity, based on the limited information the Holy Scripture gives us about this topic and on these alone, such acts or experiences are improbable.

Have you ever attended a grave site ceremony, which typically follows the funeral service? If so, you may recall the preacher or priest leading the family and the deceased's body from the hertz to the burial site. There is a black book in his hands.

As they trek toward the burial site, the clergy reads or quotes Psalm 23:4

> "Yea thou I walk through the valley of the shadow of death, I will fear no evil; for thy art with me; thy rod and staff comfort me."

Then, after a few additional words, mainly to the family of the deceased, the preacher picks up or has at his disposal dirt or dust, which is slowly sprinkled over the coffin or burial site while repeating these words:

> "And now, as we stand beside this open grave, in this silent city of the dead, we commit this body to the ground: earth to earth, ashes to ashes, dust to dust - and we commit the spirit."[35]

Where does this come from? In the Old Testament of the Bible, the Ecclesiastes writer encourages all people to "Remember Him" (referring to God) during our lifetime and before the advent of old age and death, which he frames in this manner:

> "[6] *Remember Him* before the silver cord is broken and the golden bowl is crushed, the pitcher by the well is shattered, and the wheel at the cistern is crushed; [7] then the dust will return to the earth as it was, and the spirit will return to God who gave it." Ecclesiastes 12:6-7

It is believed that the soul will depart like it entered the body. In some cases, those witnessing death note that the deceased's final act is a frantic attempt to grasp for air (a type of respiratory distress)but only to exhale and, in some cases, violently. It displays the body's natural desire and tendency for life. However, these details are not realized by every person experiencing death.

Regardless, the soul leaves the body and goes to the "unseen world." What is this place? If it is unseen, how do we know it exists? How do we know if departed souls are not floating around in the atmosphere searching for an avenue back to life and reality? How do we know that they cannot communicate after they have departed?

The Holy Scriptures provide limited but rich information that answers some questions about the afterlife and the world of departed souls. Only one passage in the Holy Scriptures gives us a few clues regarding what happens when we leave this life. Ironically, Luke (a physician by trade) records Christ's words about what happens after death.

Although noted in the New Testament, the time of the event reflects a period during the Old Testament, the time of Moses precisely. This passage is a parable. As such, some caution how much of it is literal. However, Jesus used parables to convey truth and spiritual principles. Subsequently, he never used things or stories that were not true to communicate the truth. Additionally, the Hebrew word Sheol and the Greek words used for Hell and Hades affirm and coagulate what Jesus describes in this parable, strengthening the narrative's veracity and making the story worthy of note. The passage is as follows:

> **19** "Now there was a rich man, and he habitually
> dressed in purple and fine linen, joyously living in
> splendor every day. **20** And a poor man named
> Lazarus was laid at his gate, covered with

sores, **21** and longing to be fed with the *crumbs* which
were falling from the rich man's table; besides, even
the dogs were coming and licking his sores. **22** The
poor man died and was carried away by the angels
to Abraham's bosom; the rich man also died and was
buried. **23** In Hades he lifted his eyes, being in
torment, and saw Abraham far away and Lazarus in
his bosom. **24** And he cried out and said, 'Father
Abraham, have mercy on me, and send Lazarus so that
he may dip the tip of his finger in water and cool off my
tongue, for I am in agony in this flame.' **25** But
Abraham said, 'Child, remember that during your life
you received your good things, and likewise Lazarus
bad things; but now he is being comforted here, and
you are in agony. **26** And besides all this, between you
and us there is a great chasm fixed, so that those who
wish to come over from here to you will not be able,
and *that* none may cross over from there to
us.' **27** And he said, 'Then I beg you, father, that you
send him to my father's house— **28** for I have five
brothers—so that he may warn them so that they will
not also come to this place of torment.' **29** But
Abraham said, 'They have Moses and the Prophets; let
them hear them.' **30** But he said, 'No, father Abraham,

> but if someone goes to them from the dead, they will repent!' **31** But he said to him, 'If they do not listen to Moses and the Prophets, they will not be persuaded even if someone rises from the dead." (Luke 16:19-31 NASB)

In conjunction with the Bible's keywords associated with death and the afterlife, this passage provides an overview of where the soul goes and some information about the world. Let's begin with keywords in various scriptures that give insight into death and the world of departed souls. We must acknowledge that the unseen world is a world, a place for unique habitation. Souls do not float helplessly and aimlessly around the atmosphere after departing the body. This world (obviously created by God) is designed explicitly for disembodied souls or spirits. As best as determined, it is a waiting place for such beings.

Hollywood, comedians, and people's erroneous views or perceptions generally pale compared to what happens after death. Although an oversimplification, it is worth noting that people's dogs and other animals will not be there to greet the soul upon its arrival.

Pride and narcissism are not stroked and pacified there; services for Netflix and Comcast cable are unavailable;

iHeart Radio does not play there; There is no signal for the Internet. Discover, Visa and American Express are useless; the thousands, millions, or billions of dollars a person may have selfishly harnessed and protected are out of reach. The billionaire and the homeless person are now equals. The color one's skin used to be, and its associated privileges do nothing to advance the soul. There is no marijuana for lounging in grassy meadows or bottles of Hennessey for hanging out on the corner.

Three key Greek words answer some of the most critical inquiries about life after death. These words are 1) Tartaroo, translated as Tartarus; 2) Geenna, translated as Gehenna; 3) Haides, translated as Hades. When appropriately used, each word refers to a different section of the "unseen" world or the world itself. However, any of the three words can be translated as Hell. [36] Subsequently, this fact adds to the confusion about what happens in the afterlife. In other words, all three Greek words can be translated as Hell in any text they appear. Therefore, if the reader is unaware of the distinction (which should be made by those teaching the text) between the words, they will walk away with an incomplete or erroneous understanding of that text and the events of the afterlife to which it relates. Kenneth S. Wuest (1973)does an excellent job delineating and distinguishing these words.

Subsequently, this writing adapts some of his scholarship for the sake of the argument.

First, Wuest (a New Testament Greek Scholar) notes that the Greek word Haides comes from a stem that means “to see” and, coupled with its prefix, creates a composite that means “not to see.” As such, the noun form of this word is “unseen.” Hence, the “unseen world” holds all immaterial or inanimate beings. These include the souls of humans (righteous or wicked), angels kicked out of heaven, and any demonic beings. To a greater extent, heaven is classified as an unseen world, but not the place disembodied souls go before Judgment Day; notably, as each word suggests, these are not all held in the same section of the unseen world.

When Hades is used in Luke 16:23, it refers to the section of the Unseen World reserved for the ungodly dead. The opposite side or counterpart is referred to in this text as “Abraham’s bosom,” a phrase that Israelites use about Paradise. By all indications, Paradise is a place of comfort and reward for those bound for heaven eternally. However, when the Greek word Hades is used in Matthew 16:18, it is about the entire Unseen World and should be translated as Hell, according to Wuest.[37]

The Bible refers to the lake of fire after the final judgment; Hell is translated from the word Ghenna, which was used by Christ frequently (Matt. 5:22,29, 30; 10:28; Mk.9:43, to name a few) and is used in Revelation 20:14, 15. This is the destination for ungodly people. This is the connotation used most often when the word Hell is read in the bible, which in some cases is an incorrect application.

The final Greek word for Hell is Tartarus, which specifically refers to the place reserved for fallen angels as used in II Peter 2:4. As best as is determined, this world is a part of the Unseen World but separate from where the souls of humans are held. However, the story of the rich man and Lazarus is centered on the part of the Unseen World that houses disembodied souls of men and, as such, provides additional information about life after death. Notice the following points the passage yields about death and the afterlife:

- After the soul leaves, angels direct it to the proper waiting place, at least for those bound for paradise and heaven. The text indicates that this world is divided into at least two unconnected sections. There is a vast and deep chasm between the two sections, so much so that reaching one side from the other is impossible. Think of something like the Grand

Canyon to capture the image. This is important for two reasons, one addressed below; the other is because Jewish rabbis taught that the two sections were only a "finger's breadth apart."[38] As Jesus narrates the story, He is mindful of the erroneous teaching and includes details to debunk such notion. Additionally, one side is likely dark, fiery, and disturbing, and the other is illuminated, tranquil, and comfortable. It is uncertain whether the ungodly souls are escorted to their waiting section. The text only points out that the angels carried Lazarus away. Interestingly, angels accompanied Jesus during his ascension back to Heaven (Acts 1:9-11).

Recently, at the bedside of a dying father placed on life support, his 4-year-old son entered the room with his mother. Looking at the tubes running in and out of his father, he began to question the nurse about their function. His mother explained that his dad was going to heaven to be with God. The little boy was concerned and asked how he would find his way.

How will he know how to get there? The Chaplain, also present in the room, asked, what do you think? After pondering a few seconds, he says, "Oh! The angels will show him how to get there!"

- Upon arrival, Lazarus and the rich man are conscious and able to exercise some of the same senses associated with the body, i.e., sight, sound, sensory, and emotion. Some questioned the distance between the two sections, given that the rich man and Abraham could communicate. However, one should not assume that the physics used in a material world like ours also applies to an immaterial world. It is not with human ears that they can hear each other. Although intangible, the soul appears to be recognizable.

- They have a memory of their former life and people significant to them. Additionally, we can surmise that the soul knows what transpired leading to death. This should be of no surprise. As indicated in chapter one, we have long since believed that the soul harnesses the seat of all emotions and is, in fact, the natural person. The body, though magnificent, is merely the vessel, venue, and conduit through which the tenor and desires of the soul are manifest. In their book The Spiritual Brain: A Neuroscientist's Case for the Existence of the Soul, Mario Beauregard

& Denyse O'Leary (2007) makes a research-based conclusion about the existence of the nonmaterial nature of man.[39]

- What is equally striking about the person or soul in the Unseen World is that it harnesses (primarily) the same perceptions, prejudices, and other cognitive processes held when they were alive in the body. In this scenario, although in agony, the rich man sees himself as one who should be served and Lazarus as one who should serve him. It solidifies that how we die, meaning mannerisms, thought processes, and desires, regenerate or unregenerated, is the same way we wake in the next life.[40] This is like Revelation 22:11

> "Let the one who does wrong, still do wrong; and the one who is filthy, still be filthy; and the one who is righteous, still practice righteousness; and the one who is holy still keep himself holy." NASB

The condition of our souls at death is the condition in which it resurrects on the other side. Contrary to what Catholics and other people believe, the Unseen world as a waiting place is not an opportunity to renegotiate one's spiritual condition.

There are no mediators or the option and ability to pray one's soul out of condemnation. The rich man pleads for mercy or wants to change his condition, but his request is declined. Additionally, Abraham points to his time on earth as the opportunity and period to do what was right.

Final Verdict

Death is the permanent escape from the irremediable process of deterioration, separation from a life subject to disobedience, defilement, and various forms of suffering for some. It is the gateway to the final declaration of God's matchless love and Holiness. Contrary to secularism and materialism, death is not the end but halftime for a four-quarter theocratic affair. Time is not equalized across quarters in this event but shortens and protracts as these events unfold. The Unseen world is the 3rd quarter, a period and place where man faces either a grim or gracious reality. In the third quarter, man is stripped of all tangible support garnered throughout his lifetime and returns to the state where he began his trek without anything. Notably, the Ecclesiastes writer states:

> "As he had come naked from his mother's womb, so will he return as he came. He will take nothing from the fruit of his labor that he can carry in his hand." (Eccl. 5:15).

... unless he was wise enough to make an immaterial investment in eternity. As such, he faces whatever condition he finds his core person or soul. For some, this is agony, torment, grief, and regret; for others, it is restorative, tranquil, comfortable... just downright blissful!

The dynamics detailed in The Unseen World are merely a prelude to the finale and final act of divine affairs. Everything happening before the fourth quarter prepares us for the events poised for that final period. In this context, one cannot broach the subject of death without including judgment. Let's look at the text again; "...it is appointed for men to die once, and after this comes judgment" (Heb. 9:27).

One aspect of theology many people are bewildered about is eschatological things (Study of the last things, i.e., the Second Coming of Christ, final judgment), a fitting category for judgment. We are vexed by two opposing poles or extremes, in that on one side, some exaggerate eschatology to the exclusion of other critical biblical teachings, and on the other are those who are so misguided and mystified by it that they leave it alone altogether. Whenever either side broaches the subject, everything is usually conflated and unfolds in one day, one event. For some, the Lord returns, the church or the saints, Israel, the other nations, the unbeliever, Satan, and his demons are judged, and the destruction of the current heaven and earth unfolds all in one day. God has continuously operated in phases. In addition, these usually see or understand judgment in a one-dimensional paradigm, when biblically, there are different kinds of judgments, i.e.,

- Cosmic judgment, the general judgment pronounced through the death of the entire human race (Gen. 2:7; Rom. 5:12; 6:23).
- Cataclysmic judgment, exemplified through the flood (Gen. 7-8), Sodom and Gomorrah (Gen. 19), and Bethsaida and Capernaum (Matt. 11:20 and Lk. 10:13-15).
- Current judgment of wrath on the world as featured in John 3:36 and Romans 1:18-32.
- Christians' work and behavior in the body (I Cor. 3:11-15; II Cor. 5:10). Notwithstanding, this judgment

should not be conflated (in nature or time) with the scene in Revelation 20:11-15. In the former passages, the Christian is only under judgment for works or deeds done in the body, for which we will be rewarded. There are two essential points about judgment in these passages.

- Firstly, the phrase "stand before judgment Christ" is not meant to be punitive here; it is not for sins the Christian may have committed after baptism. Christ's substitutionary sacrifice and death cover the believer's condemnation and consequences for sins.[41] Paul emphasizes no condemnation for those in Christ Jesus (Rom. 8:1). Salvation is a gift, not a reward, and not obtained through works (Eph. 2:8-10; II Tim. 1:9; Titus 3:5).

Secondly, the word "judgment" in the Corinthian passages is not used to determine salvation. This is evident from the language Paul uses in the narrative found in I Cor. 3:11-15. It is mentioned explicitly that after burning up useless works (classified as wood, hay straw), the Christian suffers a loss, but not the loss of his soul ("but he shall be saved," where the word "save" refers to salvation from Hell). The Christian's useless works will be burned by fire, not the individual. Additionally, the Greek word for "evil" in II Cor. 5:10 does not refer to sin but to something useless and does not bring glory to God.

- Eschatological Judgment (the final verdict) is what Rev. 20:11-15 is about. The White Throne Judgment does not include those who are true Christians. This is for those who are not covered by the blood of Christ because they denied Him, did not believe, and therefore rejected the Gospel. These will stand in judgment without a divine covering for their sins and will subsequently be judged by their works and deeds recorded in God's book. Only those in Christ's name are recorded in the Book of Life.

Judgment is one of those words that regularly makes people uncomfortable. People generally do not like to be judged, undergo processes where their inner workings and identity are laid bare, or experience judgment that makes them look inadequate or wrong. For many, this means keeping certain aspects of the inner self or psyche hidden.

However, when the Bible speaks about judgment or the final verdict, it routinely notes exposing the hidden things of life, a person's inner being.

For instance, Ps. 33:13-15, Ecclesiastes 12:13-14, Matthew 10:26, II Corinthians 5:10, and Hebrews 4:13 speak about those things that are private or hidden in our lives and will be exposed as part and parcel of judgment. Among these, II Corinthians 5:10 is (perhaps) the most descriptive and informative regarding this element of the judgment process. There are two interesting Greek words to this end, "appear" and "judgment" or "judgment seat." The Books mentioned in Revelation chapter 20 detail every thought, utterance, and behavior of every human that has ever lived. Numerous passages suggest that we live constantly under God's watchful eye, which, given His Omnipresence, should not be surprising. He is a holy God and Creator to whom all His creation is subject and must give an account. No part of our being or our lives is exempt from this reality.

Subsequently, those thoughts of envy and jealousy, pride, and lust that one may have believed were unknown are known by God. Those hidden moments of spousal or child abuse, as well as the sexual exploitation of women, are documented in Heaven. Atrocities committed by leaders of countries and factions are also reported. The evil of human trafficking and sordid acts of racism and prejudice have not gone unnoticed. God has noted the unscrupulous business deals, greed, and the unfair division of family inheritance. In addition, God's eye has captured the astonishing acts of forgiveness and love toward the unlovable, and other deeds of righteousness do not go unnoticed by Him.

In II Corinthians 5:10, the text says, We must all *appear*..." The word "appear" means more than just showing up. The word is phaneroo in Greek, and its root signifies one brought into the light to expose one's true character. The idea is to take the lid or cover off something, in this case -the self. Every aspect of a person's inner being is laid before the Lord. This is significant because there are five people in every person, which manifests in this manner:

- Projected self: This is the person you want everyone to know and see, but it may not be reflective of the real you.

- Public self: This person sees and knows things about you that you do not know or will not accept.

- Proper self: this is the person who knows what is right but struggles periodically

- Private self: this person will hide and protect certain things about you at all costs.

- Hidden self: this is the person no one knows, including the self, yet this person exists and impacts relationships.

We will stand before the Lord as we are. The next step is found in the word judgment seat. Originating from the Greek word Bema, it refers to a method and a place with profound divine significance. Bema describes a seat or throne and an elevated space accessible only by a series of steps. Consider the Lincoln Memorial as a vivid example. It is only accessible by steps. Psychologically, the idea of steps takes a person up and away from people and substances we have grown to depend on over time. Metaphorically speaking, we are summoned from the crowd to stand alone before God and give an account of the life lived. There are no lifelines given here. We cannot call our best friend to help answer the questions presented. This is a moment of divine urgency and responsibility, a moment that demands our full attention and preparation.

At some point, our time on Earth will end, and we will face judgment before God. Our soul will leave our body, and all material possessions will be left behind. After this, the soul enters the Unseen World, divided into two sections: Hell for the ungodly, a place of torment, and Paradise or Heaven for the Godly, a place of eternal comfort and rest. Depending on whether a person dies or the Lord returns, Angels may guide the soul to its proper place in the afterlife, offering a sense of divine guidance and reassurance.

During the soul's tenure in the Unseen world, it will have recall and emotions and can experience some of the same senses experienced in the human body. The soul cannot leave this world on its own or at will; neither can those on the outside enter or communicate with the soul. There are no second chances to correct errors or change the soul's condition. The condition in which we die is the condition into which the soul awakes. It will know whether it made it just a few seconds after the soul's permanent departure from the body.

Preparing to Meet God

In Psalm 139:16, King David makes a powerful statement that few Christians pay much attention to: "And in Your book were all written the days that were ordained for me when as yet there was not one of them." Before David was conceived and born, God had already determined how long he would live. The reality of this statement is so heavy, mind-blowing, and entirely uncomfortable for many Christians. It is loaded with powerful truths about God's sovereignty and wisdom and much about man's weakness and gullibility. The Hebrew writer's statement parallels this concept by using the words "appointed to die." Given this reality, it behooves all of us to invest in our soul's condition for the afterlife. We are taught to diligently prepare for retirement and those "just-in-case" scenarios that can potentially surface even during that period of our lives. Those who do not prepare for retirement via education, vocational training, saving, and investing money are considered unwise.

Death is the gateway to judgment, and for those in Christ, it is the unavoidable pathway that leads to the presence of God. Regardless of how long one lives in this life, it pales compared to the eternity spent on the other side. The certainty of death warrants every person to prepare adequately to prepare to meet their maker. Preparing for this life, but not the next, is irrational.

The foolishness of this is best noted in two examples given by Jesus. The first of which is emphasized in Jesus' discussion about discipleship contrasted with one's love for this life, to which He says: "For what will it profit a man if he gains the whole world, and losses his own soul? Or what will a man exchange for his soul"? Mark 8:36-37.

The second example comes from a story in which a man approaches Jesus about his brother who would not finely divide the family inheritance (Luke 12:13-14), out of which Jesus makes two profound statements. At first glance, it appears Jesus isn't concerned about the issue and quickly dismisses the man. But afterward, He makes these statements, the first of which directly responds to the brother's problem over the family inheritance. The second is about a rich man wanting more. Jesus states:

> "Beware and be on your guard against every form of greed; for not *even* when one has an abundance does his life consist of his possessions." (Lk. 12:15).

> [20] "But God said to him, 'You fool! This *very* night, your soul is required of you; *now*, who will own what you have prepared?"

Interestingly, the Ecclesiastes writer states:

> "He who loves money will not be satisfied with money, nor he who loves abundance with its income. This too is vanity." (Eccl. 5:10).

However, God is not a killjoy or one who does not want us to have and experience the best life can be. Several scriptures support this fact, two of which are noted below:

> "There is nothing better for a man than to eat and drink and tell himself that his labor is good. This also I have seen that it is from the hand of God." (Eccl. 2:24).
>
> "Furthermore, as for every man to whom God has given riches and wealth, He has also empowered him to eat from them and to receive his reward and rejoice in his labor; this is the gift of God." (Eccl. 5:19).
>
> 10 The thief comes only to steal, kill, and destroy; I came that they may have life and have *it* abundantly." (John 10:10 NASB)

As it appears here, the word abundantly refers to life in the surplus. It is from the Greek word Perissos, which means- more than enough, much or great, overflowing or exceeding.[42] Our task is not to chase this recklessly, selfishly, ungratefully, and in a way that injures others.

The fact of the matter is that both rich and poor die alike. Regardless if you are an Atheist, Materialist, or subscribe to a philosophy or way of life that extols man, demeans and dismisses God, or whether you are a devout believer, young or elderly, death is imminent. As such, time is not on our side. While one may not be able to erase all fear and pain associated with death, it is undoubtedly reduced by understanding the process and the purpose for it.

It may seem as if life marches on day by day. Even if one subscribes to that concept, the end is inevitable. God did not create humans to live independently of Him. We were made for a purpose, primarily to give glory to God. Life is about Him and less about us. He extends life and blessings from His abundant grace, but only for a pre-ordained period. After this, every soul will stand in judgment for the life lived. The burning question for every human is, what will be the final verdict?

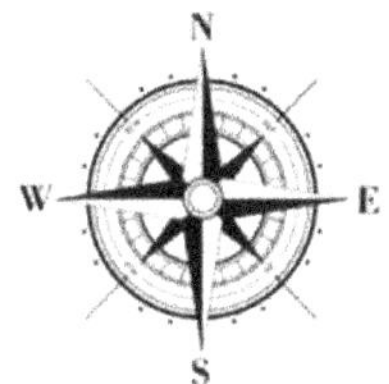

THE GUIDE POST

Seven Suggestions to Help Mitigate Unresolved Grief

1. Understand the inevitability of death as a part of our existence as opposed to the end of life.

2. View death as necessary for our fallenness and essential for eternal redemption.

3. Appreciate the distinction between "chronological and qualitative time."[43] It's not how long it takes but in what manner or way one lives.

4. Prepare for death as one prepares for retirement to ease the burden and pain of those left behind. Pray for wisdom and guidance.

5. Identify positive memories, things, and relationships about the deceased to mitigate some of the grief associated with their departure.

6. Reconnect old relationships halted or interrupted by their departure and initiate new relationships.

7. Resume normal activities, i.e., work and family commitments.

Chapter Notes and References

[1] The King of Terror: Job 18:14

[2] A phenomenon in which the dying suddenly surges with energy, clarity, and a sense of normalcy. Some refer to this as a "rally." While this process is shrouded in mystery, many believe this is a part of the dying process that provides an opportunity for the patient and the family to say goodbye or have closure. Usually, when people are aware that they are in this stage, they will request their favorite things, i.e., songs, meals, or other experiences that can help them engage in their current condition. While this might help explain the psychology of it, Dr. Craig Blinderman highlights the physiological possibilities for the notable experience. Dr. Blinderman suggests that lucidity is a direct fallout from the organs shutting down and their subsequent release of steroids that briefly energize the body before death. See the New York Times Article, 2018. Dr. Blinderman is the Associate Professor of Medicine and the Director of the Adult Palliative Medicine Service at the Columbia University Medical Center.

[3] An Indelible and Inevitable Decision, the eulogy of Sandy J Allen by Dr. E.D. Allen

[4] Centers for Medicaid & Medicare Services. www.cms.gov

[5] W.P. Wilson (1985) Death and Dying in Baker Encyclopedia of Psychology 1985

[6] Robert Kastenbaum and Ruth Aisenberg (1972) The Psychology of Death. New York: Springer p. 1

[7] Sanjay Gupta, (2009) Cheating Death the doctors and medical miracles that are saving lives

[8] God can suspend natural law and reverse death to life. Life is in Him, and death is at His will. Gen. 2:17; Jo. 1:4; 5:26; 11:25; Heb. 9:27

[9] John C. Morgan and Richard L. Morgan (2005) Psychology of Death and Dying. Wipf and Stock Publishers, pg. 19

[10] Romans 5:12-14

[11] Christopher, H. (1875) The Remedial System, pg. 382-383

[12] Ibid Wilson (pg. 282)

[13] Ibid, Christopher (pg. 382)

[14] Genesis 2:16-17

[15] Ibid, Christopher (pg. 80, 81)

[16] Exodus 3:1

[17] Exodus 3:1-6

[18] Genesis 4:3-5

[19] Ibid, Christopher pg. 96

[20] Genesis 3:17

[21] Genesis 2:7

[22] Deuteronomy 34:7

[23] The Telegraph 5, October 2016 Humans are unlikely ever to live longer than 125 years, scientists claim. Retrieved June 20, 2018

[24] Genesis 5:27 * This author is aware of the argument by Ellen Bennet, who argues that the Septuagint Genesis 5 numbers are in tenths of years, which "will explain how it was that they read **930 years** for the age of Adam instead of **93 years**, and **969 years** for Methuselah instead of **96 years** and **950 years** for that Noah instead of **95 years**"...

[25] About Kids Health (October 18, 2009) Baby's first breath. Retrieved from https://www.aboutkidshealth.ca/ Article?contentid=420&language=English

[26] Changes in the newborn at birth (October 18, 2017) Medline Plus Encyclopedia. Retrieved from: https://medlineplus.gov/ency/article/002395.htm

[27] Ezekiel 37:1-10

[28] Thayer Greek-English Lexicon of the New Testament. Pg. 282

[29] When Adam's sin is identified as the reason for every man's condemnation, what is crucial in that concept is not the actual sin he committed but the fallout from it, the corrupt condition that is now in every human born after him. This is what the Apostle Paul is explaining in Romans 5:11-ff.

[30] Acts 5:1-11

[31] Nelson's Illustrated Bible Dictionary (1986) Pg. 267

[32] The Complete Works of Flavius Josephus (1960) Kregel Publications

[33] Romans 5:10-11

[34] Stafford Betty (2011) The Afterlife Unveiled: What 'the dead' tell us about their world. Books Publishing CO.

[35] Christian Minister's Manual (1983) DeHoff Publications

[36] Kenneth S. Wuest (1973) Wuest's Word Studies From the Greek New Testament Vol. III, pg. 48

[37] Ibid

[38] Complete Biblical Library. Luke, pg. 499

[39] Mario Beauregard & Denyse O'Leary (2007) The Spiritual Brain: A Neuroscientist's Case for the Existence of the Soul. Harper One Publishing

[40] See Jo. 3:1-6

[41] The atoning work of Christ was extensive in that it includes all sin permanently. See: Hebrews 9:28; 10:11-14

[42] Ibid, pg. 1,151

[43] Ibid, Morgan & Morgan. Pg., 59

12

Recalculating, turn Right

The proverbial pursuit of happiness

Saturday morning is one of the few periods in which most people's day does not begin with a buzzing alarm clock or a melodious tune emanating from a cell phone. In my home, my daughter's euphoric chatter pleasantly suspends the serenity of slumber accustomed to the dawn of the weekend. Every morning, she wakes up animated over the pleasant things on her mind the night before or the expectations of the day ahead. In my effort to break free from a deep sleep, my eyes flicker intermittently at the ceiling as sounds of happiness drift down the corridor. Listening to her narrated dialogue from Disney movies, PBS videos, and Sesame Street, I wonder how it feels to be that happy and not have a care. She is a 15-year-old child with autism and Mosaic Down Syndrome. [1,2] Although a teenager, her disabilities confine h er cognitive function[3] to that of a three-and-a-half-year-old child. She is in a perpetual state of bliss while living in a paradoxical handicap. Her cognitive structure presents polar realities that limit her functioning yet emancipate and deregulate her soul. For instance, the limitations of her cerebral cortex make tying her shoes too complex for her to grasp. [4] In addition, her Executive dysfunctions restrict her capacity to understand or conceptualize specific thoughts and behaviors deemed normal for you and me. [5]

But the things that handicap her here are the things that protect, purify, and liberate her. Given her cognitive condition, she has no concept of evil; she does not know what it means to hate; her love is perfect and undefiled. She is the purist human I know. There are traces of God in her eyes. Happiness emanates from the purity of her soul.

What is happiness?

In contrast, people with average cognitive ability are striving to attain what my daughter and other individuals with Down syndrome already possess - happiness. The inevitable tug and scuff to be, belong, and become dominate the human agenda. Preoccupation with dissatisfaction cloaks true essentials for meaningful living. The human trek obscures authentic happiness. Dallying over what happiness looks like and how to find it, many unconsciously substitute their perception of happiness for what they believe is genuine. Cultural influences, religious beliefs, and family values are critical components of people's perception of happiness. Subsequently, happiness is subjective and relative, meaning it depends on the individual, a fact apparent by the plethora of avenues people pursue to experience happiness. Sometimes, we define happiness as positive emotions. The euphoric feeling develops after experiencing satisfaction or reaching a goal.

People seem happier when directed behavior achieves an identified end or goal. It is not always about the process; the result and the desired outcome are significant to most people. For instance, college students are not always fond of the academic process, i.e., late nights, excessive reading, papers, and exams, not to mention ongoing inconvenience to their social life. However, upon receipt of their degree, they are happy about the outcome, which, in this example, extends many years into the future.

Money, power, sexual pleasures, freedom of choice, and tangible possessions are what most people attribute to being the fundamentals of happiness.

In this context, happiness is having the capacity to do whatever you want whenever you wish. For others (although unrealistic) happiness is life with no adverse consequences. Others see happiness as the realization of dreams, a career, or the beginning of a new relationship.

Psychology defines one's assessment of happiness and satisfaction as Subjective Well-Being (SWB).It is a scientific term for happiness. As inferred by its name, SWB is unique to the individual and a self-reported measure. There are no guidelines necessarily. However, any assessment of individual happiness requires an analysis of one's personality, perception, environment, and relationship with God. God is not a common factor for those living outside the kingdom or church; sometimes, He is not as large of a factor as He should be for those living within the kingdom. The power to develop one's spiritual self, a critical step toward happiness, lies in the hands of the individual. [6]

Often, people build their happiness on temporary or inadequate things for extended satisfaction. The likely reasons so many people gravitate to things insufficient for happiness are a deficiency in understanding what

happiness

is, personality challenges, and an inadequate appraisal of their needs. The various measures lay people and professionals use to find happiness give us ideas of what makes people happy. There are cognitive approaches, measurements of an individual's emotions, and the ability to acquire coveted resources used to assess happiness.

For many, money is a significant factor in measuring happiness. One of the biggest myths about happiness is that more money will do the trick. Having swallowed that deception hook, line, and sinker, many people spend enormous time and effort accumulating as much as they can garner or earn. However, this relentless pursuit of material possessions often leads to a sense of emptiness and dissatisfaction, highlighting the futility of this approach to happiness.

In a survey by Gallup in 2006, 73% of students entering college and universities showed that one needs to become well-off financially. [7] In addition, they affirm that they are happier with more money. These are presumably out of college now and in their respective careers and a vital part of the current economic fabric of the country. The mantra, "money can buy happiness," is a pseudo-concept. Study after study shows that more money does not translate into a happier life per se.

This indicates that more and more money has a diminishing return because it makes less of a difference in happiness. [8] For instance, psychologists and sociologists investigating the human pursuit of happiness raised three significant questions: [9]

- "Are people happier if they live in rich countries?"
- "Within any country, are rich people happier?"
- "Does the happiness of a people rise over time with rising affluence?"

Although the inclination is for wealthy nations to have happier people, the correlation between the two fades after a certain income level. In addition, other reports suggest that the relationship between personal income and happiness is unimpressive. [10]

The National Opinion Research Center notes that although America's buying power has multiplied over the years, the country's reported level of happiness remains unaltered. [11] Money can make life comfortable but is insufficient for meaningful, long-term satisfaction. In addition, having too many options or choices is counter-productive and can cause more misery in the long run. Dr. Barry Schwartz, professor of psychology at Swarthmore College, notes that while freedom of choice is good, there is "diminishing marginal utility in having alternatives." he is referring to too many alternatives as opposed to none. [12] In addition, marketers study all consumers' Internet searches and shopping habits and tailor the outcome to the individual. Later, they will advertise 32 options of the same product to entice the buyer. Since emotion drives most people's shopping habits instead of intelligence, they are more likely to survey all 32 options before selecting.

Schwartz dubs these as "maximizers". They must explore every single choice before selecting and are often unsatisfied afterward. In addition, he states that more choices "requires increased time and effort and can lead to anxiety, regret, excessively high expectations, and self-blame..." [13] After much time and effort, these are often unsatisfied with their choice and are subject to repeat the process at another store. The closet of such a person is likely inundated with new dresses, shoes, or suits that still have tags on them. We do not limit this mindset, behavior, and facade to experiences at the mall. Instead, it often occurs within intimate relationships between family members, friends, or others. One's understanding and expectations of happiness influence how one approaches it, what one deems significant, and t he mechanisms used to achieve it. The Illustrated Oxford Dictionary defines happiness as "Feeling or showing pleasure or contentment; fortunate, pleasing."[14]

How people define happiness varies across cultures and religions. But the problem with modern society's definition and understanding of happiness is self-indulgent.

Happiness is a state of mind rather than the essence of an individual. So, happiness is evocative of something temporary. Subsequently, there is an ongoing scavenger hunt for happiness.

In the chemical sense, scavenger refers to a substance added to a mixture to remove or inactivate impurities. [15]

People are constantly weeding out experiences, things, and people that prevent this state of mind or adding those that ensure positive outcomes, even if only perceptional.

Notwithstanding, there are critical benefits to happiness, even temporary ones. Research shows a correlation between happiness and success.[16] Those who are happy are usually successful, and those who are glad are so glad. In addition, the Arnhem Study, longitudinal research of seniors that extends over a decade, shows that happiness may lead to increased physical activity, which expands a person's life span. The desire and pursuit of happiness are as normal as breathing and healthy for those experiencing it.

Myers points out that happiness does a world of good. He highlights the "feel-good, do-good" phenomenon noted among psychologists. When people feel good, they do good deeds, such as volunteering, donating, or helping others in intangible ways. People should encourage others to be happy and do positive things that promote happiness. I emphasize positive thinking because we cannot ignore that some things people engage in and use to promote happiness are not healthy, moral, or legal.

The Opposition to Happiness

Phantom forces are working in opposition to happiness. We need not forget that Satan, our adversary, and the people working on his agenda are not interested in our joy. Satan's interest lies in annihilating anyone who believes in and follows God through Christ, period. As noted in chapter one, underestimating and miscalculating his tactics is detrimental and will manifest in various parts of your life. [17] He studies us and learns what makes us tick, how we work, what we desire most, and why. He presents options that are not always evil on the surface. Most often, the contrary. He appeals to us with personal interests we have identified as critical to our stability and happiness; those things, experiences, and people many figures impossible not to have in their lives. He is the master deceiver, so we must know and understand the enemy. [18]

The segment of the public that is unchurched, de-churched, or who otherwise have a nonexistent relationship with God is clueless about the origin of the challenges and mayhem that play out in their lives. Those things that keep their hearts preoccupied and away from God are the tools used to masquerade true deliverance from their circumstance. Most times, they attribute the trouble periods in their lives to every source but the chastisement of God or the work of Satan. Drug issues, financial challenges, mental disorders, sexual desire, power, narcissism, domestic violence, and other forms of interpersonal conflict are small samples of the weapons in his arsenal. [19]

In other instances, drama, mayhem, and upheaval are not the modus operandi Satan is using to upend the lives of people. For example, it is the false sense of security in self, sole confidence in one's ability, excluding God or the need for a relationship with Him. [20] The Devil uses problematic relationships and circumstances, such as the troubled teenager or mounting stress from caring for an aging parent while managing a successful career that overtakes individuals.

In another practical view, inadequate self-appraisal, meaning an incorrect analysis of one's needs and wants, obscures happiness. For example, a person experiencing spiritual, psychological, and physical injury from a prior relationship may not need another one to address the vacancy and hole left in their heart. However, if their own (often misguided) appraisal of self suggests the need for another relationship, they are more likely to enter the next relationship vulnerable to similar experiences. The key here is self-awareness and understanding our needs and wants, empowering us to make better decisions for our happiness. Sometimes, the wish for happiness through a relationship can be so overwhelming that the individual will take the risk by entering the next relationship.

The happiness they seek eludes them. We await God's healing, deliverance, and timing for a new beginning. [21] Spiritual guidance and time-limited therapeutic intervention are likely necessary for healing, restoration, and prerequisites for the next relationship too soon.

Another opposition to happiness is over-self-indulgence, which leads to selfishness and isolation. Excessive self-indulgence indicates deeper issues within the individual. Happiness is not just about personal satisfaction but also about building a good living experience for oneself, extending the opportunity to others, engaging with others, and exchanging talents and gifts for their greater good. Studies show we are happier when we reach beyond self.

Myers' list of evidence-based suggestions for a happier life includes reaching beyond self by helping those in need and various acts of kindness. Do something for someone for which they can never repay you. This emphasizes the importance of community and connection in our pursuit of happiness, making us feel a sense of belonging and social responsibility.

Where Happiness Lives

In one aspect, the journey to happiness is a subjective experience because it largely depends on the individual. However, certain aspects of life ensure tranquility, healthiness, and productivity and improve relationships, contributing to happiness. Wherever these live, happiness will exist.

- **Nurturing the soul** is chief among the list of characteristics for happiness. Nurturing requires intentionality and attention to detail, such as feeding, training, cultivating, educating, and strengthening. [22] Another way to nurture your soul is to allow the Spirit of God to lead you into the deeper, uncharted areas of your heart you have yet to explore. For example, the diplomatic person, the talker who never stops long enough to learn the value of listening, or the prideful giver who is learning to appreciate the kindness and gifts of others. These are new dimensions for such people, which might usher in levels of tranquility and satisfaction unrealized. Don't fear becoming the other or evolving into someone you have never been; such an experience might make your life different. God encourages every Christian to grow and mature, which, for some people, is a new world of peace, knowledge, wisdom, and happiness. [23]

- **Healthy relationships** are another place where happiness flourishes. We are created as social beings needing companionship and close connection with others.[24] Unhealthy relationships breed unhappiness or discontent and can become destructive to an individual and others. Like-minded relationships increase understanding and communication and extend care to those involved.[25]

- **Positive thinking** is another characteristic of happiness. Keeping your head right is essential. Abandon the negativity, which will routinely rob people of their joy and inner peace. We are the sum of our thoughts. [26] Focus the mind on things that are

> pleasant and holy. [27] This does not mean ignoring issues in a person's life; on the contrary, they do not dominate the mind of a joyful person.

If you are traveling the right road in the wrong direction, turn right. I flew into Atlanta International Airport. The city was in the middle of an upgrade, with construction everywhere. I picked up the SUV from the rental agency and then drove into that old scenic city of the south, Chattanooga, Tennessee. After a week in the town, I returned to Atlanta Airport to catch my flight. Construction alters the route as I approach the usual route to the airport. I turned on the navigation system to help me get to the airport on time for my flight.

However, what the navigation system was registering did not align with what was happening on the road. Traveling in the direction I thought and knew to be exact, I kept running into a dead end created by reconstruction. I kept turning around, and as I did, the navigation system kept saying, 'Recalculating, turn right.' I can see the airport close by; planes are flying overhead, so close, but I can't get to it! Looking at my watch, I'm starting to get nervous... that window of time that ensures catching the flight on time is closing.

After so many rounds of this, out of frustration, I scream, "Dang-it! I'm turning right!" then, irritating me to the tenth power, the system says again, “recalculating turn right.” I go back in the opposite direction and pull into a convenience store to ask for directions. As I was approaching, a person was leaving the store. I stopped him and asked for clarity. He says, “You are on the right road, except instead of going straight down, because of the construction, turn right, and it will take you straight into the airport and the road for car rental returns.

The paradoxical message is that the right road may not mean you are traveling in the right direction. Although I accessed the right road, I still needed to know where I was going. I was on the right road to the airport, but reaching the ultimate direction required a right turn. Oh, how so many are on the right road but using their directions to reach the ultimate destination. Many people have found happiness doing what they love, what feels good, and what produces the desired results. Some have become so good at this they map their route to heaven. But sometimes, what feels good and seems right is not. [28] The first clue is t he ever-pressing need for more to sustain the euphoric outcome of happiness. This is a sign that something is still missing. What many expect happiness to deliver is found in something different- joy.

Joy is not a state of mind but a state of being.

Although happiness is a natural, important part of the human experience, people of faith and others conflate happiness with joy. They appear similar and sometimes interchangeable. Happiness is a state of mind often produced by dynamic and fleeting experiences. Conversely, joy is an incorporeal entity that is much more profound. It is not a state of mind or developed through passing experiences. Instead, it is a state of being, one's essence, which refers to something intrinsic and holds indispensable properties that are the catalyst characterizing or identifying an individual. It is immutable if a relationship between the distinguishing source and the individual or object exists.

This status and outcome are strategic and do not happen haphazardly, which is one reason they cannot develop through fleeting experiences or the reason those things that bring us happiness cannot bring us joy.

This joy is precious or invaluable because it is only available through cultivating a relationship with God through the vicarious death of Christ and the regenerating work of the Holy Spirit. Happiness is an experience; joy is an essence. Although pursuing happiness is right, God never intended for the fleeting experiences that constitute this state of mind to be consistently satisfied. Happiness soothes the mind, but joy soothes the soul. It is a more profound experience. If you could take our experiences and notions of happiness and configure them into a navigation system, it would say, " Recalculating, turn right." The navigation system is commonplace in the 21st-century automobile. It will let the driver know when they are off course if activated.

Suppose a person views happiness as acquiring material substances and euphoric experiences as essential components of lasting happiness and expects them to be the holy grail of satisfaction, tranquility, and peace. In that case, you are traveling in the wrong direction. There is likely no human being who does not want to be happy and completely satisfied. We can find what we seek in our relationship with God through Christ. What is most often unrecognized, even by people of faith, is that joy is the by-product of the

Holy Spirit. It is a fruit of the Spirit, and why can it not develop through any other relationship or fleeting experience? [29] It is an outcome reserved for those who believe in God, have entered a relationship with Him through Christ, and are benefactors of the presence and work of the Holy Spirit. Does this mean that Christians are the only happy people in the world? No, happiness and joy are different.

For instance, each time Jesus notes the word "joy," it is within the context of a relationship with Him and the

Father. [30] In addition, the word is used regarding completion, perfection, and confirmed satisfaction, lacking nothing and permanently connecting with said relationship.

This joy deepens and increases through sacrifice and obedience to God through Christ. The better the relationship, the more joy one will experience. Union with Christ cultivates a level of joy that produces a peace unrealized in others. [31] In Galatians 5:22, where the passage delineates the fruits of the Spirit, note that the word joy appears after the word love. [32] This is intentional. When the passage itemizes the fruit of the Spirit, they present it in a strategic order. Joy is the fallout of love. When God loves us, and that love is reciprocated through Christ, it produces joy unrivaled by any other person, relationship, or experience. [33]

The Spirit forms a triad that births love, joy, and peace. All the fruits of the Spirit are available to us because of Christ's redemptive work, which highlights why having a relationship with Him is essential. The proverbial quest for happiness or absolute satisfaction must ground itself in the reality that life is fleeting.[34] Relationship with God through Christ allows us to invest in eternity instead of what is a temporary abode.[35] You may have found the right road but traveling in the wrong direction. Recalculate, turn right. Do not let the quest to be, belong, and become obscure God's purpose for your life. [36] Losing sight of God's intended purpose for your life creates misalignment, disorder, and a constant chase for meaningfulness and happiness. God has always wanted man's tenure on earth to be as blissful as possible. [37] This is evident by the paradise in which God created him and the plethora of gifts given to men throughout the ages. [38] From the engineering brilliance of the Egyptian Pyramids to 21st-century technology serving humanity, it indicates a brilliant Creator. A hypothesis twenty years ago is now a reality. Today, we have cloned other animals and invented artificial intelligence (AI)to aid humanity's living experience. [39] We have orbiting satellites that can see the ocean floor, powerful telescopes capturing the beauty and wonder of God's universe, and the ability to see the body's inner workings. We have cars that drive themselves and social media platforms that enable instant worldwide communication. Notwithstanding, God's interest and commitment to not only man's joy but his happiness began soon after his creation. To solidify humanity's happiness and ensure man's terrestrial tenure is optimal, God gave him a gift; a gift designed to merge with his soul and one with which he would operate in stereo; a gift with immense capacity, beauty, and power: it's like divinity in motion, because this creature moves with grace and thunder, and has the capacity for love at depths unparallel to any other created being. God gave man this gift to help him, to complete him. It was to keep him from wandering and provide companionship, confidence, and inner strength. When Adam saw and accepted God's gift with great joy, he cried, "This one shall be called Woman!"[40] Pursue happiness, but find joy before your time on earth expires.

Chapter Notes and References

[1] Autism is a diagnosis made during childhood and results from altered rain circuity directly connected to neurons and communication between different brain regions. The effects of this are noted in the child's inability to appropriately interpret the thoughts and feelings of others and difficulty with speech, communication, and social interaction. For additional information, see David G. Meyers (2008) Exploring Psychology 11th Edition; Blakeslee, S. (200, February 8). Focus narrows in search of autism's cause. Retrieved from: www.nytimes.com.

[2] Mosaic Down Syndrome, aka mosaicism, is technically a rare form of Down Syndrome, which itself is the result of an extra copy of chromosome 21. Typically, physical deformities accompany the diagnosis. However, Mosaic Down Syndrome may not present significant physical deformities commonly associated with Down. MDS is a mixture of cells with 2 or 3 copies of chromosome 21. For additional information, visit www.mosaicdownsyndrome.com

[3] The capacity to know, think, recall, or remember and communicate, as well as the mental activities associated with this process.
See Myers, G. David (2008) Exploring Psychology 11th Ed, for additional information.

[4] The cerebral cortex is the body's central control and information processing. It connects the cerebral hemispheres. Ibid Myers, 2008

[5] The interruption or disruption of the dyad of cognitive process that manages other cognitive functions and behavioral control.
Executive function is a broad term used to highlight a plethora of cognitive processes or higher brain functioning, such as setting objectives, monitoring or self-evaluation, goal setting, etc.

[6] Myers, David (1993) The Pursuit of Happiness. Harper Paperbacks

[7] Myers, David (2007) Psychology of Happiness Scholarpedia, 2(8):3149 doi:10.4249/scolarpedia.3149. Retrieved from www.scholarpedia.org/article/Psychology_of_happiness

[8] Diener, E. (2019). Happiness: the science of subjective well-being. In R. Biswas-Diener & E. Diener (Eds), *Noba textbook series: Psychology.* Champaign, IL: DEF publishers. DOI:nobaproject. comsentfulness held in response to the fault.

[9] Ibid, Myers

[10] Ibid

[11] As stated in Myers (2007)

[12] Schwartz, Barry (June 2006) More Isn't Always Better. Harvard Business Review. Retrieved from: www.hbr.org/2006/06/more-isn'tt-always-better

[13] Ibid

[14] Illustrated Oxford Dictionary (2003) Revised and Updated. Pg. 271

[15] Chemicool Dictionary Retrieved from www.chemicool.com

[16] See: Psychology of Happiness: The psychology of behind happiness-how positive affect is quantified and what influences happiness. Retrieved from: www.psychologistworld.com

[17] I Peter 5:7

[18] Revelation 12:9

[19] Ephesians 6:11,12

[20] Luke 12:13-21; Col. 3:17

[21] Isaiah 40:31

[22] II Peter 3:18; Eph. 3:16-21

[23] Hebrews 5:12-6:4

[24] Genesis 2:18;

[25] Philippians 2:19-20

[26] Proverbs 23:7

[27] Philippians 4:8

[28] Proverbs 14:12

[29] Galatians 5:22

[30] John 15:11, 16:24; 17:13; I John 1:4

[31] John 16:33

[32] The word "fruit(s) is used here to signify that the following is the result of the strategic work of the Holy Spirit, which cannot be replicated at such level, type, and intensity but by the Spirit Himself. Solidifying that these experiences are only available through Christ and the Spirit. There is nothing in this world that can produce such permanent experiences or outcomes.

[33] Romans 14:17; 15:13

[34] James 4:14; Job 7:7; Ps. 39:4-6

[35] Ephesians 5:15-17

[36] Ecclesiastes 12:13

[37] John 10:10

[38] Exodus 31:3; Ephesians 4:7-8

[39] See www.govtech.com/computing/Understanding-the-Four-Types-of-Artificial-Intelligence.html for additional information

[40] Genesis 2:23

Author

E. D. Allen D Min. | PhD.

The Phantoms of Faith Series was created and written by Dr. E. D. Allen, who has decades of experience in the pastorate and over twelve years practicing mental health, including forensic psychology consultancy and practice as a Child and Family Investigator (CFI). In 2009, a court of law declared him an Expert Witness in multiple areas of behavioral health. Dr. Allen made valuable contributions to the community as a former president and CEO of two humanitarian nonprofits providing strategic services to refugees and other populations experiencing displacement.

Starting in 2024, Apollos I took on the task of further developing and writing the Phantom of Faith series, including revising the first two volumes: Hidden Challenges of People of Faith (Now known as Overcoming Hidden Challenges) and Volume II, WOMAN. With over forty years of ministry experience and study of the Holy Scripture, Apollos I is now an Exegetical Theologian who writes for the glory of God.

Available Now!
Volume II

WOMAN

Beauty Power Divinity in Motion

E. D. Allen

Revised by: APOLLOS I

Amid the many challenges facing the church and society, women's complex being and presence are topics that many struggle to appreciate. This second volume of the Phantoms of Faith emphasizes women's significant and indispensable creation. They are a "created specialty" and a priceless asset contributing to the human experience. God is glorified for the beauty, power, and divinity He instilled in the woman.

INDEX

CHAPTER ONE INDEX
THE ADAM COMPLEX

Chapter Two Index

In a Million Pieces

Chapter Three Index

Irreconcilable Differences

Chapter Four Index

Breach of Sanity

Chapter Five Indexed

Wanting More in The Land of Plenty

Chapter Six Indexed

The Cain Complex

Chapter Seven Indexed

The Hook and Hang up of Humanism

Chapter Eight Indexed

License to Leave Choosing to Stay

Chapter Nine Indexed

Held Hostage by a Moment in Time

Chapter Ten Indexed

The Liquid Handcuff

Chapter Eleven

The Final Verdict

Chapter Twelve Indexed

Recalculating, Turn Right

www.ingramcontent.com/pod-product-compliance
Lightning Source LLC
Chambersburg PA
CBHW060016030426
42334CB00019B/2067

* 9 7 8 0 5 7 8 2 2 0 2 1 5 *